Moral Dealing

DAVID GAUTHIER

Moral Dealing

CONTRACT, ETHICS, AND REASON

Cornell University Press

Ithaca and London

First published 1990 by Cornell University Press.

International Standard Book Number 0-8014-2431-3 (cloth)
International Standard Book Number 0-8014-9700-0 (paper)
Library of Congress Catalog Card Number 89-45975
Printed in the United States of America
Librarians: Library of Congress cataloging information
appears on the last page of the book.

Contents

Moral Dealing

Introduction

The essays in this collection are intended to complement the systematic development of a contractarian moral theory undertaken in my book *Morals by Agreement*. All were written during the years in which the argument of that book took shape. Some examine the thinkers that provide a historical background for my contractarian thought. Others explore issues in rationality and morality that are either not pursued, or are pursued differently, in my book. The earlier essays reveal doubts about the contractarian project that I should not want to be ignored, even if, as I hope, *Morals by Agreement* shows how they may be allayed.

Before I consider in more detail the work collected here, a few remarks relating to my approach to moral theory may be helpful. The contractarian brings good news—there is a touchstone for moral practices and political institutions. Neither a skeptic nor a dogmatic, the contractarian finds in rational agreement the test of moral and political validity. He invites us to contemplate a state of nature, in which each individual must rely on her own strength, exercised in accordance with her own judgment, in her endeavor to survive and flourish. He asks us to reflect on the inconveniences of such a state and to consider, were any of us to find herself suffering those inconveniences, whether she would not be willing to agree with her fellows to institutions and practices that, directing each person's strength to mutual advantage, would transform the state of nature into society. What rational persons would agree to, were they by their agreement to determine the terms and conditions of their future interactions, constitute the requirements of morals and politics. Thus the contractarian finds the basis of morality neither in our fellow feelings (al-

1

though he does not deny that we have such feelings), nor in any purportedly objective duty independent of our individual concerns, but in the intelligent ordering of our mutual affairs in ways that benefit each, and so are rationally acceptable to each.

The contractarian is not a utilitarian. If he were to accept a slogan, it would not be "the greatest good of the greatest number" but perhaps "the greatest good of each, compatible with the like good of everyone else." Borrowing two immensely useful phrases from John Rawls, he addresses his arguments to persons "conceived as not [necessarily] taking an interest in one another's interests" but who recognize one another as potential partners in "a cooperative venture for mutual advantage."[1] That such persons not only need, but have reason to accept, the mutual constraints of moral practices and political institutions is the contractarian's good news.

These remarks may help to dispel a crude misunderstanding of contractarianism. Neither I nor, to my knowledge, any other theorist who would accept the contractarian label would suppose that our existing moral practices and social institutions are to be explained or justified by our actually having agreed to them. It is the agreement of rational persons, choosing in advance the terms and conditions of their interaction, that is at the center of my account. Not only is actual agreement unnecessary, but it would clearly be insufficient to bear the weight of justifying a moral and political order. Indeed, whether persons are bound by their actual agreement must itself be established by considering the conditions in which rational individuals choosing their terms of interaction would consider agreement binding. The contractarian must show why it would be rational for persons to agree to moral practices and social institutions and, at least in broad outline, to what practices and institutions it would be rational for them to agree. And then he must show why such hypothetical agreement is relevant to us—why it is rational for us to comply with the practices and institutions that are its object—provided, of course, we may expect our fellows also to comply. For the contractarian, morality must be mutual.

The first group of essays reveals the historical antecedents of contractarian thought in the seventeenth and eighteenth centuries. I present Hobbes, not as the defender of a vanished political absolutism, but as the first modern moral theorist, conceiving reason as instrumental to nonrational (but not irrational) ends, and value as determined for each person by her desires and interests. Hobbes is the true

[1]Rawls [1], pp. 13, 4.

parent of contractarian morality, expressing its core when he says, "Reason suggesteth convenient Articles of Peace, upon which men may be drawn to agreement. These Articles, are they, which otherwise are called the Lawes of Nature."[2] I interpret Hume neither as the last major exponent of moral sentiment nor as the forerunner of utilitarianism but as the advocate of a contractarian account of justice. And I reveal Kant as offering, in his account of speculative reason, a parallel for understanding practical reason in a way that would undermine his own categorical imperative with the assertoric imperatives of a rationally agreed morality. In each case my account is, to a greater or lesser extent, consciously and intentionally revisionary in attempting to create the historical dimension for a contractarian understanding of our moral life.

What I find in Hobbes, Hume, and Kant, I deny in Locke. I contrast Hobbes's anthropocentric secularism with Locke's theism, recognizing in the patron saint of the Whigs the last of the great theorists of divine natural law. But I note that although Hobbes gives us, in his view of reason and value, those foundations for morality which we can accept, Locke offers us the richer moral conclusions that we wish. The loss of traditional moral and social bonds in a society rationalized by a contractarian appeal to mutual advantage is a recurring theme in several of the earlier essays collected here. That loss, and even more the loss of a sense of self, underlies the thought of Rousseau, who is still, to my mind, the most profound critic of the individualistic social order foreseen by Hobbes. In "The Politics of Redemption" I trace Rousseau's diagnosis of, and failed solution to, our personal and social ills. Implicitly if not explicitly, I argue that the author of *Du contrat social* views neither individuals nor society with the eye of a contractarian. With Locke and Rousseau, then, my account is also revisionary, in emphasizing the implicit criticisms of secular individualism that are concealed within and tend to undermine their overt acceptance of contractarian ideas.

The second set of essays adds historical, critical, and formal dimensions to the discussion of justice in *Morals by Agreement*. Throughout, my concern is with the reconciliation of justice with rationality. Hobbes's Foole, Hume's sensible knave, and Glaucon's Lydian shepherd claim reason as ally in their assault on justice; I consider how that alliance may be broken and the assault resisted. But in "Justice and Natural Endowment," I argue that Rawls fails to achieve the desired reconciliation; his conception of justice fails to be supported adequately by the maximizing view of rationality he endorses. The

[2]Hobbes [4a], ch. 13, p. 188.

conclusion to my discussion of Rawls suggests a road not taken—the reconsideration of that conception of rationality. Instead, in the next essay I develop explicitly the idea of justice as social choice, treating principles of justice as the basis for rational social decisions. I develop the contractarian view that these principles should be conceived as the outcome of a rational bargain or agreement among all of the members of society, who consider how they would adopt *ex ante,* from the perspective of the state of nature, their fundamental terms of association. "Bargaining and Justice" relates this argument to the context of that part of the mathematical theory of games known as bargaining theory, setting out what I take to be the correct formal resolution of the bargaining problem and applying it to the account of justice.

The essays grouped together under the heading "Rationality" are a somewhat heterogeneous lot. "Reason and Maximization" contains the first statement of what I consider my most significant contribution to understanding and reconciling morality and rationality: the defence of the rationality of what I call *constrained maximization.* There are circumstances, illustrated by the example of the Prisoner's Dilemma in section V of "Reason and Maximization," in which, if each person succeeds in carrying out his best response to the actions chosen by the others, then everyone does worse than if each carries out an agreed action that is not his best response to the agreed actions of the others. In such circumstances a constrained maximizer performs her agreed action providing she expects the others to do so as well; a straightforward maximizer carries out his best response. The key to my argument for the rationality of standing to one's agreement is that a person who is believed to be a constrained maximizer will be accepted as a participant in ventures advantageous to her from which a person who is believed to be a straightforward maximizer will be excluded. The expectations of others about her behavior lead them to interact with the constrained maximizer in such a way that she enjoys superior opportunities, and so does better overall, than the straightforward maximizer. Therefore, I claim, it is rational to be a constrained maximizer.

Constrained maximization of course plays the central role in chapter 6 of *Morals by Agreement.* One might suppose that the discussion there supercedes that in "Reason and Maximization." But there are sufficient differences between the two accounts, and sufficient doubt (in my own mind) that either is the best way of presenting the key ideas, that I think it worthwhile to let the two coexist. To be sure, the discussion in *Morals by Agreement* removes some of the crudity in the earlier account, in particular the implicit supposition that constrained and straightforward maximizers must both appear to their fellows in their true colors. But in the book I leave to one side the idea, central to "Reason and Maximization," of a person's choosing his conception of rationality, which is one that invites further exploration.

In "The Incompleat Egoist" I explore two quite different concerns about the rationality of egoism—that it is inconsistent and that it is self-defeating. The latter is my old problem about the rationality of morality, in a slightly different guise. The former is a quite different problem, and leads to such curious conclusions as that while *anyone* can do his best, *not everyone* can. This essay discusses egoism's failures; "Coordination" might be interpreted as exhibiting one of egoism's successes. Even for straightforward maximizers, rudimentary practices of truthfulness and promise-keeping can be defended, as resolving their coordination problems. But these problems are not addressed only to egoists; I seek to incorporate a general principle for successful coordination into a maximizing account of rational choice.

In "Deterrence, Maximization, and Rationality" I show how the idea, central to the defense of constrained maximization, that one's opportunities depend on others' expectations about one's behavior may be used in a very different context, to support the rationality of some deterrent policies, despite the costs of adhering to them should one's adversary not be deterred. That keeping one's agreements and carrying out one's threats may be given parallel rational support may seem a very mixed blessing. It seems, therefore, only fair to acknowledge that this essay in particular represents work still in progress, the exploration of particular issues that must be treated in a general theory of practical rationality. In working toward such a theory, one of my current projects focuses on the differences, rather than the similarities, between the rationale for keeping agreements and the rationale for carrying out threats. Here then I should stress the tentativeness of my defense of the rationality of deterrence.

The reader will find, in the conclusions of most of the earlier essays—those published up to 1980—expressions of unease. These differ in their emphasis and focus, but they suggest the inadequacy of a rational contractarian morality to support the bonds among persons needed for a stable society. There are two somewhat different concerns. One is stated most directly in "Why Ought One Obey God?" where I endorse Locke's insistence that the Hobbist will not admit "a great many plain duties of morality." Contractarian morality—the morality of mutual advantage—is a minimal constraint on the pursuit of one's own interest; the charge is that it is too minimal. The other concern forms the theme of the final essay, "The Social Contract as Ideology," in which I examine the corrosive effect of taking all our social relationships to be contractually based. Here I take economic man to provide the contractarian paradigm of the human individual and argue that his directly self-interested, appropriative motivation undercuts his adherence even to minimal constraints on the pursuit of his own interest. Not the scope of contractarian morality, but its motivational adequacy, is found wanting.

The appearance of these concerns in my papers led some persons to interpret me as a critic rather than a defender of contractarianism. (Such an interpretation could hardly survive the publication of *Morals by Agreement*!) But although the scope and motivational basis of the morality that a contractarian can defend are undoubtedly issues that demand attention, I have become increasingly convinced that they do not provide compelling objections to the contractarian position. My first reason for this conviction is mentioned in section VI of "Justice as Social Choice" and developed in chapter 7 of *Morals by Agreement*. By focusing on what is required for social stability, the contractarian can provide a rational defense of stronger moral constraints than would be suggested by a purely Hobbesian account. As I stated above, principles of justice may be conceived as the outcome of a rational bargain or agreement among all of the members of society, who consider how they would adopt *ex ante*, from the perspective of the state of nature, their fundamental terms of association. I argue that if the terms of association are to gain voluntary and enduring recognition, and so provide a stable basis for society, they must be accepted from the perspective of a Lockean rather than a Hobbesian state of nature—that is, a state of nature already constrained by a form of the Lockean proviso, which forbids a person from benefiting herself by interaction that worsens the situation of others.

The introduction of the Lockean proviso extends the scope of contractarian morality. I address doubts about its motivational adequacy by dethroning economic man as the contractarian paradigm and replacing him with the liberal individual. This is the theme of the final two chapters of *Morals by Agreement*. Rather than chafe unwillingly under the constraints of justice, the liberal individual recognizes that an essentially just society provides the conditions necessary to realize her own good through free participation in fair cooperation with her fellows. To the liberal individual, human relationships in a just society are not exclusively or even primarily contractual, but they offer the respect for each individual's good, the assured mutuality of benefit, and the freedom from exploitation that voluntary, rational agreement would guarantee.

But my deepest reason for endorsing a contractarian grounding of morality, despite worries about scope and motivation, is that no other account seems compatible with the maximizing conception of practical rationality, and I no longer find plausible the view, suggested in both "Justice and Natural Endowment" and "Reason and Maximization," that this conception is merely part of the particular ideology of our modern, Western society. Instead, I find myself increasingly persuaded by a view of rationality that might be part of a naturalized Kantianism. I began "The Unity of Reason" as a *jeu d'esprit*, an attempt to draft an unwilling Kant into the contractarian army, but in writing it I found myself focusing on the Kantian understanding of reason as unifying our beliefs, desires, and feelings into the experience of a single self—an individual. And this, it now seems to me, provides the deep basis of the maximizing conception of practical rationality, transcending those aspects of our self-understanding that might be considered socially relative.

These remarks are not intended as argument; rather, they point to a research program. An account of rationality as the socially invariant basis of the unity of the self, if it can be developed, will show whether I am right to think that contractarian thought can be freed from the concerns that haunt "The Social Contract as Ideology."

All of the papers in this collection have been published previously; for details consult the Author's Bibliography. They are reprinted here with corrections and editorial changes, and a few clarifications, but without substantive alterations. Most were first offered in symposia or conferences. "Thomas Hobbes: Moral Theorist" was presented at a symposium of the Eastern Division of the American Philosophical Association in 1979, with Bernard Gert as commentator. "Why Ought One Obey God? Reflections on Hobbes and Locke" was presented at a symposium of the Canadian Philosophical Association in 1976, with John King-Farlow as commentator. "David Hume, Contractarian" was presented at a conference at Dalhousie University in 1976, commemorating the joint bicentennial of the death of Hume and the first publication of Adam Smith's *Wealth of Nations,* with Virginia Held as commentator. "The Politics of Redemption" was presented at the Rousseau Bicentennial Conference at Trent University in 1978. "The Unity of Reason: A Subversive Reinterpretation of Kant" was presented at the Oberlin philosophy colloquium in 1984, with Stephen Darwall as commentator.

"Bargaining and Justice" was presented at a conference at the University of Waterloo in 1984. "Reason and Maximization" and "The Social Contract as Ideology" were first presented at the Canadian Philosophical Association Institute on Moral and Social Philosophy at the University of Toronto in 1974. The two papers that comprise

"The Incompleat Egoist" were presented as the Tanner Lectures on Human Values at Stanford University in 1983, with Kenneth Arrow, Allan Gibbard, and Gregory Kavka as commentators. "Deterrence, Maximization, and Rationality" was presented at a conference sponsored by the University of Maryland Center for Philosophy and Public Policy on "Nuclear Deterrence, Moral and Political Issues" in 1983, with Gregory Kavka as fellow symposiast and David Lewis as commentator. And, as is customary, versions of several of the papers were read to philosophy departments at universities in Canada, the United States, and England.

To the commentators mentioned above, and to all who have participated in the discussion of my work, I am most grateful. But I especially want to acknowledge the two persons who, in addition to discussing my work, persuaded me to publish this selection from it—Christopher Morris and Geoffrey Sayre-McCord. Although I will accept blame for faults in the arguments, they must accept blame if their publication is a further fault.

HISTORICAL ESSAYS

[1]

Thomas Hobbes:
Moral Theorist

That Thomas Hobbes is the greatest of English political philosophers is a commonplace claim. That he is the greatest of English moral philosophers is not a commonplace. But it is true.

I

The problematic of modern moral theory is set by three dogmas which philosophy receives from economics. The first is that value is utility—a measure of subjective, individual preference. The second is that rationality is maximization: the rational individual "will maximize the extent to which his objective is achieved."[1] The third is that interests are non-tuistic: interacting persons do not take "an interest in one another's interests."[2] Modern moral theory determines the possibility of morality in relation to these dogmas.

The majority of moral theorists have, of course, sought to establish the possibility of morality by rejecting one or more of the economists' suppositions. They have offered alternative accounts of value, or reason, or interest. But the dogmas remain, and the bolder course is to embrace them. This is what Hobbes does, establishing a place for morality as a conventional constraint on our natural behavior. The *tour de force* in his theory is the reconciliation of maximizing rationality with constraining morality. How can one be rational in accepting the constraints of the laws of nature, and so not exercising one's full right of nature? The answer requires Hobbes's account of right reason. For

Reprinted with permission of *The Journal of Philosophy*.
[1]Winch, p. 16.
[2]Rawls[1], p. 13.

his true moral theory is a dual conventionalism, in which a conventional reason, superceding natural reason, justifies a conventional morality, constraining natural behavior. And this dual conventionalism is Hobbes's enduring contribution to moral theory.

Or so I shall claim. First I shall establish Hobbes's acceptance of positions essentially equivalent to the three dogmas. Next I shall trace the argument from nonmoral nature to moral convention. Then I shall raise the objection of Hobbes's Foole, who "hath sayd in his heart, there is no such thing as Justice" (*L* 15).[3] To this point I shall traverse familiar and, in my view, uncontroversial although not uncontroverted ground. But I shall then strike out in a new direction, bypassing my former comments on the subversion of Hobbes's moral theory by his psychology[4] and his rather lame response to the Foole. For Hobbes has a better response, although, one must admit, he seems unaware of it. The elements of my presentation are all to be found in Hobbes, but what I shall present is the theory he never gave.

II

Hobbes's conceptions, although embodying the core of the economists' dogmas, lack the precision of contemporary formulations. He speaks, not of utility and preference, but of good and desire. But his position is clear:

> Whatsoever is the object of any mans Appetite or Desire; that is it, which he for his part calleth *Good:* And the object of his Hate, and Aversion, *Evill;* And of his Contempt, *Vile,* and *Inconsiderable.* For these words of Good, Evill, and Contemptible, are ever used with relation to the person that useth them: There being nothing simply and absolutely so; nor any common Rule of Good and Evill, to be taken from the nature of the objects themselves. (*L* 6)

Where the contemporary value subjectivist says that utility is the measure of individual preference, Hobbes says rather that "private Appetite is the measure of Good, and Evill" (*L* 15), thus exchanging measure and measured. But it is evident that both treat value as dependent on choice or appetite.

Hobbes's general conception of reason identifies it with "*Reckoning* (that is, Adding and Substracting) of the Consequences of generall names agreed upon, for the *marking* and *signifying* of our thoughts" (*L*

---

[3]References to *Leviathan* are shown by *L* with the chapter number; similarly for *De Cive,* with *C*, chapter number, and paragraph number.
[4]In Gauthier [10], esp. pp. 93–98.

5). We reason so that we may do what we will. Thus deliberation, which terminates in the will to do or omit some action, is but reasoning about particulars, based on desires and values (*L* 6). The instrumental role of practical reasoning in Hobbes's account is thus emphasized in his discussion of the reasonableness of justice, in which he identifies what is "against reason" with what is "against . . . benefit" (*L* 15). The measure of the reasonableness of an action is the extent to which it conduces to the agent's ends. What is this but the maximizing conception of rationality?

That persons are conceived to take no interest in one another's interests is implicit in Hobbes's account of the value of a man, which is "his Price; that is to say, so much as would be given for the use of his Power: and therefore is not absolute; but a thing dependant on the need and judgement of another" (*L* 10). A man's concern with his fellows is with their power. He takes pleasure in being valued highly by them, for this is a sign of his superiority. If their powers stand in the way to his goals, he considers them enemies (*L* 13). He may have to accommodate their interests to attain his own, but in themselves their interests are not his concern.

III

The natural condition of mankind, Hobbes insists,

> is called Warre; and such a warre, as is of every man, against every man. . . . To this warre of every man against every man, this also is consequent; that nothing can be Unjust. The notions of Right and Wrong, Justice and Injustice have there no place. . . . Force, and Fraud, are in warre the two Cardinall vertues. Justice, and Injustice are none of the Faculties neither of the Body, nor Mind. . . . They are Qualities, that relate to men in Society, not in Solitude. (*L* 13)

Natural relationships among human beings are determined entirely by might, not right, and the consequence is unlimited conflict.

That Hobbes denominates force and fraud as the cardinal virtues of man's natural condition in no way contradicts his insistence that right and wrong have there no place, for force and fraud are simply those qualities of greatest value to their possessors. Their goodness is purely subjective. What may be thought a greater problem is Hobbes's ascription to each person of the right of nature—"the Liberty each man hath, to use his own power, as he will himselfe, for the preservation of his own Nature." That Hobbes does ascribe this right to men in the state of nature is made clear by his insistence that "in such a condition, every man has a Right to every thing; even to one anothers body" (*L* 14).

But the right of nature is not in itself a moral conception. Consider first Hobbes's definition of 'right' in *De Cive:*

> It is . . . neither absurd nor reprehensible, neither against the dictates of true reason, for a man to use all his endeavours to preserve and defend his body and the members thereof from death and sorrows. But that which is not contrary to right reason, that all men account to be done justly, and with right. Neither by the word *right* is anything else signified, than that liberty which every man hath to make use of his natural faculties according to right reason. (*C* I.7)

This passage makes very clear the two main features of Hobbes's conception of right, only one of which is mentioned in *Leviathan.* What is right is what accords with reason, and the connection between right and reason is found in the crucial conception of *right reason.* We shall return to this conception; here we need note only that, in the natural condition of mankind, each man must take his own reason for right reason, and so each considers acts according with his own reason to be right. The right of nature is thus introduced as a rational, not a moral, conception.

The second feature, stated explicitly both in *De Cive* and in *Leviathan,* is that the right of nature is a *liberty.* It is not correlative with duty; my right of nature constitutes a license for me, and not a fetter on you. It determines what I *may* do. Now Hobbes holds that one may do whatever accords with reason, which implies, as we have seen, that one may do whatever conduces to one's ends. He asserts this explicitly in *De Cive*—"in the state of nature profit is the measure of right" (*C* I.10). Since in this natural condition anything may be conducive to one's ends, "Nature hath given to *every one a right to all.*" The right of nature is an unlimited permission, a blank check.

An unlimited permissive right implies the absence of all obligation or duty—of all moral constraint. In taking profit as the measure of right, Hobbes treats right as redundant; there are no *moral* distinctions within the state of nature. To suppose that men in their natural condition possess the right of nature is to view that condition from a different vantage point—from the social condition of mankind. In society right is not unlimited; it is neither what accords with each person's own natural reason, nor what is measured by consideration of each person's profit. Viewed from society, the state of nature appears as the effect of removing all limitations on right, and so as a condition of entire liberty. But it is the perspective of society, and not the condition of nature itself, which determines this appearance.

IV

The natural condition of mankind is a state of war, and this war is licensed by the right of nature. But this war is unprofitable; it lessens each person's prospect of maintaining his own life, which is his principal end. Of course, this does not show war to be irrational; the natural condition of mankind exemplifies the well-known Prisoner's Dilemma, in which individual maximizing behavior, which is by definition rational, leads to a mutually disadvantageous, sub-optimal outcome.

But if man's natural condition is unprofitable, then the unlimited right of nature, which licenses this condition of war, is equally unprofitable. Thus Hobbes insists that "as long as this naturall Right of every man to every thing endureth, there can be no security to any man, . . . of living out the time, which Nature ordinarily alloweth men to live" (*L* 14). And so we come to the second law of nature, the cornerstone of Hobbes's account of morality:

> That a man be willing, when others are so too, as farre-forth, as for Peace, and defence of himselfe he shall think it necessary, to lay down this right to all things; and be contented with so much liberty against other men, as he would allow other men against himselfe. (*L* 14)

To lay down some portion of one's originally unlimited right, is to introduce a constraint on what one may do. A permissive right creates no obligation, but the laying down of such a right is the assumption of an obligation, so that a man is

> said to be OBLIGED, or BOUND, not to hinder those, to whom such Right is granted, or abandoned, from the benefit of it: . . . and that such hindrance is INJUSTICE, and INJURY, as being *Sine Jure;* the Right being before renounced, or transferred. (*L* 14)

To lay down a right is to distinguish between what is done with right and what is done without right, between acts that are right and acts that are wrong. At this point morality enters Hobbes's account. In laying down right, man transforms his condition.

The laws of nature are the grounds of this morality. But they are not themselves moral principles:

> A LAW OF NATURE, . . . is a Precept, or generall Rule, found out by Reason, by which a man is forbidden to do, that, which is destructive of his life, or taketh away the means of preserving the same; and to omit, that, by which he thinketh it may be best preserved. (*L* 14)

The very word 'law' is misleading, as Hobbes himself admits (*L* 15). But the laws of nature differ from mere advice, in their necessity and generality; they state what one *must* do, in the pursuit of one's chief end, preservation, and they state what *each* must do, since each seeks the same end, self-preservation, in the same conditions, a war in which all have equal hope of success. So conceived, the laws of nature provide for the rational introduction of a morality that is neither individual nor natural, but mutual and conventional.

I shall define a *convention* as a regularity *R* in the behavior of persons *P* in situations *S*, such that part of the reason that most of these persons have for conforming to *R* in *S* is that it is common knowledge among *P* that most persons conform to *R* in *S*, and that most persons expect most (other) persons to conform to *R* in *S*.[5] We may distinguish between *descriptive* and *normative* conventionality; the former concerns the explanation of behavior, the latter concerns the justification of behavior. It is of course in the normative sense that Hobbesian morality is conventional. Thus my claim is that obligations, or restrictions on right, constitute regularities, and that the rationale for adherence to these regularities includes the common knowledge that most persons both adhere to and expect others to adhere to them.

The regularities in question are spelled out in the detailed list of the laws of nature which Hobbes provides. If the rationale for adherence to them is to rest on the knowledge that adherence is both usual and expected, then two conditions must be satisfied. First, each person must have reason to prefer that most persons adhere to the laws of nature, rather than that most ignore the laws; otherwise the convention would be *pointless* for those who lacked such reason. And second, each person must have reason to prefer that he or she ignore the laws of nature, given that most others ignore them; otherwise the convention would be *redundant,* since each would have reason to adhere whether others did so or not. The laws of nature are not pointless, since mutual adherence to them is necessary to bring men from a condition of war to one of peace. And they are not redundant as conventions, since, as Hobbes insists, no one has reason to adhere to them unless others do (*L* 15).

Since in Hobbes's view the laws of nature afford the only means to peace, we may say that morality constitutes a uniquely dominant set of conventions, or regularities of behavior, for men who, seeking their own preservation, must seek peace. Thus "the Science of them [the laws of nature], is the true and onely Moral Philosophy. For Morall

[5]My account of convention owes much to David Lewis, although there are differences which I shall not seek to justify here. See Lewis [1], esp. pp. 42, 78.

Philosophy is nothing else but the Science of what is *Good,* and *Evill,* in the conversation, and Society of mankind" (*L* 15).

Values are subjective, but peace is a common instrumental good, since it is a necessary means to each man's chief good, his own preservation. Reason is instrumental, but the laws of nature, which prescribe the means of peace, are addressed equally to each man's reason, and so are rational for all. Interest is non-tuistic, yet each man must give up some of the right with which he pursues his own interests, since this is the basis of the laws of nature. Thus morality, a set of conventions constraining each man's maximizing activity, and distinguishing right from wrong, is established.

V

But a major difficulty confronts Hobbes's conception of morality. The laws of nature provide a set of conventions which is dominant, and neither pointless nor redundant. But is this set *stable?* That is, given common knowledge that most persons conform to the laws of nature and expect others to conform, does each prefer that he or she also conform rather than ignore the laws? Or may not each person reason that, since peace is assured by the constraints on right accepted by others, he does best for himself by accepting no such constraints?

Hobbes faces both a *rational* and a *motivational* problem. A convention is rationally stable if and only if each person has reason to adhere to it, provided others do; it is motivationally stable if and only if each is usually moved to adhere to it, provided others do. Motivational stability is the central problem of Hobbes's political theory; our concern is rather with rational stability. And Hobbes is well aware of this concern.

The device by which we effect the mutual laying down of right required by the second law of nature is *covenant,* a "mutuall transferring of Right" in which at least one party is to perform in the future "and in the mean time be trusted" (*L* 14). The third law of nature then requires *"That men performe their Covenants made:* without which, Covenants are in vain, and but Empty words; and the Right of all men to all things remaining, wee are still in the condition of Warre" (*L* 15). Adherence to this law is justice. The question of rational stability is then the question whether justice is always rational, and this is what Hobbes's Foole denies:

> The Foole hath sayd in his heart, there is no such thing as Justice; and sometimes also with his tongue; seriously alleaging, that every mans conservation, and contentment, being committed to his own care, there

could be no reason, why every man might not do what he thought
conduced thereunto: and therefore also to make, or not make; keep, or
not keep Covenants, was not against Reason, when it conduced to ones
benefit. He does not therein deny, that there be Covenants; and that they
are sometimes broken, sometimes kept; and that such breach of them
may be called Injustice, and the observance of them Justice: but he
questioneth, whether Injustice, . . . may not sometimes stand with that
Reason, which dictateth to every man his own good; . . . This specious
reasoning is neverthelesse false. (*L* 15)

Why is the Foole's reasoning false? He need not deny that the
natural condition of mankind exemplifies the Prisoner's Dilemma, so
that universally peaceable behavior is better, for everyone, than universally warlike behavior, but warlike behavior is nevertheless each
person's best reply to the others, whether they be warlike or peaceable. What the Foole maintains is that the Dilemma recurs in considering whether to adhere to the laws of nature. In the natural condition
of mankind, anticipatory violence—seeking to forestall others by
dominating them—is licensed by the right of nature. Since mutual
anticipation creates war, Hobbes holds that it is rational for each
person to lay down the right to anticipate, provided others do so as
well. But however true this may be, it does not change the advantage
inherent in anticipation, which still maximizes each person's prospect
for survival and so is rational. If violating one's covenant enables one
to anticipate one's fellows, then it is rational. Hence, if the rational
man seems to lay down some portion of his right, it can only be to take
it up again as the occasion may suggest. But then morality is indeed in
vain. Each may pretend peace, but only the better to anticipate his
fellows. The laws of nature in themselves offer no escape from the ills
of our natural condition. The Foole's reasoning seems sound.

In his reply to the Foole, Hobbes claims that the rationality of an act
depends not on its actual outcome, but on its expected outcome, that
the rational reaction of others to the covenant-breaker is to cast him
out of society, and that, although others may err in letting the covenant-breaker live in peace, such error cannot be rationally expected
(*L* 15). However, Hobbes does not challenge the Foole's contention
that, could covenant-breaking be expected to be advantageous, then it
would be reasonable, however unjust one might call it.

Is this reply adequate? To answer this question, we must first distinguish three ways in which, in contractual situations, the respective
advantages of mutual adherence and unilateral violation may be related. First, mutual adherence may be in itself better than unilateral
violation for each person. Second, mutual adherence may be in itself

worse than unilateral violation for some persons, but better for each in virtue of external enforcement. And third, mutual adherence may be worse than unilateral violation for some parties, all things considered.

Now Hobbes does not suppose, and it is surely not plausible to suppose, that making only those covenants in which mutual adherence is better in itself for everyone than unilateral violation will prove sufficient to enable men to escape from the natural condition of war. He does, however, suppose that men can escape by making covenants in which external enforcement renders mutual adherence better for everyone than unilateral violation. If he is wrong about this, then his reply to the Foole is clearly inadequate. If he is right, then although he may claim that the Foole's objections do not show peace to be unattainable, yet he may not deny that in the attainment of peace real benefits must be forgone. External enforcement is necessarily costly;[6] so the parties to a beneficial covenant in which mutual adherence is not in itself better for each person than unilateral violation, would do better were they nevertheless to adhere without external enforcement. Hobbes must ignore this because he does not challenge the Foole's insistence that covenant-breaking, to be irrational, must be expected to be disadvantageous. And he thereby sacrifices the real point of his, or of any, conventional moral system, as introducing a constraint on taking the maximization of advantage to be the aim of rational individual behavior.

But could Hobbes avoid this sacrifice? The Foole's reasoning contains an argument seemingly fatal to moral conventionalism. If morality is to be a rational and conventional constraint on natural behavior, then it must be rationally stable, and this requires that each have reason to follow it provided others do. Since reason enjoins the maximization of advantage, morality is rationally stable only if it is most advantageous for each to follow it provided others do. But if this holds, then in what sense is morality a *constraint?* If each person's good is best furthered by some course of action, then each, rationally exercising his or her unlimited right of nature, will follow that course of action. No laying down of right is needed. The role of so-called moral conventions can then be not to constrain our behavior, but rather to enable us to coordinate that behavior to maximal advantage, effecting, like the perfectly competitive market, the harmony of non-

---

[6]As Hobbes recognizes, "But a man may here object, that the Condition of Subjects is very miserable; as being obnoxious to the lusts, and other irregular passions of him, or them that have so unlimited a Power in their hands. . . . not considering that the estate of Man can never be without some incommodity or other" (*L* 18).

tuisms. The conception of morality as a rational and conventional
constraint has thus no place. On the other hand, if each does worse, in
terms of advantage, to follow morality provided others do, then, although morality constitutes a constraint on our natural behavior, the
constraint is irrational. And so again, the conception of morality as a
rational and conventional constraint has no place.

VI

But "this specious reasoning is neverthelesse false." Hobbes has
another, and better, reply to the Foole, in his account of right reason.
To pass between the horns of the apparent dilemma set by stability—
that morality is either not a constraint or else an irrational constraint
on individual behavior—we must embrace a further element of conventionalism. Not only morality, but rationality as well, must come
within its ambit. And Hobbes shows us what is required:

> And as in Arithmetique, unpractised men must, and Professors them-
> selves may often erre, and cast up false; so also in any other subject of
> Reasoning, the ablest, most attentive, and most practised men, may de-
> ceive themselves, and inferre false Conclusions; Not but that Reason it
> selfe is always Right Reason, as well as Arithmetique is a certain and
> infallible Art: But no one mans Reason, nor the Reason of any one
> number of men, makes the certaintie; no more than an account is there-
> fore well cast up, because a great many men have unanimously approved
> it. And therefore, as when there is a controversy in an account, the
> parties must by their own accord, set up for right Reason, the Reason of
> some Arbitrator, or Judge, to whose sentence they will both stand, or
> their controversie must either come to blowes, or be undecided, for want
> of a right Reason constituted by Nature; so is it also in all debates of what
> kind soever: And when men that think themselves wiser than all others,
> clamor and demand right Reason for judge; yet seek no more, but that
> things should be determined, by no other mens reason but their own, it
> is as intolerable in the society of men, as it is in play after trump is
> turned, to use for trump on every occasion, that suite whereof they have
> most in their hand. (*L* 5)

In this passage we find the germ of Hobbes's real answer to the
Foole, as well as his fundamental argument for the necessity of a civil
Sovereign, not as absolute enforcer, but rather as arbitrator, whose
primary task is to provide the conventional standard of right reason
required to uphold the laws of nature. The Foole, in appealing to
natural reason in support of injustice, falls into inconsistency, through
his failure to appreciate the tight conceptual connection between

right and reason which is necessary to Hobbes's thought. The right of nature expresses right reason. If one lays down some portion of that right, then one also renounces the rationality that was the basis of the right laid down. If one lays down some portion of one's right to do whatever seems conducive to one's preservation and well-being, so that one may find peace, then one renounces preservation as the standard of reason, in favor of peace. The Foole appeals to that reason which dictates to every man his own good—to natural reason, so that he may show injustice to be rational. But injustice is a violation of covenant, and, in covenanting, in laying down one's right, one has renounced natural reason as the court of appeal, in favor of a reason that dictates to every man what all agree is good.

When Hobbes considers the need for a conventional standard of reason, he argues from our susceptibility to error. In the practical affairs of men, it is not error, but the subjectivity of our natural end, which renders natural reason inadequate. Each man takes his own conservation for trump, rather than peace. But this grounds the un-limited right of nature, and so the natural condition of war. Only insofar as each man takes peace as trump are the laws of nature upheld, so that war gives way to peace.

One may paraphrase Hobbes's argument for the second law of nature, as an argument for replacing natural reason, directed to indi-vidual preservation, with a conventional reason directed to peace. As long as each person appeals solely to his natural reason, there can be no security to any man of living out the time that nature ordinarily allows. Thus a man must be willing, when others are so too, as far as he shall think it necessary for peace, to lay down natural reason, and be contented with a standard of reason which allows him so much liberty against other men, as he would allow other men against himself.

That this standard is conventional follows from the fact that each person has ground for accepting it only insofar as it is common knowledge that most persons both accept and expect others to accept it. Basing reason on peace, rather than on individual preservation, is mutually beneficial, but against each person's interest should others not accept it. Thus the convention is neither pointless nor redundant. And it is rationally stable; adherence to a standard of reason based on peace is itself rationally required as a means to peace.

The problem of motivational stability is, of course, not resolved by replacing natural with conventional reason. We may grant the Foole that each person would prefer to violate the laws of nature, given that others adhere. Since men tend to be ruled by passion rather than reason, Hobbes requires the Sovereign, not only as arbiter, whose reason, accepted by all as right reason, prescribes the means to peace, but also as enforcer, whose power, authorized by all, is exercised to maintain peace. But this problem of motivation is not peculiar to Hobbes' conception of morality and does not threaten to undermine his conventionalist theory.

VII

I have now made good my initial claims. Hobbes's moral theory is a dual conventionalism, in which a conventional reason, superceding natural reason, justifies a conventional morality, constraining natural behavior. Hobbes has succeeded in demonstrating the possibility of morality, while accepting the three dogmas of the economists which define the modern moral problematic—the subjectivity of value, the instrumentality of reason, and the non-tuism of interest. If he is not only the first, but, as I believe, the only moral philosopher to have accomplished this task, then he is surely the greatest of English moral philosophers.

But if, on this three-hundredth anniversary of his death, we can recognize that Hobbes constitutes a permanent part of the heritage of moral theory, we can also recognize the difficult tasks his theory leaves us. The morality that Hobbes establishes is minimal; it represents the weakest of constraints on natural maximizing behavior—that set by considerations of mutual advantage. It is only because each person has an interest in peace that each has grounds to accept the conventional reason and morality which together override the straightforward maximization of subjective value. Much of traditional morality will not be accommodated by Hobbes's theory; must it be sacrificed? Or may we establish a stronger morality by a well-grounded relaxation of one or more of the economic dogmas assumed by Hobbes?

The most promising candidate for relaxation is the dogma of non-tuism. Not that we should abandon it, for it surely holds in many of the contexts in which persons interact. Indeed, it makes possible economic life as we know it. But we may insist that it does not constitute the whole truth about human beings, and that where it does not hold sway, a richer morality may be established on the basis of sympathetic interests—not, of course, a fictitious universal sympathy, but real particular sympathies. Most important, we may suppose that without these sympathies, and the richer morality and genuine sociability which they make possible, human society as we know it would disintegrate into something approaching Hobbes's nightmare vision of the natural condition of mankind.

Hobbes shows us that moral and social relationships are possible among persons in contexts in which they take no interest in one another's interests. Properly understood, this is one of the great liberating insights on which a free and democratic society is based. But Hobbes's absolute Sovereign stands as an awful warning to those who, like Hobbes himself, suppose that human society needs *no* basis in sympathetic interests. The task left to the moral and social theorist today is to establish the proper bounds of the moral and rational conventionalism that was first conceived by Thomas Hobbes.

[2]

Why Ought One Obey God?
Reflections on Hobbes and Locke

I

Lastly, those are not at all to be tolerated who deny the being of God. Promises, covenants, and oaths, which are the bonds of human society, can have no hold upon an atheist. The taking away of God, though but even in thought, dissolves all.

These words, from Locke's *Letter concerning Toleration*, ring unconvincingly in our ears. They affirm that the bonds of human society hold only those who believe in God. This affirmation breaks into two propositions:

(1) The bonds of human society are promises, covenants, and oaths.
(2) Promises, covenants, and oaths hold only those who believe in God.

Much might be said about the first proposition, but not here.[1] Whether it rings unconvincingly in our ears, surely the second does, and it is this which I shall address. The supposition that moral conventions depend on religious belief has become alien to our way of thinking. Modern moral philosophers do not meet it with vigorous denials or refutations; usually they ignore it.[2] If the dependence of

Reprinted with permission of the *Canadian Journal of Philosophy*.
[1]The first proposition suggests a rather literal version of social contractarianism. Substituting hypothetical contractarianism, as defended by John Rawls, or as dissected in several of my recent papers, would not affect Locke's affirmation.

[2]The phrase "modern moral philosophers" is intended to evoke G. E. M. Anscombe's paper "Modern Moral Philosophy." Anscombe's discussion of the "*law* conception of ethics" and her suggestion that the status of the notion of "obligation" in recent moral thought is "the interesting one of the survival of a concept outside the framework of

moral conventions on religious belief was necessary for Locke, it is almost inconceivable for us.

"The taking away of God, *though but even in thought, . . .*" It is with thought that we are concerned, with man's conceptions, and most especially his moral conceptions. What lies beyond thought may be relevant to the validation of these conceptions, but validation falls outside my inquiry. Whether there is a God does not affect the argument of this paper, although it may affect the consequences to be drawn from this argument. Here we are concerned with the conception of God, and the role which this conception plays in moral thought. And Locke insists that this role is central.

"The taking away of God . . . *dissolves all.*" These are measured words, which convey Locke's exact intent. They express the core of his moral and political thought. Much of the time they are not in the forefront of that thought, for Locke largely addresses those who share his conviction. But some of the time they come to the fore, since Locke was aware, uncomfortably, of those who did not share that conviction. In particular, Locke was aware of Hobbes.

Locke can be read, and often is read, from our presumptively superior vantage point. We know where his argument leads, and thus can discern its true significance. Hence we suppose that Locke was not really trying to justify individualistic contractarianism by tying it to the natural law of God, but rather that he was defending capitalistic appropriation.[3] Having ourselves abandoned God for Mammon, we read that abandonment back into Locke, and then find, not only that he is the grandfather of the ideology of capitalism, but also that he is the wolf, Hobbes, in sheep's clothing.[4]

Locke would have been unsurprised. Having taken away God, we have dissolved all—all of what Locke understood as morality. And the result is precisely Hobbism. Locke shares his individualism, his emphasis on self-preservation, his subjectivist, hedonic value theory, with his predecessor. And if these are all, then morality fails: "an Hobbist with his principle of self-preservation whereof him self is to be judge, will not easily admit a great many plain duties of morality."[5]

---

thought that made it a really intelligible one" are directly relevant to the underlying argument of the present enquiry.

[3]Macpherson [2] is of course the classic statement of this view of Locke. According to Macpherson, Locke's achievement is that he "provides a positive moral basis for capitalist society" (p. 221). It is interesting to find that Macpherson is alive to complaints about ahistorical interpretations of Locke; he objects on this ground to those who read "modern liberal-democratic beliefs" back into Locke.

[4]Cox offers the most extended statement of this view; see esp. pp. 18–28, 136–147. He is following in the footsteps of Leo Strauss; a typical statement is "It is on the basis of Hobbes's view of the law of nature that Locke opposes Hobbes's conclusions" (p. 231).

[5]Locke MS, quoted in Dunn, pp. 218–219.

If Locke minus God equals Hobbes, then Hobbes plus God equals Locke. And if among our modern commentators are some who read God out of Locke, there are also some who read God into Hobbes. Hobbes tells us that "the true Doctrine of the Lawes of Nature, is the true Morall Philosophie" (*L* 15).[6] Howard Warrender then says, "If it is denied that God plays an essential role in Hobbes's doctrine, the laws of nature in the State of Nature cannot be taken to be more than prudential maxims for those who desire their own preservation."[7] Again, the taking away of God dissolves all morality.

Warrender's comment, directed to Hobbes, has for us a further significance. We are concerned with the alleged dependence of moral conventions on religious belief. If we accept Warrender's argument, then it would seem that this dependence is required, at least for that framework of thought, shared by Hobbes and Locke, within which the science of the laws of nature is identified with moral philosophy. If we find it difficult even to understand Locke's insistence that the taking away of God dissolves all, then surely we must find it difficult to understand this framework. And yet, modern moral and political philosophers still appeal to Hobbes and Locke. Kurt Baier compares his conception of morality with that of Hobbes.[8] Robert Nozick revives the doctrine of natural law in a form which he traces to Locke.[9] Baier, of course, does not interpret Hobbes in the theistic manner of Warrender, and Nozick deliberately avoids querying the underpinning of the Lockean system. But perhaps God is lurking there, unwanted and even unconceived, yet not unneeded.

My first concern in this paper is to place the role of God in the thought of Hobbes and Locke. I shall argue that they differ in a manner which I consider characteristic of the difference between secular and religious outlooks. My next concern is to explore the implications of this difference for our understanding of morality. I shall agree with Locke that moral convention depends on religious belief, given his conceptual framework. But I shall argue that Hobbes, within his different framework, is quite able to construct a purely secular morality.

This is not all. If it were, then we might dismiss Locke as holding an outworn theism, and embrace Hobbes's secularism. But I want at least to suggest that Locke is correct about two further matters. First, he is right to insist that "a great many plain duties" cannot be accommo-

---

[6]Quotations from Hobbes's *Leviathan* are indicated by *L*, followed by the chapter number.
[7]Warrender, p. 99.
[8]Baier, pp. 308–315.
[9]Nozick, p. 9.

dated within the secular morality available to Hobbes and those who share Hobbes's outlook. Second, Locke is right to insist that the taking away of God does indeed dissolve those duties. The morality available to Locke is thus not only conceptually different, but also materially different, from that of a Hobbist.

All this is important if we are to understand more recent moral thought. There is a Hobbist, secular morality, and there is a Lockean, religious morality. But what modern moral philosophers have wanted is a Lockean, secular morality, beginning with the individualism which Hobbes and Locke share with us, and leading, without introducing God, to the "many plain duties" which Locke affirms.[10] If my suggestions are correct, such a morality is not to be found.

II

Locke's thought contains a set of tight conceptual connections among morality, law, God, nature, and reason.

(1) *Morality and law:* a "moral relation" is defined as "the conformity or disagreement men's voluntary actions have to a rule to which they are referred, and by which they are judged of." "*Morally good and evil,* then, is only the conformity or disagreement of our voluntary actions to some law, whereby good or evil is drawn on us from the will and power of the law-maker" (*E* II.28.4).[11]

(2) *Morality, law, and God:* of three kinds of law distinguished by Locke, "The *divine law* . . . is the only true touchstone of moral rectitude" (*E* II.28.8).

(3) *Law, God, and nature:* the divine law is "promulgated to them [men] by the light of nature, or the voice of revelation" (ibid.). So promulgated, the divine law is the law of nature. "The *Rules* that they [men] make for other Mens Actions, must, as well as their own and other Mens Actions, be conformable to the Law of Nature, i.e. to the Will of God, of which that is a Declaration" (*2T* 135).[12]

(4) *Law, nature and reason:* the law of nature is identified with the law of reason (*1T* 101; *2T* 96) and with Reason itself: "The *State of Nature* has a Law of Nature to govern it, which obliges every one: And Reason, which is that Law" (*2T* 6).

(5) *Reason and God:* reason is "*the Voice of God in him* [man], . . ." , (*1T* 86),

---

[10]Modern moral philosophers do not actually say that this is what they want. But I believe that it is illuminating to read them from this assumption. John Rawls erects the most impressive edifice.

[11]Quotations from Locke's *Essay concerning Human Understanding* are indicated by *E*, followed by the book, chapter, and paragraph numbers.

[12]Quotations from Locke's *Two Treatises of Government* are indicated by *1T* or *2T*, followed by the section number.

"the common Rule and Measure, God hath given to Mankind" (2*T*
11), that "which God hath given to be the Rule betwixt Man and
Man, and the common bond whereby humane kind is united into
one fellowship and societie" (2*T* 172).

From these interconnected conceptions we may move in two directions: to the content of the law of nature, and to its binding force. I
shall make brief reference to the first presently. Since the law of
nature is the expression of the will of God, the second concern directly raises the question which serves us for a title: why ought one
obey God?

Locke answers this question, which must be crucial given the structure of his moral and political thought, very briefly. His answer is
formulated first in the sixth of the *Essays on the Law of Nature*,[13] but we
may focus on his later and essentially similar formulations in the *Essay
concerning Human Understanding* and the second *Treatise on Government:*

> That God has given a rule whereby men should govern themselves, I
> think there is nobody so brutish as to deny. He has a right to do it; we are
> his creatures. He has goodness and wisdom to direct our actions to that
> which is best; and he has power to enforce it by rewards and punish-
> ments, of infinite weight and duration, in another life: for nobody can
> take us out of his hands. (*E* II.28.8)
>
> The *State of Nature* has a Law of Nature to govern it, which obliges
> every one: And Reason, which is that Law, teaches all Mankind, who will

[13]*Essays on the Law of Nature VI:* "Are men bound by the law of nature? Yes." The crux
of Locke's argument is in this passage:
We say that the law of nature is binding on all men primarily and of itself and by its
intrinsic force, and we shall endeavour to prove this by the following arguments:
   (1) Because this law contains all that is necessary to make a law binding. For God,
the author of this law, has willed it to be the rule of our moral life, and He has made
it sufficiently known, so that anyone can understand it who is willing to apply
diligent study and to direct his mind to the knowledge of it. The result is that, since
nothing else is required to impose an obligation but the authority and rightful
power of the one who commands and the disclosure of his will, no one can doubt
that the law of nature is binding on men.
   For, in the first place, since God is supreme over everything and has such authority and power over us as we cannot exercise over ourselves, and since we owe our
body, soul, and life—whatever we are, whatever we have, and even whatever we
can be—to Him and to Him alone, it is proper that we should live according to the
precept of His will. God has created us out of nothing and, if He pleases, will
reduce us again to nothing: we are, therefore, subject to Him in perfect justice and
by utmost necessity.
   In the second place, this law is the will of this omnipotent lawmaker, known to us
by the light and principles of nature; the knowledge of it can be concealed from no
one unless he loves blindness and darkness and casts off nature in order that he
may avoid his duty (Locke [2], pp. 187, 189).

but consult it, that being all equal and independent, no one ought to harm another in his Life, Health, Liberty, or Possessions. For Men being all the Workmanship of one Omnipotent, and infinitely wise Maker; All the Servants of one Sovereign Master, sent into the World by his order and about his business, they are his Property, whose Workmanship they are, made to last during his, not one anothers Pleasure. (*2T* 6)

Locke distinguishes three aspects of the obligation to obey God in these passages. First, he refers to God's power, indeed to his omnipotence, as the basis for the enforcement of the law of nature. Locke insists that sanctions are necessary if law is to be binding (*E* II.28.6), but he does not argue that sanctions alone create obligation; power, without right, may compel, but does not obligate.

Second, Locke refers to God's wisdom, and indeed to his omniscience, in directing our actions to what is best. What is best would seem to be determined by the interests, the pleasures and pains, of mankind. Law, Locke says, is "*the direction of a free and intelligent Agent* to his proper Interest, and prescribes no farther than is for the general Good of those under that Law" (*2T* 57). "Good and evil . . . are nothing but pleasure or pain, or that which occasions or procures pleasure or pain to us" (*E* II.28.4). But Locke does not suggest that God's wisdom and goodness, in directing our actions to what is best, provide the basis of our obligation to obey the law of nature. He admits that "Could they [men] be happier without it, the *Law*, as an useless thing would of it self vanish" (*2T* 57), yet it is not the usefulness of the law which makes it binding.

Rather, third, the obligation to obey God, and so the law of nature, Locke clearly derives from the right of God, the Creator, over his creation. We are obliged to obey him because we are all his creatures, his workmanship, his property.

It is as creator that God provides law for all his creation. In the first of the *Essays on the Law of Nature* Locke says:

The third argument [which proves the existence of a law of nature] is derived from the very constitution of this world, wherein all things observe a fixed law of their operations and a manner of existence appropriate to their nature. For that which prescribes to every thing the form and manner and measure of working, is just what law is. . . . This being so, it does not seem that man alone is independent of laws while everything else is bound. On the contrary, a manner of acting is prescribed to him that is suitable to his nature; for it does not seem to fit in with the wisdom of the Creator to form an animal that is most perfect and ever active, and to endow it abundantly above all others with mind, intellect, reason, and all the requisites for working, and yet not assign to it any work, or again to make man alone susceptible of law precisely in order that he may submit to none.[14]

All creation is subject to law, each creature in that manner appropriate to its nature. We find an equivocation in the application of the concept of law both to descriptions of the workings of things and to prescriptions for the workings of men; Locke finds no equivocation. Man being rational, his law is the command of reason, so that man is given law in a prescriptive manner, but the law he is given, like the law given all other things, is the directive appropriate to his created nature.

From our standpoint the derivation of man's obligation to obey God from God's creation of man requires argument. Creation and obligation are not intrinsically or necessarily connected. But this is the fundamental measure of the difference between Locke's conceptual framework and our own. His framework is theocentric; everything depends on God, for its being, for its nature, and so for its rule. And each thing depends on God in the manner appropriate to its nature, so that man, as rational, depends rationally on God. Reason is God's voice in man, the rule God has given to mankind. No argument from creation to obligation is needed from Locke's perspective. Creation establishes man's dependence on God, and so his dependence on God's rule; man's created nature establishes the mode of this dependence. Rationality establishes rational dependence, which is obligation to prescriptive law.

The binding force of the law of nature is thus found in man's relation to God, as creature to creator. The fundamental content of this law is preservation. Locke insists that "the *fundamental Law of Nature* being *the preservation of Mankind,* no Humane Sanction can be good, or valid against it" (*2T* 135). Preservation of the individual is subordinated to preservation of the species; "the *first and fundamental natural Law* . . . is *the preservation of the Society,* and (as far as will consist with the publick good) of every person in it" (*2T* 134).

Each individual's primary concern is to preserve himself. The positive obligation that each has to do "as much as he can, *to preserve the rest of Mankind,*" depends on the condition that "his own Preservation comes not in competition" (*2T* 6). But concern with one's own preservation is not a license to destroy others; Locke never suggests, as does Hobbes, that "every man has a Right to every thing; even to one anothers body" (*L* 14). Indeed, self-preservation is fundamentally not a right but a duty. "Every one . . . is *bound to preserve himself*"; Man "has not Liberty to destroy himself" (*2T* 6). When Locke speaks of my

[14]Locke [2], p. 117.

"Right to destroy that which threatens me with Destruction," he derives this right from *"the Fundamental Law of Nature, Man being to be preserved"* (2T 16). Law and duty, not right, is the foundation of Locke's ethics.

III

Turning from Locke to Hobbes, we must consider how far Hobbes's thought exhibits a parallel set of conceptual connections among morality, law, God, nature, and reason.

(1) *Morality, law and nature:* "the Science of them [the laws of nature], is the true and onely Moral Philosophy" (*L* 15).

(2) *Law, nature and reason:* "A LAW OF NATURE . . . is a Precept, or generall Rule, found out by Reason" (*L* 14). "The laws mentioned in the former chapters, as they are called the laws of nature, for that they are the dictates of natural reason."[15]

(3) *Reason and God:* "God Almighty hath given reason to a man to be a light unto him."[16]

(4) *Law, nature and God:* "there may be attributed to God, a two-fold Kingdome, *Naturall,* and *Prophetique:* Naturall, wherein he governeth as many of Mankind as acknowledge his Providence, by the naturall Dictates of Right Reason" (*L* 31).

These passages may suggest a framework of thought very similar to that of Locke. But they do not adequately represent Hobbes's position. We need also to consider these further excerpts:

(5) *Reason:* "REASON . . . is nothing but *Reckoning* . . . of the Consequences of generall names agreed upon, for the *marking* and *signifying* of our thoughts" (*L* 5); "All the voluntary actions of men tend to the benefit of themselves; and those actions are most Reasonable, that conduce most to their ends" (*L* 15).

(6) *Reason, law and God:* "These dictates of Reason, men use to call by the name of Lawes; but improperly: for they are but Conclusions, or Theoremes concerning what conduceth to the conservation and defence of themselves; whereas Law, properly is the word of him, that by right hath command over others. But yet if we consider the same Theoremes, as delivered in the word of God, that by right commandeth all things; then are they properly called Lawes" (ibid.).

(7) *Law, God and nature:* "there being no Court of Naturall Justice, but in the Conscience onely; where not Man, but God raigneth; whose Lawes . . . in respect of God, as he is the Author of Nature, are

---

[15]Hobbes [2], 1.5.1.
[16]Ibid., 1.5.12.

Naturall; and in respect of the same God, as he is King of Kings, are *Lawes"* (*L* 30).

Taking all of these passages together, we may suppose that two, quite different positions are present in Hobbes's thought. On the one hand, moral philosophy is the science of rational precepts concerning preservation or conservation, within a natural order created but not otherwise affected by God. On the other hand, moral philosophy is the science of those precepts commanded by God as King of Kings. Does Hobbes hold both, or indeed either, of these views?

To answer this, let us return to our initial question: why ought one obey God? This question is never raised in *Leviathan,* where Hobbes considers only God's right to rule:

> The Right of Nature, whereby God reigneth over men, and punisheth those that break his Lawes, is to be derived, not from his Creating them, as if he required obedience, as of Gratitude for his benefits: but from his *Irresistible Power.* I have formerly shewn, how the Soveraign Right ariseth from Pact: To shew how the same Right may arise from Nature, requires no more, but to shew in what case it is never taken away. Seeing all men by Nature had Right to All things, they had Right every one to reigne over all the rest. But because this Right could not be obtained by force, it concerned the safety of every one, laying by that Right, to set up men . . . by common consent, to rule and defend them: whereas if there had been any man of Power Irresistible; there had been no reason, why he should not by that Power have ruled, and defended both himselfe, and them, according to his own discretion. To those therefore whose Power is irresistible, the dominion of all men adhaereth naturally by their excellence of Power. (*L* 31)

But this argument is insufficient for Hobbes's purposes. The right of nature, as he defines it, is merely permissive, a liberty, determining what one may do, but implying no obligation or duty on others. But God's right to rule must surely be a claim right, with a consequent obligation on the part of men to obey.

In *De Cive* Hobbes proceeds to establish an obligation, to obey the holder of the natural right to rule. I have argued elsewhere that Hobbes deliberately omitted this account of man's obligation to obey God from *Leviathan,*[17] but since no alternative account is open to him, we may consider the argument of *De Cive* here:

> Now if God have the right of sovereignty from his power, it is manifest that the *obligation* of yielding him obedience lies on men by reason of

[17]Gauthier [10], pp. 188–199.

their weakness. . . . there are two species of *natural obligation*. . . . [The first is irrelevant.] The other, when it [liberty to resist] is taken away by hope or fear, according to which the weaker, despairing of his own power to resist, cannot but yield to the stronger. From this last kind of obligation, that is to say, from fear or conscience of our own weakness in respect of the divine power, it comes to pass that we are obliged to obey God in his natural kingdom; reason dictating to all, acknowledging the divine power and providence, *that there is no kicking against the pricks.*[18]

Although no covenant is introduced, Hobbes's account of our obligation to obey God parallels his introduction of the covenanted obligation to obey a conqueror. In both cases we yield from weakness, rationally accepting an obligation of obedience in the interest of our preservation.

The laws of nature are *laws* insofar as God is King of Kings, that is, insofar as he is omnipotent. They are laws because they are his commands, and we, insofar as we are rational, cannot but yield obedience to them. But none of this matters to the structure of Hobbes's moral and political theory.

Hobbes is no atheist. He accepts the existence of God as a fact. But what is the practical or moral relevance of this fact? God is omnipotent, and so threatens our existence. We must, to maintain ourselves as best we can, accept his rule and oblige ourselves to obey him. This is to act in accordance with the second law of nature, insofar as it enjoins a man "*as farre-forth, as for Peace, and defence of himselfe he shall think it necessary, to lay down . . . [his] right to all things*" (L 14), to lay down, that is, some portion of his initially unlimited permissive right of nature. Thus the second law of nature, as the command of God, obliges us only because the same second law, as a dictate of reason, requires us to oblige ourselves to obey God. The ultimate validity of the second law therefore turns on its status as a rational precept, not on its status as a divine command.

Moral obligation does not depend on God. It arises whenever, in accordance with the rational requirements of the laws of nature, we grant away some portion of our initially unlimited right. We do this in our relationship with God, but we do it also in our relationships with our human fellows, to secure ourselves against their power.

Hobbes's presentation of his argument parallels its logical structure. The laws of nature are introduced as theorems of reason, and only afterwards as commands of God. The obligation to obey the temporal sovereign is established in terms of these theorems of reason, and only at the conclusion of Hobbes's political argument is man's rela-

---

[18]Hobbes [1], XV.7.

tionship with the spiritual sovereign introduced. Although Hobbes is no atheist, he is what we may call a practical atheist—as indeed we, his successors, all are. God makes no difference to the structure of Hobbes's moral and political system, and indeed, since God in his commands simply reinforces the laws of nature, God makes no difference even to the content of Hobbes's system.

But, we may ask, does Hobbes even present a moral system? If the laws of nature are but rational requirements for preservation, then is not Warrender right to insist that they are mere maxims of prudence? If they are not truly laws, then as Locke says, "Man would not be able to act wrongfully, since there was no law issuing commands or prohibitions, and he would be the completely free and sovereign arbiter of his actions."[19] Locke insists that the binding force of the laws of nature cannot be explained if every man's own interest is taken to be their basis.[20]

Hobbes's laws of nature are more than principles which prescribe the necessary means to self-preservation. They are precepts which each man is rationally required to follow, provided every other man does so. And this double generality—that the laws apply to every man but to each only insofar as they apply to every other man—distinguishes the laws of nature from mere principles of prudence, and establishes their moral significance. In a crucial passage Hobbes explains:

> The Lawes of Nature oblige *in foro interno;* that is to say, they bind to a desire they should take place [which we may gloss as a desire they be accepted by all]: but *in foro externo;* that is, to the putting them in act, not alwayes. For he that should be modest, and tractable, and performe all he promises, in such time, and place, where no man els should do so, should but make himselfe a prey to others, and procure his own certain ruine, contrary to the ground of all Lawes of Nature, which tend to Natures preservation. And again, he that having sufficient Security, that others shall observe the same Lawes towards him, observes them not himselfe, seeketh not Peace, but War; & consequently the destruction of his Nature by Violence. (*L* 15)

To follow the laws of nature is not to act directly in accord with immediate interest. Mutual adherence to the laws is the "cooperative" outcome of a multilateral Prisoner's Dilemma, optimal, better for each than mutual violation, which is the "competitive", directly self-in-

---

[19]Locke [2], p. 121.
[20]Locke [2], VIII: "Is every man's own interest the basis of the law of nature? No," p. 205.

terested outcome.[21] I have argued elsewhere that what distinguishes this type of morality is that each person benefits more from the cooperative behavior of others than he loses by refraining from competitive behavior.[22] Hobbist moral principles are thus those maxims which it is in the interest of each to adopt, as overriding the direct pursuit of the objects of his own appetites, provided his adoption is both the necessary and the sufficient condition of their adoption by others.

Hobbist morality is entirely conventional, and strictly instrumental in relation to each individual's ends. Hobbes and Locke agree that men exist within the order of nature, but for Locke, although not for Hobbes, the order of nature is a moral order. For Hobbes, men must create a moral order, because without it they are unable to achieve security. Morality is then neither an expression of man's nature, nor an expression of the natural order within which he finds himself, but rather the product of his rational capacity to impose costs on himself, for the sake of greater benefits. And these benefits relate only to individual conservation and delectation; they do not, and cannot, themselves possess any moral significance. For Locke, morality confers value on man's non-moral ends; preservation is a duty. For Hobbes, morality takes its entire value from these non-moral ends, having no value of its own to confer upon them.

Locke, like many more recent thinkers, never grasps the real nature of Hobbism. For him, the only possibilities are recognition of the laws of nature as divine commands, or pursuit of immediate advantage. Hobbes does not adequately clarify his "middle way," partly because his defective psychology forces him to the implausible claim that morality is directly, rather than indirectly, advantageous to each individual.[23] But the real structure of his argument reveals a conception of morality which addresses the condition of the self-interested, secular individual who faces the conflicts of naked egoism.

IV

To confirm the differences between Locke's theocentrism and Hobbes's anthropocentrism, I propose now to ask them another question: what considerations provide reasons for acting? The conception of a reason for acting is, of course, not to be found in their writings,

[21]The Prisoner's Dilemma is by now well established in philosophical literature. For a very brief account, see my "Reason and Maximization," below, p. 221.

[22]Gauthier [4], pp. 461–464, 468–470.

[23]Hobbes is thus led to his discussion of "the Foole" (*L* 15). See my account in Gauthier [10], pp. 61–62, 76–98.

but we may nonetheless consider how each would understand it, consistently with what is found in those writings.

By a reason for acting, I denote a consideration with practical force which directly affects the rationality of action. To speak of practical force is to insist that the consideration must be capable of playing an explanatory role; reasons for acting must be capable of being reasons why one acts. The reverse does not hold; explanatory reasons may be irrelevant to, or may even detract from, the rationality of action. Reasons for acting are thus a proper subset of reasons why one acts.

If a consideration is capable of being an explanatory *reason*, then it must be possible to act on it intentionally. Otherwise it would not belong to that subset of causes which are also reasons. One may say that what one does intentionally, one wants to do; hence to act on a reason is to want so to act. One may then be tempted to suppose that one can have a reason to do only what one wants, or in other words, that reasons why one acts, and so reasons for acting, must be or be derived from the wants and desires of the agent.

But this is not so. One need not have a reason to do anything one wants to do, except that in treating a consideration as a reason for acting, one *thereby* wants to act on it. We must sharply distinguish the view that we have certain wants, which thereby become or may become our reasons for acting, from the quite different view that we find certain considerations to be reasons for acting, which thereby become, or may become, what we want.

I shall say that a reason for acting is *internal* to an agent, insofar as its status as a reason depends on its prior connection with that agent. And I shall say that a reason for acting is *external* to an agent, insofar as its status as a reason is independent of, or prior to, its connection with that agent. If a person's own wants and desires provide her directly with reasons for acting, then such reasons are internal. If, on the other hand, the wants and aims of other persons provide her directly with reasons for acting, then such reasons are external. Let me state, quite dogmatically, a fundamental theorem of practical rationality: internal reasons for acting do not entail external reasons, or vice versa. I shall not attempt here to defend the view that internal reasons are perfectly acceptable.[24]

One might suppose that the distinction between internal and external reasons corresponds necessarily to the distinction between the

[24]The most developed attack on the acceptability of internal reasons is offered by Nagel. My terminology differs from Nagel's, but I think that my internal reasons are a subset of the reasons he classifies as subjective. Opposed to subjective reasons are objective ones, which, he concludes after an intricate argument, are "the only acceptable reasons" (p. 96).

wants of the agent and all other factors, considered as reasons for acting. But this supposition rests on a particular conception of human nature. If one were to hold, with Aristotle, that man by nature has an *ergon,* a function or role,[25] then one would suppose that this *ergon* as part of each person's nature, provides him with reasons for acting, whether or not his actual wants accord with it. And if one were also to hold, with Plato, that desire is an inferior part of human nature, which should be mastered by the rational individual,[26] then one would suppose that desires provide reasons for acting, not directly in virtue of being part of human nature, but only insofar as they receive the endorsation of man's superior faculties. It may be foolishness to us to suppose that wants provide only external reasons for acting, and that other factors can and must provide internal reasons, but it was not foolishness to the Greeks.

Within the tradition of possessive or appropriative individualism, internal reasons for acting must be, or must be derived from, the wants of the agent. The plausibility of the more extreme but mistaken claim that all reasons for acting must, as a matter of logical or conceptual necessity, rest on wants, arises from taking for granted this conception of man. If each man is an independent appropriator, then natural human activity must be a function of appropriative desires, themselves perhaps founded on more basic desires for preservation. Reason plays an instrumental role on this conception of man, so that appropriative desire is the natural and final ground of all rational action. If, as is commonly done, we identify Locke with this individualistic tradition, then we shall have to conclude that in his account reasons for acting, or at least internal reasons for acting, must be derived from and only from the agent's wants and desires.

We may draw this conclusion, but we must draw it carefully, without oversimplifying the complexities which Locke's theocentrism introduces into his account. Although he says that "If it be . . . asked, what it is moves desire, I answer, Happiness, and that alone" (*E* II.21.41), and he continues, "What has an aptness to produce pleasure in us is that we call good, and what is apt to produce pain in us we call evil; for no other reason but for its aptness to produce pleasure and pain in us, wherein consists our happiness and misery" (*E* II.21.42), yet we may not straightforwardly conclude that since "all good be the proper object of desire" (*E* II.21.43), therefore desire gives rise to our reasons for acting.

For Locke, the function of reason is to acquaint us with God's law, so

---

[25]*Nicomachean Ethics* 1097b25 ff.
[26]Cf. *Republic* 441e–442b.

he must relate our desires to the divine will, as the ultimate basis of all reasons for acting. Thus he argues:

> For the desire, strong desire of Preserving his Life and Being having been Planted in him, as a Principle of Action by God himself, Reason, *which was the Voice of God in him,* could not but teach him and assure him, that pursuing that natural Inclination he had to preserve his Being, he followed the Will of his Maker, and therefore had a right to make use of those Creatures, which by his Reason or Senses he could discover would be serviceable thereunto. (*1T* 86)

God, as author of our being, has planted our reason, our desires, and our sensations in us. Reason, together with our sensations, makes us aware of God, and of our dependence on him; Locke establishes this in the *Essays on the Law of Nature*. This dependence has its practical consequences; only in relating a ground of action to God does reason approve it. Hence when reason considers our desires—those factors which naturally and directly motivate us—it regards them as providing reasons for acting, not in themselves, but in virtue of their divine origin. It is because God has planted a desire in me, as part of my nature, that it comes to be my reason for acting. Desires give rise to reasons for acting, not in themselves but nevertheless because of their prior connection with the agent, and so, in terms of our distinction, provide internal reasons for acting.

But if reason validates our desires by relating them to their divine origin, it also, together with our sensations, makes us aware of God's will, and of his law of mankind. This law is the "Rule betwixt Man and Man" (*2T* 172), making each person "know how far he is left to the freedom of his own will" (*2T* 63). Hence the law of nature imposes a constraint on each individual's pursuit of happiness, a constraint derived from God's concern with the preservation of all mankind, which the law commands.

When Locke states that we are "sent into the World . . . about his [God's] business," so that each of us is bound "not to quit his Station wilfully" (*2T* 6), one might suppose that Locke is ascribing a role to man, independent of his wants, which gives rise to further internal reasons for acting. But this would be a misinterpretation; our awareness of God's business, and of our station, is not an awareness of our own nature, but of God's edicts. We apprehend God's business as affording us reasons for acting, because we apprehend it as part of his will for us, contained in his law. Although Locke agrees with Aristotle that the universal order includes a role for man, he treats this role as related externally to the individual, constraining his pleasure-based will, and so as providing external reasons for acting.

Hobbes presents a simpler account, for he unequivocally embraces the position that all reasons for acting are internal, resting on the agent's wants, and that no reference to God, or to any other being, is required to establish these wants as reasons. Hobbes begins with an account of human motivation, and his subsequent treatment of rationality is strictly derivative from it. To show some consideration to be a reason for acting is to relate it, directly or indirectly, to man's basic motivations. Thus the first step in Hobbes's discussion of those considerations which determine what we ought to do, the introduction of the unlimited, permissive right of nature, is established by relating this right to each man's concern for his own preservation, and for the means required best to assure it. The unlimited right of nature is simply the reformulation, in the language of reason, of Hobbes's claim that "in the first place, I put for a generall inclination of all mankind, a perpetuall and restlesse desire of Power after power, that ceaseth onely in Death" (*L* 11). The two subsequent steps in the argument, the limitation of the right of nature, or assumption of obligation, in accordance with the prescriptions of the laws of nature, and the authorization of the sovereign to enforce the laws of nature and the obligations assumed under them, are both established by demonstrating the insufficiency of the preceding step, and the consequent necessity of the new step, given only each individual's concern with his own end, "which is principally their owne conservation, and sometimes their delectation only" (*L* 13).

V

I shall turn now to some of the fundamental consequences for moral theory which are entailed by the contrasting standpoints of Locke and Hobbes. In particular, I shall focus on the autonomy of the moral agent, and on the overriding character of moral requirements.

A person is autonomous, a law unto himself, if and only if reasons for acting require the endorsation of his will. A person is morally autonomous if and only if he is morally bound by and only by his own will. Since Locke supposes that the law of nature provides what I have termed external reasons for acting, it may seem evident that his system provides no place for moral autonomy. External reasons for acting oblige independently of any connection with the will, and so cannot require its endorsement.

But this argument needs more careful elaboration. To talk of the will is of course to invite difficulties, for the concept is notoriously obscure, but we may at least distinguish Hobbes's conception, in which the will is *"the last Appetite in Deliberating"* (*L* 6) from Kant's, in which "the will is nothing but practical reason."[27] If we accept Kant's view, then the rational apprehension of certain considerations as reasons for acting is the rational willing of those considerations. And so autonomy is not violated by the existence of external reasons so apprehended. External reasons have no prior connection with the agent, but, in a Kantian framework, they oblige only as apprehended and willed by the agent.

Locke's conception of the will is, of course, closer to that of Hobbes than to that of Kant. He does not reduce the will to an appetite, but he supposes that the will is determined, not by reason, but by uneasiness, a form of desire (*E* II.21.31). The apprehension of the law of nature as the rational ground of human action is therefore not equivalent to the willing of that law.

As we noted in considering Locke's view of reasons for acting, he insists that the law of nature limits man's will. Locke returns several times to this point.

> For God having given Man an Understanding to direct his actions, has allowed him a freedom of Will, and liberty of Acting, as properly belonging thereunto, within the bounds of that Law he is under. (*2T* 58)

And in speaking of the right every man has to enforce the law of nature in the state of nature, Locke contrasts will and reason:

> And thus in the State of Nature, *one Man comes by a Power over another;* but yet no Absolute or Arbitrary Power, to use a Criminal when he has got him in his hands, according to the passionate heats, or boundless extravagancy of his own Will, but only to retribute to him, so far as calm reason and conscience dictates, what is proportionate to his Transgression. (*2T* 8)

Man is not a law unto himself, but a subject of God's law. God's law is apprehended by man's reason, and is promulgated in the interest of mankind, but it is not expressive of man's own will, or based on his individual interest. Thus our initial conclusion is correct; Locke rejects moral autonomy.

Hobbes, on the other hand, uncompromisingly affirms the autonomy of the individual. A man is morally bound only by his own will. Obligations are self-imposed, "there being no Obligation on any man, which ariseth not from some Act of his own; for all men equally, are by Nature Free" (*L* 21). Each man places himself under obligation only by his own acts of covenant, acts whereby he denies himself some

[27]Kant [3], p. 80.

portion of his initially unlimited right of nature, in return for similar denial by those with whom he covenants. If men in Hobbist society are bound inescapably to the sovereign, and to the sovereign of sovereigns, God, yet they are bound entirely by chains of their own making, expressive of their own will, and based on their own individual interest.

Hobbes is able to affirm autonomy, however, only by supposing that morality overrides individual interests in the minimum possible way. A man's direct and immediate pursuit of his own conservation and delectation is overridden by the laws of nature only insofar as it is in his interest that everyone's similar pursuit of conservation and delectation be so overridden. The only checks which anyone accepts rationally on the exercise of self-interest are those which, imposed on everyone, enable him better to attain his principal ends.

No man can oblige himself not to resist when his survival is directly threatened:

> For . . . no man can transferre, or lay down his Right to save himselfe from Death, Wounds, and Imprisonment, (the avoyding whereof is the onely End of laying down any Right,) and therefore the promise of not resisting force, in no Covenant transferreth any right; nor is obliging. (*L* 14)

Checks on the exercise of self-interest which do not better enable a man to secure his conservation could only be curbs on, and not expressions of, his individual will.

Locke, it will be remembered, accuses the Hobbist of not admitting "a great many plain duties of morality." We have established the basis of this accusation, in showing that Hobbist morality can override interest only to secure greater mutual advantage. No man can be expected to sacrifice more, by his moral actions, than he can expect to benefit, from the moral actions of others. For Locke, and for most of us, this is not enough.

Moral autonomy and the overriding character of moral requirements are not reconciled satisfactorily either by Hobbes or by Locke. Given the individualistic conception of man, in which human nature is characterized by desire, for appropriation, and ultimately for self-preservation, the will must be determined by appetite. Man can then be autonomous only insofar as appetite is accepted as his proper basis, and his only ultimate proper basis, for action. A morality based on appetite can be only a morality of the Hobbist type—a morality the laws of which curb the pursuit of advantage only better to secure advantage. A stronger morality, of the Lockean variety, requires a basis in some power outside of and superior to man, and thereby cancels human autonomy in overriding man's appetite-based will.

VI

Our argument has been concerned with differences between Hobbes and Locke at the level of moral theory; before concluding, we should draw at least one implication at the level of moral practice. I have endorsed Locke's insistence that Hobbes's doctrine will not admit many plain duties; let us, then, consider a fairly plain duty. Let us consider the morality of refraining from preemptive war.

Hobbes and Locke agree that war is the great evil in human affairs. For Hobbes, it is that "Warre, where every man is Enemy to every man," which makes

> the life of man, solitary, poore, nasty, brutish, and short. . . . And Reason suggesteth convenient Articles of Peace, . . . which otherwise are called the Lawes of Nature. (*L* 13)

For Locke:

> To avoid this State of War (wherein there is no appeal but to Heaven, and wherein every the least difference is apt to end, where there is no Authority to decide between the Contenders) is one great *reason of Mens putting themselves into Society.* (*2T* 21)

Nevertheless, war stands on a very different footing in their accounts.[28] Hobbes insists that in the state of nature it is rational to resort to preemptive violence:

> And from this diffidence of one another [endemic to the state of nature], there is no way for any man to secure himselfe, so reasonable, as Anticipation; that is, by force, or wiles, to master the persons of all men he can, so long, till he see no other power great enough to endanger him: And this is no more than his own conservation requireth, and is generally allowed. (*L* 13)

It is rational to seek peace, but where agreement on peace is not to be found, it is rational to engage in unlimited war:

> it is a precept, or generall rule of Reason, *That every man, ought to endeavour Peace, as farre as he has hope of obtaining it; and when he cannot obtain it, that he may seek, and use, all helps, and advantages of Warre.* (*L* 14)

[28]See Cox, pp. 164–171, 184–189, for an opposed interpretation of Locke, which would make preemptive violence justifiable for him as for Hobbes.

For Locke, only defensive war can be rational. He argues,

> And one may destroy a Man who makes War upon him, or has discovered an Enmity to his being, for the same Reason, that he may kill a *Wolf* or a *Lyon;* because such Men are not under the ties of the Common Law of Reason, have no other Rule, but that of Force and Violence, and so may be treated as Beasts of Prey. (2*T* 16)

In other words, those who initiate war have abandoned the rule of reason for that of unjust force; only as a response to such a rejection of reason is force just and rational.

If morality is an agreed rule for mutual preservation, then where there is no agreement on preservation, there is no morality. In the state of nature there is no such agreement; hence Hobbes concludes logically that "where there is no Common-wealth, there nothing is Unjust" (*L* 15). Preemptive war falls outside the framework of morality; we may condemn it from the vantage point of those who have agreed to peace, but we may not condemn those who lack such agreement if they engage in it.

If, on the other hand, morality is an imposed rule for common preservation, then morality binds in the state of nature as in society. Locke correctly insists that "Truth and keeping of Faith belongs to Men, as Men, and not as Members of Society" (2*T* 14). War, as inimical to common preservation, is irrational and immoral from every standpoint, and preemptive war may be condemned, not only from the vantage point of those who have agreed to peace, but also for those who, lacking such agreement, must be prepared to defend themselves, but may not otherwise "take away, or impair the life, or what tends to the Preservation of the Life, Liberty, Health, Limb or Goods of another" (2*T* 6).

Although it is easy to find instances of preemptive war throughout human history, only in the nuclear age has it been openly advocated as a justifiable practice. We may find in this one piece of evidence for a shift, in our society, from Lockean to Hobbist rationalizations. If we have lost the conceptual basis of Locke's thought, while embracing Hobbes's secular individualism, this shift should not surprise us. I cannot consider here whether it is, indeed, pervasive.

VII

Why ought one obey God? We are unwilling to be his creatures; indeed, we are unable to be his creatures because we have forgotten the meaning of the status of creaturehood. Locke's theocentrism is an answer we no longer understand, but insofar as it is an answer to the question of the foundations of morality, our failure to understand does not remove the problem.

That there is no kicking against the pricks is an answer we can understand, but of course Hobbes's truer answer to why one ought to obey God is that obedience to God is no more than adherence to those rational precepts which he calls the laws of nature. And that answer to the question of the foundations of morality we can also understand; morality is founded in advantage.

But it was not the foundations of this morality—the morality of advantage—that we were seeking. As I have suggested, modern moral philosophers want to begin with the conception of man as an individual appropriator, and derive a Lockean, strongly overriding morality within the framework of Hobbist secularism and autonomy.

Locke's affirmation of God will not satisfy us. But we must realize that if, and since, it does not satisfy us, in embracing Hobbes's practical atheism we cannot deny its consequences for morality. Perhaps this should be our conclusion. But if, in turn, Hobbist morality does not satisfy us, then we must realize that we have no adequate conceptual foundations for the conventions of morality, or for the bonds of human society which these conventions maintain. "The taking away of God . . . dissolves all."

[3]

David Hume, Contractarian

I

David Hume's moral and political inquiries comprise three theories: a theory of moral sentiment, a theory of property and justice, and a theory of government and obedience. My concern is with the latter two, and my basic thesis is that, contrary to what may seem Hume's explicit avowals, these theories are both contractarian. In supporting this thesis I shall accept the following ground rules:

(1) My interpretation will not contradict Hume's actual anti-contractarian avowals. I shall argue that he rejects—and for good reason—that understanding of contractarianism dominant in the Whig opinions of his time. But that rejection is inconclusive if there are, as I shall try to show, other, and deeper, ways of developing a contractarian position.

(2) My interpretation will not question the evidently noncontractarian character of Hume's theory of moral sentiment. Thus I shall be committed to a distinction between that theory, which I shall usually call Hume's moral theory, and his theory of property and justice. Since Hume treats justice as a moral virtue, these theories must be connected, but connection is not identification.

(3) Contractarianism is a species of normative conventionalism, but my interpretation will not reduce to triviality by identifying species with genus. In particular, utilitarianism may also be understood as a species of conventionalism, and my subordinate thesis is to refute the view that Hume is a proto-utilitarian.

(4) My interpretation will rest on the *Essays, Moral, Political, and Literary,*

Reprinted with permission of *The Philosophical Review.*

and on the *Enquiry Concerning the Principles of Morals* (henceforth *Essays* and *Enquiry*). References to the *Treatise of Human Nature* will be subordinate, or comparative. Were my purpose either to glean from Hume an approach to contemporary issues in moral theory, or to place Hume in a history of contractarian thought, my reliance on his later works would be perverse, for, at least in my view, the *Treatise* is at once more profound and more contractarian. But my purpose here is to interpret Hume, and in this endeavor I find myself bound by his explicit description of the *Treatise* as "the juvenile work, which the Author never acknowledged," by his statement that he later corrected "some negligences in his former reasoning and more in the expression," and most especially by his injunction that "the following Pieces [which include the *Essays* and the *Enquiry*] may alone be regarded as containing his philosophical sentiments and principles."[1] Others have chosen to disregard Hume's Advertisement on these matters; I shall prefer to establish that interpretation of his argument which Hume could not but find himself obliged to acknowledge.

II

Some terminological clarification is a necessary preliminary. Hume's understanding of *property* and *justice* are closely linked; indeed, he sometimes uses the terms interchangeably.[2] But I shall say that for Hume property is determined by a system of rules for the possession and use of objects, so that my property is what, in accordance with the rules, I possess and use, and my exclusive property, what I alone possess and use. Justice, then, is the virtue determined by such a system, so that just behavior consists in adherence to the rules governing the possession and use of objects. For Hume, a theory of property and justice explicates the rationale for systems of rules determining possession and use.

I shall use *government* (or *magistracy*) and *obedience* (or sometimes *allegiance*) in a manner parallel to property and justice. Government is determined by a system of rules for the enforcement of justice, that is, for Hume, rules for the enforcement of the system of rules governing the possession and use of objects. And obedience is the virtue determined by the system of government, so that obedient behavior consists in adherence to the rules for the enforcement of the system of property. For Hume, a theory of government and obedience expli-

---

[1] *Advertisement* from Hume [3], vol. II.
[2] E.g., "what rules of justice or property would best promote public interest" (*Enquiry*, sec. III, pt. II).

cates the rationale for systems of rules for the enforcement of rules which determine possession and use.

Implicit justification for the controversial features of this usage will arise in the exposition of Hume's position. But the key assumption should be evident. Rules establishing property authorize certain modes of behavior with respect to objects, and forbid other modes. Rules establishing government authorize certain modes of behavior with respect to persons, and forbid other modes. But behavior with respect to objects and behavior with respect to persons are interdependent. The particular interconnection, assumed by Hume, requires the system of government to be dependent on the system of property. Since my purpose is to interpret Hume's argument, and not to evaluate it, I am allowing that assumption to appear in the use of the primary terms, property and justice, government and obedience. And I shall give primary attention to the theory of property; only after exhibiting its contractarian character will I turn secondarily and more briefly to Hume's theory of government.

III

My interpretation of Hume requires an analysis of *convention,* and a distinction, within the genus of conventionalist normative theories, of several variants, including the *contractarian* and the *utilitarian.* About convention I must be dogmatic. My account owes much to reflection on the analysis offered by David Lewis, but I can not explicate, much less defend, either the similarities or the differences in this paper.[3]

Very briefly, I propose to regard a convention as a regularity R in the behavior of persons P in situations S, such that part of the reason that most of these persons conform to R in S is that it is common knowledge (among P) that most persons conform to R in S and that most persons expect most (other) persons to conform to R in S. What essentially distinguishes a convention from other regularities of behavior among the members of groups is that almost every person's reason for conforming to the regularity includes his awareness and expectation of general conformity. Typically, this reason will relate to interest, and will include both a preference for general conformity, rather than the expected outcome of general nonconformity, and a preference for personal nonconformity unless there is general conformity.

If most persons do not prefer general conformity to R in S, or at

[3]See Lewis [1], esp. pp. 42, 78.

least do not consider such conformity desirable, in relation to the
expected outcome of general nonconformity, then R is a *pointless* convention, one which serves no purposes shared by the persons P. An
account which treats property or government as a pointless convention may be *descriptively* conventionalist but cannot be *normatively* conventionalist, since it denies that property or government has a rationale as a convention.

If most persons do not prefer personal nonconformity to R in S, or
at least do not consider such nonconformity undesirable, unless others conform, then R is a *redundant* convention, in that most persons
would have reason to conform to R even without the common knowledge that most persons do so conform and expect such conformity.
An account which treats property or government as a redundant
convention may again be descriptively conventionalist, but can not be
normatively conventionalist, since it affords a rationale for property
or government as a nonconventional regularity.

There can be little dispute that Hume's theories of property and
government are ostensibly conventionalist. Clear evidence is found in
passages such as the following:

> If by convention be meant a sense of common interest, which sense each
> man feels in his own breast, which he remarks in his fellows, and which
> carries him, in concurrence with others, into a general plan or system of
> actions, which tends to public utility; it must be owned, that, in this sense,
> justice arises from human conventions. (*Enquiry*, app. III)

Reference to "common interest" and "public utility" makes clear
that Hume does not suppose that justice arises from a pointless convention; reference to "concurrence with others" suggests that Hume
does not consider the convention redundant. I shall not have occasion
to refer further either to pointlessness or to redundancy, since nothing in Hume's account suggests that either of these weaknesses affects
his conventionalism. Henceforth, then, I shall take all mention of
convention to exclude these possibilities.

To assist us in delimiting the sphere of contractarian theories, let us
consider a favorite example in Hume. In the *Enquiry*, appendix III, he
writes, "Thus, two men pull the oars of a boat by common convention
for common interest, without any promise or contract."[4] The situation envisaged is very simple; each man has two possible actions, to
row, or not to row. Each prefers the outcome if both row, that is, if
each conforms to the convention of rowing, to the outcome if neither

---

[4]The same example appears in the *Treatise*, bk. III, pt. II, sec. III.

rows, or indeed, to any other possible outcome. Hence general conformity is preferred, not only to the expected outcome of general nonconformity, but to the expected outcome of conformity to any other possible convention—for example, that only the first man in the boat would row.

Each prefers not to row, unless the other rows. That is, each prefers personal nonconformity in the absence of general conformity. But also, each prefers to row if the other rows. (We assume that the boat will not move, or will move only in circles, if but one man rows.) Thus each prefers to row if and only if the other rows. Personal conformity to the convention of rowing is each person's most preferred response to conformity by the other, and each person's least preferred response to nonconformity.

To the extent to which R is not seriously dispreferred to any alternative regularity R' for behavior in S by persons P, R is a *dominant* convention in S. If for certain situations there is a single dominant convention, the character of which is evident to the persons involved, then they may be expected to adopt it without any formal agreement, such as might result from a bargain among them. And to the extent that conformity to R is not seriously dispreferred to nonconformity, given conformity by others, R is a *stable* convention in S.[5] If a convention is stable, then persons who adopt it will have no need for a *covenant*,[6] that is, for assurance by each that he will do his part provided the others do theirs, since direct interest in conformity will provide a sufficient guarantee. A dominant, stable convention is a device which serves to coordinate the actions of two or more persons in situations in which their preferences converge on the choice of a mode of behavior *and* on adherence to the mode chosen.

In Hume's example, rowing is both dominant and stable. By way of contrast, suppose that the two men were in a boat which required but one oarsman. Then if we suppose that each would prefer that the other row, no convention would be dominant. And if we suppose that the boat could be rowed, either by one or by both men, then a convention requiring one to row would be stable, but a convention requiring both to row would be unstable, in that each would prefer nonconformity assuming conformity by the other.

Since a dominant, stable convention requires neither bargain nor covenant, it affords no room for contract. Were the conventions estab-

---

[5]See my "The Social Contract as Ideology," below, pp. 334–337. As distinguished there, a *type I* situation permits a dominant, stable convention. In a *type II* situation, there is no dominant convention; in a *type III* situation, any stable convention is not optimal.

[6]My use of *covenant* is taken from Hobbes [4], ch. 14.

lishing property and government similar to Hume's convention of rowing, then we should have to conclude that his theories were not contractarian. I shall argue that his accounts of property and government show that his example is insufficiently complex to capture the significant characteristics of just or obedient behavior. But I shall argue more than this, for not all conventions which are either non-dominant or unstable are in fact contractual. If in some situations no possible convention is dominant, so that each regularity R is seriously dispreferred to some alternative R' by some persons, then we must consider how the opposed preferences of those concerned are reconciled, in deciding whether the resulting convention is contractual. And if conformity to a convention is not each person's preferred response to the conformity of others, then we must consider how adherence is assured, in deciding whether the convention is contractual.

Typically, contractual conventions are characterized by devices which have already been mentioned—bargain and covenant. Within the framework of this discussion, I intend by a *bargain* an agreement, entered into by each person on the basis of his own interests, which results in the selection of a convention. I intend by a *covenant* also an agreement, entered into by each person on the basis of his own interests, which assures, with or without enforcement, mutual adherence to a convention. What is common to bargain and covenant, and what is necessary to a contractual convention, is the appeal to each person's interests. Generalizing, I shall use the phrase *interested recognition* to refer to any process such as bargaining, in which the resolution of opposed preferences necessary to select a convention is effected through an appeal to the interests of each. And I shall use the phrase *interested obligation* to refer to any device, such as a covenant, in which adherence to a convention against immediate interest is assured through an appeal to interest.[7] (The apparent paradox involved here will be discussed in section VII.) Thus a convention is a contract if and only if either it is selected from alternatives by a process of interested recognition or it commands adherence on the basis of interested obligation.

Hume is frequently interpreted as a proto-utilitarian. But utilitarianism, insofar as it may be assimilated to moral conventionalism, appeals neither to interested recognition nor to interested obligation, although it introduces conventions which are neither dominant nor

---

[7]My use of *interested obligation* is less restricted than that of Hume, as will be seen in sec. VII infra. For discussion of this dual relation to interest, see Gauthier [4] and "Reason and Maximization," below, esp. pp. 220–233.

stable. Given opposed individual preferences among possible conventions, the utilitarian selects that one which maximizes total utility or well-being. Although each person's interests are taken into account, and in one sense taken equally into account, in the selection of a convention, yet the process of selection involves, not interested recognition by each, but recognition of a single moral standard defined as a function of individual interests.[8]

Should the convention so selected prove unstable, in requiring some persons to conform against their own interests, given the conformity of others, then the utilitarian appeals to an obligation based directly on the standard of total well-being. He does not argue from the position of the individual who is required to act against his own interests, an argument typically contractarian, and which may be found in Hume.[9] Rather, the utilitarian insists that each person, having had his interests included in the determination of total utility, is now obligated without further appeal to those interests.

The utilitarian considers overall well-being a sufficient condition for the conventions of property. The contractarian considers the well-being of each individual a necessary condition for such conventions. This difference will play a decisive role in my interpretation of Hume, so I shall conclude these preliminary remarks by clarifying it. Suppose that we wish to ascertain if some convention of property and justice is acceptable among some group of persons. We evaluate each feasible set of circumstances in which this group may find itself in terms of the utility of each member. Then a utilitarian will consider a property convention acceptable if there is some feasible set of circumstances in which it affords the group a total utility greater than the total utility of any circumstances attainable in its absence. A contractarian, on the other hand, will consider a property convention acceptable only if

[8]One can provide a decision-theoretic grounding for average utilitarianism which in effect assimilates the utilitarian position to contractarianism. See, for example, "Can the Maximin Principle Serve as a Basis for Morality? A Critique of John Rawls' Theory," in Harsanyi [2], pp. 37–63, and other papers in part A of this volume. But of course, not all utilitarians would accept this grounding (which seems to me to fail for reasons which I hope to discuss in another paper).

[9]Hume's argument may be found in his discussion of the *natural obligation* to justice in the *Treatise*, bk. III, pt. II, sec. II. The crucial passage is:

'Tis certain, that no affection of the human mind has both a sufficient force, and a proper direction to counter-balance the love of gain, and render men fit members of society, by making them abstain from the possessions of others. . . . There is no passion, therefore, capable of controlling the interested affection, but the very affection itself, by an alteration of its direction. Now this alteration must necessarily take place upon the least reflection; since 'tis evident, that the passion is much better satisfy'd by its restraint, than by its liberty, and that in preserving society, we make much greater advances in the acquiring possessions, than in the solitary and forlorn condition, which must follow upon violence and an universal licence.

there is some feasible set of circumstances in which it affords each member of the group no less utility, and some members more utility, than is afforded either by the existing circumstances, or than by any set of circumstances voluntarily attainable in the absence of any property convention. A sufficient condition of utilitarian acceptability is that a convention maximize total utility; a necessary condition of contractarian acceptability is that a convention increase the utility of some, and decrease the utility of none.

I shall argue that Hume's theories of property and government clearly reflect the latter condition for the acceptability of a convention. Only when everyone may reasonably expect to benefit, does Hume suppose that the circumstances of justice or of obedience obtain. His theories therefore have a starting point fundamentally different from those of a utilitarian, who supposes that the circumstances of justice or of obedience obtain whenever overall benefit may be realized even should this benefit be secured at the expense of some persons.

IV

Hume's explicit strictures on the original contract must be our next concern. For in showing Hume to be a contractarian, I do not intend to show him to be inconsistent, and so I must remove the apparent, but evident, stumbling block of his anticontractarian views. "New discoveries are not to be expected in these matters. If scarce any man, till very lately, ever imagined that government was founded on compact, it is certain that it cannot, in general, have any such foundation" (*Essays*, Pt. II, no. XII, *Of the Original Contract*).

But there are several species of contractarian theory. We should first distinguish *original contractarianism*—the theory that the origin of property and government is to be found in a contractual convention among human beings. This theory may extend to the claim that an original contract provides the rationale for existing society, but primarily it concerns the origin of society, and need not attempt either to explain or to justify present systems of property and government.

If the binding force of the original contract is called into question, the answer tends to introduce a second species of contractarian theory—*explicit contractarianism*. On this view the appeal to a contract serves, not to explain the origin or existence of systems of property and government, but rather to defend (or to attack) their legitimacy. Government is legitimated by, and only by, actual agreement, sometimes among all those who constitute political society, but more often between subjects and their rulers.[10] This agreement will reflect the actual abilities, aims, interests, and powers of those party to it. But for it to reflect a free choice between the existing system of property or government and possible alternatives, it must not be constrained by those powers institutionalized in actual social arrangements. Explicit contractarianism demands actual agreement, but not in circumstances which are weighted in favor of the existing order.

This is evidently an unrealistic requirement. And so the contractarian may be led to a further modification of his position—*tacit contractarianism*.[11] This view is also indifferent to questions of origin or explanation. It establishes the legitimacy of existing systems of property and government by contending that the acceptance, by anyone, of the advantages arising from enforced rules determining use and possession, implies his consent to the systems which uphold those rules. The rules confer benefits; the systems impose costs necessary to those benefits; accepting the benefits, then, one must accept the costs. The choice expressed in tacit agreement is thus between existing society, with its institutionalized powers, and either emigration or anarchy. Not only the actual abilities and interests of the members of society, but the existing social arrangements, constrain choice for tacit contractarianism. Thus if the explicit position fails to conform to the practice of the world, the tacit position conforms all too well, in sacrificing any real concern with free consent.

If this sacrifice is judged too great, then we are led to a fourth (and final) species of the theory—*hypothetical contractarianism*. On this view, systems of property and government are legitimated in terms of the consent they would receive from *rational* persons in a suitably characterized position of free choice.[12] The theory does not suppose that this choice is or ought to be expressed in actual agreement, and does not require that the choice enter into actual belief about the rationale of society. A system of property and government is justified if it *would* be the object of agreement among rational persons in a suitable choice situation, whether or not actual persons consider the system justified. Although such hypothetical agreement must reflect the real interests of those party to it, it abstracts not only from the existing institutional

[10]The two forms of agreement distinguished here correspond to the distinction between the social contract proper and the contract of government; cf. Gough, pp. 2–3.

[11]See John Locke's distinction between express and tacit consent, *Second Treatise of Government*, sec. 119.

[12]The idea here is of course based on John Rawls's conception of the original position; see Rawls [1], esp. pp. 17 ff.

structures which constrain tacit consent, but also from the use, by individuals and groups, of force or fraud, and from the appeal against real interest to present desire, both of which would constrain explicit consent. Hypothetical contractarianism thus involves the resolution of opposed individual preferences by a process which depends solely on the interested recognition of those concerned.

With these four species of contractarian theory in mind, let us turn to Hume's arguments in the *Essay Of the Original Contract.*[13] He beings by granting the thesis of original contractarianism, insofar as it applies to the origin of government.

> The people . . . voluntarily, for the sake of peace and order, abandoned their native liberty, and received laws from their equal and companion. . . . If this . . . be meant by the *original contract,* it cannot be denied, that all government is, at first, founded on a contract.

But this proves nothing about the origin of existing governments, or about the grounds of existing allegiance.

> Almost all the governments, which exist at present, or of which there remains any record in story, have been founded originally, either on usurpation or conquest, or both, without any pretence of a fair consent, or voluntary subjection of the people.

Hume proceeds to argue that the view

> that all men are still born equal, and owe allegiance to no prince or government, unless bound by the obligation and sanction of a *promise* . . . [which] is always understood to be conditional, and imposes on [them] no obligation, unless [they] meet with justice and protection from [their] sovereign . . . [which] advantages the sovereign promises . . . in return

is contrary to the views and practices of all the world. Although people consent to the authority of whomever they consider to be their lawful sovereign

> they never imagine, that their consent made him sovereign. They consent; because they apprehend him to be already, by birth, their lawful sovereign.

[13]Hume's earlier criticism of contractarian theory in the *Treatise,* bk. III, pt. II, sec. VII, does not differ in any essential respects.

Hume does not

> exclude the consent of the people from being one just foundation of government where it has place. It is surely the best and most sacred of any. I only pretend, that it has very seldom had place in any degree, and never almost in its full extent. And that therefore some other foundation of government must also be admitted.

Explicit contractarianism is thus rejected by Hume. Although he accepts consent as a possible title, and as the best of titles, to government, yet he does not deny legitimacy to governments otherwise upheld. This conforms to the essentially empirical character of Hume's moral and political inquiries, to his assumption that what is required is to systematize and explain men's actual normative views, rather than to impose on theoretical grounds views which men do not in fact hold. Thus Hume insists that the direction of fit between consent and legitimacy is usually the reverse of what is required by explicit contractarianism, so that in fact legitimacy secures consent, rather than consent conferring legitimacy.

Tacit contractarianism fares no better in Hume's argument. He insists that one can not infer that when a usurper succeeds in obtaining power

> the people, who in their hearts abhor his treason, have tacitly consented to his authority, and promised him allegiance, merely because, from necessity, they live under his dominion.

The tacit contractarian claims that the benefits of government cannot be had without acceptance of its costs—the duties of justice and obedience. But although this be true, it does not follow that acceptance of these benefits from the person who actually has *power* to confer them thereby commits one to consent to his *right* to confer those benefits, and hence to one's duty to obey him in return. No doubt Hume would agree that the person who willingly accepts the benefits of government must recognize an obligation to obey some authority, but not necessarily the existing claimant to that authority, even if de facto he be holder of the requisite power.

Finally, Hume insists that there is no

> necessity . . . to found the duty of *allegiance* or obedience to magistrates on that of *fidelity* or a regard to promises, and to suppose, that it is the consent of each individual, which subjects him to government; when it appears, that both allegiance and fidelity stand precisely on the same

foundation, and are both submitted to by mankind, on account of the apparent interests and necessities of human society.

The justification for both allegiance and fidelity is the same so that an appeal to contract is as superfluous in theory as it is irrelevant in practice.

The explicit contractarian supposes that we are bound only by our own free consent. Hume replies that our consent binds us, only because of our interest in being thereby bound; consent obligates, because the stability of society requires that it should, and our interests require the stability of society. But we are bound to obedience for the same reason; the command of the magistrate obligates, because the stability of society requires that it should, and our interests require the stability of society.

Nothing in this argument is incompatible with hypothetical contractarianism. For this view agrees with Hume that government exists to serve the interests of the citizens, so that its legitimacy depends ultimately on its serving those interests, and their obligation to obey is founded in interest. The hypothetical contract gives precise expression to a particular way in which the conventions of property and government, and our obligations to conform to them, may be supposed to be founded in human interests. The question then is whether the connection between interest and government in Hume's thought is appropriately expressed by a hypothetical contract. Nothing in Hume's strictures against other species of contractarian thought serves to answer this question. The utilitarian equally expresses a particular way in which government may be related to human interests. Only Hume's positive account of the rationale for the conventions of property and government can show whether his thought is contractarian, or utilitarian, or neither.

Before turning to that positive account, we may pause briefly to remark that Hume's anti-contractarian arguments were of course addressed to the Whig doctrine current in his day, which supposed that the explicit consent of the people, or more correctly, of their elected representatives in the House of Commons, was the foundation of their duty of obedience to the sovereign. This doctrine may be viewed as an ancestor of the position that only democratic government is legitimate, since it alone rests on explicit consent. The practice of the world has in some ways come closer to embracing explicit contractarianism since Hume's time. Of course, the measures used to elicit consent have introduced the powers of existing society into the circumstances in which the choice among forms of society is made, and actual bargaining among groups has severely constrained individual participation in the process of agreement.[14] One might at least question whether the ideals of explicit contractarianism are better realized by liberal democrats in the twentieth century than by eighteenth-century Whigs.

V

Hume's account of justice in the *Enquiry* begins with the claim "that public utility is the *sole* origin of justice, and that reflections on the beneficial consequences of this virtue are the *sole* foundation of its merit." This claim may seem to pose an immediate challenge to a contractarian interpretation of Hume's theory of property and justice. For first, in insisting that public utility is the sole origin of justice, Hume may seem to be espousing the view that overall utility is the measure of justice, and this is at least a quasi-utilitarian position. And second, in deriving the merit of justice from its beneficial consequences, Hume may seem to be equating the foundation of justice with the source of the morality of justice, so that his theory of justice would be merely part of his moral theory, which is unquestionably noncontractarian.

In reply to this reading of Hume's claim, I shall insist that public utility is to be understood as *mutual expected utility,* so that a rule or practice has public utility if and only if each person reasonably expects that rule or practice to be useful to himself. Thus in insisting that public utility is the origin of justice, Hume is not appealing to total utility, as would a utilitarian, but rather to mutual advantage, as befits a contractarian.

I shall also insist that beneficial consequences are not to be equated with public utility, so that the foundation of the merit of justice is to be distinguished from the origin of justice. Central to Hume's moral theory is the thesis that whatever has beneficial consequences receives moral approbation.[15] Whatever, then, is generally useful, or useful on the whole, receives overall moral approbation, and so may be denominated a virtue. Since justice has mutual expected utility, it must be generally useful, and so receives moral approbation. We may thus say,

---

[14]See "The Social Contract as Ideology," below, for discussion of the place of contractarianism in our thought about social relationships.

[15]See, for example, Hume's discussion in *Enquiry,* sec. V, pt. I:
Usefulness is agreeable, and engages our approbation. . . . But, *useful?* For what? For somebody's interest, surely. Whose interest then? Not our own only: For our approbation frequently extends farther. It must, therefore, be the interest of those, who are served by the character or action approved of; and these we may conclude, however remote, are not totally indifferent to us.

with Hume, that the beneficial consequences of justice establish its moral merit.

But to say that justice has public utility, or is mutually advantageous, is to say more than to say merely that justice is generally useful, or that justice has beneficial consequences. It is, of course, to say that each person may expect beneficial consequences *for himself* from justice. This additional factor does not enter into the moral approbation accorded to justice. That beneficial consequences extend to each person does not affect our moral sentiments, except insofar as overall, more beneficial consequences arise. However, it is this additional factor which is essential to *justice;* it is not the beneficial consequences themselves, but the expectation of benefit by each person, that is just-making. Thus we may again say, with Hume, that public utility, understood as mutual expected advantage, is the origin of justice.

Hence we distinguish public utility as the origin of justice, from general utility, or overall advantage, as the basis of our moral approbation of justice. Arrangements may be expected to be useful to each person; therefore they are just. These arrangements may also be expected to have beneficial consequences; therefore they receive moral approval, and justice is a virtue. In this way Hume's contractarian theory of justice may be clearly distinguished from his noncontractarian theory of morality. His initial claim should then read, with words added [thus]: "That public utility [i.e., mutually expected advantage] is the *sole* origin of justice, and that reflections on the generally beneficial consequences of this virtue are the *sole* foundation of its merit [i.e., moral approbation]."

But so far this is mere assertion, not argument. I have set out the interpretation which I intend to establish by an appeal to Hume's texts. First, however, it is worth noting that if my interpretation is sound, then Hume's theory occupies in some important respects a middle ground between the theories of Hobbes and Locke. For all three, government is contractarian in its rationale. For Hobbes and Hume, but not for Locke, property and justice are also contractarian. For Hobbes, but not for Hume or Locke, moral approbation is contractarian in rationale. Hume and Locke of course differ in their accounts of the basis of morality, since Locke derives it from divine natural law, whereas Hume, who like Hobbes is a conventionalist about natural law, bases morality on natural sentiment.[16] What is perhaps most controversial about these comparisons, and so about my

---

[16]See "Why Ought One Obey God?" above for discussion of some of the differences between Hobbes and Locke; on Hobbes on natural law see pp. 34–35.

interpretation, is that with respect to property and justice, Hume is in essence a Hobbist.

In examining Hume's text, we shall consider first whether mutual advantage is a necessary condition for the convention of property or whether overall advantage is sufficient. Hume develops his account of justice in the *Enquiry* by distinguishing six sets of circumstances in which justice would be useless, and no rules determining property would arise, or be maintained. Analysis of these situations will show how he is to be understood.

The first two sets of circumstances lend themselves equally to contractarian or utilitarian interpretation. Hume first supposes a situation of natural superabundance, in which the objects of all of our desires are provided without need for our efforts. He next supposes a situation of universal fellow-feeling, in which each person has the same concern for the interests of all of his fellows as for his own. In both of these circumstances, Hume insists, there would be no rules of property. In the first situation, maximum overall satisfaction would result from each person seeking his own; in the second situation, each person's own satisfaction would be maximized by the common pursuit of overall satisfaction. Conventions would serve purely to coordinate the endeavors of different individuals, and would be both dominant and stable.

In the second set of circumstances, human beings are natural utilitarians, directly motivated by concern for overall well-being. But that natural utilitarians would have no use for property and justice does not show that actual human beings, who are not natural utilitarians, accept the conventions of property on utilitarian grounds. Hume's natural utilitarians may represent a moral ideal, but we can make no direct inferences from that ideal to our own situation.

After considering circumstances in which abundance or benevolence makes justice superfluous, Hume turns to circumstances in which extreme scarcity or excessive rapaciousness leads each individual to a concern with his own self-preservation which must override all conventions. Hume's treatment of these situations strongly suggests that mutual advantage is the necessary condition of justice. Consider his argument:

> Suppose a society to fall into such want of all common necessaries, that the utmost frugality and industry cannot preserve the greater number from perishing, and the whole from extreme misery; it will readily . . . be admitted, that the strict laws of justice are suspended, . . . and give place to the stronger motives of necessity and self-preservation. . . .

The use and tendency of that virtue is to procure happiness and security: . . . But where the society is ready to perish from extreme necessity, no greater evil can be dreaded from violence and injustice; and every man may now provide for himself by all the means, which prudence can dictate, or humanity permits. (*Enquiry*, sec. III, pt. I)

What Hume is saying, I suggest, is that in conditions of extreme scarcity, the institution of property ceases to be mutually advantageous, and the rules of justice are then suspended. However, morality does not lapse altogether, for even in these circumstances humanity may lead us to moderate our treatment of our fellows, so that we do not press small gains for ourselves at the expense of their lives.

A defender of the utilitarian interpretation might reply that in the circumstances envisaged, no *overall* advantage is secured by the institution of property, so that justice lapses. But Hume's argument proceeds from the standpoint of each individual; when the social order maintained by justice becomes useless to him, then he must seek his own survival by whatever means are prudent and humane.

However, we can not rest our case on these examples. For when Hume considers a man fallen among thieves, among whom "a desperate rapaciousness" prevails, he supposes that "his particular regard to justice being no longer of use to his own safety or that of others, he must consult the dictates of self-preservation alone, without concern for those who no longer merit his care and attention." We should want Hume to tell us what this man should do, were his regard to justice of no use to his own safety, but of some use to the safety of others. If he should still adhere to the dictates of justice, then mutual advantage can not be necessary to the rationale of justice. If he should consult the dictates of self-preservation, then total advantage cannot be sufficient.

The fifth set of circumstances concerns the relation between human beings and inferior creatures. Hume's position here is decisively against total advantage, and for mutual advantage.

Were there a species of creatures intermingled with men, which, though rational, were possessed of such inferior strength, both of body and mind, that they were incapable of all resistance, and could never . . . make us feel the effects of their resentment; the necessary consequence . . . is that we should be bound by the laws of humanity to give gentle usage to these creatures, but should not . . . lie under any restraint of justice with regard to them, nor could they possess any right or property, . . as no inconvenience ever results from the exercise of a power, so firmly established in nature, the restraints of justice and property, being totally *useless,* would never have place in so unequal a confederacy.

There is no reason to suppose that a convention of property would not be of substantial benefit to the inferior creatures who find themselves among us, and no reason to suppose that this benefit might not outweigh the costs to us. We could certainly contrive a convention of which this would be true. But we should have no basis for establishing it, since there is no advantage *to ourselves* in so doing. If total advantage were sufficient, then justice might enter into our relation with these inferior creatures. But it does not. Mutual advantage is necessary, and its absence rules out conventions of property and justice.

Morality is not ruled out. Hume insists that humanity requires us to use inferiors gently; "compassion and kindness [are] the only check, by which they curb our lawless will." Since moral approbation extends to whatever is generally beneficial, we approve what benefits them, but this is sharply distinguished from considerations of justice.

Finally, Hume considers the situation of persons who have neither the desire nor the need for society. Did "each man . . . love himself alone, and . . . depend only on himself and his own activity for safety and happiness, he would, on every occasion, . . . challenge the preference above every other being, to none of which he is bound by any ties, either of nature or of interest." Property and justice could have no place among such men. But, Hume argues, the conjunction of the sexes in fact gives rise to the family, and thereby to those rules "requisite for its subsistence . . . ; though without comprehending the rest of mankind within their prescriptions. Suppose that several families unite together into one society, . . . the rules . . . enlarge themselves to the utmost extent of that society; but becoming then entirely useless, lose their force when carried one step farther." And the process continues. Justice extends as far as, and no farther than, mutual convenience and advantage are recognized. Human history represents the progressive but slow "enlargement of our regards to justice, in proportion as we become acquainted with the extensive utility of that virtue."

Hume's discussion of justice proceeds negatively, by exhibiting the circumstances in which it would be of no use. The circumstances Hume selects are those in which some of those involved could not reasonably expect to benefit from adherence to conventions of property. This is not sufficient to confirm a contractarian interpretation of Hume, since the positive features of a contractarian position—interested recognition and obligation—have yet to be identified in his account. But his reliance on mutual advantage—the advantage of all those concerned—as necessary to conventions of property and justice, is consistent with, and indeed suggestive of, a contractarian position, and inconsistent with utilitarianism.

VI

In section III, I defined a convention as a contract if and only if either it is selected from alternatives by a process of interested recognition or it commands adherence on the basis of interested obligation. In this section and the next, I shall consider whether Hume's theory of property and justice satisfies either or both of these contractarian requirements. First, how are the conventions or rules which constitute a system of property selected?

Hume's basic supposition is that the need for rules determining rights in use and possession is sufficiently strong and evident that it effectively overrides opposed preferences among different rules, dictating the simplest form of agreement.

> Public utility is the general object of all courts of judicature; and this utility too requires a stable rule in all controversies; but where several rules, nearly equal and indifferent, present themselves, it is a very slight turn of thought which fixes the decision in favour of either party. (*Enquiry*, app. III)

To this passage Hume appends a long footnote in which he discusses the grounds for choosing among different rules.

> That there be a separation or distinction of possessions, and that this separation be steady and constant; this is absolutely required by the interests of society, and hence the origin of justice and property. What possessions are assigned to particular persons; this is, generally speaking, pretty indifferent; and is often determined by very frivolous views and considerations. We shall mention a few particulars.

The particulars include present possession, labor, inheritance, accession, precedent, analogy. All of these involve a connection of the imagination; some relationship connects a person with an object, and this relationship "naturally draws on the relation of property."

Hume's argument, then, is that the expected benefit, to each person, of a system of property, in comparison with no system, is very great, so that each has a strong interest in reaching and maintaining agreement with his fellows on some system. On the other hand, the expected differential benefit, to any person, between any two systems of property, is comparatively small, so that each is much more concerned with agreement on some system, than with the choice among possible systems. This concern then results in acceptance of "the most obvious rule, which could be agreed on." What is obvious turns on "connexions of the imagination," so that the basis for agreement among persons is to be found in that feature, which is a member of the set of possible circumstances each of which picks out a particular rule, and which has a stronger effect on the imagination of those concerned than any other member of this set.

Elsewhere, I have characterized the appeal to such a feature as the appeal to *salience*.[17] A rule is required to connect objects as property to persons in situations of type S. Each possible rule appeals to some feature of S. Among these features, we suppose that there is one, f_I, which establishes a stronger imaginative connection between particular objects and particular persons than any other feature, at least for most individuals. Each person, then, whether or not he shares this direct imaginative apprehension, will expect most others to respond to it, and so the feature f_I provides the salient basis for agreement on that rule which appeals to it.

Salience is a coordinating device. Hume conceives the problem of selecting among rules as one of coordination, rather than bargaining. Bargaining, the typical contractarian device, is a relatively costly procedure for reaching agreement, suitable only when our differential preferences among possible conventions are strong in comparison with our interests in the selection of some convention rather than none. But the absence of bargaining does not affect the fundamentally contractual character of the procedure. For selection by salience, as Hume employs it, is based on interested recognition. Each person, given his own interests, recognizes that salience is relevant to the possibility of agreement on conventions of property. Each regards the appeal to present possession, to labor, to precedent, and so forth—the appeal, that is, to the various specific salient features which determine particular rules of possession and use—as in his own interest, insofar as it resolves opposed preferences among ways of affording "a separation and constancy in men's possessions" at less expected cost than any other form of appeal.[18]

[17]See "Coordination," below, pp. 285–291, for a discussion of salience. See also the discussion of focal points in Schelling, chs. 3 and 4.

[18]Note that under some circumstances, total utility might be considered the most salient feature differentiating possible conventions, so that under such circumstances, an appeal to total utility would accord both with Hume's arguments and with the contractarian requirement of interested recognition. But this appeal would not be utilitarian in spirit, for total utility would not be supposed to justify the selection of a convention, but rather to permit easiest agreement on a convention.

It will be noted that the use of salience to select among possible conventions and rules is highly conservative in its effects. This conservatism, of course, reflects Hume's insistence that, while a system of property is essential, the choice among systems is of much less importance. In a critical discussion of Hume's theory we might wish to question this insistence. We might question whether present possession, inheritance, precedent, would command the interested recognition of all concerned. But such questions would only express our doubt that Hume has chosen the appropriate contractarian device to select among systems of property and justice. The basis in interested recognition, essential to contractarian thought, would only be confirmed by this critique.

VII

In the preceding two sections we have established, first, that Hume supposes that property and justice are determined by conventions accepted in the expectation of mutual advantage, and, second, that he supposes that the particular choice among conventions is accomplished through the interested recognition of those salient features which discriminate among the several possibilities. Next, then, we must consider the grounds of adherence to the conventions so chosen. This will lead both to an examination of Hume's account of the obligation to be just, and to a consideration of his theory of government, which to this point has been largely neglected in our argument.

Hume beings his account of the need for government by considering our interest in being just:

> All men are sensible of the necessity of justice to maintain peace and order; and all men are sensible of the necessity of peace and order for the maintenance of society. Yet, . . . such is the frailty or perverseness of our nature! It is impossible to keep men, faithfully and unerringly, in the paths of justice. Some extraordinary circumstances may happen, in which a man finds his interests to be more promoted by fraud or rapine, than hurt by the breach which his injustice makes in the social union. But much more frequently, he is seduced from his great and important, but distant interests, by the allurement of present, though often very frivolous temptations. This great weakness is incurable in human nature. (*Essays*, pt. I, no. V, *Of the Origin of Government*)

In section III, I defined a convention as stable if, given conformity by others, one's own conformity is not seriously dispreferred to nonconformity, and I argued that a stable convention, as such, is not contractual and does not require the support of obligation. The passage just quoted suggests that Hume supposes that for the most part, the conventions of property and justice would be stable were men to be guided by consideration of their real overall interests. But this would be too much to expect from human nature. Thus Hume is led to consider both obligation and enforcement, as supports for our real interest in justice.

Two species of obligation enter into the argument of the *Enquiry*— moral obligation and interested obligation.[19] Were Hume consistently to maintain the view that only extraordinary circumstances cause our real interests to diverge from the dictates of justice, then we might expect the latter to suffice. Given the real benefits of just behavior, one is obligated, against present temptation, to conform to the conventions determining property. But Hume's actual discussion of our interested obligation to be just reveals a rather different picture.

> Treating vice with the greatest candour, and making it all possible concessions, we must acknowledge that there is not . . . the smallest pretext for giving it the preference above virtue, with a view of self-interest; except, perhaps, in the case of justice, where a man . . . may often seem to be a loser by his integrity. And though it is allowed that, without a regard to property, no society could subsist; yet . . . a sensible knave, in particular incidents, may think that an act of iniquity or infidelity will make a considerable addition to his fortune, without causing any considerable breach in the social union. . . . That *honesty is the best policy*, may be a good general rule, but is liable to many exceptions; and he, it may perhaps be thought, conducts himself with most wisdom, who observes the general rule, and takes advantage of all the exceptions. (*Enquiry*, sec. IX, pt. II)

Hume's sensible knave, like Hobbes's Foole,[20] perceives the fundamental instability involved in justice. Each person prefers universal conformity to the conventions of property, to the expected outcome of general nonconformity. But each person also prefers, in many particular situations, not to conform, even if others do conform. Each expects to benefit from the just behavior of others, but to lose from his own; hence, whenever his own injustice will neither set an example to others, nor bring punishment on himself, his interests will dictate that injustice.

[19]Interested obligation is discussed in the *Enquiry*, sec. IX, pt. II. The phrase "moral obligation" occurs, I believe, but once in the *Enquiry*, in sec. IV, and is quoted later in this section of my paper.
[20]See Hobbes [4], ch. 15.

Recognizing the force of the sensible knave's argument, Hume continues the passage quoted above:

> I must confess that, if a man think that this reasoning much requires an answer, it would be a little difficult to find any which will to him appear satisfactory and convincing.

His further remarks constitute an appeal to our moral sentiments, tacitly admitting that there is no sufficient interested obligation to justice.[21]

But before concluding that Hume's theory of property does not provide a contractarian ground for just behavior, we should consider whether the moral obligation to justice has a basis in interest. The *Enquiry* contains only brief references to this obligation, but these relate it clearly to public utility.

> These reflections are far from weakening the obligations of justice. . . . For what stronger foundation can be desired or conceived for any duty, than to observe, that human society, or even human nature, could not subsist without the establishment of it; and will still arrive at greater degrees of happiness and perfection, the more inviolable the regard is, which is paid to that duty? (*Enquiry,* sec. III, pt. II)

Hume is then led to the strong claim that the obligation to justice is proportionate with its utility. For he says that when we consider the relations of societies, "the observance of justice, though useful among them, is not guarded by so strong a necessity as among individuals; and the *moral obligation* holds proportion with the *usefulness."* (*Enquiry*, sec. IV)

If we are to interpret Hume's view of moral obligation correctly, we must attend carefully to this reference to usefulness. Clearly it is not the usefulness of the particular action, performance of which is obligatory, which is in question. This is the sphere of interested obligation, which we have seen to be insufficient. Rather, what Hume must intend is the usefulness of the convention which gives rise to the obligation. Insofar as it is useful, so that general conformity to it is preferred to the expected outcome of general nonconformity, then there is a moral obligation to conform to it. This interpretation may be confirmed by Hume's discussion in the *Essay of the Original Contract:*

> The *second* kind of moral duties are . . . not supported by any original instinct of nature, but are performed entirely from a sense of obligation,

---

[21] In the *Treatise*, Hume discusses an obligation to justice based on interest, which he there calls *natural obligation*, and which in effect covers the interested part of moral obligation, as I characterize it here. See n. 9 above.

when we consider the necessities of human society, and the impossibility of supporting it, if these duties were neglected. It is thus *justice* or a regard to the property of others, *fidelity* or the observance of promises, become obligatory.... For as ... every man loves himself better than any other person, he is naturally impelled to extend his acquisitions as much as possible; and nothing can restrain him in this propensity, but reflection and experience, by which he learns the pernicious effects of that licence, and the total dissolution of society which must ensue from it. His original inclination, therefore, . . . is here checked and restrained by a subsequent judgment or observation.

Each person reflects, not on the consequences of his own failure to conform to the conventions of property, but on the consequences of general failure. And this reflection gives rise to a judgment, representing conformity as obligatory, which checks the inclination not to be just. Both the obligation and the inclination, it should be noted, rest on interest. The inclination not to be just rests on the interest, expressed by the sensible knave, in taking advantage of "the exceptions"—in violating the rules of justice when violation would go uncopied and unpunished. The obligation to be just rests on the interest, which each man shares with his fellows, in maintaining the rules of justice rather than abandoning all conventions of property. Although in the absence of any checks the former interest will tend to dominate the latter, Hume supposes that reflection will lead us to weigh our interest in maintaining society more heavily than our interest in pursuing direct advantage.

But this account does not explain why our obligation to be just is denominated *moral*. Somewhat speculatively, I suggest that moral obligation, for Hume, arises from a coincidence between an object of our moral sentiments and an object of our reflective interests. A convention which is generally useful receives our moral approbation. Insofar as an individual has himself an interest in general conformity to such a convention, this interest combines with his moral approbation to give rise to a sufficient moral ground for his own adherence to the convention, provided others adhere as well. If the individual also has a direct interest in violating the convention, this moral ground represents itself as an obligation, overriding such contrary considerations. The force of this moral obligation is then proportionate, not to the degree of moral approbation, which depends only on the total utility of the convention, and not to the extent of his particular interest in performing the obligatory act, which may be negative, but to the extent of his interest in upholding the convention requiring the act, so that as this latter interest diminishes, the moral obligation diminishes correspondingly.

Justice is the virtue necessary to the maintenance of the conventions of property. Insofar as property is generally useful, justice receives everyone's moral approbation. Insofar as an individual has an interest in maintaining the system of property, his interest combines with his approbation to make justice morally obligatory for him. The force of this obligation varies with the utility, to him, of the conventions of property. Insofar as he finds these essential within his own society, but only convenient in relations among societies, he is strictly obligated to respect the rights and possessions of his fellows but only weakly obligated to respect the rights and possessions of strangers.

On this interpretation, moral obligation differs from any strictly interested obligation, in appealing to our moral sentiments. However, it differs from moral approbation, in appealing also to the interests of the person obligated. And this appeal is not to his interest in performing the act to which he is obligated, but to his interest in maintaining the conventions which require the act. Such an appeal is typical of contractarian theory.

Since moral obligation combines an appeal to interest with an appeal to moral approbation, Hume, after admitting that there is no sufficient interested obligation to justice, reintroduces an appeal to moral sentiment. Recognizing that the maxim: Follow the general rule but take advantage of all the exceptions, cannot strictly be refuted, he shifts his ground and considers the man of moral feeling, saying, "If his heart rebel not against such pernicious maxims, if he feel no reluctance to the thoughts of villainy and baseness, he has indeed lost a considerable motive to virtue; and we may expect that his practice will be answerable to his speculation" (*Enquiry,* sec. IX, pt. II).

Hume's account of our obligation to be just, to conform to the conventions of property, is thus not purely contractarian, insofar as it reflects his theory of moral sentiment. But insofar as it also reflects his theory of property, it has a strong contractarian component. Although justice is not sufficiently upheld by a directly interested obligation, it is upheld by an obligation which, in a larger sense, conforms to the contractarian requirement, in being the effect of moral sentiment on what is acknowledged from the standpoint of individual interest.

VIII

Hume's theory of government supplements and parallels his theory of property. A brief sketch will therefore suffice. As we noted in the preceding section, Hume singles out the inability to resist the temptation of immediate desire as a weakness incurable in human nature. "Men must, therefore, endeavour to palliate what they cannot cure" (*Essays,* pt. I, no. V). The palliative is government. Men "must institute some persons, under the appellation of magistrates, whose peculiar office it is, to point out the decrees of equity, to punish transgressors, to correct fraud and violence, and to oblige men, however reluctant, to consult their own real and permanent interests." Thus to the interested and moral obligations which we have examined, Hume now adds a further obligation, effected by countering the allurement of present temptation with the laws and punishments of authority. "In a word, OBEDIENCE is a new duty which must be invented to support that of JUSTICE; and the tyes of equity must be corroborated by those of allegiance."

We may ask, with Hume, how the introduction of a new duty will help. If justice does not motivate us, then why should obedience? Interest and temptation may overcome both. But Hume replies that the institution of government affords men the opportunity to exercise power, an opportunity which they eagerly seize, and so obedience, unlike justice, easily finds partisans determined to maintain it, because they serve their immediate interests thereby. And ordinarily, those who wish to secure the obedience of their fellows can best do so by "the impartial administration of justice." Hence those who exercise power tie men to obedience, and in order to exercise power, they in turn are tied to justice.

The visible interest of the magistrate in securing obedience leads to a visible interest in his subjects in offering obedience, since the magistrate has power to enforce conformity to his commands. But the relation of magistrate and subject is not conceived by Hume as resting solely on power, even though it begins with power. "Habit soon consolidates what other principles of human nature had imperfectly founded; and men, once accustomed to obedience, never think of departing from that path, in which they and their ancestors have constantly trod, and to which they are confined by so many urgent and visible motives."

Since government exists to uphold property, and obedience exists to enforce justice, we need not hesitate to interpret Hume's theory of government in the same manner as his theory of property. The convention determining property rests on mutual benefit. But it is insufficient to confirm men in the advantages of settled possession, without a further convention establishing magistracy or government. The mutual interest men have in establishing property thus extends also to a mutual interest in establishing government. Corroboration of this interpretation is easily found; witness the continuation of the discussion of moral duties in the *Essay of the Original Contract:*

> The case is precisely the same with the political or civil duty of *allegiance*, as with the natural duties of justice and fidelity. Our primary instincts

lead us, either to indulge ourselves in unlimited freedom, or to seek
dominion over others: And it is reflection only, which engages us to
sacrifice such strong passions to the interests of peace and public order.
A small degree of experience and observation suffices to teach us, that
society cannot possibly be maintained without the authority of magistrates, and that this authority must soon fall into contempt, where exact
obedience is not paid to it.

But there are costs to government which make it, for Hume, very
much a second-best arrangement. Only because men are unable to act
steadfastly in their real interests, is it necessary. In the *Essay of the
Origin of Government* Hume represents the costs of magistracy in terms
of "a perpetual intestine struggle . . . between AUTHORITY and
LIBERTY; . . . A great sacrifice of liberty must necessarily be made in
every government; yet even the authority, which confines liberty, can
never, and perhaps ought never, in any constitution, to become quite
entire and uncontroulable." Absolute authority, a Hobbist authority,
would be purchased at too great cost; men can secure the benefit of a
settled distinction of possessions without subjecting themselves to a
ruler able to override all such distinctions at mere pleasure.

Hume argues that the constraints of justice are to be overridden
when the conventions of property cease to be mutually advantageous.
Similarly, we should want the constraints of obedience to be overridden when the conventions of magistracy cease to be mutually advantageous. But magistracy, unlike property, has power to enforce its
rules, and obedience, unlike justice, becomes habitual and less easily
ignored by men. Hence Hume concludes his brief discussion of the
struggle between authority and liberty with the remark "that a circumstance [authority], which is essential to the existence of civil society, must always support itself, and needs be guarded with less jeal-
ousy, than one [liberty] that contributes only to its perfection, which
the indolence of men is so apt to neglect, and their ignorance to
overlook."

IX

The last major questions which confront a contractarian interpretation of Hume concern the role of interested recognition in choosing
among possible conventions of government and the role of interested
obligation in insuring adherence to the particular convention selected. About the latter I have little to say. It is evident that the power
of magistracy will give rise to a more direct obligation to conform,
based solely on interest, than is found in the case of justice. Otherwise,

we may suppose that the same coincidence of moral approbation and individual interest in the maintenance of conventions, which gives rise to the moral obligation of justice, will equally give rise to the moral obligation to obedience. I turn, then, to the choice among possible conventions of government.

In the *Essay of the First Principles of Government,* Hume maintains that opinion, not force, must be the ultimate basis of the magistrates' authority. I interpret his view to be that the opinion of the many (the governed) is the essential condition for the force of the few (the magistrates) to be effective in society. Three forms of opinion are relevant—opinion of interest, of right to power, and of right to property.

Hume says little about the last, which is peripheral to our concerns.[22] Opinion of interest includes "the sense of the general advantage which is reaped from government; together with the persuasion, that the particular government, which is established, is equally advantageous with any other that could easily be settled" (*Essays,* pt. I, no. IV).

But the advantageousness of the established order is by no means the only ground for our opinion that we are obliged to uphold it. Hume holds that we suppose ourselves obliged to obey certain persons, and not others, because we suppose those first persons to have a right to command our allegiance, a right to power. "What prevalence [this] opinion . . . has over mankind, may easily be understood, by observing the attachment which all nations have to their ancient government, and even to those names, which have had the sanction of antiquity. Antiquity always begets the opinion of right."

In the *Essay of the Coalition of Parties,* Hume outlines the argument of the monarchical party at the time of the civil war. Although he is not speaking in his own person, but rather in the person of a seventeenth-century royalist, his statement that "according to the established maxim of lawyers and politicians, the views of the royalists ought . . . to have appeared more solid, more safe, and more legal" may permit us to suppose that he endorses the argument, which, I should hold, is of the first importance to an appreciation of his own political thought. Here is the crucial passage:

> The only rule of government . . . known and acknowledged among men, is use and practice: Reason is so uncertain a guide that it will always be exposed to doubt and controversy: Could it ever render itself prevalent

[22]Hume's main concern in considering right to property is to deny that right to property and right to govern coincide; although there is a strong connection between the system of property and the choice of magistrates, the one does not fully determine the other.

over the people, men had always retained it as their sole rule of conduct: They had still continued in the primitive, unconnected, state of nature, without submitting to political government, whose sole basis is, not pure reason, but authority and precedent. Dissolve these ties, you break all the bonds of civil society, and leave every man at liberty to consult his private interest, by those expedients, which his appetite, disguised under the appearance of reason, shall dictate to him. The spirit of innovation is in itself pernicious, however favourable its particular object may sometimes appear. (*Essays*, pt. I, no. IV)

And one further excerpt is essential:

The true rule of government is the present established practice of the age. That has most authority, because it is recent: It is also best known, for the same reason.

The ultimate appeal, in determining right to power, and so the choice among conventions of government, is the present established practice.

An appeal to antiquity may appear to conflict with an appeal to present practice. What connects them is the key term "established." Opinion of right to power is not determined by an antiquarian appeal to practices which prevailed in the distant past but have fallen into desuetude. Opinion of right to power is equally not determined by what prevails at the present moment without regard to what has occurred previously. Rather, this crucial opinion is determined by present practice which is established, and which therefore can be traced back to antiquity. In the absence of such established practice, no government can possess a clear and unquestionable title to the exercise of power, and no person can possess a secure title to the use and possession of land and goods.

But where, in Hume's account, is there place for the selection of governments or governors on the basis of interested recognition? If opinion of interest supports the established government as equally advantageous with any realistic alternative, then is not existing authority founded on a dominant convention, one not seriously dispreferred to any other? And if there is a dominant convention, then there are no opposed preferences to resolve, no real selection to make among possible governments or governors.

Hume was well aware of the existence of controversy over the determination of the right to power. The passages quoted above, in support of the claim that opinion of right rests primarily on established practice, are found in a discussion of political conflict in England. And Hume was of course aware that such conflict reflected opposed individual interests and preferences. When he argues that governmental authority must be established on the opinion that the existing government is equally advantageous with any realistic alternative, he does not set aside the existence of conflict and contention. Rather, he holds that government must be supported by the opinion that no alternative would afford greater mutual advantage—that the established government is, at least from a practical point of view, optimal. But different individuals will still have clear preferences for alternatives, although they will not agree on any one alternative. In such a situation, Hume supposes that opposed individual preferences are best resolved by an appeal to salience. Established authority captures the imagination. The actuality of past obedience carries the imagination to accept the duty of future obedience.

Each person has a strong interest in effective government. Different persons have differing preferences with respect to the forms of authority, or the persons who exercise authority. But most persons will grant that no alternative to the existing government would be mutually preferable. The appeal, then, of longstanding authority to the imagination provides a focal point for the convergence of men's preferences for some authority, despite their differing individual preferences concerning that authority, so that all can agree that the established government has the right to power. Prescriptive title commands interested recognition.[23]

Thus we find the contractarian appeal to the mutual advantage of conventions, and to the interested recognition of established conventions, underlying Hume's theory of government. Mutual advantage requires the settled distinction of possessions, or property, and the orderly enforcement of that distinction, magistracy or government. Interest leads to the recognition of present established practice, as that way of resolving questions about the rules of property and government which most readily commands acceptance. But as we have seen, neither the content nor the binding force of the conventions of property and government is founded directly on advantage. We adhere to what is established because of its practical salience. In considering what we should do, we are led by the exercise of imagination to the memory of what we have done, and associate future decision with past action.

We may admit the value of Hume's prescriptive appeal without fully accepting its accompanying conservatism. In effect, he supposes that

[23]Those puzzled by "prescriptive" may be aided by this definition from the *Shorter Oxford English Dictionary*, p. 1573: "Derived from or founded on prescription or lapse of time"; and the definition of "prescription," "The action of prescribing or appointing beforehand."

the utility of upholding established practice takes precedence over the utility of the practice itself. Although he suggests that changes in the conventions of property or of government would afford no gains sufficient to outweigh the costs of abandoning settled rules and procedures, we may associate his defense of the *status quo* with the limited horizon of his own social position. And so we may hold that the admittedly disruptive effects of change can and should be neutralized by accommodating change to tradition, so that alteration is represented as development. Present practice may be established, not by conceiving it as the unchanged heir of past tradition, but by showing it as the development of that tradition in changing circumstances. If human institutions are viewed as shaping and altering man's world, then present practice may be considered as the adaptation of past practices to the changes which those practices themselves effected in the world. In this way, a continuing modification of practice, guided by criteria of mutual advantage, may be accommodated to the requirement that practice be legitimated, not by its utility but by its establishment.

X

Hume's men, like those of Hobbes and Locke and Bentham, are possessive individualists.[24] They are, no doubt, among the more civilized and humane representatives of that tradition, exhibiting benevolence as well as self-love, although, as Hume happily reminds us, "the present theory . . . enters not into that vulgar dispute concerning the *degrees* of benevolence or self-love, which prevail in human nature" (*Enquiry*, sec. IX, pt. I).

The world of possessive individualists is not benign. Their natural condition is marked by great inconveniences. The overcoming of these inconveniences, the emergence of possessive individualists from their wanderings in the wilderness of the state of nature into the promised land of civil society, is the great theme of moral and political thinkers in the developmental era of our capitalist society. Central to that theme is the role of self-interest.

This paper was first presented to a conference honoring the bicentenary of Hume's death together with the bicentenary of the publication of Adam Smith's *Wealth of Nations*. That juxtaposition serves to remind us that, when Hume wrote, the Invisible Hand had yet to place its fingerprints on economic and social thought. Were all the

---

[24]Possessive individualists are, of course, creatures of C. B. Macpherson; see Macpherson [2].

world a perfectly competitive market, then self-interest would pose no problem, and the early utilitarian thinkers whose enthusiasm led them to embrace this wondrous belief were able to rejoice in the perfect coincidence of the happiness of each with the happiness of all.

But Hume is sensibly aware of men's interest in curbing interest. It is this awareness which makes his thought contractarian, for the essence of the social contract is found in the mutual advantage of restraining the pursuit of advantage. In the world outside the marketplace, where the Invisible Hand is powerless to direct self-interested men to a stable competitive optimum, the social contract is the conceptual constraint necessary to prevent a society of possessive individualists from being overcome by externalities and returning to the chaos of the state of nature. But how shall the contract prevail?

Hume's illustrious predecessors offer answers which are comfortless to us. Hobbes:

> Covenants being but words, and breath, have no force to oblige, contain, constrain, or protect any man, but what it has from the publique Sword; that is, from the untyed hands of that Man, . . . that hath the Soveraignty.[25]

Locke:

> Promises, covenants, and oaths, which are the bonds of human society, can have no hold upon an atheist. The taking away of God, though but even in thought, dissolves all.[26]

Either the public sword or the divine power is required to turn the headlong rush of possessive individualists from competitive chaos. But if, as Hume insists, the public sword rests on opinion, and if the deity, too, is the creature of opinion, then what can make mutual advantage prevail? What is the basis of right?

Although a Scot, Hume's answer is peculiarly English, finding in the resources of common law and history the forces which promote our mutual well-being. If all is opinion, then Hume will embrace opinion itself. Mutual advantage prevails through our opinion of right, formed by "authority and precedent. Dissolve these ties, you break all the bonds of civil society" (*Essays*, pt. II, no. XIV).

Property and government are the greatest of the creatures of opinion. Brought into being by the historical acts and speeches of men,

---

[25]Hobbes [4], ch. 18.
[26]Locke [3].

they exist subject to all the vicissitudes of the temporal. The realm of generation is the realm of corruption, but also of duration. Settled possession endures and becomes property; orderly regulation endures and becomes magistracy. The politics of interest endure and become the politics of right. Opinion is all; there is and can be no appeal against the present established practice of the age.

[4]

The Politics of Redemption

I

Our inquiry begins in that recreated beginning, that redeemed garden, the Elysium of Clarens.[1] To Saint-Preux, it is the gift of a nature which surpasses all human effort.

> Ce lieu, quoique tout proche de la maison, est tellement caché par l'allée couverte qui l'en sépare, qu'on ne l'aperçoit de nulle part. L'épais feuillage qui l'environne ne permet point à l'œil d'y pénétrer, et il est toujours soigneusement fermé à clef. À peine fus-je au-dedans, que, . . . je ne vis

Reprinted with permission of the University of Ottawa Press.

Source: This paper should be read as offering a hypothesis about Rousseau's political theory, based primarily on a study of the *Discours sur l'inégalité, Économie politique, La Nouvelle Héloïse, Émile, Contrat social, Lettres de la Montagne,* and *Gouvernement de Pologne,* supplemented by the *Essai sur l'origine des langues* which remained unpublished by Rousseau, the "Geneva manuscript" of the *Contrat social,* and the unfinished *Émile et Sophie,* and *Constitution pour la Corse.* If the hypothesis seems to fit these works, then it should be related more closely to the *Discours sur les sciences et les arts* and read against the autobiographical writings; these tasks remain to be undertaken.

Textual references are in the first instance to Rousseau [4], [5], and [7], identified respectively as *E, NH,* and *V.* These are all in modern French; I have modernized quotations from *Émile et Sophie* and the *Essai sur l'origine des langues* to conform. I have also provided references to Rousseau [6], identified as *OC;* this edition does not include the *Essai sur l'origine des langues,* identified as *OL* and to which I provide only chapter references.

Numerous writings on Rousseau have influenced me, but the only ones consciously in my mind in writing this paper (apart from one or two issues raised by Vaughan in Rousseau [7]) were Berman and Shklar.

[1]Clarens, in Switzerland, is the estate of Wolmar, husband of Julie. Saint-Preux, Julie's lover (and originally tutor) before her marriage, and now friend of the family, provides a long description of Clarens as a model community. The Elysium is Julie's creation and her special retreat.

plus en me retournant par où j'étais entré, et, n'apercevant point de porte, je me trouvai là comme tombé des nues.

. . . Ce lieu est charmant, . . . mais agreste et abandonné; je n'y vois point de travail humain. Vous avez fermé la porte; l'eau est venue je ne sais comment; la nature seule a fait tout le reste; et vous-même n'eussiez jamais su faire aussi bien qu'elle. (*NH*, 353–354; *OC*, II, 471–472)

But Saint-Preux is deceived. Elysium recreates nature, but the recreation is human artifice, as Julie, responding to his rapture, makes all too clear.

Il est vrai . . . que la nature a tout fait, mais sous ma direction, et il n'y a rien là que je n'aie ordonné. (*NH*, 354; *OC*, II, 472)

Tout ce que vous voyez sont des plantes sauvages ou robustes qu'il suffit de mettre en terre, et qui viennent ensuite d'elles-mêmes. D'ailleurs, la nature semble vouloir dérober aux yeux des hommes ses vrais attraits, auxquels ils sont trop peu sensibles, et qu'ils défigurent quand ils sont à leur portée: elle fuit les lieux fréquentés; . . . Ceux qui l'aiment et ne peuvent l'aller chercher si loin sont réduits à lui faire violence, à la forcer en quelque sorte à venir habiter avec eux; et tout cela ne peut se faire sans un peu d'illusion. (*NH*, 359–360; *OC*, II, 479–480)

A little illusion. Elysium is the very triumph of artifice, the work of man with all signs of the workman removed. "Je n'aperçois aucun pas d'hommes," says Saint-Preux. "Ah!" replies Wolmar, "c'est qu'on a pris grand soin de les effacer" (*NH*, 359; *OC*, II, 479). Here in the garden we penetrate to the heart of Rousseau's conceptions of man, nature, and society.

The story of humankind—the story of man's development or socialization—is the story of the fall from natural man, at one with himself and with nature, to perfected man,[2] who disfigures both self and nature.[3] From this fall none has escaped, not even those such as the Corsicans, who are least bound by the chains of civilization.[4] Even they desire what is not for their good. Even they must be recreated, so that Corsica may be another Elysium. For if Rousseau's story of human development is to be a tale not only of the fall but also of the

---

[2]According to Rousseau, perfectibility distinguishes man from other animals. See discussion in sec. 3 infra.

[3]"Il défigure tout" (*E*, 35; *OC*, IV, 245).

[4]"Les Corses sont presque encore dans l'état naturel et sain; mais il faut beaucoup d'art pour les y maintenir, parce que leurs préjugés les en éloignent: ils ont précisément ce qui leur convient, mais ils veulent ce qui ne leur est pas bon" (*V*, II, 355; *OC*, III, 950).

redemption, then it too must continue to a triumph of artifice which restores man to himself, effacing its own work in its act of recreation. Society must parallel the achievement of Elysium:

> Ce lieu solitaire, où le doux aspect de la seule nature devait chasser de mon souvenir tout cet ordre social et factice qui m'a rendu si malheureux! (*NH*, 364–365; *OC*, II, 486)

But can society redeem what human socialization has corrupted? Can man be redeemed by artifice—"un peu d'illusion"?

Our inquiry will turn to Rousseau's account of the history of humankind, but our concern will be to trace, not the origin of inequality, but rather the disappearance of liberty. In understanding why man enslaves himself in perfecting himself, we shall understand the predicament in which, according to Rousseau, we find ourselves, and the problem which his social theory endeavours to resolve.

We shall then move to the attempted resolution, to the artificers on which it depends, and to the artifice of a free society. As Julie does violence to nature in rescuing it from disfigurement, so Rousseau's greater artificers—the Legislator, the Tutor, Wolmar—do violence to man in rescuing him from the development he inflicts upon himself. Our concern will be, not so much with the necessity of this violence, as with its sufficiency. After posing us the stark picture of the man who "est né libre, et partout il est dans les fers," Rousseau may be able to answer his question "Qu'est-ce qui peut le rendre [i.e., ce changement] légitime?" (*V*, II, 23–24; *OC*, III, 351). But his answer fails before his own maxim: "Tout est bien sortant des mains de l'Auteur des choses, tout dégénère entre les mains de l'homme," (*E*, 35; *OC*, IV, 245). Everything degenerates, even in the hands of the best men. Julie may recreate nature in her Elysium, but not even Wolmar can recreate Julie.

II

Although Rousseau's conception of liberty is central to our argument, I cannot subject the host of contexts in which it figures to an exhaustive analysis, so I must be somewhat dogmatic. In my view the core account, clearly expressed in *Émile*, is that liberty lies in the sufficiency of power to desire.

> L'homme vraiment libre ne veut que ce qu'il peut, et fait ce qu'il lui plaît. Voilà ma maxime fondamentale. (*E*, 99; *OC*, IV, 309)

If one's desires exceed one's powers, then one cannot fulfill those desires and one feels enslaved by them. It is this inadequacy of power which is presupposed in Rousseau's insistence that "l'impulsion du seul appétit est esclavage" (*V*, II, 37; *OC*, III, 365).

This account of liberty illuminates Rousseau's conceptions of happiness, wealth, and human action, each of which is related to the proportion between power and desire.[5] Should desires exceed powers, one is miserable, poor, and inactive through despair. Should powers exceed desires, one is rich but inactive through indolence, or active only through duty and habit. A surfeit of happiness marks a danger to man's condition; we shall find cause to reflect with Rousseau on Julie's words, "Mon ami, je suis trop heureuse; le bonheur m'ennuie" (*NH*, 528; *OC*, II, 694).

Power, and hence liberty, depend on one's natural forces.

> Ta liberté, ton pouvoir, ne s'étendent qu'aussi loin que tes forces naturelles, et pas au-delà; tout le reste n'est qu'esclavage, illusion, prestige. (*E*, 98; *OC*, IV, 308)

Rousseau's words—slavery, illusion, prestige—are significant; they indicate those modes of human existence which are contrasted with liberty. If the slave finds his satisfaction only through conforming to the will of others, the man who seeks prestige finds his satisfaction only through maintaining the approbation of others. Both are treated by Rousseau as dependent and unfree, for both find their satisfaction hostage to the alien wills of others. The man whose satisfaction depends on illusion may seem to avoid this dependence, but in linking him with those who are unfree, Rousseau warns us not to accept too readily the seductions of a social theory which bases redemption on illusion. We must ask if he heeded his own warning.

The insistence that dependence on another is incompatible with liberty comes to occupy a central place in Rousseau's argument.[6] Indeed, Rousseau frequently formulates his conception in this essentially negative way:

[5]Happiness: "Plus l'homme est resté près de sa condition naturelle, plus la différence de ses facultés à ses désirs est petite, et moins par conséquent il est éloigné d'être heureux" (*E*, 94; *OC*, IV, 304).

Wealth: "Il n'y a point de richesse absolue. Ce mot ne signifie qu'un rapport de surabondance entre les désirs et les facultés de l'homme riche" (*NH*, 400; *OC*, II, 529–530).

Action: "Celui qui vit sans désirs, et celui qui sait ne pouvoir obtenir ce qu'il désire, restent également dans l'inaction. Il faut, pour agir, et qu'on aspire à quelque chose et qu'on puisse espérer d'y parvenir" (*V*, II, 345; *OC*, III, 938).

[6]"Quiconque dépend d'autrui, et n'a pas ses ressources en lui-même, ne saurait être libre" (*V*, 308; *OC*, III, 903).

La liberté consiste moins à faire sa volonté qu'à n'être pas soumis à celle d'autrui; elle consiste encore à ne pas soumettre la volonté d'autrui à la nôtre. (*V*, II, 234; *OC*, III, 841)

But this may seem to place undue weight on the relations between persons. What does it matter, one may ask, if I depend on others, when my own forces are insufficient to satisfy my desires? Grant that the most perfect liberty requires that power be adequate to desire; why is the greatest threat to liberty not then the slavery to desire which is manifest whenever desire outreaches power?[7]

Rousseau's account of human development answers these questions. It also explains other aspects of his conception of liberty—his insistence that liberty depends on submission to law,[8] and that moral liberty may be equated with obedience to a law that one prescribes to oneself.[9] We turn, then, to those parts of Rousseau's story of the fall of man which exhibit his conception of liberty and which relate to the prospect of redemption.

III

The natural or original condition of man is simple, self-sufficient, and stable. *Amour de soi*, the fundamental ground of all human action,[10] leads him to seek to satisfy his needs for food, drink, shelter, and sex; and in the original state of nature, few obstacles impede such satisfaction. *Pitié*, a natural repugnance at suffering, and especially at the suffering of those whom one discerns to be like oneself,[11] serves to direct one's efforts away from those actions which would harm others, so that man is inspired with "cette . . . maxime de bonté naturelle, . . . : *Fais ton bien avec le moindre mal d'autrui qu'il est possible*" (*V*, I, 163; *OC*, III, 156). Since man's original condition is primarily solitary, *pitié* is but an infrequent curb on the promptings of *amour de soi;* little that one man does has effects, good or bad, on any other.

Natural man, "l'homme sauvage," satisfies Rousseau's fundamental

---

[7]This view is suggested in *Émile et Sophie;* see discussion in sec. 9 infra.

[8]"J'aurais voulu vivre et mourir libre, c'est-à-dire tellement soumis aux lois, que ni moi ni personne n'en pût secouer l'honorable joug" (*V*, I, 126; *OC*, III, 112).

[9]"On pourrait . . . ajouter à l'acquis de l'état civil la liberté morale, qui seule rend l'homme vraiment maître de lui; car l'impulsion du seul appétit est esclavage, et l'obéissance à la loi qu'on s'est prescrite est liberté" (*V*, II, 37; *OC*, III, 365).

[10]"La source de nos passions, l'origine et le principe de toutes les autres, la seule qui naît avec l'homme et ne le quitte jamais tant qu'il vit, est l'amour de soi" (*E*, 275; *OC*, IV, 491).

[11]How do we discern others to be like ourselves? Rousseau does not say, but cf. *OL*, ch. 9, where he suggests that the activation of *pitié* requires the development of imagination.

condition for being free. His powers are perfectly proportioned to his needs. He has no cause, then, to seek either to extend his powers, or to diminish his desires.[12] But, having no cause to change, he does not manifest in his life what Rousseau considers the distinguishing characteristic of human beings:

> La faculté de se perfectionner, faculté qui, à l'aide des circonstances, développe successivement toutes les autres, et réside parmi nous tant dans l'espèce que dans l'individu. (*V*, I, 150; *OC*, III, 142)

Perfectibility plays a profoundly ambivalent role in Rousseau's argument. Despite the positive connotation of its name, it is, he insists,

> la source de tous les malheurs de l'homme; . . . c'est elle qui le tire, à force de temps, de cette condition originaire dans laquelle il coulerait des jours tranquilles et innocents; . . . c'est elle qui, faisant éclore avec les siècles ses lumières et ses erreurs, ses vices et ses vertus, le rend à la longue le tyran de lui-même et de la nature. (ibid.)

But this description of its effects anticipates developments in the human condition which Rousseau has yet to describe and explain.

After long ages, this original, free, and agreeable condition of human kind begins to destabilize. Rousseau tells us little about the causes of this destabilization, passing over the crucial beginnings of this momentous development in a single sentence—"À mesure que le genre humain s'étendit, les peines se multiplièrent avec les hommes" (*V*, I, 170; *OC*, III, 165). The pressure of increasing population upsets the balance between man's desires and his powers. On the one hand, those who remain in the forests where survival was originally easy find themselves competing with more and more of their fellows for resources which, under the pressure of increasing demand, are no longer in plentiful supply. On the other hand, those who leave the forests to avoid this competition for scarce goods find themselves driven to environments ever less conducive to human survival—"Des années stériles, des hivers longs et rudes, des étés brûlants, qui consument tout" (ibid.). Greater efforts, and greater powers, are required to secure the same satisfaction. Thus although these first changes do not affect man's desires, his powers to satisfy his desires are effectively

---

[12]"Qui ne voit que tout semble éloigner de l'homme sauvage la tentation et les moyens de cesser de l'être? Son imagination ne lui peint rien; son cœur ne lui demande rien. Ses modiques besoins se trouvent si aisément sous sa main, et il est si loin du degré de connaissances nécessaire pour désirer d'en acquérir de plus grandes, qu'il ne peut avoir ni prévoyance ni curiosité" (*V*, I, 151; *OC*, III, 144).

diminished by increasing density of population and increasing environmental hardships. Primitive liberty is endangered.

New activities are required for survival. Men begin to fish and hunt. And these new activities bring with them new ideas.[13] Human perfectibility begins the long course of its self-actualization. This actualization involves a continued interaction among power, intelligence, and desire. Faced with greater obstacles to the satisfaction of his original needs, man must increase his powers. This increase brings with it a development of his intelligence and his awareness. As his ideas enlarge, his desires also increase. These new, greater desires require yet greater powers to ensure their satisfaction, and so the process continues—powers, ideas, and desires each expanding in what seems an unending spiral. Once the original stable balance between desire and power is upset, man faces a succession of changes, as each new effort to satisfy his desires results in new desires to satisfy. The results are the emergence of the first form of human society—family life, and the beginnings of individual property.[14]

But with these new conditions, a new equilibrium between desire and power is established. Why the spiralling interaction among powers, ideas, and desires comes again to a point of stability, Rousseau does not explain. Perhaps of crucial importance is his supposition that the *units* in this stage of human development—families—have little contact one with another, just as the units in the original human condition—individual persons—had little contact. Each family, then, provides an horizon, both of powers and of ideas, within which the expansion of desires must be confined.

Thus Rousseau emphasizes, not so much the increase in man's wants from his original condition, but the limitation in these wants in relation to later stages in human development. Even so, he notes that the seeds of slavery are spreading:

Dans ce nouvel état, avec une vie simple et solitaire, des besoins très bornés, et les instruments qu'ils avaient inventés pour y pourvoir, les hommes, jouissant d'un fort grand loisir, l'employèrent à se procurer plusieurs sortes de commodités inconnues à leurs pères; et ce fut là le

---

[13]"Cette application reitérée des êtres divers à lui-même, et des uns aux autres, dut naturellement engendrer dans l'esprit de l'homme les perceptions de certains rapports. . . .

"Les nouvelles lumières qui résultèrent de ce développement augmentèrent sa supériorité sur les autres animaux, en la lui faisant connaître" (*V*, I, 170; *OC*, III, 165).

[14]"Ces premiers progrès mirent enfin l'homme à portée d'en faire de plus rapides. Plus l'esprit s'éclairait, et plus l'industrie se perfectionna. . . . Ce fut là l'époque d'une première révolution qui forma l'établissement et la distinction des familles, et qui introduisit une sorte de propriété" (*V*, I, 172; *OC*, III, 167).

premier joug qu'ils s'imposèrent, sans y songer, et la première source de maux qu'ils préparèrent à leurs descendants. (*V*, I, 173; *OC*, III, 168)

The new goods become needs, and as needs, "l'on était malheureux de les perdre, sans être heureux de les posséder" (ibid.).

Human speech makes its appearance in this epoch. In the *Discours* Rousseau suggests that language originates within the family.[15] But in the fuller account of the *Essai sur l'origine des langues*, he suggests that language develops in the first intercourse among families, an intercourse which is originally necessitated by the material conditions of life, but which takes its true character from the passions aroused in the young when they meet in the course of bringing their animals to water.

> Dans les lieux arides où l'on ne pouvait avoir de l'eau que par des puits, il fallut bien se réunir pour les creuser, ou du moins s'accorder pour leur usage. Telle dut être l'origine des sociétés et des langues dans les pays chauds.
>
> Là se formèrent les premiers liens des familles, là furent les premiers rendez-vous des deux sexes. . . . Là, des yeux accoutumés aux mêmes objets dès l'enfance commencèrent d'en voir de plus doux. Le cœur s'émut à ces nouveaux objets. . . . L'eau devint insensiblement plus nécessaire, le bétail eut soif plus souvent: on arrivait en hâte, et l'on partait à regret. . . . Là se firent les premières fêtes: les pieds bondissaient de joie, le geste empressé ne suffisait plus, la voix l'accompagnait d'accents passionnés. (*OL*, ch. 9)

Now it is in these fêtes around the watering places that human beings begin to develop a comparative, rather than an absolute, conception of themselves, and to concern themselves not merely with the satisfaction of their needs, original or acquired but also with their status relative to their fellows.

> Chacun commença à regarder les autres et à vouloir être regardé soi-même, et l'estime publique eut un prix. Celui qui chantait ou dansait le mieux, le plus beau, le plus fort, le plus adroit, ou le plus éloquent, devint le plus considéré: et ce fut là le premier pas vers l'inégalité, et vers le vice en même temps. De ces premières préférences naquirent d'un côté la vanité et le mépris, de l'autre la honte et l'envie; et la fermentation causée par ces nouveaux levains produisit enfin des composés funestes au bonheur et à l'innocence. (*V*, I, 174; *OC*, III, 169–170)

---

[15]"On entrevoit un peu mieux ici comment l'usage de la parole s'établit, ou se perfectionna, insensiblement dans le sein de chaque famille" (*V*, I, 173; *OC*, III, 168).

Here we find the real danger to the liberty of man. If his desires come to exceed his powers, he is no longer free, but his slavery endures only so long as his powers remain inadequate; by expanding his powers, or curbing his desires, he may regain his liberty. But if his desires come to depend for their satisfaction on the opinions of others, then no mere expansion of his powers or contraction of his desires will suffice to restore liberty. He is no longer free, because his satisfaction depends on the will of another, and he can no longer be free, because that will must forever be alien to his own. He may be able to force others to minister to his material needs, but he can only force them to *appear* to minister to his spiritual needs; he may command the appearance of their opinions, but not the opinions themselves.

Yet this danger is still, in Rousseau's view, largely potential. In this first stage of human society vanity exists, but its effects are mild.[16] Familial society preserves a mean between the indolence of the savage, who need do little to meet his few needs and thus satisfy the promptings of *amour de soi,* and the frantic activity of civilized man, who must exert himself constantly to meet the passions which depend on *amour-propre.*

The connection between *amour de soi* and *amour-propre* is crucial and difficult. In his notes to the *Discours* Rousseau says:

> Il ne faut pas confondre l'amour-propre et l'amour de soi-même, deux passions très différentes par leur nature et par leurs effets. L'amour de soi-même est un sentiment naturel qui porte tout animal à veiller à sa propre conservation, et qui, dirigé dans l'homme par la raison et modifié par la pitié, produit l'humanité et la vertu. L'amour-propre n'est qu'un sentiment relatif, factice, et né dans la société, qui porte chaque individu à faire plus de cas de soi que de tout autre, qui inspire aux hommes tous les maux qu'ils se font mutuellement, et qui est la véritable source de l'honneur. (*V,* I, 217; *OC,* III, 219)

Were this his last word on the relation between *amour de soi* and *amour-propre,* Rousseau would have set himself an evidently impossible task, by his own standards, in proposing to redeem man through a recreated society from the ills which socialization has brought. For there can be no society without *amour-propre.*

A consciously social relationship among human beings requires that

[16]"Ainsi, quoique les hommes fussent devenus moins endurants, et que la pitié naturelle eût déjà souffert quelque altération, ce période du développement des facultés humaines, tenant un juste milieu entre l'indolence de l'état primitif et la pétulante activité de notre amour-propre, dut être l'époque la plus heureuse et la plus durable" (*V,* I, 175; *OC,* III, 171).

each person party to it conceive oneself in relation to the other parties. But this is to conceive oneself, not absolutely, in oneself, but relatively, in terms of others. As long as one's conception of oneself is absolute and noncomparative, than *amour de soi* concerns itself only with the satisfaction of one's equally noncomparative desires. But as soon as one's conception of oneself becomes relative, based on a comparison with others, then *amour de soi* must concern itself with those passions proper to this relative self, and these passions have as their object one's superiority; the relative self necessarily seeks to be better than others. *Amour de soi* is thus transformed into *amour-propre* within *any* social context. Rousseau insists on this information in *Emile:*

> Mon Émile n'ayant jusqu'à présent regardé que lui-même, le premier regard qu'il jette sur ses semblables le porte à se comparer avec eux; et le premier sentiment qu'excite en lui cette comparaison est de désirer la première place. Voilà le point où l'amour de soi se change en amour-propre, et où commencent à naître toutes les passions qui tiennent à celle-là. (*E,* 305–306; *OC,* IV, 523)

If, as Rousseau says in the Notes to the *Discours, amour de soi* is in itself the source of all virtue; if, as we have just argued, in society *amour de soi* is necessarily transformed into *amour-propre;* and if, as Rousseau also says, *amour-propre* is the ground of all human ills; then what hope can there be for humankind? By this reasoning we seem led to agree with those who suppose Rousseau to be a romantic advocate of man's primitive condition, demanding that we cast off the chains of society to return to savage solitude. But Rousseau insists that these chains may be made legitimate. *Amour de soi* is, in itself, compatible with the natural goodness which Rousseau consistently ascribes to man in his original condition, but, despite what he says in the note quoted, it is not, in itself, the source of virtue—a very different characteristic, and one yet to be defined in our discussion. Indeed, when we come to characterize Rousseau's conception of virtue, we shall show that it proves to be a transmutation of *amour-propre,* just as *amour-propre* is a transmutation of *amour de soi.*[17]

But here our concern is with the ills caused by *amour-propre.* In the first, familial society, its force is insufficient to upset the balance be-

---

[17]Virtue may be derived indirectly, from *amour de soi,* as the source of all our passions (see n. 10 supra). But such a derivation, which would require *amour-propre* as intermediary, cannot be what Rousseau intends, in contrasting *amour de soi,* as the source of virtue, with *amour-propre,* as the source of all our ills. Rousseau's position here seems to me to contradict his usual view—a conclusion which I accept reluctantly, since in my judgment he maintains a single, consistent thesis about man and society throughout his writings.

tween desire and power which makes that society the happiest and stablest in the course of human development. And indeed, Rousseau supposes that, in itself, *amour-propre* would not upset this balance. It is the material circumstances of human life, and in particular the development of agriculture and metallurgy, which introduce real inequalities among persons and thereby give *amour-propre,* as the passion which concerns such inequalities, the opportunity to manifest its full power.

I shall not dwell on the growth of inequality, which is sufficiently clear in Rousseau's familiar and very powerful account. Let us consider, rather, the condition of man when *amour-propre* has run rampant, when man has been perfected, but depends for his well-being, not so much on the exercise of his newly acquired capacities, but on their effects in exciting the good opinion of others.[18] What if one lacks the characteristics which secure esteem? Then, as Rousseau says, one must appear to have them:

> Il fallut, pour son avantage, se montrer autre que ce qu'on était en effet. Être et paraître devinrent deux choses tout à fait différentes; et de cette distinction sortirent le faste imposant, la ruse trompeuse, et tous les vices qui en sont le cortège. (*V,* I, 178; *OC,* III, 174)

What one is has ceased to be important; what one appears to be—what one is in the eyes of one's fellows—is now what is essential. And so all are enslaved:

> D'un autre côté, de libre et indépendant qu'était auparavant l'homme, le voilà, par une multitude de nouveaux besoins, assujetti pour ainsi dire à toute la nature, et surtout à ses semblables, dont il devient l'esclave en un sens, même en devenant leur maître: riche, il a besoin de leurs services; pauvre, il a besoin de leurs secours; et la médiocrité ne le met point en état de se passer d'eux. (*V,* I, 178–179; *OC,* III, 174–175)

Worse even than the imbalance between our desires and our powers is this new distinction between what one is, and what one appears to be. For the latter comes to embrace the former. We must consider a

---

[18]"Voilà donc toutes nos facultés développées, la mémoire et l'imagination en jeu, l'amour-propre intéressé, la raison rendue active, et l'esprit arrivé presque au terme de la perfection dont il est susceptible. Voilà toutes les qualités naturelles mises en action, le rang et le sort de chaque homme établi, non seulement sur la quantité des biens et le pouvoir de servir ou de nuire, mais sur l'esprit, la beauté, la force ou l'adresse, sur le mérite ou les talents; et ces qualités étant les seules qui pouvaient attirer de la considération, il fallut bientôt les avoir ou les affecter" (*V,* I, 178; *OC,* III, 174).

yet bleaker picture of the descent of man. Rousseau has maintained that "le premier sentiment de l'homme fut celui de son existence" (*V*, I, 169; *OC*, III, 164). This sentiment is expressed directly in man's original existence, for "le sauvage vit en lui-même" (*V*, I, 195; *OC*, III, 193). In society, however, each man takes the sense of his existence only from his fellows:

> L'homme sociable, toujours hors de lui, ne sait vivre que dans l'opinion des autres; et c'est, pour ainsi dire, de leur seul jugement qu'il tire le sentiment de sa propre existence. (ibid.)

Liberty, as we have said, depends primarily on the sufficiency of one's powers for the satisfaction of one's desires. But here we have penetrated to a yet deeper level. Not only one's satisfaction, but the very sense of one's own existence, one's self-identity, is no longer in one's own power. One is what others believe one to be. Apart from those beliefs, one is nothing. The slave preserves his identity against his master; the social man take his identity from his fellows; in himself, he is a void. We have reached the end point in Rousseau's story of man's fall.

IV

Rousseau's published works offer no connected argument to link his account of man's socialization and fall to his account of man's redemption. To fill this gap we must turn to the draft of the *Contrat social* usually called the "Geneva manuscript," in which the second chapter, "De la Société générale du Genre humain," explains the need for artifice to rescue man from the ills occasioned by his historical social relationships.

The chapter begins with a brief characterization of man's passage from liberty to slavery, brought about by the disproportion between individual needs and individual powers which has rendered each dependent on his fellows. In this account Rousseau emphasizes the effects of unlimited desire.[19] The man who is ruled by *amour-propre* can never be content, since his desire is always for *more*.[20] Once one no

---

[19]"La force de l'homme est tellement proportionnée à ses besoins naturels et à son état primitif que, pour peu que cet état change et que ces besoins augmentent, l'assistance de ses semblables lui devient nécessaire; et quand enfin ses désirs embrassent toute la nature, le concours de tout le genre humain suffit à peine pour les assouvir" (*V*, I, 447; *OC*, III, 281–282).

[20]Cf. Samuel Gompers' answer when asked what labor wanted: "More!"

longer seeks an absolute level of satisfaction, each relative level can and must be surpassed, as long as one's power and one's intelligence are capable of expansion.

But Rousseau does not suggest that the solution to man's enslavement is to return to the liberty of his original condition. Despite the ills which our perfectibility brings upon us, Rousseau does not abandon the positive connotation of the term. If social man, as he is, is vicious, yet original man, although good, is not, and cannot be, virtuous.[21] Rousseau does not explain the nature of virtue at this point in his argument. As with liberty, I must be somewhat dogmatic in my explication; taking my cue again from *Émile,* I shall say that Rousseau equates virtue with self-mastery.

> Qu'est-ce donc que l'homme vertueux? C'est celui qui sait vaincre ses affections; car alors il suit sa raison, sa conscience; il fait son devoir; il se tient dans l'ordre, et rien ne l'en put écarter (*E,* 583; *OC,* IV, 818).

In the next section we shall examine this conception more positively, considering the object of self-mastery, but this merely formal account will suffice to indicate what Rousseau finds lacking in the savage. The savage is not dominated by his passions, but equally he does not dominate them; he lives in natural harmony with them. The virtuous man recreates that harmony, consciously reestablishing the balance of desire and power in his soul. Thus virtue is necessarily linked to liberty.

If we require the assistance of our fellows in order to satisfy the needs we acquire in perfecting ourselves, then why do we not unite our wills with theirs? Why does society, instead of enslaving each man to the alien wills of others, not liberate all men by providing a common power sufficient to satisfy the desires and needs of all? The immediate answer is all too obvious:

> Loin que l'intérêt particulier s'allie au bien général, ils s'excluent l'un l'autre dans l'ordre naturel des choses; et les lois sociales sont un joug que chacun veut bien imposer aux autres, mais non pas s'en charger lui-même. (*V,* I, 450; *OC,* III, 284)

---

[21] "Notre entendement ne saurait se développer; nous vivrions sans rien sentir, nous mourrions sans avoir vécu; tout notre bonheur consisterait à ne pas connaître notre misère; il n'y aurait ni bonté dans nos cœurs ni moralité dans nos actions, et nous n'aurions jamais goûté le plus délicieux sentiment de l'âme, qui est l'amour de la vertu" (*V,* I, 449; *OC,* III, 283).

The independent man freely admits the benefits which society could bring, but he sees no possibility of realizing them.[22] Rousseau's argument here is a familiar one in political theory. Although each man is able to recognize the benefits of mutual adherence to the law of society which dictates the common good, as compared with the costs of the violence and domination by force which result from the actions of men who consider only their own interests, yet each man is also able to recognize that the benefits, to him, arise only from the adherence of *others* to the law of society, whereas his own adherence imposes costs upon him, and each man, of course, expects every other man to reason in a similar manner.

This problem—the game-theoretic problem of the Prisoner's Dilemma, the economist's problem of external inefficiencies and public bads—is exacerbated for Rousseau by his insistence on the rôle of *amour-propre*. If the goods which men pursue were only *naturally* scarce, then conflict among them, although perhaps inevitable, under the particular material conditions of human existence, could at least be assuaged in a world of ever increasing production. But if the goods which men pursue are *intrinsically* scarce, so that a gain by one must be a loss for another, then no such assuagement is possible. And Rousseau recognizes that the goods pursued by *amour-propre* are of the latter kind:

> L'amour-propre, qui se compare, n'est jamais content et ne saurait l'être, parce que ce sentiment, en nous préférant aux autres, exige aussi que les autres nous préfèrent à eux; ce qui est impossible. (*E*, 276–277; *OC*, IV, 493)

Rousseau's problem may seem not dissimilar to Hobbes's. Although Rousseau disagrees with Hobbes's assessment of natural man,[23] he accepts the state of war, not as part of the true state of nature, but as the outcome of man's descent into slavery. But Hobbes's solution, which is to afford each the security of knowing that others will obey the law, can not suffice for Rousseau. Hobbes's men compete because they recognize each other as obstacles to the attainment of scarce material goods required for physical preservation.[24] Rousseau's men compete primarily because they are motivated by *amour-propre*, by the

---

[22]"Tout ce que vous me dites des avantages de la loi sociale pourrait être bon, si, tandis que je l'observerais scrupuleusement envers les autres, j'étais sûr qu'ils l'observeraient tous envers moi. Mais quelle sûreté pouvez-vous me donner là-dessus? et ma situation peut-elle être pire que de me voir exposé à tous les maux que les plus forts voudront me faire, sans oser me dédommager sur les faibles?" (*V*, I, 450; *OC*, III, 285).

[23]*V*, I, 159–160; *OC*, III, 153–154.

[24] Hobbes [4], ch. 13; cf. Gauthier [10], pp. 14–20.

desire to be superior to their fellows. Hobbesian men seek glory because they are insecure; overcome their insecurity and most of them will forego glory, and the rest may be compelled to abandon it. Rousseauian men seek glory because their desires are no longer directed at material preservation, as in the original state of nature, but rather aim at spiritual supremacy. And the quest for glory is a zero-sum game, condemning men to the condition of universal war.

At the end of his discussion of the lack of a true "société générale" among men, Rousseau writes:

> Loin de penser qu'il n'y ait ni vertu ni bonheur pour nous, et que le ciel nous ait abandonnés sans ressource à la dépravation de l'espèce, efforçons-nous de tirer du mal même le remède qui doit le guérir. Par de nouvelles associations, corrigeons, s'il se peut, le défaut de l'association générale. Que notre violent interlocuteur juge lui-même du succès. Montrons-lui, dans l'art perfectionné, la réparation des maux que l'art commencé fit à la nature; . . . Éclairons sa raison de nouvelles lumières, échauffons son cœur de nouveaux sentiments, et qu'il apprenne à multiplier son être et sa félicité, en les partageant avec ses semblables. (*V*, I, 454; *OC*, III, 288)

We require "l'art perfectionné"—art perfected to redeem man perfected. We have found this art brought to the aid of nature in Elysium; can it be brought to the aid of humankind? Can it transform the search for glory, so that it is a source of union rather than division?

At one level, this art is expressed in the social contract. Recognizing that there is no natural community among men, we put ourselves, "sous la suprême direction de la volonté générale" (*V*, II, 33; *OC*, III, 361), thereby creating the community to redeem what the socialization of man has heretofore disfigured. But this well-worn path is not our particular concern. Rather, we must consider the "nouvelles lumières" and "nouveaux sentiments"—the changes which must be effected in human beings to give content to the general will and so make community possible. And this brings our argument once again to *amour-propre*, and the problem of its transformation into virtue.

V

Wolmar, the "Legislator" of Clarens,[25] presents an account of *amour-propre* quite different from that which we have encountered previously in our inquiry:

[25]In calling Wolmar a Legislator I have in mind Julie's description of his activity (*NH*, 274; *OC*, II, 371–372) quoted in sec. 6 infra.

Je conçus que le caractère général de l'homme est un amour-propre
indifférent par lui-même, bon ou mauvais par les accidents qui le modi-
fient, et qui dépendent des coutumes, des lois, des rangs, de la fortune,
et de toute notre police humaine. (*NH,* 369; *OC,* II, 491)

Are the ill effects of *amour-propre,* not the inevitable consequences of
its emergence from *amour de soi,* but rather the result of the particular
circumstances in which it has been manifest in human life? Not only
does Wolmar suggest this view, but Rousseau makes it a crucial part of
the argument of *Émile.* Focusing on the first comparison which Émile
makes between his fellows and himself, Rousseau claims:

Voilà le point où l'amour de soi se change en amour-propre, et où com-
mencent à naître toutes les passions qui tiennent à celle-là. Mais pour
décider si celles de ces passions qui domineront dans son caractère
seront humaines et douces, ou cruelles et malfaisantes, si ce seront des
passions de bienveillance et de commisération, ou d'envie et de con-
voitise, il faut savoir à quelle place il se sentira parmi les hommes, et
quels genres d'obstacles il pourra croire avoir à vaincre pour parvenir à
celle qu'il veut occuper. (*E,* 306; *OC,* IV, 523–524)

The Tutor is unable to prevent the emergence of *amour-propre,* but he
is able to arrange the circumstances of Émile's life so that its effects
will be benign rather than baleful.

Of course, we can not suppose that Rousseau considers it merely
accidental that in the actual history of mankind *amour-propre* has been
the source of ill. Even if it is in itself a neutral characteristic, which in
the right hands can be harnessed for good, yet only "l'art perfectionné," the triumph of artifice makes this possible. The material
circumstances of human life, which have determined the actualization
of man's faculty of perfectibility, have also determined *amour-propre* as
the instrument of man's fall. Only by overcoming nature can it be the
instrument of redemption.

But how? How may *amour-propre* be linked to virtue? The key is
again to be found in *Émile:*

Étendons l'amour-propre sur les autres êtres, nous le transformerons
en vertu, et il n'y a point de cœur d'homme dans lequel cette vertu n'ait
sa racine. (*E,* 329; *OC,* IV, 547)

Amour-propre becomes virtue by redirecting it, so that its object is not
the individual but the group of which he is a member. The man who
considers himself in relation to his fellows, and seeks to outdo them, is
their enemy. The man who identifies with his group in relation to the

world outside is no longer the enemy of his fellows but rather their companion and loyal ally. If *amour-propre* were extended to all humankind, then, as Rousseau says, it would become "l'amour de la justice,"[26] and there could be a general society of the human race. But this ultimate transformation of *amour-propre* into the purely generalized sentiment of justice, the love of humankind which manifests itself in seeking happiness for all members of the species, is a remote ideal. Rousseau's usual thought is more limited; our fellows are not all humankind, but the members of a particular community—our fellow citizens.

We may ask why the redirection of the object of *amour-propre* has the effect of transforming it into virtue, given the conception of virtue as self-mastery or self-rule which we found present in Rousseau's thought. The answer would seem to be that a conscious concern with the interests of a group, which is required by the extension of *amour-propre*, requires the control of our own particular passions, so that they conform to those interests. Self-mastery does not simply serve the interests of the individual; rather, it plays its primary rôle in enabling us to cooperate fully with our fellows. And so we may conceive virtue as, negatively, mastery over our particular passions which, positively, leads us to consider and to act for the well-being, not of ourselves, but of all those with whom we identify ourselves through transformed *amour-propre*. Indeed, virtue consists in adherence to the general will, since that will expresses the interests common to the members of a community, in rules which take the form of laws prescribed by all. As obedience to self-prescribed law, virtue is identical with moral liberty.[27]

The transformation of *amour-propre* into virtue is effected through pride. Pride and vanity are, we may say, the two species of *amour-propre*, the former found in the "great-souled" men characteristic of societies in their vigorous youth, the latter found in the small-minded, civilized men who are omnipresent today.[28] Although both pride and vanity occasion conflict among men,[29] here their resemblance ceases. Vanity is directed towards superficial and ephemeral goods and gives

[26]"Moins l'objet de nos soins tient immédiatement à nous-mêmes, moins l'illusion de l'intérêt particulier est à craindre; plus on généralise cet intérêt, plus il devient équitable; et l'amour du genre humain n'est autre chose en nous que l'amour de la justice" (*E*, 329; *OC*, IV, 547).

[27]See n. 9 supra.

[28]"Vous verrez d'où vient à notre amour-propre la forme que nous lui croyons naturelle; et comment l'amour de soi, cessant d'être un sentiment absolu, devient orgueil dans les grandes âmes, vanité dans les petites, et dans toutes se nourrit sans cesse aux dépens du prochain" (*E*, 278; *OC*, IV, 494).

[29]My argument is that pride occasions conflict primarily among peoples, not individuals. But Rousseau is less than explicit on this point.

rise to endless petty and selfish clashes among individuals. It must be eradicated from the souls of men, if they are to constitute a true community. In its place must be pride, which is directed towards those objects which are truly fine and deserving of estimation, the power and the freedom of the community.[30] Pride is thus the source of group-feeling, of *amour de la patrie,* which serves to unite as well as to divide men. And it is this transformation into *amour de la patrie* which links *amour-propre* with virtue.

Rousseau's clearest account of this transformation is found in the *Économie politique.*

> Il semble que le sentiment de l'humanité s'évapore et s'affaiblisse en s'étendant sur toute la terre. . . . Il faut en quelque manière borner et comprimer l'intérêt et la commisération pour lui donner de l'activité. . . . Il est certain que les plus grands prodiges de vertu ont été produits par l'amour de la patrie: ce sentiment doux et vif, qui joint la force de l'amour-propre à toute la beauté de la vertu, lui donne une énergie qui, sans la défigurer, en fait la plus héroïque de toutes les passions (*V,* I, 251; *OC,* III, 254–255).

Amour de la patrie—pride directed toward the institutions, practices, and concerns which unite men as citizens—is the sentiment which brings human beings into that conscious concern with their fellows, and that conscious regulation of their own passions, which serve to distinguish virtue from mere natural goodness. Those who are motivated by *amour de la patrie* do not cease to compete with their fellows, but their competition is directed not toward the amassing of commodities but to the service of their common mother. The obstacles which each must overcome, to achieve the status which his pride demands, are the very objects which the vain man seeks; thus *amour-propre,* transformed into *amour de la patrie,* takes on a moral character quite opposite to that with which it began.

This transformation also reconciles *amour-propre* with liberty. For when men are motivated by *amour de la patrie,* the balance between desire and power can be restored, albeit in a new form, so that men, ceasing to be dependent on the alien wills of others, but becoming dependent on the general will of their country, are free in effecting that will which expresses the passions and the interests common to them.

---

[30]"L'opinion qui met un grand prix aux objets frivoles produit la vanité; mais celle qui tombe sur des objets grands et beaux par eux-mêmes produit l'orgueil. . . . Comme il n'y a rien de plus réellement beau que l'indépendance et la puissance, tout peuple qui se forme est d'abord orgueilleux" (*V,* II, 344–345; *OC,* III, 938).

Of course, no single individual has the power to satisfy the pride which directs him to the cause of his country. But this pride, unlike the particular passions which divide individuals, unites fellow citizens, so that each may include the capacities of his fellows in considering the adequacy of his power to the satisfaction of his pride. Although each is dependent on others, yet each is dependent only in those respects in which his will is united with the wills of those others. Thus there are neither masters nor slaves, but only citizens.

Law, as the expression of the general will, is the condition of freedom, for law expresses the demands of each man's *amour-propre*, transformed into *amour de la patrie*, and thus directed only on the common concerns of all the citizens. But we must note—law is the condition of freedom *only* for those in whom this transformation has taken place.

But how may this new freedom be brought about? For Rousseau, there is no historical dialectic which can effect such a change in human beings. History does not redeem humankind, as Marx supposes. Indeed, the history of man, within the confines of his natural development, is at an end. There is no new transformation, no further stage in human progress, which will operate within history to restore the liberty which civilized men have lost. Only an irruption into history can effect the transformation needed if human beings are to be united in true community. We turn now to consider the persons to whom Rousseau entrusts this irruption, and with it, our redemption.

VI

> Les lois ne sont proprement que les conditions de l'association civile. Le peuple soumis aux lois en doit être l'auteur; il n'appartient qu'à ceux qui s'associent de régler les conditions de la société. Mais comment les régleront-ils? . . . De lui-même le peuple veut toujours le bien, mais de lui-même il ne le voit pas toujours. . . . Il faut lui faire voir les objets tels qu'ils sont, quelquefois tels qu'ils doivent lui paraître. . . . Les particuliers voient le bien qu'ils rejettent; le public veut le bien qu'il ne voit pas. Tous ont également besoin de guides. Il faut obliger les uns à conformer leurs volontés à leur raison; il faut apprendre à l'autre à connaître ce qu'il veut. . . . Voilà d'où naît la nécessité d'un Législateur. (*V*, II, 50–51; *OC*, III, 380)

This passage from the *Contrat social,* more perspicuously placed in the "Geneva manuscript" as the culmination of the first book, introduces the *deus ex machina* required by Rousseau to institute the redemptive society. Throughout his political works, from the *Économie politique* to the *Considérations sur le gouvernement de Pologne,* Rousseau emphasizes the importance of the Legislator. His model is historical; he discusses, in that last work, the great legislators of antiquity—Moses, Lycurgus, Numa.[31]

What task did these legislators accomplish? To give laws is, for Rousseau, to create the will which alone can make law—the general will.[32] And to create the general will is to create a people. It is to shape the desires, passions, and interests, of those who are to constitute a community,[33] focusing their attention exclusively on those activities and practices which unite them, and which distinguish them from other peoples. And this shaping of passion and domination of opinion which transforms a multitude into a people requires the Legislator to concern himself primarily with education, conceived as the entire process whereby the young are socialized into citizenship.

> Par où donc émouvoir les cœurs, et faire aimer la patrie et ses lois? L'oserai-je dire? Par des jeux d'enfants: par des institutions oiseuses aux yeux des hommes superficiels, mais qui forment des habitudes chéries et des attachements invincibles. (*V*, II, 427; *OC*, III, 955)

Rousseau has learned well the lesson of the *Republic;* education, not economics, is the chief concern of the true community, the community that will redeem its members.

> Je finis cette partie de l'*économie* publique par où j'aurais dû la commencer. La patrie ne peut subsister sans la liberté, ni la liberté sans la vertu, ni la vertu sans lescitoyens. Vous aurez tout si vous formez des citoyens.... Or, former des citoyens n'est pas l'affaire d'un jour; et, pour les avoir hommes, il faut les instruire enfants. (*V*, I, 255; *OC*, III, 259)

---

[31]"Le même esprit guida tous les anciens Législateurs dans leurs institutions. Tous cherchèrent des liens qui attachassent les citoyens à la patrie et les uns aux autres: et ils les trouvèrent dans des usages particuliers, dans des cérémonies religieuses qui par leur nature étaient toujours exclusives et nationales; dans des jeux qui tenaient beaucoup les citoyens rassemblés; dans des exercices qui augmentaient avec leur vigueur et leurs forces leur fierté et l'estime d'eux-mêmes; dans des spectacles qui, leur rappelant l'histoire de leurs ancêtres, leurs malheurs, leurs vertus, leurs victoires, intéressaient leurs cœurs, les enflammaient d'une vive émulation, et les attachaient fortement à cette patrie dont on ne cessait de les occuper" (*V*, II, 429–430; *OC*, III, 958).

[32]"Elles [les lois] sont des actes de la volonté générale" (*V*, II, 49; *OC*, III, 379).

[33]"Quiconque se mêle d'instituer un peuple doit savoir dominer les opinions, et par elles gouverner les passions, des hommes" (*V*, II, 437; *OC*, III, 965–966).

For Rousseau, as for Plato, education penetrates to the inmost core of the being of each citizen. Man must achieve a second nature, a sense of self-identity which ties him inseparably to his community.

> Les bonnes institutions sociales sont celles qui savent le mieux dénaturer l'homme, lui ôter son existence absolue pour lui en donner une relative, et transporter le *moi* dans l'unité commune; en sorte que chaque particulier ne se croie plus un, mais partie de l'unité, et ne soit plus sensible que dans le tout. Un citoyen de Rome n'était ni Caïus, ni Lucius; c'était un Romain; même il aimait la patrie exclusivement à lui. (*E*, 39; *OC*, IV, 249)

As we have seen, the man governed by *amour de soi* lives in himself, enjoying an absolute, independent existence. But once *amour de soi* is transformed into *amour-propre*, one lives only relatively to others, and independent existence becomes empty. The very sentiment of one's existence must be found in the opinions of others. The Legislator is therefore compelled to effect a complete transformation of each individual, giving him an existence appropriate to that sentiment. The citizen must bear no trace of the original, absolute, independent being proper to him as a natural man. He must indeed be given an existence relative to others, but he must not come to find the sentiment of that existence in the opinions of those whom he conceives as alien to himself, with desires and wills entirely independent of his own, for that would render him a slave. Rather, he must be made to identify himself as an indivisible part of a single, greater whole, taking the sentiment of his existence from the opinions of those with whom he shares common institutions and practices, which manifest the desires, the opinions, and the will common to all. And it is the Legislator who must bring this about, as Rousseau explains very clearly in the *Économie politique*:

> Si . . . on les exerce assez tôt à ne jamais regarder leur individu que par ses relations avec le Corps de l'État, et à n'apercevoir, pour ainsi dire, leur propre existence que comme une partie de la sienne, ils pourront parvenir enfin à s'identifier en quelque sorte avec ce plus grand tout, à se sentir membres de la patrie, à l'aimer de ce sentiment exquis que tout homme isolé n'a que pour soi-même, à élever perpétuellement leur âme à ce grand objet, et à transformer ainsi en une vertu sublime cette disposition dangereuse d'où naissent tous nos vices. (*V*, I, 255–256; *OC*, III, 259–260)

The radical break between individual and communal existence is emphasized again in *Contrat social*. The words Rousseau uses here, as elsewhere, in describing the task of the Legislator, are of the first importance if we are to grasp the import of his thought, for they underline how little he shares the views of the romantic advocates of natural man. Whatever man has been, what he must become is a product of "l'art perfectionné," a totally socialized being—or he is nothing.

> Celui qui ose entreprendre d'instituer un peuple doit se sentir en état de changer pour ainsi dire la nature humaine, de transformer chaque individu, qui par lui-même est un tout parfait et solitaire, en partie d'un plus grand tout, dont cet individu reçoive en quelque sorte sa vie et son être. . . . Il faut, en un mot, qu'il ôte à l'homme ses forces propres pour lui en donner qui lui soient étrangères, et dont il ne puisse faire usage sans le secours d'autrui. . . . en sorte que, si chaque citoyen n'est rien, ne peut rien, que par tous les autres, et que la force acquise par le tout soit égale ou supérieure à la somme des forces naturelles de tous les individus, on peut dire que la législation est au plus haut point de perfection qu'elle puisse atteindre. (*V*, II, 51–52; *OC*, III, 381–382)

Each person must lose all of his natural powers, acquiring in their place social powers, whose exercise depends on the cooperation of others. But then has the Legislator not instituted the most complete servitude? Each person is rendered totally impotent to satisfy his desires. Rousseau has insisted that liberty requires the sufficiency of one's powers to the satisfaction of one's desires, and that these powers must depend on one's own natural forces, so that their exercise is not subject to the wills of others. How may liberty and citizenship be reconciled?

The liberty of the citizen is achieved by the shaping of his will. He is free, because the Legislator has given him a new nature. To make the powers of each individual depend entirely on the cooperation of others would be slavery, were the will of each individual not identical with the will of others. The task of the Legislator is to ensure this identity. To the citizens, then, the powers of her fellows are her own, since neither she nor they has any existence, any desires, any opinions, any will, apart from the community. Each is utterly dependent, but only on that greater whole from which she takes the sense of her own existence, and so the conception of her own liberty.

Liberty depends on the adequacy of power to the satisfaction of desire; the Legislator institutes an order among men in which this adequacy is assured, insofar as such assurance is possible in this changing world. In *Nouvelle Héloïse*, Julie represents the activity of Wolmar in this light:

L'ordre qu'il a mis dans sa maison est l'image de celui qui règne au fond de son âme, et semble imiter dans un petit ménage l'ordre établi dans le gouvernement du monde. . . . On y reconnaît toujours la main du maître et l'on ne la sent jamais; il a si bien ordonné le premier arrangement qu'à présent tout va tout seul, et qu'on jouit à la fois de la règle et de la liberté. (*NH*, 274; *OC*, II, 371–372)

This passage is central to Rousseau's argument.[34] The order which Wolmar has established at Clarens, the order of the ideal familial society, corresponds both to the order in the soul of the Legislator and to the order found in the universe as a whole. Society is both macrocosm and microcosm—a greater person, and a lesser nature. The same liberty which man exhibits as part of the universal order—the liberty which rests on the identity between the order in man's soul and the order in the universe—is thus to be found in the true society. And this liberty is manifest not in the absence of rule but in the presence of a rule such that society is self-sustaining—"tout va tout seul." Artifice has recreated nature.

But we may suspect this recreation. The citizen is free only because he has been appropriately molded. Can this be true freedom? The activity of the Legislator, like that of the divine Creator whose order he imitates, may be thought incompatible with the liberty of his creation.

VII

To understand more clearly the relation between the Legislator and the redeemed citizens whom he creates, we may examine the analogous relation between the Tutor and the redeemed individual whom he also in effect creates. Both Legislator and Tutor are primarily educators; the one educates public man, the other private man. But the discussion of private education, in *Émile*, develops quite explicitly the nature of a relationship which in effect combines extreme dependence with what, Rousseau nevertheless insists, meets his criterion of liberty. In one sense we find Émile utterly dependent on his Tutor, just as the inhabitants of Clarens are dependent on Wolmar, and the citizens of Sparta on Lycurgus. And yet Rousseau wants to argue that Émile, the inhabitants of Clarens, and the citizens of Sparta are all truly free.

The child cannot be truly free, because his powers are inadequate

[34]It is however omitted from the recent abridged translation of *La Nouvelle Héloïse;* see Rousseau [5a].

to meet his basic needs. Indeed, this inadequacy is what makes him a child. Thus Rousseau insists that Émile's needs be met *as needs*.[35] Beyond this, the child must learn to depend solely on his own powers. Otherwise he will rapidly descend into the servitude of apparent mastery—expecting the power of others to be directed to his pleasure, and thus depending on their favor for his satisfaction. But more, not only must the child not become dependent through dominating others, he must also not become dependent through being dominated by them. The Tutor must then not control Émile by attaching arbitrary consequences to Émile's actions—favors and frowns which Émile recognizes as emanating from the Tutor's own will. Rather, the Tutor must exercise his control by ensuring that the natural consequences of Émile's actions affect appropriately the development of his desires and his powers.[36]

Rousseau does not suppose that the Tutor should merely let nature, or, perhaps more accurately, existing society, take its course. As he makes very clear, the Tutor must so arrange the situations in which Émile finds himself that the actual consequences of his actions will have the desired developmental effects. In other words, although Émile is not directly dependent on the will of his Tutor, and recognizes no connection between the consequences of what he does and what is subject to the Tutor's will, yet he is indirectly dependent, in that the Tutor wills the entire framework within which Émile's actions "naturally" have the consequences which the Tutor intends.

Thus Rousseau says:

> Prenez une route opposée avec votre élève; qu'il croie toujours être le maître, et que ce soit toujours vous qui le soyez. Il n'y a point de assujettissement si parfait que celui qui garde l'apparence de la liberté; on captive ainsi la volonté même. . . . Sans doute il ne doit faire que ce qu'il veut; mais il ne doit vouloir que ce que vous voulez qu'il fasse; il ne doit pas faire un pas que vous ne l'ayez prévu; il ne doit pas ouvrir la bouche que vous ne sachiez ce qu'il va dire. (*E*, 150; *OC*, IV, 362–363)

By making the child dependent only on things, but by determining the nature of this dependence, one not only preserves the appearance of liberty for the child, so that subjectively, he considers himself free, but one comes also to a mastery over him quite different from render-

---

[35]"N'accordez rien à ses désirs parce qu'il le demande, mais parce qu'il en a besoin" (*E*, 101; *OC*, IV, 311).

[36]"Maintenez l'enfant dans la seule dépendance des choses, vous aurez suivi l'ordre de la nature dans le progrès de son éducation. N'offrez jamais à ses volontés indiscrètes que des obstacles physiques ou des punitions qui naissent des actions mêmes, et qu'il se rappelle dans l'occasion" (ibid.).

ing him dependent on one's will—one comes to a mastery of *his* will. Émile acts in accordance with his own will, but that will accords with the Tutor. Thus the Tutor is able to determine—and, as Rousseau makes clear, to determine completely—Émile's actions, without violating the condition essential to liberty, that one not be dependent on the alien will of another. Since Émile's dependence on the will of the Tutor is entirely mediated through Émile's own will, and since the dependence is, at this stage of Émile's development, entirely unconscious, Émile is not enslaved. And indeed, since the Tutor is able to shape Émile's passions to fit his powers, Émile is enabled to attain a positive liberty.

As Émile matures he ceases to require others to minister to his physical needs. However, he has yet to acquire true control over his passions; he is not yet virtuous. He is unable to secure his freedom, not only against external domination, but against internal domination by forces which he is impotent to satisfy. Thus he enters into a new phase of his relationship with the Tutor, in which he consciously takes his will freely from the Tutor's law:

> Je veux obéir à vos lois, je le veux toujours, c'est ma volonté constante; si jamais je vous désobéis, ce sera malgré moi: rendez-moi libre en me protégeant contre mes passions qui me font violence; empêchez-moi d'être leur esclave, et forcez-moi d'être mon propre maître en n'obéissant point à mes sens, mais à ma raison. (*E,* 426; *OC,* IV, 651–652)

And with his mastery over Émile's will firmly established, the Tutor's basic task is accomplished:

> Je lui laisse, il est vrai, l'apparence de l'indépendance, mais jamais il ne me fut mieux assujetti, car il l'est parce qu'il veut l'être. Tant que je n'ai pu me rendre maître de sa volonté, je le suis demeuré de sa personne; je ne le quittais pas d'un pas. Maintenant je le laisse quelquefois à lui-même, parce que je le gouverne toujours. (*E,* 435–436; *OC,* IV, 661)

The original man, the savage, is free, we have seen, because he lives within himself. He enjoys *real* liberty—the liberty of a being whose powers are *naturally* proportioned to the satisfaction of his desires, which themselves are pure givens, reflecting the needs of his condition. But for civilized man, real liberty is impossible. The emergence of *amour-propre* forces us to live outside ourselves. We must find the sense of our own self-identity in some object beyond our individual selves. Living in relation to that object, our individual powers can never be proportioned adequately to the satisfaction of our desires.

And so our liberty can only be apparent—the liberty of a being who, through artifice, takes not only the sense of his existence, but his very will, from a greater whole in which power and desire are commensurate. Our liberty depends on a shaping of our will which itself is subject neither to our desire nor to our power—a shaping which confers that appearance of independence identified by Rousseau with the independence of the citizen.

Left without guidance or control, men live a purely reflected existence, each mirrored in the others. Émile is able to live freely only in relation to his Tutor, by identifying with the rule which the Tutor has established. Citizens are able to live freely only in relation to their community, by identifying with the institutions and practices established by the Legislator. Their existence, although dependent, avoids dependence on what, according to Rousseau, we ultimately find alien—the opaque wills of others. Rather, their dependence is their identity; Émile internalizes the Tutor's rule; the citizen internalizes the social order. This internalization is and must be induced. We may even say that it is forced, and this is indeed what Rousseau intends, when he reminds us in *Contrat social* that we may be forced to be free.[37] He does not suppose that we can be physically constrained to be free. In tracing his argument, what we have found is that liberty demands spiritual constraint—the shaping of passion, opinion, and will. We have found that in the citizen both dependence and freedom are perfected, and in their perfection, made one.

VIII

The Legislator creates citizens, but they must live without him. How are they to do this? After considering their rôles, we shall turn to our final concern—is the life of the citizen possible? Is there a political redemption?

Although the Legislator proposes laws to his community, he does not enact them. He is not sovereign; sovereignty resides, for Rousseau, only in the body of citizens. The general will is the will of that body, and the laws are its edicts, addressed to itself. The Legislator proposes; the citizens dispose.[38]

The Legislator does, of course, ensure the acceptance of his proposals. The general will, the will common to the citizens which makes them one body, is his creation. He may say of the people, what the

[37]"Que quiconque refusera d'obéir à la volonté générale y sera contraint par tout le Corps: ce qui ne signifie autre chose sinon qu'on le forcera d'être libre" (*V*, II, 36; *OC*, III, 364).
[38]*V*, II, 48–54; *OC*, III, 378–384.

Tutor says of Émile, that he has made himself "maître de sa volonté," so that "je le gouverne toujours."

But what is the rôle of the citizen in the absence of the Legislator? Essentially, it must be to remain faithful to what the Legislator has proposed, and what the citizens, through the general will, have in consequence enacted. There is a temptation, particularly if one focuses exclusively on the *Contrat social*, to misinterpret Rousseau here, and to suppose that he conceives the ideal polity as a participatory democracy. For sovereignty is exercised by the citizens, and Rousseau considers how this may be done, sketching the procedures to be followed to ensure that the true voice of the general will is heard.[39] And this may lead one to suppose that the primary activity of men in the true community is political, that their primary task is to assemble in order to formulate the general will.

From this perspective, one may find it difficult to understand Rousseau's support for the "droit négatif" in his analysis of the constitutional structure of Geneva.[40] He argues, on the one hand, that the *Conseil général*, the council of all the citizens of Geneva, is sovereign, and that its sovereignty is the necessary condition of the legitimacy of the Genevan polity. But he maintains, on the other hand, that this council has no right to initiate legislation, that it may consider only those propositions put to it by the *petit Conseil*, the executive body, or government in the special sense which Rousseau attaches to this term.[41] This right of the *petit Conseil* to initiate legislation is the "droit négatif" which Rousseau defends.

Rousseau insists that the rule of law is incompatible with the constant innovation which would result from affording the citizens an unrestricted right to initiate legislation.[42] One might suppose this a concession to expediency. Rousseau knew well that the *Conseil général*

---

[39]*V*, II, 42–43, 102–106; *OC*, III, 372–373, 438–441.

[40]Rousseau does not defend the "droit négatif" claimed by the *petit Conseil*, which extended to an absolute veto on Representations by the citizens against the administration of the law. See Vaughan's discussion, *V*, II, 178–183.

[41]"Qu'est-ce donc que le Gouvernement? Un corps intermédiaire établi entre les sujets et le souverain pour leur mutuelle correspondance, chargé de l'exécution des lois et du maintien de la liberté, tant civile que politique" (*V*, II, 65; *OC*, III, 396).

[42]"Car, le Gouvernement ayant un droit négatif contre les innovations du Législateur, et le peuple un droit négatif contre les usurpations du Conseil, les lois seules règnent, et règnent sur tous" (*V*, II, 288; *OC*, III, 894). (Rousseau's use here of "Législateur" does not conform to his usual usage, since it is the sovereign, the *Conseil général*, to which he refers. By "Conseil" he intends, of course, the *petit Conseil*.)

"L'aversion des nouveautés est donc généralement bien fondée; . . . et le Gouvernement ne peut apporter un trop grand obstacle à leur établissement: car, quelques utiles que fussent des lois nouvelles, les avantages en sont presque toujours moins sûrs que les dangers n'en sont grands" (*V*, II, 239; *OC*, III, 846).

did not claim the right to initiate, and that such a right could not be considered conformable to the Genevan constitution. But there is ample evidence that the stability assured by denying the sovereign body of citizens the right to initiate legislation is indeed a fundamental demand of Rousseau's theory. For as we have seen, he insists that "Les lois ne sont proprement que les conditions de l'association civile."[43] Once these conditions, the constitution of society, become established, then any further legislation must involve an alteration of the basic social bonds. And any such alteration may be expected to have a destabilizing effect.[44]

Rousseau's analysis of the constitutional structure of Geneva is an application of the political theory developed in *Contrat social*. But the ideas of that theory were present in his dedication of the *Discours sur l'inégalité* to the Genevan republic, in which he described the country he would have chosen for himself:

> J'aurais cherché un pays où le droit de législation fût commun à tous les citoyens; car qui peut mieux savoir qu'eux sous quelles conditions il leur convient de vivre ensemble dans une même société? . . .
> J'aurais désiré que, pour arrêter les projets intéressés et mal conçus et les innovations dangereuses qui perdirent enfin les Athéniens, chacun n'eût pas le pouvoir de proposer de nouvelles lois à sa fantaisie; que ce droit appartînt aux seuls magistrats.[45]

Liberty does not express itself in political activity, in the art of formulating and enacting laws. Rather, this art is the condition of liberty, and liberty itself is the fruit of living under laws, conforming one's will to them so that life is tranquil and stable. Liberty is not an activity but a habit.[46] Hence when Rousseau applies his political theo-

[43]Quoted in sec. 6 supra.

[44]"Depuis que la constitution de votre État a pris une forme fixe et stable, vos fonctions de Législateur sont finies. La sûreté de l'édifice veut qu'on trouve à présent autant d'obstacles pour y toucher qu'il fallait d'abord de facilités pour le construire. Le droit négatif des Conseils, pris en ce sens, est l'appui de la République" (*V*, II, 235; *OC*, III, 843).

[45]The passage continues: "Qu'ils en usassent même avec tant de circonspection, que le peuple, de son côté, fût si réservé à donner son consentement à ces lois, et que la promulgation ne pût s'en faire qu'avec tant de solennité, qu'avant que la constitution fût ébranlée on eût le temps de se convaincre que c'est surtout la grande antiquité des lois qui les rend saintes et vénérables; que le peuple méprise bientôt celles qu'il voit changer tous les jours; et qu'en s'accoutumant à négliger les anciens usages, sous prétexte de faire mieux, on introduit souvent de grands maux pour en corriger de moindres" (*V*, I, 127–128; *OC*, III, 113–114).

[46]"Car il en est de la liberté comme de ces aliments solides et succulents, ou de ces vins généreux, propres à nourrir et fortifier les tempéraments robustes qui en ont l'habitude, mais qui accablent, ruinent et enivrent les faibles et délicats qui n'y sont point faits" (*V*, I, 127; *OC*, III, 112–113).

ry to the analysis or the reform of actual political institutions, he constantly emphasizes the need for stability, the need to retain existing laws and usages:

> Braves Polonais, prenez garde: prenez garde que, pour vouloir trop bien être, vous n'empiriez votre situation. En songeant à ce que vous voulez acquérir, n'oubliez pas ce que vous pouvez perdre. Corrigez, s'il se peut, les abus de votre constitution; mais ne méprisez pas celle qui vous a faits ce que vous êtes. . . .
>
> Qu'il soit aisé, si l'on veut, de faire de meilleures lois; il est impossible d'en faire dont les passions des hommes n'abusent pas, comme ils ont abusé des premières. (*V*, II, 426; *OC*, III, 954–955)

The problem is not that better laws cannot be devised. The problem is that political reform requires a change in the passions of men, and the opinions on which these passions depend. It is these which determine whether or not there is a true basis for law. In the absence of the Legislator, who will form these passions? Who will decide men's opinions? Better to maintain the opinions and passions which men have, if these afford any basis at all for community, rather than to seek to impose new ones.

The ultimate political task is the creation of citizens. Once this is accomplished, the citizens can only carry out the laws which are the very ground of their existence. Redeemed men can, perhaps, be patriots. They can, perhaps, be just. They can display virtue. But they are not true Legislators. Rousseau never forgets this essential point.

The life of the citizen is, from one standpoint, an active one. Rousseau supposes that the members of society should be constantly occupied with the grand objects of civic life. But from another, and perhaps deeper, perspective, the life of the citizen is profoundly passive. "Le commerce produit la richesse; mais l'agriculture assure la liberté" (*V*, II, 311; *OC*, III, 905). No life is more conservative, more stable, more tranquil, than the agricultural.

IX

After the marriage of Émile and Sophie, the Tutor abdicates his authority over his former pupil.[47] But he does not take his leave, and some months later, learning that he is to become a father, Émile says to the Tutor, "Tant que je vivrai, j'aurai besoin de vous. J'en ai plus besoin que jamais, maintenant que mes fonctions d'homme commen-

[47]"J'abdique aujourd'hui l'autorité que vous m'avez confiée, et voici [Sophie] désormais votre gouverneur" (*E*, 628; *OC*, IV, 867).

cent" (*E*, 629; *OC*, IV, 868). These words are troubling. Has not Émile
been educated to live as a man? Should he not be able to enter into the
world, where "tout va tout seul?"

Alas, as the sequel makes clear, even the best education is not
enough. After several years Émile and Sophie take up residence in
Paris; the manner of their lives changes; Émile's habits degenerate;
Sophie becomes pregnant by another man. Émile leaves her and,
after various wanderings, is enslaved by the Barbary pirates.[48] Reflecting on his new condition, he reasons:

> Soumis par ma naissance aux passions humaines, que leur joug me soit
> imposé par un autre ou par moi, ne faut-il pas toujours le porter, et qui
> sait de quelle part il me sera plus supportable? . . . Il n'y a de servitude
> réelle que celle de la nature. Les hommes n'en sont que les instru-
> ments. . . . Si la liberté consistait à faire ce qu'on veut, nul homme ne
> serait libre; . . . celui qui sait le mieux vouloir tout ce qu'elle [i.e., la dure
> nécessité] ordonne est le plus libre, puisqu'il n'est jamais forcé de faire ce
> qu'il ne veut pas. (*OC*, IV, 917)

Here we have not only Émile, but seemingly Rousseau, turned up-
side down. The only real servitude is that of nature—dependence on
another is simply another form of dependence on one's passions—
true freedom is the acceptance of necessity—these are not the doctrines which we have been considering. But of course, Rousseau does
not suppose simply that "la liberté consistait à faire ce qu'on veut."[49]
Émile here expresses the position of the Stoic, who agrees with Rousseau that one is free only if one's powers are sufficient to satisfy one's
desires, but places the primary cause of man's lack of liberty, not in the
emergence of an *amour-propre* which enslaves us to the opinions of
others, but rather on our passions which uncontrolled bring us into
conflict with "la dure nécessité."

Émile et Sophie is an unfinished work. But its subtitle, *Les Solitaires*,
together with the accounts of those with whom Rousseau discussed
the projected story,[50] make sufficiently clear the impossibility of
Émile, despite his ideal education, living happily and freely in the
civilized world. Away from the constant presence of a Tutor, not even
the most carefully socialized individual is capable of living among
men as they are, without either succumbing to corruption, or resign-
ing himself to an acceptance of his complete impotence as the sole
ground of liberty.

But would the sustaining presence of the Tutor overcome this di-

---

[48]Thus the story of *Émile et Sophie*, Rousseau's unfinished sequel to *Émile*.
[49]See the discussion of liberty in sec. 2 supra.
[50]*OC*, IV, clxi–clxvi.

lemma? Let us consider once again the redeemed world of Clarens, the estate shaped by Wolmar which exhibits both the order of the redeemed soul and the order of the universe. After her description of Wolmar's activity as "Legislator," Julie relates her own work to his:

> Chacun des deux est précisément ce qu'il faut à l'autre; il m'éclaire et je l'anime; nous en valons mieux réunis, et il semble que nous soyons destinés à ne faire entre nous qu'une seule âme, dont il est l'entendement et moi la volonté. (*NH*, 276; *OC*, II, 373–374)

As the will corresponding to Wolmar's understanding, Julie in effect embodies the general will of Clarens in her person. For her there should be no conflict between private will and general will, no need that she be forced to be free. And yet, with the return of Saint-Preux, we find her writing to him, "Mon ami, je suis trop heureuse; le bonheur m'ennuie" (*NH*, 528; *OC*, II, 694).

Rousseau appends a note:

> Quoi, Julie! aussi des contradictions! Ah! je crains bien, charmante dévote, que vous ne soyez pas non plus trop d'accord avec vous-même. Au reste, j'avoue que cette lettre me paraît le chant du cygne.

Rousseau is, after all, in a position to know. And surely enough, Julie is soon on her deathbed, writing her last to Saint-Preux. As she comes to the end, the "vous" with which she has faithfully addressed him since terminating their affair becomes once more "tu," and we read:

> La vertu qui nous sépara sur la terre nous unira dans le séjour éternel. Je meurs dans cette douce attente: trop heureuse d'acheter au prix de ma vie le droit de t'aimer toujours sans crime, et de te le dire encore une fois! (*NH*, 566; *OC*, II, 743)

Wolmar has failed to redeem Julie. The ideal world of Clarens is not enough; her soul demands more; her passions can be satisfied, not by being the general will for which Wolmar is the Legislator, not, admittedly, by abandoning virtue for her love of Saint-Preux, but only by a reconciliation of desire and virtue beyond the grave, in an eternal life.

Wolmar, who kindly encloses Julie's last words to Saint-Preux in a letter of his own, admits:

> J'ai beau savoir que celle qui l'a écrite est morte, j'ai peine à croire qu'elle n'est plus rien. (*NH*, 548; *OC*, II, 720)

Wolmar has been presented as an unbeliever, who rejects the possibility of life beyond the grave. His redemptive activity is of this world. The doubts which he here expresses are perhaps not so much theological in their basis as political. Julie's death throws into question not so much his disbelief in another life as his belief in the sufficiency of this life. If the perfect society can be created, if Clarens can provide its occupants with an order in their lives which corresponds to the order in the soul of the man who is at one with himself and with nature, then an eternal life is superfluous; redemption on earth is possible. But if society, however perfect, lacks a sufficient hold on its members, if it can not transform their passions so that it satisfies them, if even the best of mortals finds passion and virtue irreconcilable in this life, then only a redemption beyond the grave, among the angels, can free us from being slaves of our passions to the very end.

Rousseau's imagination betrays him. Both Julie and Émile, despite the efforts of Wolmar and the Tutor, fail to attain the liberty which seemed promised for them: The only liberty for Émile is in solitude or in Stoic resignation; the only liberty for Julie is in another world. Neither is, nor can be, a truly recreated human being.

The lesson of imagination, it may be urged, is not the lesson of reason. The failure of Émile and Julie need not be the failure of humankind. Let the Legislator work his magic with us; let him give us a collective existence which will transform our *amour-propre* into virtue; let us be free!

Our century has shown the seductiveness of that appeal. But does not Rousseau himself warn us against such a possibility? Our language has its origin in our individual passions. This is one of Rousseau's profoundest insights. Our first words are *aimez-moi*.[51] But having learned such a speech, we have already acquired the conception of the *moi individu* which is fatal to the task of the Legislator. He must teach us another language, rooted in our collective passions. But can he eradicate our first tongue? Can we unlearn our first words? Can the sentiment of our collective existence obliterate that original sentiment of individual existence which lies behind speech? Do not Caïus and Lucius emerge from behind the Roman mask when they speak, and then begin to act out their individual lives?

Rousseau's imagination senses what his reason would deny—that there is, and can be, no politics of redemption. The recreated society, the society which transforms the individuality relativized by *amour-propre* into a collective sentiment infused by *amour de la patrie*, the society which fills the void of individuals living only in the opinions of others—all this is but part of a dream, a dream of a Sparta and a

---

[51]*OL,* ch. 9. My assumption is that Southern languages are prior to Northern, an assumption conformable to ch. 2, as well as to the *Discours sur l'inégalité.*

Rome which history never knew, a dream in which the garden of Elysium fades into that other garden which humankind had lost before Rousseau's story began,[52] a dream which turns to nightmare as the liberty of the citizen becomes the liberty of the slave in the galleys of the Barbary pirates.

Rousseau has no solution to offer us to the problem of man perfected and enslaved. But in his statement of the problem, in his portrayal of us as beings who have, indeed, lost the sense of living in ourselves, and who know how to live only mirrored in the opinions of others, Rousseau has touched, and was the first to touch, the deepest of the themes of our modern social thought. Rousseau's achievement is in secularizing the fall of man, and in placing that fall within the context of human development, in which we are perfected in losing our liberty. Rousseau's failure is in offering a political redemption for that fall, in perfecting liberty itself, supposing that if man's actual socialization had enslaved him, an alternative socialization would liberate him. Whether for better or worse, no artifice, transforming *amour-propre* into virtue, can finally obliterate the *moi individu*. Disfigured, but not denatured, we humans live, as Rousseau, despite himself, finally knew that we must live, unredeemed.

---

[52]Cf. *OL*, ch. 9. God taught Adam to speak, but this first language was forgotten with the dispersal of Noah's children. Rousseau's story of human development begins, in effect, after the Flood.

[5]

The Unity of Reason:
A Subversive Reinterpretation of Kant

I

Infidelity to the text is not a traditional virtue of interpretation. It is, however, essential to the present commentary, which addresses certain of Kant's remarks to Theorems II and III in the *Critique of Practical Reason.*[1] For my aim is to achieve a subversive reinterpretation of Kant's account of the nature and role of practical reason.

A subversive reinterpretation exploits elements and ideas present in a text to lead the reader in a direction manifestly different from and even opposed to that in which the author seeks to go. But this new direction is not randomly selected. On the one hand, it must reveal something about the author's own journey. Success as reinterpretation requires that the author create the opportunity for the violence done his text. On the other hand, it must lead the reader to some new understanding. Interpretation is a public act. Fidelity to the text is sacrificed, not for the commentator's mere delectation, but in a philosophic cause.

I want then to lead you to a truer understanding of the role of reason in ethics. Kant is to serve as an unwilling recruit in this task. And yet he points the direction in which we shall travel, not only in the particular remarks in the *Critique of Practical Reason* from which we begin, but more surprisingly in his account of the speculative em-

Reprinted with permission of the University of Chicago Press. Copyright © 1985.
[1]Quotations from Kant [1] are identified by *CPrR* with pagination from the Royal Prussian Academy edition. Quotations from Kant [2] are identified by *CPR* with pagination from the second edition (B). Quotations from Kant [3] are identified by *Gr* with pagination from the Royal Prussian Academy edition.

ployment of reason. For I shall argue that there is a plausible practical parallel to much of the core of that account, which may be exploited to give a more unified view of the role of reason than Kant himself offers.

What Kant denies reason in its speculative employment, he permits it, and indeed requires of it, in its practical employment.[2] We are warned "that we must never venture with speculative reason beyond the limits of experience" (*CPR* B, xxiv), while being told "that there is an absolutely necessary *practical* employment of pure reason—the *moral*—in which it inevitably goes beyond the limits of sensibility" (*CPR* B, xxv). Thus Kant speaks of the "speculative restriction and practical extension of pure reason" (*CPrR*, 141). Our subversive reinterpretation rejects this practical extension, arguing that Kant had available an account of the practical role that would have imposed restrictions parallel to those he demands for speculative reason. The metaphysical consequence of our reinterpretation is of course that God and immortality (though not, as we shall see, freedom) pass beyond not only theoretical knowledge but practical faith. The ethical consequence, of more interest to us here, is that the Categorical Imperative, which expresses the pure unconditional rational necessity of moral law in a form appropriate to human beings, is replaced by an assertoric imperative which expresses the conditional rational necessity to human beings of moral law.

II

"To be happy is necessarily the desire of every rational but finite being, and thus it is an unavoidable determinant of its faculty of desire" (*CPrR*, 25). Happiness is not merely an object of desire. It occupies a privileged place marked out by that word, of core importance to Kant, "necessarily." Elsewhere, Kant says that "happiness is the satisfaction of all our desires" (*CPR* B, 834). It is, then, necessary in being the proper object of desire—or more precisely, of the desire of a rational but finite being.

Kant does not say either that all rational beings desire happiness or

[2]As Darwall makes clear, my interpretation of the implications of this contrast for Kant's account of reason is far from unproblematic. The speculative role of reason, for Kant, is to unify what is given in the manifold of intuition so that knowledge is possible. But may one not suppose that the practical role of reason, even as exemplified in the Categorical Imperative, is to unify what is given in the manifold of desire so that (rational) action is possible? And so may not the contrast, which Kant himself draws, be compatible with a deeper unity, which I deny? A full response to this line of argument would require showing that the Categorical Imperative is *not* suited to playing this unifying role, and I do not attempt this here.

that all finite beings desire happiness. We humans, in whom rationality and finitude are combined, are distinguished from those rational but self-sufficient beings who exhibit contentment with their existence as something inborn, rather than something to be attained. They do not desire happiness but enjoy it; they have no desires. We humans are also distinguished from those finite but nonrational beings who lack any conception of contentment with their existence. They have desires, but they do not desire happiness because they are unable to think of the satisfaction of all their desires; they are unable to unify their desires in thought.

As finite beings, lacking self-sufficiency, we have desires; as rational beings, we unite our conception of these desires in thought and so conceive of happiness as the proper object of desire. Rationality, applied to finitude, necessitates the idea of the satisfaction of all our desires and so necessitates the idea of happiness.

"Contentment with our existence . . . is . . . a problem imposed upon us by our own finite nature as a being of needs" (*CPrR*, 25). Need is the practical expression of our finitude, or lack of self-sufficiency. Need gives rise to desire. Let us reflect on our text in the light of what Kant argues elsewhere. In the *Critique of Pure Reason* he examines the conditions of knowledge for a rational but finite being; he insists that knowledge supposes the possibility of objects being given in intuition. Can we extend this parallel?

We recall that "to man at least," objects are given in intuition only "in so far as the mind is affected in a certain way. The capacity . . . for receiving representations through the mode in which we are affected by objects, is entitled *sensibility*" (*CPR* B, 33). And sensibility has a form, "which so determines the manifold of appearance that it allows of being ordered in certain relations" (*CPR* B, 34). The pure forms of sensibility are space and time; for us, all objects of knowledge must be given in space or in time.

As intuition requires sensibility, so desire requires need. As space and time are the conditions of our speculative apprehension of objects, so need, we may suppose, is the condition of our practical apprehension. Apart from need, objects would not be grasped by us as of interest or concern; knowledge of them would be possible but would not dispose us to act in relation to them.

A being capable of intellectual intuition would have knowledge without being given objects through sensibility; such a being would be self-sufficient with respect to the possession of truth. For him the exercise of speculative reason would be direct, and not mediated and restricted, as it is for us, by what is given in sensible intuition. Similarly a being self-sufficient with respect to the possession of happiness or contentment would act without being given objects through need; she would act not to attain but to express happiness. For her the exercise of practical reason would be direct, and not mediated and restricted, as it is for us, by what is given as an object of desire.

We have now reached a recognizably un-Kantian position. Developing the parallels between knowledge and action, intuition and desire leads us to suppose that, whatever role practical reason might play, it has no pure employment that gives rise to action, any more than speculative reason has a pure employment that gives rise to knowledge. And so we must ask why Kant supposes that reason has a role in the practical or moral realm that he denies it in the speculative or theoretical realm. This will lead us in two directions. First, we shall consider why Kant's insistence on the necessity of our desire for happiness does not lead him to find a role for practical reason in relating action to desire, which is parallel to the role he finds for speculative reason in relating knowledge to intuition. And second, we shall consider why, even if Kant were to acknowledge such a parallel, he would continue to insist that the moral realm requires a further role, in which the exercise of practical reason is not limited by what is given as an object of desire. But of course, as we examine Kant's position, we shall be interpreting it, subversively, to develop a similarity between the speculative and practical roles of reason.

III

Although Kant admits that happiness is a necessary object of desire, he denies that it gives rise to a practical law. He insists that "all the elements which belong to the concept of happiness are without exception empirical" (*Gr*, 418), and "just because this material ground of determination can be known by the subject only empirically, it is impossible to regard this demand for happiness as a law, since the latter must contain exactly the same determining ground for the will of all rational beings and in all cases" (*CPrR*, 25). I shall not ask whether Kant's argument here is fully consistent with his acceptance of pragmatic practical law, "derived from the motive of *happiness*" in the first *Critique* (*CPR* B, 834). Rather I shall claim that his argument provides no ground for rejecting the idea of a practical law based on happiness.

That such a law would provide a determining ground for the will only of rational but finite beings, and not all rational beings as such, is not a disqualification, given Kant's general willingness to relate the necessity of law to the conditions of possible experience. If happiness is the necessary object of desire, then it necessarily conditions our practical experience. This is of course not to say that happiness must be the basis of practical law, but only that it is suited to be such a basis.

But, Kant insists, the content of happiness is known only empirically. Each particular need, satisfaction of which is part of happiness, serves as a ground of the will, but since we have no a priori knowledge of such needs, the particular practical principles connecting action to the will on the basis of need are merely empirical. They lack the necessity of law. They express a merely contingent relationship between the physical necessity expressed in laws of nature, and happiness. They give rise to merely hypothetical imperatives, indicating the necessary means to contingent ends.

A law states a necessary synthetic connection. If this connection is between a person, or her will, and an action as something to be done by the person, then the law is practical. A practical law prescribes an action as rationally necessary for a person who has not already implicitly willed the action. Now Kant seems to suppose that a principle prescribing happiness as an end would be synthetic and necessary but not practical, whereas a principle prescribing some action as a means to happiness, if it were necessary, would be practical but not synthetic. Thus happiness cannot give rise to practical law.

Kant claims that we are necessarily motivated to seek our happiness. But this is not a practical necessity; happiness is not given us as a rationally required object. Happiness, as Kant has said, is "an unavoidable determinant of [the] faculty of desire" (*CPrR*, 25); we do seek happiness, but we do not choose to seek happiness. That we seek happiness is, it would seem, a natural necessity.

We do choose the means to happiness. Kant argues that, since we lack a determinate conception of happiness, we are never able to show that some action is a necessary means to or condition of happiness. But suppose we could show this. Then the proposition prescribing this action would indeed state a practical necessity, but only in virtue of the fact that we had already willed the end, happiness, to which the action was the necessary means. And Kant holds, "Who wills the end, wills . . . also the means which are indispensably necessary and in his power. So far as willing is concerned, this proposition is analytic" (*Gr*, 417). That we seek the means to happiness is, then, a practical but analytic necessity.

Reason, insofar as it enters into our practical concern with happiness, plays a purely instrumental role. This is to make it, as Hume insists, the slave of the passions; it is to deny to reason any distinctive practical role. Since Kant does not suppose that the practical role of reason is related to happiness, he would not be dismayed by this consequence of his argument. But his denial that happiness gives rise to practical law and his rejection of any distinctive practical role for reason in relation to happiness reflect his failure to grasp the implications of his conception of happiness as the satisfaction of all our desires. For, so conceived, happiness is not given to us as an object of desire, but must be constructed from the particular desires arising out of our needs. And this task affords a practical role to reason.

The desires of a finite being do not manifest simultaneous needs but, rather, needs that occur at different and overlapping periods of time. Occurrent need, as the direct determinant of desire, does not itself pose the problem of happiness, or contentment with our existence, that arises when we conceive of "our own finite nature as a being of needs." Such a conception requires grasping our needs as united into a single whole—as the needs of one person. Only so conceived do they give rise to the thought of happiness as a single object of desire. An animal has desires corresponding to its needs, but it is incapable of thinking of each as "I desire." Neither its intuitions nor its desires constitute a single experience because it lacks the rational capacity to unite what is given separately.

In considering what is required for us to think of happiness as the object of desire, we should be reminded of the role Kant assigns to the pure concepts of the understanding. They play a unifying role, bringing the manifold of intuition into a single, knowable experience. As Kant states, "In so far as the manifold representations of intuition are *given* to us, they are subject to the [formal conditions of space and time]; in so far as they must allow of being *combined* in one consciousness, they are subject to [conditions of the original synthetic unity of apperception]. For without such combination nothing can be thought or known" (*CPR* B, 136–137). And these conditions are of course the Kantian categories, the concepts "which prescribe laws *a priori* to appearances, and therefore to nature, the sum of all appearances" (*CPR* B, 163).

The understanding is the rational faculty that gives rise to knowledge. The pure concepts of the understanding, the categories, unite the manifold of intuition to make knowledge possible. The will is the rational faculty that gives rise to action; indeed, Kant defines the will as "nothing but practical reason" (*Gr*, 412). Thus we should expect there to be pure concepts of the will that unite the manifold of desire to make action possible. Kant does not meet our expectation here, but we may nevertheless ask what these pure concepts would be. Action involves a choice among alternatives. For choice to be possible, the desires of the actor must be unified in such a way that they determine a single alternative from those possible actions that are available to her. The actor's desires must be so related that they determine a preferential ordering of the set of alternative possible actions, from which she may then select a maximal element. The familiar ideas of the theory of rational choice correspond to the pure concepts of the will.

In a single choice the existence of a maximal element is an analytic necessity; the chosen element may always be interpreted as maximal. But a series of choices may not reveal a single preferential ordering of alternative possible actions. Taken together, they may not express the unified desires of an individual rational actor. The possibility of being able to unite disparate desires so that they determine the same actions is not given in the concept of desire or in that of need. Without this unity, ongoing rational action, based on choice, is impossible. But since this unity is not given to the actor in her desires, it depends on the activity of her will, just as the unification of intuitions necessary for knowledge of objects depends on the activity of her understanding. Action, like knowledge, requires an activity of reason that is synthetic and that is constitutive of rather than based on experience, and so a priori.

Happiness, the satisfaction of all desires, is given as the end of action not, as Kant seems to have supposed, by natural necessity, but as the result of the activity of the will, or practical reason, in unifying the manifold of desire to determine a single action. The action so determined takes happiness as its end. Of course, given the possibility of conflict among desires reflecting distinct needs, happiness may not be fully attainable; none of the possible actions need satisfy every desire. But that action most preferred on the basis of the actor's unified desires will maximize their satisfaction and so bring about her greatest possible happiness.

Since it is reason that unifies the manifold of desire to make choice possible, it is reason that prescribes the performance of that action maximizing the actor's satisfaction. The requirement that one seek happiness thus depends on the synthetic a priori activity of practical reason. And so it would seem to be the practical law, based on happiness, whose possibility Kant denies. Kant notes correctly, "To be happy is necessarily the desire of every rational but finite being" (*CPrR*, 25). But he fails to recognize that this necessity reflects the activity of the will in unifying what is given by differing needs arising at differing times. Without practical reason, there could be no conception of happiness as the single object of desire. Kant does not discern the parallel between the activities of will and understanding and so he does not recognize that, just as the pure concepts of the understanding prescribe a law a priori to appearances, so the pure concepts of the will prescribe law a priori to our choices.

IV

We have introduced the idea of a practical law based on happiness by exploiting a set of parallels, implicit in Kant's position but unnoticed by him, between intuition and desire, understanding and will, knowledge and action. But even if its Kantian base is accepted, such a law may seem an unwelcome intruder, at odds with Kant's developed view of rational action. In particular, it may seem in conflict with Kant's insistence on the autonomy of the rational actor.

Kant supposes that, were there a practical law based on happiness, "it would not have the necessity which is conceived in every law, . . . unless we hold this necessity to be not at all practical but only physical, maintaining that our action is as inevitably forced upon us by our inclination as yawning is by seeing others yawn" (*CPrR*, 26). Leaving aside Kant's curious example, we may note that to suppose that action is forced on us by inclination is to assume a direct link between occurrent need and action at the time of its occurrence. A being who responded directly to distinct, temporally given needs would not thereby exhibit the characteristics of a unified actor. She would not take happiness, the satisfaction of all her desires, as her objective. Should there be unity in her life, it would reflect a preestablished harmony, no doubt explicable in evolutionary terms but not subject to her will, her conscious control.

If an actor brings her need-based desires into a single framework, so that they direct her to her maximum overall satisfaction, then she is not inevitably determined to respond directly to each of her needs. As we have seen, the necessity of happiness as the object of desire is not natural but practical, determined by the unifying activity of practical reason. Thus such an actor is autonomous, acting on the basis of the practical law given by her exercise of practical reason. If there is a problem in reconciling practical necessity with natural necessity, or human freedom with causality, then it arises as much for the actor who acts autonomously to maximize her own happiness as for the actor who acts to fulfill the moral law. Kant's emphasis on and concern with autonomy is retained by our reinterpretation.

But a practical law based on happiness does not purport to be a *moral* law. The principle of maximizing satisfaction expresses the fulfillment and not the constraint of natural desire. One could, no doubt, pay morality extra to make it mean what one likes, but a

morality that consisted solely in the pursuit of happiness would constitute both a conceptual and a practical departure from our ordinary
understanding and would leave the place presently occupied by morality vacant.

Our subversive reinterpretation of Kant is not intended to leave out
a place for morality. In providing that place, we shall focus on two
characteristics of morality as Kant conceives it. First, we shall accept
Kant's insistence on the relation between morality and rationality, so
that the ground of moral obligation must be found in the pure concepts of practical reason. Of course, we treat these concepts as parallel
in the speculative and practical roles of reason, so we seek to ground
morality in concepts that correspond to the pure concepts of understanding. And second, we agree with Kant that the happiness of the
actor cannot be the direct basis of moral motivation. If there is a
moral law, then it must be related to practical reason in a quite different way than is the law of maximizing satisfaction. But what can this
relation be, if we are not willing to suppose, with Kant, that practical
reason can of itself, and without any basis in need, serve as the ground
of practical law? We shall answer this by reflecting on a further argument offered by Kant against the possibility of a practical law based on
happiness. And we shall find that we must revise our initial argument,
so that, while there is indeed a practical law based on the synthetic
activity of reason in unifying our desires, it is not the simple maximizing principle that we have so far supposed but serves rather to constrain our pursuit of happiness.

V

"It is . . . astonishing how intelligent men have thought of proclaim-
ing as a universal practical law the desire for happiness, and therewith
to make this desire the determining ground of the will merely because
this desire is universal. Though elsewhere natural laws make everything harmonious, if one here attributed the universality of law to this
maxim, there would be the extreme opposite of harmony, the most
arrant conflict, and the complete annihilation of the maxim itself and
its purpose" (*CPrR*, 28). What is new and significant in this argument
is Kant's insistence that a law of happiness would be destructive of
harmony—indeed, would be simply destructive. Now it may be un-
clear why Kant attributes this arrant conflict to the supposition that
the desire for happiness constitutes a practical *law*. For if, as he has
insisted, to be happy is an unavoidable determinant of the faculty of
desire, then it would seem that the destructive effect of happiness is
assured, law or no law. But perhaps Kant wants to claim that practical

law can stand guard against the desire for happiness, curbing its destructive tendency, whereas a law based on happiness would give conflict free rein. This idea, that practical law checks the excesses of the endeavor to satisfy all one's desires, will enable us to reinsert morality into a framework from which it may appear to have been expunged.

But this is to anticipate. First we should ask Kant why a law based on happiness would lead to conflict. And his answer is that "the wills of all do not have one and the same object, but each person has his own (his own welfare), which, to be sure, can accidentally agree with the purposes of others who are pursuing their own, though this agreement is far from sufficing for a law because the occasional exceptions which one is permitted to make are endless and cannot be definitely comprehended in a universal rule" (*CPrR*, 28). Kant then goes on to exhibit not the harmony of convergence but, rather, the pseudo-harmony of conflict in his examples, "a married couple bent on going to ruin, 'Oh, marvelous harmony, what he wants is what she wants'; or like the pledge which is said to have been given by Francis I to the Emperor Charles V, 'What my brother wants (Milan), that I want too.'"

Kant's argument seems to be that a law based on individual happiness would be destructive, whereas a law based on universal happiness would be indefinitely defeasible. I agree; neither egoism nor utilitarianism affords an adequate basis for practical law. But Kant implicitly assumes these alternatives are exhaustive insofar as basing a practical law on happiness is concerned. This I deny. Here we must examine the logical structure of interaction to determine more precisely why the attempt by each person to maximize her own satisfaction engenders conflict and how this attempt might be curbed without appealing to anything other than each person's maximizing aim.

Consider two conditions that might be related to the supposed maximizing principle of practical reason:

(1) Each person should maximize her happiness, given the actions of other persons.
(2) Each person should maximize her happiness, given the amount of happiness received by other persons.

The first is naturally understood as a condition on choice or behavior; each seeks to do as well for herself as possible, given what others do. The second is naturally understood as a condition on outcomes; each gets as much as possible, given what others get. In any interaction, a set of actions each of which satisfies the first condition is said to be in equilibrium; each action is a best response to the others, so that no person has reason to change her behavior. An outcome that satisfies the second condition is optimal (in the Pareto sense); no person could do better unless some other person were to do worse. Now the idea that a law based on happiness would lead to conflict may be expressed more precisely by the claim that a law prescribing a best response for each person must, in some situations, lead to an outcome that is not optimal. Each will maximize her happiness given the actions of her fellows but receive less happiness than she could given what her fellows receive. That this claim is correct is shown by the familiar example of the Prisoner's Dilemma. Even though it is always possible for the optimality condition to be satisfied and—if we allow probability distributions over actions as further actions—always possible for the equilibrium condition to be satisfied, yet it is not always possible for both conditions to be satisfied.

Kant's argument would then seem to be that a law based on happiness engenders conflict whether it is based on individual happiness, and so satisfies the equilibrium condition, or based on universal happiness, and so satisfies the optimality condition, except that it allows each person to exempt herself when her happiness would otherwise suffer. In the first case, the application of the law itself would lead to conflict whenever no equilibrium outcome was optimal. In the second case, the permitted exceptions to the law would lead to conflict whenever no optimal outcome was in equilibrium. And since no equilibrium outcome is optimal just if no optimal outcome is in equilibrium, conflict would arise in the same situations whether individual or universal happiness is supposed to be the basis of law.

VI

Kant is not alone in thinking that what we shall call, anachronistically, the idea of the Prisoner's Dilemma, creates problems for our understanding of practical rationality. Let us consider briefly a modern dress version, as it were, of the issue. In his paper "Truth, Invention, and the Meaning of Life," David Wiggins raises the question of "practical rationality for all conceivable rational agents."[3] Noting that "a great deal of time and effort" has been directed to establishing a priori the properties of an objective intelligence, Wiggins claims, "What was not . . . to be expected was that the most elementary part of the subject should immediately collide—as it has—with a simple and . . . unanswerable paradox—the so-called 'Prisoner's Dilemma.'" The paradox, in Wiggins's view, is that "a general principle of decision-theoretic

[3]Wiggins, p. 363.

prudence, generalizable to any agent whatever caught in the relevant circumstances, will lead in a wide variety of applications to what must be agreed by everybody to be a situation which is worse than it might have been for each participant if he had not acted on the generalizable principle—or if there had been another generalizable decision-theoretic principle to recommend (which there is not)."[4]

The generalizable decision-theoretic principle to which Wiggins refers is, of course, the familiar principle of expected utility maximization which, with 'happiness' substituted for 'utility,' is the putative practical law rejected by Kant for the very reason Wiggins gives—that it engenders conflict, or leads to a situation worse for everybody than might have obtained had the principle not been followed. And Wiggins claims, as does Kant, that there is no alternative principle to be recommended.

Wiggins goes on to note that in treating the Prisoner's Dilemma as a paradox we are supposing "that it *should* have been possible to construct an *a priori* theory of rationality or prudence such that . . . rationality is definable both independently of morality and ideals of agency and in such a way as to have independent leverage in these ancient disputes."[5] Now Kant supposes that rationality is definable independently, if not of ideals of agency, yet at least of morality, and in such a way that we can then derive morality from it. But Kant accomplishes this only by bypassing entirely the set of concerns that give rise to the Prisoner's Dilemma and ascribing to reason in its practical employment a role that he rightly denies it in its speculative use. His a priori theory of practical rationality introduces "unconditional practical law" as "merely the self-consciousness of a pure practical reason" (*CPrR*, 29). Our task is to reinterpret Kant to meet Wiggins's requirement that practical rationality be characterized in a way independent of morality and yet as having leverage in deriving morality, without allowing pure practical reason a role unparalleled by speculative reason.

Wiggins sees the Prisoner's Dilemma as an insuperable obstacle to the accomplishment of this task. On the contrary, the structural feature of interaction revealed by the Dilemma—the incompatibility between the equilibrium and optimality conditions—is precisely what makes it possible to understand practical rationality in such a way that, on the one hand, the Dilemma is rationally resolved and, on the other hand, morality is derived as unproblematically rational.

To show this, let us begin by getting clear about the a priori require-

[4]Ibid., p. 363n.
[5]Ibid., p. 364n.

ments on our account of practical rationality. Wiggins supposes that it seemed that there should be an account that moved from "a set of concerns" to "a way that they might be best brought about."[6] But this would lead to a directly maximizing requirement on principles of action, which satisfies the equilibrium but not the optimality requirement, and the Dilemma reveals the unprofitability and inappropriateness of this approach. Instead, we require first of all a principle that, suitably generalized, yields outcomes satisfying the second, optimality condition and does so in such a way that, in any situation in which all persons follow the principle, each may expect to do better than if all followed a maximizing principle satisfying the equilibrium condition. Second, although I shall say nothing about this here, we require a procedure enabling rational persons to decide among alternative principles satisfying the first requirement. Third, and crucial to our present argument, we must relate rationality not to thinking directly about how best to bring about a set of concerns, but to thinking about how one should act so that one will be best placed to bring about one's concerns, whatever those concerns may be.

An ideally rational actor is one who chooses in such a way that he maximizes the satisfaction of his desires, where choice is taken to be cost free and where the actor is neither weak-willed nor epistemically imperfect. Now it is tempting to pass from this characterization to what may appear a mere rewording: an ideally rational actor is one who chooses to maximize the satisfaction of his desires. But the second is not equivalent to the first and so is not a correct formulation of ideally rational choice. A person who chooses in such a way that he maximizes the satisfaction of his desires does not always choose to maximize their satisfaction. This is the deep lesson of the Prisoner's Dilemma.

Let us spell it out. Consider a person who chooses to maximize satisfaction. Whenever he is in a Prisoner's Dilemma or PD situation, he cannot expect the outcome to be optimal unless he is interacting with a sucker, who lets herself be exploited. Now suckers are unlikely to do well in the struggle for survival, so that our maximizer may not expect to find many around. He must then expect suboptimality in most interactions in which the two conditions are not jointly satisfiable.

Consider another person whose choices are related to her expectations about those with whom she interacts. She chooses on the basis of a principle satisfying the optimality condition when she expects others to do so as well, subordinating any temptation to exploit them, but is no sucker, maximizing when she expects others to choose on the basis

[6]Ibid., p. 364.

of a principle satisfying the equilibrium condition. Now if she is usually able to form correct expectations about others and to enable them to form correct expectations about herself, she may expect optimal outcomes in most PD situations in which others are like-minded. She may then expect to do better, in terms of overall satisfaction, than those who choose directly to maximize their satisfaction. For her restraint opens up opportunities for mutual benefit unavailable to those who make directly maximizing choices.

The first person chooses to maximize the satisfaction of his desires. The second person chooses in such a way that she maximizes the satisfaction of her desires. The first suffers from PD interactions; the second benefits from them. Or at least, the first suffers except in a world of suckers; the second benefits except in a world where her fellows are not like-minded. We take the second person to be fully rational. And in so conceiving practical rationality, we satisfy Wiggins's desideratum that it be definable independently of morality and yet in such a way that it permits the derivation of morality. For insofar as choosing in such a way that one maximizes satisfaction requires that, on occasion, one forgo maximizing choices, the element of constraint that traditionally characterizes moral obligation is introduced as a requirement of practical rationality.

We must now withdraw our previous proposal that the principle of maximizing happiness, or the satisfaction of our desires, is a practical law. Kant is right; such a law would be destructive, in leading to suboptimal, mutually disadvantageous outcomes in PD situations. But we are not therefore led to agree with Kant and Wiggins that no practical law based on happiness is possible. The correct law must ensure that the person who conforms to it may expect to maximize her happiness; it therefore constrains her choices when she is among like-minded persons in PD situations. But we shall not attempt to formulate the correct law here. Although based on each person's concern with happiness, its prescriptions are not straightforwardly directed to individual happiness, as in egoism, or to universal happiness, as in utilitarianism, or to universal happiness "with exceptions." Our subversive reinterpretation simply points to a principle, based on each person's rational concern to choose in such a way that she maximizes her happiness, as the law that Kant should have recognized.

VII

Kant's notorious examples of moral duties (as set out in the *Groundwork*) will not all be accommodated by our subversive reinterpretation. But both promise keeping and mutual assistance do fit nicely under a practical law adherence to which maximizes the actor's expectations of happiness. And they fit in quasi-Kantian ways.

Promising plays two district roles. First, it is a device for coordinating actions. We want to meet and I promise to be in my office at 2 P.M., thus facilitating the selection of a place and time for our meeting. But beyond coordination, promising is a device for commitment, for giving others an assurance of our future behavior that is decoupled from the calculations we should otherwise make. To induce you to aid me in harvesting my field this week, I promise to aid you next week. Here more than coordination is involved; before you will lend me a hand, you want to be assured that I will lend you a hand, and will not, once you have aided me, simply recalculate, whether egoistically in terms of my own happiness, or in utilitarian fashion in terms of universal happiness, before I decide whether to aid you. You must take my word as my bond, believing that I will treat keeping my promise as an overriding consideration. And only insofar as it induces this belief in you is my promise fully effective.

Now the invocation of an overriding consideration is ruled out by conceptions of rationality that identify rational choice with adherence to a simple maximizing principle, whatever may be the value to be maximized. Promising can be no more than a coordinative device for persons who suppose that they should choose to maximize happiness, whether their own or everyone's. But if one supposes that one should choose in such a way that one maximizes happiness, and even that one maximizes one's own happiness, then the rationale for a commitment device is quite straightforward. Given normal expectations about interaction, every person may expect *ex ante* that she will do better if she has some verbal device for committing herself and so giving others an assurance of her future behavior decoupled from the calculations she would otherwise make.

It is certainly possible to make a false promise, purporting to commit oneself and intending others to believe one to be committing oneself, yet not intending to adhere to one's purported commitment should it prove contrary to normal calculations. And Kant is surely wrong to insist that such false promising must be contrary to reason. But he is quite right to claim that there is a practical law requiring promise keeping and that there could not be a law prescribing false promising as a universal practice.

Given the basic practical law prescribing that one so choose that one may expect to maximize one's happiness, and the consequent need for a commitment device, the practical law prescribing adherence when one invokes that device follows immediately. This law is circumvented, but not broken, by justifiable cases of false promising. But these cases are necessarily parasitic. There could not be only a universal practice of pretending to invoke overriding considerations. For such pretense requires a practice in which persons believe themselves actually to be invoking overriding considerations.

There is a longer story to be told about the rationale of promising—but not here. Let us turn to mutual assistance. Suppose that I propose to assist you only when it is to my advantage to do so. Now we could imagine a practical law that so restricted assistance. There could be a universal practice of giving assistance only when the giver as well as the recipient could expect to benefit. But would such a practice be rationally willed?

Any practice of assistance in which the costs to the giver are less than the benefits to the recipient must provide an average net benefit greater than that provided by the practice of giving assistance only at no cost to the giver. But not everyone need expect *ex ante* to be better off as a result of this increase in average benefit. A practice requiring women to assist men when total benefits outweigh total costs, but not requiring men to assist women, would increase average net benefit but not the *ex ante* expected benefit of any woman, when compared with the practice of giving only cost-free assistance. However, given normal expectations about interaction, it is reasonable to suppose that some practices of assistance in which benefits outweigh costs will offer each party to them increased expected benefit *en ante*. And if so, then some such practices will be willed by each person, concerned with his own happiness, for otherwise as Kant notes, "he would rob himself of all hope of the help he wants for himself" (*Gr*, 423). We cannot say here precisely what will be required in the way of mutual assistance, but we may note that Kant, speaking of "meritorious duties to others" (*Gr*, 430), leaves the matter equally vague.

VIII

What of the Categorical Imperative? Our subversive reinterpretation has conjured it back into the limbo from which it should never have emerged. For the Categorical Imperative is the legacy of those dogmatic slumbers from which Kant was not awakened. His achievement in curbing the pretensions of speculative reason is marred by his willingness to encourage the excesses of practical reason. Indeed, his very purpose in denying that pure reason in its speculative employment can attain knowledge is to allow that same reason in its practical employment to ground faith.

The Categorical Imperative is a synthetic a priori practical proposition. It is synthetic because in it "the willing of an action is not derived analytically from some other willing already presupposed (for we do not possess any such perfect will)" (*Gr*, 420). For Kant, the willing required by the Categorical Imperative is given in the idea of a rational will as such but not in the idea of a rational will subject to inclination—the will of a rational but finite being. There are objective practical laws, but for us they are subjectively contingent.

In this account, the practical employment of reason is based, not on the requirements of action, but on an ideal of pure practical rationality. This is exactly the reverse of Kant's account of the speculative employment of reason, which is based, not on an ideal of pure speculative rationality, but on the requirements of knowledge. The role of the understanding is to fill the gap between sensible intuition and knowledge. But the role of the will is not, according to Kant, to fill the gap between desire and action.

I have argued that practical reason does fill this gap. For human action—the conscious, deliberate, ongoing activity that requires choice among alternatives—to be possible, the will must unify the manifold of desires that arise from diverse needs, so that a single object, happiness, is determined. Without reason there would be no such action but only mere animal responsiveness to immediate need.

In exhibiting the practical role of reason in directing human beings to happiness, I have not shown that no pure practical employment of reason is possible. I have not disproved Kant's claim that there is an objective principle of pure practical rationality. But in showing that not only practical law but also moral law can be understood without resort to such a principle, I hope to have undermined the plausibility of Kant's position. The same good sense that leads us to deny that pure speculative reason can ground knowledge should lead us to deny that pure practical reason can ground action.

More positively, the unifying activity of reason gives us a unified account of reason in its speculative and practical employments. Just as an event is explained by subsuming it under physical law, so an action is justified by subsuming it under practical law. Kant's official account of rational justification terminates in a dead end, but his help, albeit unwitting and unwilling, has launched us on a more rewarding journey.

JUSTICE

[6]

Three against Justice: The Foole, the Sensible Knave, and the Lydian Shepherd

I

Justice, the virtue of the self-interested, is the virtue that curbs self-interest. Honesty, if not always the best policy, is the best police. But can interest be so easily reined? Theorists of justice, presenting a rationale for it as the self-interested curb on each person's pursuit of her own benefit, find themselves creating their own antagonists, personifications of the deep threat posed to justice by an apparent union of reason and interest.[1] These adversaries, the *personae* of injustice, are our principal characters.

First there is Hobbes's Foole, who "hath sayd in his heart, there is no such thing as Justice; . . . seriously alleaging, that every mans conservation, and contentment, being committed to his own care, there could be no reason, why every man might not do what he thought conduced thereunto" (*L* 15, p. 72). The Foole has more to say, but this is sufficient to suggest his character. He is an extreme individualist, taking each person's conservation and contentment—interest—as that person's sole concern. He sees no reason why each should not do

Reprinted with the permission of *Midwest Studies in Philosophy.* Copyright © 1982 by the University of Minnesota.

[1]The theorists are Hobbes, Hume, and Plato in the person of Glaucon. Quotations from their works appear as follows: *De Cive* (in English translation) as *DC* followed by chapter and paragraph; page references to Hobbes [1a]. *Human Nature* as *HN* followed by chapter and paragraph; page references to Hobbes [3]. *Leviathan* as *L* followed by chapter; page references to Hobbes [4]. *The Questions concerning Liberty, Necessity, and Chance* as *Qu;* page references to Hobbes [5]. *An Enquiry concerning the Principles of Morals* as *E* followed by section; page references to Hume [2]. *A Treatise of Human Nature* as *T* followed by book, part, and section; page references to Hume [1]. And *Republic* as *R.*

what seems best to further her own interest, *and therefore he denies
justice.* Here we have our core problem posed by the first antagonist.

Next there is Hume's sensible knave, who "may think that an act of
iniquity or infidelity will make a considerable addition to his fortune,
without causing any considerable breach in the social union and confederacy" (*E* IX, p. 282). The sensible knave, a smoother man than the
Foole, avoids the hyperbole of denying justice, but treats it only as
policy, "a good general rule, . . . liable to many exceptions." But justice
as policy is not justice as virtue. The essential challenge to justice,
conceived as the virtue that curbs self-interest, is reaffirmed.

Last there is a shepherd, servant to the king of Lydia. While meeting with his fellows to prepare their monthly report to the king, he
discovered the power of his new-found ring to make him invisible.
"Aware of this, he immediately contrived to be one of the messengers
to the king. When he arrived, he committed adultery with the king's
wife and, along with her, set upon the king and killed him. And so he
took over the rule" (*R* 360a–b). The point of this parable, and its
implications for justice, are drawn for us by Glaucon. "Now if there
were two such rings, and the just man would put one on, and the
unjust man the other, no one, as it would seem, would be so adamant
as to stick by justice and bring himself to keep away from what belongs to others and not lay hold of it, although he had license to take
what he wanted from the market without fear, and to go into houses
and have intercourse with whomever he wanted, and to slay or release
from bonds whomever he wanted, and to do other things as an equal
to a god among humans" (*R* 360b–c).

The ring of Gyges, in making one equal to a god among humans,
puts one beyond the reach of justice and injustice. What then is justice
but the reminder of our human weakness? The answer is that it is
indeed the reminder, in being also the remedy for that weakness.
Justice is the virtue that curbs the self-interest of those who are not
also self-sufficient. If this conclusion seem too negative, let us remember that sociability is a disposition appropriate only to those who
are not self-sufficient. We may equally consider justice the virtue that
in curbing self-interest makes possible our human sociability.

II

Conclusion in hand, let us return to our premises. The Foole is
Hobbes's antagonist. It is time to bring the protagonist into our
argument.

The Hobbesian condition of mere nature is one of radical insufficiency. Human beings, as all other animals, are characterized by a set

of motions—those which Hobbes calls "vital motion." Human action, which Hobbes calls "voluntary motion," is primarily directed to the maintenance and sustenance of vital motion (see *L* 6, p. 23; *HN* 7.1, p. 31). At any given time a person exhibits a certain level of vital motion. An increase in that level heightens the quality and lengthens the probable extent of his life; a decrease lowers the quality and shortens the probable extent. We may say that a condition is minimally sufficient only if it is one in which a person is able to maintain his level of vital motion. (This is a static characterization, reflecting Hobbes's own inattention to children and the aged. To do full justice to the underlying idea we should consider the internal dynamic of vital motion, so that for a child minimal sufficiency requires its enhancement, whereas for an aging person minimal sufficiency is compatible with its natural diminution.) A radically insufficient condition is one in which the actions that persons undertake in their endeavor to maintain existing vital motion create a pattern of interaction that actually impedes such motion. Under radical insufficiency the best efforts of each to maintain himself are frustrated by the impact of the similar efforts of others.

Each person, seeking to sustain and strengthen his own vital motion, must of course exercise some effect on the vital motions of others. According to Hobbes, these effects are naturally negative; each tends to weaken his fellows. This is not an expression of human ill will; rather, the powers of persons in the state of nature are opposed, so that each rightly considers it advantageous to diminish the powers of his fellows so that his own may be more effective (see *HN* 8.4, p. 38; *L* 13, p. 61). But this conflict, endemic to the Hobbesian state of nature, does not itself entail radical insufficiency. Hobbes's natural condition of humankind is radically insufficient because the total diminution of vital motion that each person inflicts on his fellows is greater than the enhancement that each is able to achieve for himself. Given the important assumption of physical equality, that "the weakest has strength enough to kill the strongest" (*L* 13, p. 60), it follows that each must expect natural interaction to be inimical to his endeavor to protect and strengthen himself. As Hobbes says, "there can be no security to any man . . . of living out the time, which Nature ordinarily alloweth men to live" (*L* 14, p. 64). Each would prefer solitude to the interaction that characterizes the state of nature.

The natural condition of human beings is a theoretical construct. As Hobbes makes clear in the preface to *De Cive*, "to make a more curious search into the rights of states and duties of subjects, it is necessary . . . that they be so considered as if they were dissolved" (*DC*, pp. 98–99). The natural condition of humankind is, then, the result of conceiving interaction in the absence of all moral and political relationships. Its *purely* theoretical character is revealed by its radical insufficiency; were moral and political relationships to be dissolved in reality, the survival of humankind would be threatened.

Given that the natural, amoral, apolitical, asocial condition of human beings is potentially fatal, what alternative to it may be found? This is Hobbes's great problem, but it is not in principle a problem unique to his thought. For it is a particularly dramatic form of the general problem endemic to human interaction—the problem of negative externalities.

In any interaction the marginal costs and benefits to any person must bear one of three possible relationships: marginal benefits may be greater than, equal to, or less than marginal costs. An excess of marginal benefits over costs indicates the presence of a positive externality. We may suppose that in general such an excess arises from interaction that is not purely instrumental—interaction among persons who take an interest in one another's interests. Hobbes ignores such interaction; his account of human nature leaves little place for the supposition that persons take anything but an instrumental interest in one another (see *L* 13, p. 61). We shall bring noninstrumental interest into our argument later, for it would seem to be part of any ideal of human sociability. But for the present we ignore it, considering only the possibility of a human society lacking all sociability. This has its own ideal, expressed in the requirement that for each person in any interaction or set of interrelated interactions, marginal benefits be no less than marginal costs.

If marginal benefits are less than costs, there must be a negative externality, an external inefficiency. The internalization of such inefficiencies, and so the attainment of the ideal of nonsociable society, is the primary problem faced in all human interaction. Hobbes differs from other social theorists most especially in his insistence that this problem arises in the most acute form possible—that in natural human interaction not only are marginal costs for each in excess of benefits, but total costs are in excess of total benefits. Human beings do not merely fail to achieve an optimal or efficient outcome—an outcome that affords each the greatest benefit compatible with the benefits afforded others—but human beings are worse off than they would be in a state of solitude. Read as a response to this problem, Hobbes's gloomy theory of society may take on greater appeal.

The first three laws of nature provide Hobbes's three-step rational resolution to the problem created by the radical insufficiency of the natural human condition. This resolution consists of the moralization of nature, the reintroduction of moral relationships among persons, these relationships now being grounded and rationalized by an appeal to the insufficiency of the natural amoral condition.

The first law of nature, that every person ought to endeavor peace, specifies the objective that must be realized (*L* 14, p. 64). Hobbes characterizes the state of nature in terms of its primary negative externality when he describes it as a state of war, of every person against every person (*L* 13, p. 62). The internalization of this externality is peace.

The second law of nature then prescribes the change in individual interaction necessary if peace is to supplant war. Each person, in exercising the so-called right of nature, the liberty "to use his own power, as he will himselfe, for the preservation of his own Nature" (*L* 14, p. 64), is led to impose costs on others greater than the benefit he secures for himself. Each therefore must "be willing, when others are so too, . . . to lay down this right to all things; and be contented with so much liberty against other men, as he would allow other men against himselfe" (*L* 14, pp. 64–65). In other words, the liberty that each person should continue to enjoy, so that peace may prevail, must be determined, not by each person's calculation of the benefit to himself which he may obtain by his own actions, but rather from each person's calculation of the overall benefit to himself that he may expect from the interaction of all.

We may set out the requirement of the second law of nature in graphic form. The benefits each person may secure for himself may be represented as a function of the extent of his liberty. At zero liberty, each secures zero benefits; as liberty increases, each secures increasing benefits but, we may reasonably suppose, at a decreasing rate. The costs each faces may be represented as a function of the extent of the liberty of others. At zero liberty for others, each faces zero costs; as liberty increases, each faces increasing costs and, we may suppose, at an increasing rate. If we make the simplifying assumption that the extent of an agent's liberty is equal to the average extent of the liberty of those with whom he interacts, we may represent benefits and costs as a function of this average extent of liberty, and by summing benefits with costs we may also represent the net benefit or cost to each person of interaction with others, as a function of the average extent of liberty. We show this in Figure 1. Average liberty is plotted along the X-axis; benefits and costs are plotted on the YY'-axis. The curve C_1 shows the benefits secured by the individual as a function of liberty; C_2 shows the costs imposed on the individual as a function of liberty; C_3 shows net benefit to the individual. What the second law of nature requires is that each be willing to agree to that extent of liberty, *L*, which maximizes expected net benefit, *B*.

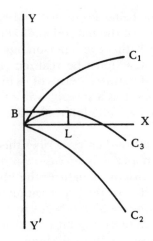

Figure 1

Hobbes supposes that the reciprocal reduction in liberty, or equivalently the reciprocal assumption of obligation, which is required to
maximize net benefit, is to be achieved by a network of agreements or
covenants among interacting persons (see *L* 14, pp. 66 ff). These
covenants are essentially negative; each agrees to renounce certain of
his rights, to stand out of the way of others, in return for their reciprocal renunciations (see *L* 14, p. 65). This negative emphasis is
inherent in Hobbes's insistence that the condition of nature is characterized by an excess of costs over benefits. In effect each person
agrees not to impose this excess. Note that there is no suggestion in
Hobbes's argument that any person should refrain altogether from
imposing costs on others. Given Hobbes's conception of human
nature, this would rule out all interaction. Rather, what the second
law of nature requires is that persons reciprocally desist from straightforwardly self-regarding behavior at that point at which the marginal
cost imposed on others exceeds the marginal benefit obtained.
    In our analysis of the second law of nature we have made two
important assumptions: that persons are equal in their capacity to
inflict and their susceptibility to suffer costs; and that liberty is to be of
equal extent for all. The first assumption will come into question
when we turn to Glaucon and the Lydian shepherd. The second
enters crucially into the rationale for the second law of nature. For it is
important to note that however much liberty others enjoy, each person maximizes his own net benefit by maximizing the extent of his
own liberty. To take the liberty of others as given is to assume certain
fixed costs, so that one's net benefits become an increasing function of
one's liberty.

It follows that each person will be tempted, and seemingly with good reason, to violate his covenants, to ignore the limitations on the exercise of his natural liberty to which he has agreed. Each will be tempted to seek a greater and unequal liberty for himself. If this temptation is not resisted, then, as Hobbes says, "Covenants are in vain, and but Empty words; and the Right of all men to all things remaining, we are still in the condition of Warre" (*L* 15, p. 71). Thus Hobbes is led to the third step in his resolution of the problem of radical insufficiency, the third law of nature, "That men performe their Covenants made" (ibid.).

This law addresses an issue quite different from that with which the second law is concerned. The second law determines the point of rational agreement—the point at which equal persons, concerned with their own conservation and contentment, will agree to limit their liberty in interaction. The third law concerns adherence to this point of agreement—adherence to the limitations rationally required by the second law.

Although the laws and the issues they address differ, they are of course related. Simplifying greatly, we may say that if one does not intend to adhere to one's agreements, and so does not intend to follow the third law, then one does not sincerely enter the agreements, as required by the second law. To put the second law into effect, then, one must also put the third law into effect; in agreeing to a limitation on one's liberty, one must intend that one adhere to the limitation. The third law contains, as Hobbes says, "the Fountain and Originall of JUSTICE" (ibid.). To be unjust is to act without right; the person who violates his covenant and exercises a liberty that he has foregone, acts without right and so is unjust. The third law demands that one be just, and this requirement may be read back into the requirement of the second law. Justice is thus the virtue that, exhibited in their interactions, enables human beings to overcome the radical insufficiency of their natural condition.

In introducing the third law of nature, Hobbes's theory begins to become unstuck. We may understand why by retracing our steps and noting what is missing from the argument we have outlined. We began with the costs of natural interaction, noted the need for peace to make these costs tolerable, and showed that peace required a limitation of liberty effected by mutual agreement. We then discovered a derivative problem, arising because of the temptation to violate such agreement. The third law addresses this problem; it enjoins nonviolation. But we have not offered an argument for this law parallel to the argument for the second law.

The second law has a direct maximizing rationale; it enjoins one to select that point of equal liberty which maximizes one's expected net benefit. A rational utility-maximizer, faced with the problem of selecting a point of equal liberty, will follow the second law. The third law lacks this rationale; instead, it imposes a constraint on maximizing behavior. It enjoins one to adhere to the agreed point of equal liberty, even though the exercise of greater liberty would maximize one's net benefit. A rational utility-maximizer, faced with the problem of selecting a point of liberty for himself, will not follow the third law.

This is the burden of the argument of Hobbes's Foole. Given that everyone's conservation and contentment is committed to his own care, "therefore also to make, or not make; keep, or not keep Covenants, was not against Reason, when it conduced to ones benefit. He [the Foole] does not therein deny, that there be Covenants; and that they are sometimes broken, sometimes kept; and that such breach of them may be called Injustice, and the observance of them Justice: but he questioneth, whether Injustice . . . may not sometimes stand with that Reason, which dictateth to every man his own good" (*L* 15, p. 72).

The response Hobbes offers to the Foole in *Leviathan* tends to miss the point of the objection. In effect Hobbes insists that covenants are binding only because it is in one's interest, based on reasonable expectations, to keep them (*L* 15, p. 73). Given that one expects others to adhere to their covenants and to penalize those who do not adhere, then one expects to benefit by adherence. This reply replaces moral by political constraints, so that injustice lies in ignoring expected penalties rather than in violating one's covenant. There is a theory of justice to be developed here, one which begins from the mutual benefits of agreement, proceeds to a rationale for punishment as required to ensure adherence to such agreement, and then treats justice simply as prudent behavior in the context of such punishment. Liberty is externally restricted by the sovereign source of punishment, but each retains the natural right to do whatever in his judgment is most conducive to his benefit. But this is not the theory that Hobbes seems to espouse, and which the Foole attacks. On Hobbes's account, one proceeds from the mutual advantageousness of agreement to the view that justice is the virtue disposing persons to adhere to such agreement, and then one may rationalize punishment as deserved by injustice. Justice constitutes an internal restriction on liberty; each no longer has the full natural right to do whatever in his judgment is most conducive to his benefit. Hobbes cannot defend this latter theory by an appeal to the former. Justice as prudent calculation is not justice as moral disposition.

The account that the Foole rejects treats justice as the virtue of the self-interested. Self-interest alone leads persons to agreement on the basis of the second law of nature, and justice is then the curb on the continued pursuit of self-interest necessary for such agreement to be effective. The Foole insists that any curb on self-interest is contrary to reason. In failing to challenge this insistence, Hobbes fails to meet the deep threat posed to justice by the apparent union of reason and interest.

III

It may be supposed that the problem raised by the Foole is grounded either in Hobbes's excessively unflattering portrait of human beings or in his equally negative account of the natural condition of humankind. To show this supposition to be unfounded, we shall consider a formally similar account of justice based on a much less negative portrayal of human beings and their condition, and find a formally similar problem. We turn to our second protagonist, David Hume.

Hume enumerates six sets of circumstances in which, he insists, "the cautions, jealous virtue of justice would never once have been dreamed of" (*E* III, p. 184). The adjective Hume employs in characterizing the virtue are instructive, for "cautious" and "jealous" should prepare us for an account that, once again, treats justice as the virtue of the self-interested. Justice, Hume proceeds to inform us, would be useless if:

(1) External conveniences existed in abundance and were attainable without effort.
(2) Each person were to feel the same consideration for others as for herself.
(3) External conveniences were found in such paucity that most must perish and all must be in misery.
(4) Those with whom we interact were to exhibit "a desperate rapaciousness" (*E* III, p. 187) without regard to long-term consequences or to public order.
(5) Those with whom we interact were, although rational, yet "of such inferior strength . . . that they were incapable of all resistance, and could never . . . make us feel the effects of their resentment." (*E* III, p. 190)
(6) Each person were to possess "every faculty, requisite both for his own preservation and for the propagation of his kind." (*E* III, p. 192)

The first two sets of circumstances that exclude justice are ones in which interaction would not be expected to give rise to negative externalities. Were all goods present in abundance and available without labor, no one would have reason to impose costs on others. And were each as concerned with her fellows as with herself, each would exert herself to maximize total overall benefit; full benevolence would lead to the utilitarian paradise. In the former set of circumstances self-interest would need no constraint; in the latter it would be sufficiently constrained in each person's motivation by her concern for others.

The third and fourth sets of circumstances may seem to distinguish Hume's account of justice from Hobbes's. For one may note that the Hobbesian natural condition of humankind is characterized by just the extremes of scarcity and rapaciousness that, Hume insists, exclude all consideration of justice. Yet it is these features of the natural human condition that demand justice as their remedy. However, there is no real difference here between Hobbes and Hume. For Hobbes would agree that in an actual condition of extreme scarcity and rapaciousness justice has no place. The condition of mere nature is a state of war, and "the notions of Right and Wrong, Justice and Injustice have there no place" (*L* 13, p. 63). That justice is part of the remedy for the ills of the state of nature does not make it part of that state. Hume insists that if others are rapacious, one "can have no other expedient than to arm himself, to whomever the sword he seizes, or the buckler, may belong: To make provision of all means of defence and security: . . . he must consult the dictates of self-preservation alone" (*E* III, p. 187). Hobbes argues to exactly the same effect in considering what one should do in a condition of war in which others do not, or will not, endeavor peace.

The second law of nature provides for constraints on interaction in those circumstances in which mutual benefit is possible and all are willing to seek it. Given sufficient scarcity, no mutual benefit is possible; to escape the present stroke of death every person must be for herself alone. And although the rapacity of others does not rule out the possibility of mutual benefit, it does show their unwillingness to seek it. For scarcity there is no remedy save a greater supply of goods. For rapacity the remedy is that prudence which grounds, but does not constitute, justice.

The fifth set of circumstances shows the importance of assuming equality in power among persons. Given sufficient inequality, the total benefits that the stronger can secure for themselves by the exercise of an unconstrained liberty are greater than the total costs that the weaker can inflict upon them. And more to the point, the increase in benefit to the stronger as the average extent of liberty increases exceeds the increase in their costs. Net benefit for the stronger group is maximized at the position of maximum liberty. They have no reason to agree to any limitation on their liberty.

The sixth set of circumstances exhibits the connection between in-

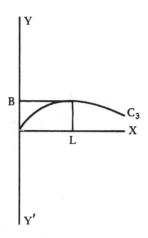

Figure 2

dividual insufficiency and justice. Creatures who are able, through their individual efforts, to maintain their level of vital motion and so preserve themselves, and, insofar as they fail eventually through aging, to reproduce themselves and so maintain their species' level of vital motion, have no instrumental concern with their fellows. To them, others of their kind are neither helps nor hindrances. Hume claims, surely correctly, that such creatures would be purely solitary, having no concern whatsoever for their fellows. They would form no conception of their behavior as assuming a liberty of action in relation to others of their kind, much less the conception of constraining that liberty. Justice is conceivable to the self-interested only insofar as they are not self-sufficient.

But now suppose that none of these six sets of circumstances obtains. Does it follow that human beings, apart from the constraints of justice and the framework of society, are in a natural condition of radical insufficiency? Not at all. Radical insufficiency requires that for each person, the total costs of interaction exceed the total benefits. But the need for justice arises when the marginal costs of interaction would exceed the marginal benefits.

In Figure 1 the radical insufficiency of the natural condition of humankind is shown by the fact that as liberty increases beyond L, the curve C_3 representing net benefit not only falls but eventually crosses the X-axis, and takes on values representing negative net benefit, or net cost. Our analysis of justice, however, does not depend on net benefit taking negative values for a sufficient extent of liberty. Consider Figure 2, labeled in the same manner as Figure 1. In the condition

that it represents, interaction always has positive value; the curve
showing net benefit never falls below the X-axis. Thus for maximum
liberty, total benefits exceed total costs. But marginal benefits are less
than marginal costs for all degrees of liberty greater than L. Even if
interaction is profitable overall, human beings may have reason to
accept curbs on their liberty in order to maximize net benefit.

We may therefore consider restrictions on liberty in a more positive
light than is suggested by Hobbes's account. As Hume maintains,
"The common situation of society is a medium amidst all these extremes [i.e., the sets of circumstances in which justice would have no
place]. We are naturally partial to ourselves, and to our friends; but
are capable of learning the advantage resulting from a more equitable
conduct. Few enjoyments are given us from the open and liberal hand
of nature; but by art, labour, and industry, we can extract them in
great abundance. Hence the ideas of property become necessary in all
civil society: Hence justice derives its usefulness to the public: And
hence alone arises its merit and moral obligation" (*E* III, p. 188). For
Hume justice lies not only in the performance of covenants, but more
generally in a respect that ensures the stability of property, restricting
its transference to mutual consent (see *T* III.II.VI, p. 526). Hume is
no doubt overly sanguine in supposing that the benefits of any system
of stable possession are sufficiently great that it matters little who
possesses what (see *E,* app. III, p. 309n). We might wish a closer
inquiry into how expected net benefit might be maximized for the
average person. But we need not dispute Hume's fundamental insight, that the rules of justice provide the framework for the activities
of production and exchange that constitute the primary advantage of
society over the condition of nature.

Hume's argument thus does not require treating the natural condition of humankind as one of radical insufficiency, in which interaction
is more costly than solitude. Given that we require the assistance of
one another, we are sensible of the advantages of human interaction.
But we come to recognize that in the absence of agreed and stable
possessions, this interaction, even if sufficient for bare survival, is
nevertheless less advantageous than might be. And this provides a
place for the virtue of justice, as a disposition to accept those curbs on
our self-interested behavior which are necessary to maintain a system
of stable possession and voluntary exchange.

Hume supposes that we enter sympathetically into the interests of
others—that interests are, as it were, contagious so that they spread
from their original possessor to those who come into contact with her
(see *T* III.III.I, pp. 575–578). This affords each person a motive for
just behavior entirely lacking in Hobbes's account. For the general

advantageousness of the system of property and agreement upheld by justice elicits our sympathetic approval. However, the particular advantages of injustice are not thereby denied. Each person, although approving the general benefits secured by justice, must also be sensible that any constraint on her own behavior is contrary to her individual benefit. And so we find a place for the sensible knave.

"Having explained the moral *approbation* attending merit or virtue," Hume says, "there remains nothing but briefly to consider our interested *obligation* to it, and to inquire whether every man, who has any regard to his own happiness and welfare, will not best find his account in the practice of every moral duty" (*E* IX, p. 278). This seems an entirely reasonable question to put, and in no respect more reasonable than in connection with justice. But what follows in Hume's discussion is of great significance to an understanding both of justice itself and of justice in relation to the other moral virtues. For Hume finds no difficulty in accommodating those other virtues to human interests. In his argument he does, of course, appeal to a sociability foreign to Hobbes's conception of human nature, in order to defend virtues that are no part of Hobbes's conception of morality. Given that our fellows' interests are sympathetically communicated to us and so become our own, we find that the virtues other than justice express and promote the full range of our concerns. They are the dispositions a person would select, if we "suppose that he has full power of modelling his own disposition, and let him deliberate what appetite or desire he would choose for the foundation of his happiness and enjoyment" (*E* IX, p. 281).

But justice is not so easily accommodated. "Treating vice with the greatest candour, and making it all possible concessions, we must acknowledge that there is not, in any instance, the smallest pretext for giving it the preference above virtue, with a view of self-interest; except, perhaps, in the case of justice, where a man, taking things in a certain light, may often seem to be a loser by his integrity" (*E* IX, p. 282). It may seem paradoxical that the virtue of the self-interested person should be the one most difficult to accommodate to self-interest. But the paradox is merely apparent, for justice curbs the unrestricted rule of self-interest, whereas the other virtues, resting on our sympathetic identification with the interests of others, maximize our happiness. They do not curb self-interest but rather instruct it in the means necessary to the greatest happiness of sociable and sympathetic creatures.

Thus the sensible knave tells us. "That *honesty is the best policy*, may be a good general rule, but is liable to many exceptions; and he, it may perhaps be thought, conducts himself with most wisdom, who observes the general rule, and takes advantage of all the exceptions" (*E* IX, pp. 282–283). And what is Hume's response? "I must confess that, if a man think that this reasoning much requires an answer, it would be a little difficult to find any which will to him appear satisfactory and convincing" (*E* III, p. 283). This has the virtue, lacking in Hobbes's reply to the Foole, of recognizing the real problem; it has the candor to admit that Hume has found no real answer. He then moves to the sentiments on which his general account of morality, although not his theory of justice, is founded: "If his heart rebel not against such pernicious maxims, if he feel no reluctance to the thoughts of villainy or baseness, he has indeed lost a considerable motive to virtue; and we may expect that his practice will be answerable to his speculation" (ibid.). We may indeed. But the sensible knave sees himself as no villain, but rather as one who recognizes that in deciding what to do, ignoring the constraints of justice, when possible, is the interested policy.

IV

The Foole and the sensible knave have focused on a problem about the virtue of justice. Reason and interest direct us to accept limitations on our liberty which reason and interest then seem to direct us to subvert. So far we have not given serious attention to considerations that might challenge the stance of our antagonists. We have noted an absence of argument in the replies of Hobbes and Hume, who seem to have been more effective in creating their own opponents than in answering those opponents' charges. But perhaps more can be said, and indeed more has been said by both Hobbes and Hume.

Justice is opposed by an alliance of reason and interest. We may therefore look to each of these, to see if it can be detached from this alliance, and made to join forces with, or at least not to oppose, justice. And to this end it is worth adverting to two passages—one in Hobbes's discussion with Bishop Bramhall on the *Questions Concerning Liberty, Necessity, and Chance,* the other in Hume's *Treatise of Human Nature.*

Hobbes agrees with Bramhall that "moral goodness is the conformity of an action with right reason" (*Qu*, p. 193), a position from which the Foole would hardly dissent. But what is right reason? Here Hobbes disagrees with Bramhall, although this disagreement is not germane to our present concern, and also with the Foole. "All the real good, which we call honest and morally virtuous, is that which is not repugnant to the law, civil or natural; for the law is all the right reason we have, and, (though he, as often as it disagreeth with his own reason, deny it), is the infallible rule of moral goodness. The reason whereof is this, that because neither mine nor the Bishop's reason is right reason fit to be a rule of our moral actions, we have therefore set up over ourselves a sovereign governor, and agreed that his laws shall be unto us, whatsoever they be, in the place of right reason, to dictate to us what is really good" (*Qu*, p. 194).[2]

The Foole, in his attack on Hobbes, appeals to that natural reason "which dictateth to every man his own good" (*L* 15, p. 72). Hobbes's reply must be to appeal to that conventional reason which "is no otherwise certainly right than by making it so by our approbation of it and voluntary subjection to it" (*Qu*, p. 193). The second law of nature, in directing us to give up some portion of natural right, must also direct us to give up a corresponding portion of natural reason. For as Hobbes insists in *De Cive*, reason is the foundation of right: "Neither by the word *right* is anything else signified, than that liberty which every man hath to make use of his natural faculties according to right reason" (*DC* 1.7, p. 115). As I have argued elsewhere, the Foole, in appealing to natural reason, fails to appreciate the tight conceptual connection between right and reason that is central to Hobbes's thought, and that affords Hobbes his defense against the Foole's argument.[3] Against the Foole's practice, of course, only the sovereign may be able to offer a defense.

We noted in section II that the second law of nature has a direct maximizing rationale. Each person does best to agree to limit her liberty to that extent which maximizes expected net benefit, provided others do so as well. This rationale must extend to limiting natural reason, insofar as otherwise it directs one to subvert one's agreement and exercise an unlimited liberty. In place of natural reason, one must accept the conventional reason of the law, which directs one to adhere to one's covenants.

The Foole insists that any curb on self-interest is contrary to reason. The reply is that both interest and reason curb themselves, in directing persons to agreement on the basis of the second law of nature. Although contrary to natural reason, justice is grounded in the right reason which is law.

Whereas the Foole fails to appreciate the redirection of reason implicit in Hobbes's argument, the sensible knave fails to appreciate the redirection of interest advanced by Hume. Hume begins by noting that " 'Tis certain, that no affection of the human mind [other than self-interest] has both a sufficient force, and a proper direction to counter-balance the love of gain, and render men fit members of

---

[2] I am grateful to Tommy Lott for directing my attention to this passage. That I overlooked it in "Thomas Hobbes: Moral Theorist," above, is a serious fault.

[3] See ibid., pp. 20–21.

society, by making them abstain from the possessions of others" (*T* III.II.II, p. 492). After developing this point by considering such particular affections as benevolence, and showing their insufficiency, he concludes that "there is no passion . . . capable of controlling the interested affection, but the very affection itself, by an alteration of its direction. Now this alteration must necessarily take place upon the least reflection; since 'tis evident, that the passion is much better satis-fy'd by its restraint, than by its liberty, and that in preserving society, we make much greater advances in the acquiring possessions, than in the solitary and forlorn condition, which must follow upon violence and an universal licence" (ibid.).

Hume's argument here may seem open to an obvious objection. In order to preserve society the interested passion must indeed be re-strained. But each benefits by the restraint exhibited by others, not by her own. Taking the behavior of others as given, the net benefit one receives is, as we noted in section II, an increasing function of the extent of one's own liberty, or of the absence of real restraint.

But this objection is less convincing than it may appear. Hume may reply that the interested passion must be curbed if persons are to be fit for society. Each of us has an interest in being a member of society, and so each of us has an interest in being a just person, a person whose initial self-interest is redirected in favor of the demands of justice. What the least reflection reveals is, not the advantage to each in having others restrained by justice, but the advantage of being herself so restrained.

In any particular interaction, the clever Foole or the truly sensible knave must expect to do better than the just person, for the sensible knave will not be disposed to just behavior but will regard justice as mere policy. The knave will adhere to the requirements of justice as long as, but only as long as, self-interest does not reveal an exception of which she may take advantage. However, the clever Foole or truly sensible knave still mistakes her true interest. For in being a knave she makes herself unfit for society—a person to be excluded from, rather than included in, the mutually advantageous arrangements that society affords.

This brings us back to a passage in Hobbes's reply to the Foole which we have so far neglected. "He therefore that breaketh his Cove-nant, and consequently declareth that he thinks he may with reason do so, cannot be received into any Society, that unite themselves for Peace and Defence, but by the errour of them that receive him; nor when he is received, be retayned in it, without seeing the danger of their errour; which errours a man cannot reasonably reckon upon as the means of his security" (*L* 15, p. 73). Only the just person, disposed to adhere to agreements and to respect the property of others, is fit to be included in society.

We may not expect that this argument will finally silence the adversaries of justice. The Foole and the sensible knave may reply that it is the semblance of being a just person, and not the reality, that pays. One must convince others that one has redirected one's interest, and abandoned natural for conventional reason, but all this may and should be but a smokescreen. In a full inquiry into justice this further argument would need examination, but since it is neither advanced by our antagonists nor combated by Hobbes or Hume we here leave it to one side.

Because justice arises from a redirection of interest, Hume is able to claim that "the question . . . concerning the wickedness or goodness of human nature, enters not in the least into that other question concerning the origin of society; . . . For whether the passion of self-interest be esteemed vicious or virtuous, 'tis all a case; since itself alone restrains it: So that if it be virtuous, men become social by their virtue; if vicious, their vice has the same effect" (*T* III.II.II, p. 492). At the core of becoming social is the acquisition of the disposition to just behavior. Hume claims then that justice needs no root other than interest together with "the degrees of men's sagacity or folly" (ibid.).

Clearly this view sets justice significantly apart from other virtues. And this suggests one of the major conclusions that our inquiry reveals—that the theory of justice is quite distinct from other parts of the theory of morality. Justice stands in a quite different relationship to interest than do other virtues, and it is misleading to group it with them under the single and simple rubric of morality.

Morals, as commonly conceived, embrace at least three quite distinctive subjects. First, there are those concerns arising from an ideal of human nature or human activity. These concerns relate to those values of human fulfillment that cannot be treated merely as instrumental to conservation and contentment. Perhaps these allegedly objective values are chimerical; here I may plead that I do not know. Second, there are concerns arising from the noninstrumental interests human beings take in their fellows, and indeed also in other living beings. These concerns relate to those directives for behavior which are based on other-directed interests. As Hume argues, many of the traditional virtues fall into this area; they arise from the sympathetic identification between persons. And third, there are concerns arising from the negative externalities endemic to unrestricted interaction. These concerns relate to those curbs on behavior necessary if the externalities are to be internalized. They presuppose neither a noninstrumental interest in others nor an ideal of human activity apart from a concern with individual satisfaction. It is this third area of concern which we examine in theories of justice, and it would seem to contain no essential reference to those other areas traditionally grouped with it in morality.

But a sharp dividing line between justice and other virtues is also misleading. The theory of justice, as developed by Hobbes and, at least in its main emphases, by Hume, abstracts from human sociability. But the role of justice in human affairs cannot be understood apart from that sociability. Or so we shall argue, as we turn our attention from the Foole and the sensible knave to the third of our antagonists, the Lydian shepherd.

V

Glaucon introduces the parable of the Lydian shepherd in presenting an account of justice which he wishes Socrates to refute. Whether he is right to wish this is a matter to which we shall return. But first let us consider Glaucon's statement of the view, expressed as what "they say." "They say that doing injustice is naturally good, and suffering injustice bad, but that the bad in suffering injustice far exceeds the good in doing it [i.e., the marginal costs of being the victim of an unjust action exceed the marginal benefits of performing a similar action]; so that, when they do injustice to one another and suffer it and taste of both, it seems profitable—to those who are not able to escape the one and choose the other [i.e., those who satisfy Hobbes's and Hume's requirement of equality]—to set down a compact among themselves neither to do injustice nor to suffer it. . . . And this . . . is the genesis and being of justice; it is a mean between what is best— doing injustice without paying the penalty [as advocated by the Foole and the sensible knave]—and what is worst—suffering injustice without being able to avenge oneself. The just is in the middle between these two, cared for not because it is good but because it is honored due to a want of vigor in doing injustice. The man who is able to do it and is truly a man would never set down a compact with anyone not to do injustice and not to suffer it. He'd be mad" (*R* 358e—359b). The Lydian shepherd, possessor of the ring of Gyges, illustrates the truth of what they say; his ring makes him superior to his fellows so that he escapes from the circumstances of justice.

There is a problem evident in Glaucon's statement, which treats injustice as natural but justice as conventional—its genesis and being lying in an agreement to avoid injustice. It would be better to say that, finding the benefits of certain forms of behavior to be less than the costs of suffering those forms when practiced by others, persons agree among themselves to desist from them, denominating them unjust, and their avoidance just. On this revised account both injustice and justice would be conventional. Glaucon, in applying 'injustice' to certain natural behavior, is in effect reading the conventional label back into the preconventional situation. Indeed, in this respect his usage parallels Hobbes's ascription of the right of nature to persons in their natural condition.

Our inquiry into Hobbes and Hume will have made Glaucon's position familiar, as our parenthetical interjections in what "they say" will make clear, and we may therefore be less ready to demand that it be refuted. What we must note, however, is that the problem posed by the Lydian shepherd is quite different from that posed by our previous antagonists. The relation between the shepherd and his fellows parallels the relation between humans and inferior rational beings which, Hume maintains, falls outside the scope of justice. The shepherd's capacity to make himself invisible enables him to wreak what is conventionally termed injustice on others, without those others having any effective means of retaliation. He has therefore no reason to agree to any curb on his liberty to do as he pleases. Although he is willing to take advantage of any restraint shown by others, yet for him marginal benefits exceed costs, even in purely unrestrained interaction. If the rationale for justice is to be found in self-interest, surely the shepherd would be mad to accept it.

The Lydian shepherd thus challenges not *adherence* to rules or rights to which he has rationally agreed, but rather the very *agreement* itself. His quarrel is not with Hobbes's third law of nature but with the first and second laws; he lacks reason to endeavor peace. Is he then, as Glaucon hopes Socrates will show him to be, wrong to place himself outside the bounds of justice? And is he wrong to consider justice a second-best disposition, a mean between the truly desirable capacity to inflict what one pleases on others without fear of retaliation, and the most undesirable inability to avoid or to retaliate against what others inflict—a mean which most persons accept because of their weakness, but which his fortunate invisibility enables him to avoid?

If there is a single clue to the answer to these questions, it may be found in Glaucon's explication of the parable, when he speaks of the ring of Gyges enabling one to act "as an equal to a god among humans" (*R* 360c). Not only does the Lydian shepherd place himself outside the bounds of justice, he places himself outside the bounds of human life. He interacts with his fellows as a god because he does not fear their reprisal. Of course, since he combines the desires of a man with the powers of a god, it is not surprising that his behavior appears to us as unjust. The true god would have neither the desires nor the limitations that cause one to act as a human among humans; he would lack any conception of justice.

Justice is a peculiarly human virtue. It arises from self-interest and the lack of self-sufficiency. It is the virtue of beings who, because they stand in need one of another, conceive of the benefits that may result from their interaction, yet who, because they frequently face situations in which unrestricted interaction yields marginal costs in excess of benefits, recognize the need to constrain their behavior. But this virtue sits uneasily with certain ideals that such beings may form—an ideal of self-sufficiency, or an ideal of interaction from which externalities are naturally absent. For the conditions that make justice needed by human beings would not obtain were either of these ideals realized. And this seems to make justice a second-best disposition, accepted because neither ideal is possible.

We may, then, share Glaucon's concern and seek a redefinition of justice that will afford it an intrinsic value absent if its place is restricted to the particular nonideal conditions of human life. We might suppose ourselves ready to embark on what seems the quest of Plato's *Republic*. But this supposed quest embodies a profound error; the value of justice is in no way impugned by conceiving it as the virtue necessary to human interaction, but as irrelevant to an ideal that, were it realized, would transcend human nature and the conditions of human life. Persons are not self-sufficient and are self-interested; these are not accidental features of human nature but are partially constitutive of it. Human beings live, and must live, in the circumstances of justice.

Hobbes demonstrates that the rationale for justice requires no appeal to human sociability. But his argument reveals no incompatibility between the two. Indeed, we may suppose that both the disposition to be just and the disposition to be sociable are in part grounded in a lack of self-sufficiency. Human need one for another not only grounds an awareness of the mutual advantages of social interaction but also gives rise to that sympathetic communication of interests which converts the need for society into a desire for sociability. Justice and sociability both serve as curbs on the unrestrained pursuit of self-directed interests, but they do so in different ways. Justice overrides individual interest to promote agreed mutual benefit; sociability adds a concern with the interests of others to the original self-concern.

But there is more than mere compatibility between justice and sociability. Indeed, we may argue that justice provides a norm for sociable behavior, a norm adherence to which makes full and true sociability possible. For in the absence of the constraints of justice, sociability is vulnerable to deep and pervasive exploitation—of which no doubt the most striking example in contemporary consciousness concerns the relationships between the sexes.

The sociable person shares the interests of his fellows. He directs his efforts toward their gratification, as well as to the gratification of his own proper interests. Indeed, he may be led to neglect his own concerns in attending to those of his fellows. And he may not receive from others a comparable attention in return. In this way his sociability may be exploited. And the traditional nurturing and caring roles assigned to women in our society, and in many other societies, exhibit this exploitation. For did God not make Eve a helpmeet for Adam?

Justice, in requiring that marginal costs not exceed benefits for any person involved in interaction, opposes this exploitation of sociability. In a just society, the noninstrumental interests that persons take in one another, the attentions each pay to the concerns of his fellows, are sources of mutual benefit and enrichment over and above the payoffs of merely interested cooperation. And without this enrichment, true sociability is surely lacking. A one-sided sacrifice, even if carried out in the name of sociable and sympathetic feeling, even if presented under the guise of nurture and care, must prevent full mutual respect between those who give and those who take. We have come to be openly aware of the partially concealed contempt that so often lies behind the facade of relationships between men and women, and we may identify this contempt as stemming from a lack of justice in those relationships, a justice which would ensure full mutuality of benefit.

Thus if justice represents the apex of a society lacking sociability, it represents also the cornerstone of that mutual concern which is not only the remedy for human weakness—the remedy for individual insufficiency—but also the source of human enrichment and fulfillment. Hobbes's unflattering picture of human nature is less than the whole truth, but is a truth that we do ill to ignore; even if we love our neighbor, we also love ourselves, and we need the constraints of justice to remind us not to benefit at our neighbor's expense.

The just person has much to learn from his encounter with the antagonists. From his debate with the Foole he learns not to deliberate solely in terms of the direct maximization of net individual benefit, if he would be admitted to the society of others. From his debate with the sensible knave he learns to redirect his interest to express a concern with that society, if he would remain within it. From his debate with the Lydian shepherd he learns to beware of conferring more than human powers on those with human desires, for they cannot then be bound by justice. And he learns that although justice may not require sociability, yet there is no true sociability without justice. If the just person learns these lessons properly, he will not, I think, have reason to join with Glaucon, in complaining of the account of justice that he presents, and which is advanced by Hobbes and Hume.

[7]

Justice and Natural Endowment: Toward a Critique of Rawls's Ideological Framework

I

The reconciliation of morality with rationality is the central problem of modern moral philosophy. It is easy to achieve this reconciliation by fiat, to select a conception of rationality and a conception of morality so that the two fit. What is of greater interest and value is to attempt this reconciliation beginning with our intuitive conceptions of rationality and morality. *A Theory of Justice* claims to achieve this, for that part of morality which constitutes the realm of justice.

Rawls's theory of justice

> generalizes and carries to a higher level of abstraction the familiar theory of the social contract [11]. . . . On the contract view the theory of justice is part of the theory of rational choice [47]. . . . The guiding idea is that the principles of justice for the basic structure of society are the object of the original agreement. They are the principles that free and rational persons concerned to further their own interests would accept in an initial position of equality as defining the fundamental terms of their association [11].

Thus the connection between rationality and justice is to be established in terms of an act of choice in an initial position of equality. In addition to an account of rationality and justice, then, the theory must provide an account of what Rawls usually refers to as the "initial situation" (121). The hypothesis, which makes the theory a genuine

Reprinted with permission of *Social Theory and Practice*.
Note: Page citations from Rawls [1] are in parentheses.

theory, is that an account can be given of these factors which both matches our considered judgments about them, and relates them so that the conception of justice would be embodied in the principles chosen by rational men in the initial situation.

Rawls explicitly recognizes the importance of this hypothesis with respect both to justice and to the initial situation. He suggests that

> it seems natural to think of the concept of justice as distinct from the various conceptions of justice and as being specified by the role which these different sets of principles, these different conceptions, have in common. (5)

The theory must then provide that

> account of a person's sense of justice . . . which matches his judgments in reflective equilibrium. . . . This state is one reached after a person has weighed various proposed conceptions and he has either revised his judgments to accord with one of them or held fast to his initial convictions (and the corresponding conception). (48)

Furthermore,

> there are . . . many possible interpretations of the initial situation. . . . But . . . there is one interpretation of the initial situation which best expresses the conditions that are widely thought reasonable to impose on the choice of principles yet which, at the same time, leads to a conception that characterizes our considered judgments in reflective equilibrium. This most favored, or standard, interpretation I shall refer to as the original position. (121)

And so the theory of

> justice as fairness is the hypothesis that the principles which would be chosen in the original position are identical with those that match our considered judgments and so these principles describe our sense of justice. (48)

But Rawls's account of rationality is significantly different from his account of justice and of the initial situation. He does not suggest that he is concerned with a particular conception of rationality, among the various possible conceptions which one might entertain, but rather with the concept itself.

> The concept of rationality invoked here . . . is the standard one familiar in social theory. Thus in the usual way, a rational person is thought to

have a coherent set of preferences between the options open to him. He ranks these options according to how well they further his purposes; he follows the plan which will satisfy more of his desires rather than less, and which has the greater chance of being successfully executed. (143)

Rawls makes, explicitly, one special assumption,

that a rational individual does not suffer from envy. He is not ready to accept a loss for himself if only others have less as well. (143)

This is part of the standard view, if "loss" is understood in relation to the purposes or desires of the agent. A better formulation of the special assumption is that there are certain *primary goods,* and

the persons in the original position . . . prefer more rather than less primary goods. (93)

No one's purposes are served by accepting less primary goods for herself, if only others have less as well.

The concept of rationality familiar in social theory identifies rationality with the maximization of individual utility. Rawls, then, accepts this identification, subject to the special assumption that there is a class of goods such that an increase in these goods always represents an increase in utility. This account of rationality is not advanced as a particular conception, competing with others as an adequate formulation of our concept of rational man, but as expressing that concept itself. Hence the view, common in medieval thought, that the role of reason is to acquaint man with the divine law for human conduct must be not only mistaken but also *conceptually* mistaken.

An *ideology* may be characterized, in part, by the identification of a particular conception of rationality with the concept itself. Hence Rawls's assumption of that conception of reason that is prevalent in, and indeed fundamental to, our society both characterizes his own *ideological framework* and identifies it, in one essential respect, with what I shall neutrally term the *liberal individualist* framework. In the present argument, then, I suggest a basis for a critique of that framework.

The argument has the following structure. In section II, I introduce the central features of Rawls's conception of justice, and his account of the initial situation. In section III, I show how the maximizing conception of rationality, in conjunction with the conception of the original position, seems to lead to the difference principle which characterizes Rawls's conception of justice. However, in sections

IV and V, I show that a consideration of man's natural endowment, in relation first to the absence of society and then to man's social potential, requires revisions in the difference principle. In section VI, I examine the effect of these revisions on the type of society instituted by the adoption of the principles of justice, showing that contrary to Rawls's view, this proves to be civil or private society. Finally, in section VII, I mention an alternative conception of society and its relation to man's natural endowment, as the starting point for a critique of the maximizing conception of practical rationality.[1]

II

Rawls formulates the general conception of justice which is derived from his theory in this way:

> All social primary goods—liberty and opportunity, income and wealth, and the bases of self-respect—are to be distributed equally unless an unequal distribution of any or all of these goods is to the advantage of the least favored. (303)

This general conception is used to derive a special conception which Rawls takes to be applicable to our actual circumstances. Among the primary goods, "fundamental rights and liberties" are distinguished from "economic and social benefits" (63). The former are to be equally available to all; the latter are to be distributed in accordance with what Rawls terms the *difference principle*. In the most general form in which Rawls presents this principle—a form more general than that in which he employs it, yet less restrictive in its assumptions about actual conditions—the principle states that

> in a basic structure with n relevant representatives, first maximize the welfare of the worst-off representative man; second, for equal welfare of the worst-off representative, maximize the welfare of the second worst-off representative man, and so on until the last case which is, for equal welfare of all the preceding $n - 1$ representatives, maximize the welfare of the best-off representative man. We may think of this as the lexical difference principle. (83)

The difference principle, which I shall use in this most general, lexical form, distinguishes what Rawls calls democratic equality from

[1] The position which I develop here as a corrective to Rawls's views may be found, in a positive formulation based on game-theoretic concepts, in Gauthier [6] and elsewhere, especially Gauthier [5].

liberal equality. Both liberal and democratic equality nullify "the influence of social contingencies," but the liberal conception

> still permits the distribution of wealth and income to be determined by the natural distribution of abilities and talents. Within the limits allowed by the background arrangements, distributive shares are decided by the outcome of the natural lottery; and this outcome is arbitrary from a moral perspective. There is no more reason to permit the distribution of income and wealth to be settled by the distribution of natural assets than by historical and social fortune (73–74).

The democratic conception, based on the difference principle, does not permit wealth and income to be determined by natural talents. Hence Rawls's

> conception of justice . . . nullifies the accidents of natural endowment . . . leaving aside those aspects of the social world that seem arbitrary from a moral point of view. (15)

To anticipate, the particular aim of my argument is to show that this *nullificatory* feature of Rawls's conception of justice is incompatible with its *contractual* basis. I shall argue that if we accept the contractual framework, required by Rawls's maximizing conception of rationality, we are led to a conception of justice more closely resembling the liberal conception which Rawls would reject. Insofar as this liberal conception fails to satisfy our considered judgments and hence our sense of justice, rationality and morality are not reconciled.

The contractual basis of Rawls's thought requires, as we have seen, a specification of the initial situation in which the principles of justice are to be chosen. The favored specification is referred to as the original position. In the original position each person is assumed to be rational, and so is assumed to seek to maximize her well-being, subject to the constraint that she is free from envy. Each is subject and knows she is subject, to what Rawls terms "the circumstances of justice," which

> may be described as the normal conditions under which human cooperation is both possible and necessary. . . . Hume's account of them is especially perspicuous. . . . For simplicity I often stress the condition of moderate scarcity (among the objective circumstances), and that of mutual disinterest or individuals taking no interest in one another's interests (among the subjective circumstances). Thus, one can say, in brief, that the circumstances of justice obtain whenever mutually disinterested persons put forward conflicting claims to the division of social advantages under conditions of moderate scarcity. (126–128)

The persons in the original situation have a good deal of general knowledge about their situation, but they have no particular knowledge. They are to choose under a "veil of ignorance" which ensures that

> no one knows his place in society, his class position or social status; nor does he know his fortune in the distribution of natural assets and abilities, his intelligence and strength, and the like. Nor, again, does anyone know his conception of the good, the particulars of his rational plan of life, or even the special features of his psychology such as his aversion to risk or liability to optimism or pessimism. (137)

There is more that is unknown about the nature and circumstances of the particular society. But what is essential to my argument may be summarized from the passage quoted: *no one knows who he is.* And since no one knows who he is, or in what circumstances he will be, each man is everyman—or no man. Thus

> it is clear that since the differences among the parties are unknown to them, and everyone is equally rational and similarly situated, each is convinced by the same arguments. Therefore, we can view the choice in the original position from the standpoint of one person selected at random. If anyone after due reflection prefers a conception of justice to another, then they all do, and a unanimous agreement can be reached. (139)

This sufficiently specifies the original position. The next task is to show why rational persons in this position are supposed to choose Rawls's conception of justice, and more specifically, the lexical difference principle.

III

In examining the derivation of the difference principle as the object of choice by rational persons subject to the circumstances of justice in the original position, I shall not trace Rawls's own argument. An analysis of that argument would require an essay in itself and would, I believe, reveal certain weaknesses which my own account is intended to avoid. Thus I depart from Rawls, not to weaken the statement of his case so that it will prove more amenable to criticism, but to present the lexical difference principle in the most favorable light possible.

In the derivation, it is essential to focus on two different standpoints. First, of course, is the standpoint of the reasoner in the original position, choosing "behind a veil of ignorance" (12). But second, there is the standpoint of the reasoner after the principle is chosen, the resulting society is instituted, and the veil of ignorance is lifted. I want to insist that a principle establishing the terms of association must be rational, not only prospectively but also retrospectively. By this I mean, not that the choice made in ignorance be the choice one would make, if one could, when one is aware of the actual circumstances governing the outcome, but that awareness of the outcome should not lead one to judge the original choice irrational, when one in imagination reimposes the constraints under which it was made. The choice must be rationally acceptable, in this sense, to each representative person after the veil of ignorance is lifted. This requirement is, it seems to me, implicit in Rawls's insistence "that the original position be interpreted so that one can at any time adopt its perspective" (139).

Consider first the method of rational choice for a person who knows who he is. Such a person would choose those principles which would maximize his expected benefits. He would attach, to each possible set of principles an expected future, which would be the probability-weighted average of the possible futures which might result from adoption of the principles. Then to each expected future he would assign a value, or utility, indicating its expected benefits to him. He would then choose those principles which maximized this value.

But in the original position no one knows who he is, so it is everyman's reasoning that we must attempt to formulate. If everyman were to reason in a manner similar to a particular person, then he would attach, to each possible set of principles, a set of expected futures— one member of the set representing the expected future of each possible representative person, each person who he might turn out to be. To each such expected future he would assign a value, representing its expected benefits to the person in question. To each set of expected futures he would then assign an expected value, representing the probability-weighted average of the values of its members (the probabilities here corresponding to the likelihood of being each of the possible persons). This last expected value is then what he would maximize by his choice of principles. And thus he would choose the principle of average utilitarianism, and not the difference principle.

Rawls discusses average utilitarianism at some length (section 28), but without presenting objections to it that are, in my view, fully convincing. The best argument against it, and in favor of the difference principle, seems to me to arise from a consideration of the situation of the person who finds himself to be least advantaged, when the veil of ignorance is lifted. Unless all are equal, there must be some representative person who finds both that no one is worse off than he is, and that his utility is less than the probability-weighted average which he expected. How is he to convince himself that his choice of principles was rational?

Insofar as his misfortune depends on the actual circumstances, this poses no real problem. He had reason to expect the circumstances to be otherwise, more favorable to his well-being. He can envisage himself under those other circumstances, enjoying greater well-being. This expected alternative makes his actual sacrifice of well-being acceptable to him; the outcome is unlucky, no more. He recognizes that, given the information available to him, the choice that he made was best.

But insofar as his misfortune depends on who he is, the situation in which he now finds himself is a quite different one. For even if the supposition that he had reason to expect to be another, more favored, person is intelligible, yet he can not now envisage *himself* as that other person, enjoying greater well-being. He can of course envisage himself in the circumstances of another person, but this is not the alternative he expected, for *ex hypothesi* his well-being, and thus his circumstances, are to depend on who he is. He can also envisage some other person enjoying greater well-being, and this indeed is the relevant expected alternative, but it does not now make his sacrifice of well-being acceptable to him. Now that he knows who he is, he does not suppose that the choice which he made was best for him. He realizes instead that his ignorance of who he was rendered him unable to make a best choice for himself.

This argument is, as I have said, not to be found in Rawls. But he does suggest some part of it (173–175), especially in his insistence that

> the expectation finally arrived at in the reasoning for the average principle seems spurious . . . : it is not, as expectations should be, founded on one system of aims. (175)

If everyman chooses those principles which lead to the maximization of average expected utility, he does not *thereby* choose those principles which maximize the expected utility of any of the representative persons who he may turn out to be. It is not, of course, possible for him to choose principles which would maximize the expected utility of all of these persons, for the outcome which would maximize one representative person's expected utility does not in general coincide with the outcome which would maximize some other person's expected utility. What alternative then is open to everyman?

Everyman must choose principles in such a way that when the veil of ignorance is lifted, each representative person will consider that he would rationally so have chosen. Given the assumed connection between rationality and maximization of benefit, one condition which everyman's choice of principles must satisfy is that the outcome determined by the principles be such that no representative person could expect to receive greater benefits, without some other person expecting to receive lesser benefits. For if someone finds that he could have expected to do better, at no expected cost to anyone else, then he will not consider that he has chosen rationally. Optimality in the Pareto sense, or efficiency, as Rawls prefers to term it, is thus a condition on everyman's choice.

But there are usually many Pareto-optimal outcomes, and, so, many principles which would satisfy this condition. A second condition on everyman's choice is then required and arises from the initial equality of each person. Everyman may not choose principles which favor the well-being of one person over another, if his choice is to be acceptable to each representative person. Although the persons are free from envy, and hence do not value the benefits they receive by comparing them with those received by others, the rational acceptability of a principle assigning a particular person a given set of expected benefits will depend on the relationship of that set to the sets of benefits assigned to other persons. A person will not consider everyman's choice rationally acceptable, if the principles chosen afford him expected benefits less than those expected by some other person, except insofar as the inequality could not be rectified by increasing his own benefits, but *only* by reducing the benefits of the more favored person.

The least advantaged person will therefore consider the choice of principles rational, only if there are no alternative principles which could afford him greater benefits, while he remains the least advantaged person, and no way in which he could cease to be the least advantaged person, without someone else becoming at least as disadvantaged as he now is. Everyman, then, must choose principles such that the least advantaged representative person does as well as possible. The position of the second least advantaged may then be considered, and so on; thus it is evident that everyman must choose the lexical difference principle, to determine the procedure by which benefits are to be distributed among the members of society. Or, in other words, everyman must select those principles whose adoption institutes a society in which optimal benefits are produced and distributed equally, if equal distribution is optimal, and if not, distributed so that the least-favored representative person does as well as possible, and compatibly with this so that the second least-favored person does as well as possible, and so on. Thus it seems that Rawls's claim to derive his conception of justice, involving the difference principle, from the maximizing conception of rationality and the original position of ignorance is upheld. But in the next two sections I argue that Rawls does not characterize satisfactorily the way in which the lexical difference principle is to be applied to the distribution of benefits, and that a more satisfactory account puts the principle in a very different light.

IV

The lexical difference principle is to regulate the distribution of those primary social goods which are classified as economic and social benefits. Some of these goods are the creation of society. But others, in particular economic benefits, must be available in some measure under any circumstances. Hence we may ask, how are these goods to be distributed in the absence of agreement on a principle of distribution? What if there is no social contract?

To ask this is to ask about the "no agreement point" (147). Rawls distinguishes two views of this point, which he terms "general egoism" and "the state of nature." He supposes that the original position itself corresponds to the state of nature (12) but holds that general egoism is the outcome of no agreement. Unfortunately, he does not discuss general egoism in terms of the behavior of rational persons. However, I shall assume that by general egoism is meant that condition in which each person seeks directly to secure as much as possible for herself. The distribution of primary social goods, insofar as they exist apart from agreement and society as instituted by agreement, is the result of egoistic activity on the part of each person.

This distribution can not be expected to be equal. The persons who make up society differ in their natural endowment, and differences in natural endowment will affect differentially peoples' ability to secure economic goods for themselves in the condition of general egoism. Hence the "no agreement point" will provide a different level of well-being for different persons, albeit a low level for everyone.

Behind the veil of ignorance, no one knows her natural abilities and talents, and hence no one knows what she would obtain in the absence of agreement. Yet each knows that she has certain natural abilities and talents, and that people differ in this endowment, so that in the absence of agreement people would secure different levels of well-being. It is therefore possible for everyone to take account of the "no agreement point" in their reasoning, even though no particular person knows how it will affect her.

The rationale for agreement is provided by the circumstances of justice. People "view society as a cooperative venture for mutual advantage" (520). Through cooperation they are able to produce more of the primary goods which each wants. I shall term those primary goods produced through cooperation the *social surplus;* it is that portion of the total quantity of primary social goods which would not be produced without cooperation. The content of the agreement people make must ensure the production and provide for the distribution of this social surplus.

We may distinguish three limiting ways in which the social surplus might be distributed:

(1) The distribution may redress the natural imbalance of primary goods which each would receive as a consequence of her natural talents and abilities, in the condition of general egoism. The total quantity of primary goods would then be distributed to maximize the minimum share, in accordance with the lexical difference principle.

(2) The distribution may ignore the natural imbalance of primary goods, and maximize the minimum share of the social surplus. The lexical difference principle would still regulate distribution, but it would be applied, not to the total quantity of primary social goods, but only to the quantity produced as a result of social cooperation.

(3) The distribution may be proportionate to the shares of primary social goods which each would secure for herself under general egoism.

The third of these possibilities constitutes what seems to me the most plausible interpretation of natural aristocracy, although it is an interpretation differing from Rawls's (74). On this view society ought to benefit each person in accordance with her natural talents and abilities, where these assets are estimated by the success of each in providing for herself in the absence of society. Rather than nullify the accidents of natural endowment, this mode of distribution takes these accidents to be the basis of social desert.

The first possibility is the opposite of the third; instead of taking natural endowment as the basis of desert, it regards natural endowment as undeserved. Thus it requires that natural inequalities be redressed, insofar as this can be achieved by an optimal outcome. This is indeed the mode of distribution favored by Rawls:

We may observe that the difference principle gives some weight to the considerations singled out by the principle of redress. This is the principle that undeserved inequalities call for redress; and since inequalities of birth and natural endowment are undeserved, these inequalities are to be somehow compensated for. . . . Now the principle of redress has not to my knowledge been proposed as the sole criterion of justice. . . . But whatever other principles we hold, the claims of redress are to be taken into account. It is thought to represent one of the elements in our conception of justice. . . . Thus although the difference principle is not the same as that of redress, it does achieve some of the intent of the latter principle. . . . We see then that the difference principle represents, in effect, an agreement to regard the distribution of natural talents as a common asset and to share in the benefits of this distribution whatever it turns out to be. (100–101)

But it is surely mistaken to hold that natural inequalities are undeserved. They are not deserved, they do not accord with desert, but equally they are not undeserved, they are not contrary to desert. In distributing the social surplus, natural inequalities, as shown by the differential abilities of people to secure benefits for themselves in the position of no agreement, should be ignored.

Redress, or nullification of the accidents of natural endowment, is not a constituent of any principle to which rational persons concerned to further their own interests would agree to regulate the distribution of the fruits of their cooperation. If each person is to agree freely, on equal terms, to cooperate with her fellows, then each will expect an equal share of the benefits which are to be achieved as a result of cooperation. When the veil of ignorance is lifted, and each is aware, both of what primary social goods she could have expected under general egoism and of what goods she can expect as a result of the society instituted by agreement, then each will want as many *additional* goods as possible to accrue to herself. A person will not consider her agreement rational if her share of these additional goods is less than that of some other person, unless (for no person is envious) greater equality could be achieved only by reducing the share of that other person, and not by increasing her own. Thus the person who receives the smallest share of the social surplus will consider the agreement rationally acceptable only if it is not possible for the least-favored person to receive a larger share. The principle agreed to must then require the maximization of the minimum share of the social surplus, and, compatibly with this, the maximization of the second minimum share, and so on; it must be the lexical difference principle applied strictly to the social surplus, without regard to the inequalities in the distribution of those benefits attainable in the absence of agreement.

An individual utility-maximizer will not consider it rational to accept a lower level of well-being in society simply to maximize average benefit; this is one of the crucial objections to average utilitarianism. But equally, such a person will not consider it rational to accept a smaller share of the benefits of cooperation—the social surplus—simply to increase overall equality of benefit. The conception of rationality which Rawls accepts without question leads people to agreement on principles of cooperation which maximize the *social* minimum.

V

Among the conceptions of justice criticized by Rawls is the view

that equal justice means that society is to make the same proportionate contribution to each person's realizing the best life which he is capable of. (510)

Rawls considers this conception, which he finds in the writings of Frankena and Findlay (510n), objectionable, not only because of practical difficulties in applying the standard, but

A more important difficulty is that the greater abilities of some may give them a stronger claim on social resources irrespective of compensating advantages to others. One must assume that variations in natural assets will affect what is necessary to provide equal proportionate assistance to those with different plans of life. But in addition to violating the principle of mutual advantage, this conception of equality means that the strength of men's claims is directly influenced by the distribution of natural abilities, and therefore by contingencies that are arbitrary from a moral point of view. (510–511)

If we suppose that our sense of justice is characterized by those principles which would be agreed to by rational utility-maximizers, then we must agree that violation of the principle of mutual advantage is unacceptable. Indeed, mutual advantage provides one of the arguments behind the insistence that the lexical difference principle must be applied to the social surplus; if it were applied to the total sum of primary goods it would be in principle possible for some person well favored under general egoism to receive no benefit from society. But mutual advantage is not violated if the difference principle is applied, not to the absolute quantity of primary social goods which each representative person is to receive, but rather to the proportionate contribution made by these goods to each person's well-being. The question is how to measure a person's share of primary social goods. Should the principle of distribution maximize the minimum *quantity* of these goods, or should it maximize the minimum *extent* to which any person's best life is realized?

Differences in natural endowment will affect not only the level of benefits people can provide for themselves in the absence of agreement, but also the possible levels of benefits which can be provided through cooperation. Let us then attempt to develop a measure of the potential social effects of differences in natural endowment.

Consider, abstractly, all possible arrangements for producing and distributing a social surplus. Negative distributions are not permitted; under each arrangement, each person must expect benefits at least equal to those he would expect in the absence of agreement. Hence a weak requirement of mutual advantage will be satisfied. Now we may suppose that different arrangements will affect both the total size of the surplus produced, and the share of the surplus which each representative person receives. We may restrict our attention to those arrangements which are Pareto-optimal, or efficient; each representative person will have his well-being maximized by some optimal arrangement.

Differences in natural talents and abilities will manifest themselves as differences in the maximum levels of well-being which different persons can attain. If we compare the well-being which accrues to the naturally intelligent, strong, and enterprising, under that arrangement maximally beneficial to such persons, with the well-being which accrues to the naturally dull, weak, and lazy, under that arrangement maximally beneficial to them, we shall find the former to be greater. Indeed, we may find that the naturally gifted do better than the naturally deprived, even under those arrangements which maximize benefits to the deprived, for it may well be that in order to maximize the absolute quantity of social goods accruing to the deprived, the gifted, who are primarily responsible for producing the social surplus, must be rewarded with an even greater quantity of these goods.

I shall term the maximum well-being which each representative person can expect, under that optimal social arrangement most favorable to him, his *social potential*. Social potential is then a measure of the potential social effects of differences in natural endowment. Behind the veil of ignorance, no person knows what his social potential is, but each knows that he has a social potential, and that social potential differs from person to person. Hence everyman may take social potential into account in his reasoning.

We may distinguish three limiting ways in which social potential may be considered in distributing the social surplus:

(1) Social potential may be ignored, so that the social surplus is distributed directly in accordance with the lexical difference principle. Rawls's interpretation of the difference principle would differ from this only in distributing all primary social goods, and not only the social surplus.

(2) The social surplus may be distributed to maximize the minimum degree to which any person's social potential is fulfilled; thus the lexical difference principle would apply to the proportionate contribution of primary social goods to well-being.

(3) Social potential may be taken as the criterion of desert, so that the social surplus may be distributed to maximize the satisfaction of the person with greatest social potential, and so on.

The third of these possibilities again seems to provide a form of aristocracy, perhaps "social aristocracy," to distinguish it from the natural aristocracy mentioned in the previous section. Natural talents and abilities are taken as indicative of merit, and so rewarded. This view runs counter to our intuitive conception of justice, and also would not be accepted by rational persons in an initial condition of equality.

But such persons would consider the first possibility to be equally unsatisfactory, because it tends to nullify the effects of natural abilities, treating them as undeserved. We are, it must be remembered, considering what principles of association will be adopted by free and rational persons concerned to further their own interests. Each person will expect to receive as much benefit from society as any other person, except where such equality could be achieved only by a reduction in the other's benefits. But how will each measure the benefit he receives? The natural measure, I suggest, is provided by social potential. If one person achieves almost the best life of which he is capable, and another receives social goods which permit him but a small fraction of his potential best life, then the first will be judged to benefit more, whatever the actual quantity of primary social goods which each receives.

Consider once again the situation when the veil of ignorance is lifted. Under Rawls's interpretation of the difference principle, natural endowments are to be taken as a common asset, so that the ratio of benefit received to talent employed and effort expended will decrease, as talent and effort increase. Hence the naturally gifted man will find his talents and efforts directed primarily to the advantage of the naturally deprived. But he will see no reason why he should not benefit from his own capacities to the same extent as anyone else. He will consider any other arrangement unfavorably discriminatory in relation to his natural endowment. Thus he will not consider it rational to agree to principles which require him to accept a lesser proportionate benefit, simply to increase overall equality of absolute benefit.

I conclude, then, that people who are rational in the sense assumed by Rawls, and who find themselves subject to the circumstances of justice in a position of original equality, will agree to a system of social cooperation regulated by a difference principle which specifies that each is to receive such benefits as he would expect apart from agreement, and, in addition, each is to receive that share of the social surplus of primary goods which ensures that the lowest level of realization of social potential is maximized, and, for equal lowest levels, that the second lowest level of realization of social potential is maximized, and so on. The object of rational agreement is the lexical difference principle applied to the distribution of the social surplus proportionate to social potential. I shall henceforth refer to this as the *proportionate difference principle*.

VI

The proportionate difference principle gives rise to a very different type of society from that envisaged by Rawls. Rawls supposes "that a society is well-ordered when it is not only designed to advance the good of its members but when it is also effectively regulated by a public conception of justice" (4–5). Rawls argues that the principles chosen in the original position give rise to a well-ordered society, for these principles are both accepted by all the members of the society as the basis of their conduct and embodied in the institutions of the society. Thus he is able to say that "justice as fairness is framed to accord with this idea of society" (454). The amendments which I have made in the difference principle do not affect this characterization. The proportionate difference principle, as the object of rational agreement in the original position, can equally give rise to a well-ordered society, in which the good of its members is secured through the optimal production of benefits, and justice is served in the distribution of these benefits to maximize the minimum level of fulfillment. The public conception of justice is different from that advocated by Rawls, but there is no reason to suppose that it will be less effective in regulating the activities of individuals, and the structure of the society's institutions.

But Rawls further supposes that

> The principles of justice are related to human sociability. The main idea is simply that a well-ordered society (corresponding to justice as fairness) is itself a form of social union. Indeed, it is a social union of social unions. Both characteristic features are present: the successful carrying out of just institutions is the shared final end of all the members of society, and these institutional forms are prized as good in themselves. (527)

Rawls is thus able to distinguish the type of society instituted through the choice of principles embodying the conception of justice as fairness from what he terms "private society."

> Its chief features are first that the persons comprising it . . . have their own private ends which are either competing or independent, but not in any case complimentary. And second, institutions are not thought to have any value in themselves. . . . Thus each person assesses social arrangements solely as a means to his private aims. . . . Everyone prefers the most efficient scheme that gives him the largest share of assets. (521)

As he goes on to point out: "The theory of competitive markets is a paradigm description of this type of society" (521–522).

Private society, or civil society as (Rawls notes) Hegel terms it, is of course the form of society depicted in the classical contract theories of Hobbes and Locke. But Rawls wants to disassociate his use of the contractual model from its historical connection with this type of society. Kant, not Hobbes, is after all Rawls's paradigm. Thus he says:

> It is sometimes contended that the contract doctrine entails that private society is the ideal, at least when the division of advantages satisfies a suitable standard of reciprocity. But this is not so, as the notion of a well-ordered society shows. (522)

This argument is, however, fallacious. It is not the conception of a well-ordered society, but of a society based on justice as fairness, which is to be distinguished from the notion of private society. Of course a well-ordered society need not be a private society, but as I show presently, a private society may be well ordered. Rawls's argument, then, must be that the contract doctrine does not entail private society because in a suitably defined state of nature, the product of the contract is a society regulated by the conception of justice as fairness. But the argument of the preceding sections of this paper has shown that the social contract does not lead to the conception of justice expressed in Rawls's difference principle, but rather to the conception expressed in the proportionate difference principle. We must therefore ask whether a society based on this principle is a social union, or rather a private society.

The answer is clear. It is precisely a competitive market society, the paradigm of private society, which is characterized by the proportionate difference principle. For the competitive market is the mechanism by which an optimal social surplus is produced and distributed in accordance with the contribution which each person makes. The one restriction which the proportionate difference principle imposes is that each person's initial position in the market must reflect only her natural endowment, and not such factors as inherited wealth. But this is only to say that the principle carries individualism to its extreme. It breaks down the inheritance relationship which is maintained in existing market societies but which in fact contradicts the individualist suppositions which constitute the rationale of these societies.

If it be agreed that the proportionate difference principle is in fact the object of agreement by free and rational persons in an initial position of equality, then the contract doctrine, properly interpreted, does require private society. Furthermore, since the proportionate difference principle leads to a well-ordered society, the contract doctrine requires a well-ordered private society. Not all forms of private society need be well ordered; a market society in which the initial position of each person depends largely on her inheritance need not satisfy a public conception of justice. And of course not all well-ordered societies are private. But social union, or any other well-ordered non-private society, cannot be derived from an agreement among rational persons in the circumstances of justice.

At this point one might entertain an objection to this argument. A defender of Rawls, who nevertheless accepted the derivation of the proportionate difference principle from Rawls's premises, might then insist that the appropriate conclusion to be drawn from the derivation is that Rawls's account of the initial situation must be amended. The proportionate difference principle is derived by supposing that in the initial situation everyone knows that there are differences in natural endowment, although no one knows her own endowment. To yield Rawls's conclusion, and so to make social union compatible with the contract doctrine, the initial situation should be redescribed to make such knowledge unavailable.

But would such an amended account of the initial situation be satisfactory? The original position must be such that the choice made in it by rational people will continue to be rationally acceptable to them when the veil of ignorance is lifted. It is surely evident that such persons, concerned to further their own interests, will not consider a set of social institutions acceptable if these institutions do not give appropriate recognition to differences in natural endowment. Viewing society as the means for producing and distributing an optimal social surplus, rational people will accept principles of distribution only if they restrict their scope to the surplus and apportion it in accordance with the contribution each makes to its production.

Hence it is not Rawls's account of the initial situation but rather his account of rationality which prevents the derivation of his conception of justice. The proportionate difference principle is the necessary result of the maximizing conception of rationality, and is the basis of private society, of a strongly individualist form of competitive market society. The instrumental conception of rationality which Rawls assumes leads to an instrumental conception of human society, a conception which Rawls wishes to reject. Rawls's ideological framework leads to the liberal individualist conception of justice and of society, not to democratic equality and the conception of social union.

VII

The proportionate difference principle expresses that conception of justice which is required by the maximizing conception of rationality fundamental to our society. If rationality and morality are to be reconciled within our own ideological and social framework, then this is the form which the reconciliation must take, insofar as the realm of justice is concerned. It is not the reconciliation which Rawls proposes, but that in itself is no argument against it. If affording each person those benefits which maximize the minimum level of fulfillment leads to conclusions which match our judgments in reflective equilibrium, then we have an adequate alternative to Rawls's theory of justice.

Now I have not argued, and in this paper I do not propose to argue, either for or against the adequacy of the revised conception of justice embodied in the proportionate difference principle. But suppose we find it inadequate. Suppose we find that justice as fairness fits our reflective judgments better than this alternative. Yet justice as fairness is incompatible with the maximizing conception of rationality. What positions are open to us?

There are, I believe, but three. The first is to maintain the conception of justice as fairness while admitting it to be, not independent of rationality, but actually incompatible with it—irrational. This option is perhaps heroic, but absurd. The second is to revise one's conception of justice, and so of morality, to conform to the maximizing conception of rationality. One abandons the attempt to achieve reflective equilibrium, and simply accepts those judgments about justice required by the proportionate difference principle, however much they depart from one's intuitions. This is the only possible response within the ideological framework assumed by Rawls, and by other proponents of the economic and social theories familiar in our society. The third response is to recognize that the maximizing account of rationality is not, as Rawls describes it, the concept of rationality, but only a conception, and to seek to bring one's conception of rationality into reflective equilibrium with one's conception of morality. But this alternative involves transcending the conceptual horizons of our society. In questioning what not only social theory but also social practice takes to be the concept of rationality, it questions our everyday awareness of ourselves as individuals-in-society.

That everyday awareness involves conceiving the individual, with his natural endowment, as being essentially apart from society, however dependent he may be on society for his actual existence and well-being. It involves conceiving society instrumentally, as private society, as a means to the satisfaction of nonsocially characterized individuals. It involves the supposition that human activity is to be understood primarily in terms of the attainment of individual well-being. And practical rationality then is conceived, and must be conceived, as the activity of determining what to do, in order to maximize individual benefits. In short, the status assigned to the individual and his natural endowment, the conception of society, and the conception of rationality, are all linked into a single, unified account of what it is to be human, based on the liberal individualist ideological framework.

Perhaps the most evident weak point in this account is the separation of man's natural endowment from the structure of society—a separation which plays such a crucial role in the derivation of the proportionate difference principle. We need not deny that there are some extra-social differences among persons, based on genetic structure, but we may suppose these of much lesser importance in characterizing an individual than socially determined differences. Instead of thinking of an individual's abilities and talents as a natural endowment brought to society, we may think of it as largely a social creation. The individual is then conceived not as a being essentially apart from society but rather as the product of society. And society is conceived not primarily as an instrument for increasing the well-being of individuals but rather as the framework within which human beings, with their characteristic differences in mental, physical, and emotional qualities, are created. Human activity is then to be understood primarily as the activity of creating human beings—not, of course, merely by physical reproduction but by the social development of human individuality. The ultimate form of this activity is self-determination, the shaping of oneself through the shaping of society. And practical rationality may then be conceived not as the activity of maximizing individual benefits but as the activity of conscious self-determination.

There are of course other ways of conceiving practical rationality. My concern is not to propose a particular alternative to Rawls's view, but rather to suggest that the question of our conception of rationality must be put on the agenda of moral philosophy. Rawls's argument, by its welcome rigor in comparison with the arguments of most moral philosophers, enables us to see that the attempt to reconcile morality with rationality leads to a critique of practical rationality. And such a critique cannot stop short of an examination of the ideological framework within which we find our conceptions of man and society, reason and morality.

[8]

Justice as Social Choice
(in part)

I

What the good is to an individual, the just is to society. The parallel is aptly formulated by John Rawls: "Just as each person must decide by rational reflection what constitutes his good, that is, the system of ends which it is rational for him to pursue, so a group of persons must decide once and for all what is to count among them as just and unjust."[1] It may seem that we can extend the parallel by adding at the end of Rawls's statement, "that is, the system of ends which it is rational for them to pursue." But this may mislead; and individual's good may perspicuously be characterized as a system of ends, but it is an open and controverted question whether the justice of a society is also a system of ends.

The rational individual pursues her good; the rational society pursues (its) justice. The principles in accordance with which the rational individual pursues her good are the subject of decision theory, the theory of individual choice. The most widely accepted view at present is that these are principles of expected-utility maximization. The underlying idea is quite simple. An individual's good is determined by her considered preferences over the possible outcomes of the courses of action, or more generally ways of life, available to her. We introduce a numerical measure of these preferences, *utility*, so that we may replace the idea of pursuing a system of ends with the more precise one of maximizing a single quantity. The rational individual, in pursuing her

[1]Rawls [1], pp. 11–12.

good, may be represented as seeking to maximize her utility. The further complications of *expected* utility I here leave to one side.

Given our parallel between individual good and social justice, we should be able to determine the principles in accordance with which the rational society pursues justice. These then would be the subject of the theory of collective decision, or social choice. In this way the theory of justice would be part of the theory of rational choice.

Once again we echo a position advanced by Rawls.[2] But his account of the connection between justice and rational choice differs from ours. Rawls treats the principles of justice as the *solution* to a problem of individual decision. Put any person behind the veil of ignorance; confront her with the problem of selecting principles for the basic structure of society; the principles she chooses are the principles of justice. But if this were the sole connection, the theory of justice would not be part of the theory of rational choice. Rawls's theory of justice, like a theory of investment, makes use of rational-choice procedures. Arriving at the principles of justice, as arriving at investment strategies, requires solving certain decision problems. The principles used to solve these problems are of course themselves part of the subject of the theory of rational choice. But their application is no part of that theory.

In claiming that the theory of justice is part of the theory of rational choice, I am not claiming that the principles of justice are arrived at by a procedure that requires us to solve a problem or problems of rational decision. It may be that the principles of justice are arrived at in this way; indeed, I shall go on to argue that they are. But this is not the present claim, which is rather that the principles of justice are principles for *making* rational choices. They are not principles for rational choice by an individual seeking her good, but principles for rational choice by a society—a group of individuals—seeking justice, and so derivatively principles for choice by each person as a justice-seeking member of the society. It is the role of the principles of justice in the making of decisions or choices, not their role as the outcome of a choice, that makes the theory of justice part of the theory of rational choice.

On the view that we are advancing, meta-ethical questions, at least in the domain of justice, reduce to meta-choice questions. The principles of justice have the same status as the principles of rational choice, whatever that status may be. 'Ought'-judgments, in the domain of justice, are simply judgments about what is rational for individuals as members of a society to do or to choose. Of course, I do not

2See ibid., p. 16.

claim that this captures all of our ordinary thinking about ethical judgments. Rather, it salvages what is rational in the ragbag of our everyday ethical attitudes. Incorporating the theory of justice into the theory of rational choice is an exercise in rational reconstruction, and questions of meta-ethics or meta-justice must be suspended until the reconstruction is completed.

II

As justice is to good, so social choice is to individual choice. If we think of the pursuit of justice as the pursuit of a system of ends, then we may suppose that the theory of social choice should be modeled on that of individual decision. We may suppose that, just as the individual may be represented as seeking to maximize some quantity, usually termed utility, so society may be represented as seeking to maximize a quantity, usually termed *welfare*. An individual attains her good, to the extent possible for her to do so, by maximizing utility; a society attains justice, to the extent possible for it to do so, by maximizing welfare. This easy identification of justice with welfare should arouse suspicion; we shall indeed reject it. But let us pursue this supposed parallel between individual and social choice—a parallel well entrenched in the literature—in somewhat more detail.

Extending the parallel between individual good and social justice, we suppose that the latter is determined by society's preferences over the possible outcomes of the available alternative social policies. We introduce welfare as a numerical measure of these preferences. The principles of social choice, and so of justice, will then be principles of expected-welfare maximization. But we shall of course want the preferences of society to be positively related to the preferences of the individuals who compose it. Social-choice theorists then face two alternatives.

First, the social preference ordering may be based on, and only on, the information provided by the individual preference orderings. This excludes the introduction of any interpersonal measure of preference, since such a measure is not recoverable from the individual orderings. And it raises the dread specter of Kenneth Arrow with his impossibility theorem.[3] Given weak conditions—conditions that require a positive connection between social and individual preference, that exclude a dictator, and that require that the social ordering over every subset of alternatives be recoverable from the individual orderings over those alternatives—Arrow demonstrates that no social-

[3]See Arrow, esp. ch. 5.

choice rule will yield a social-preference ordering for each set of individual preference orderings.

The impact of this devastating result may be weakened by allowing social choice to bypass a social-preference ordering, so that the rule for social choice must yield a nonempty set of socially best alternatives for each set of individual preference orderings. But the rules that pass suitably modified versions of Arrow's conditions and yield a social-choice set are disappointingly few. Indeed, for plausible conditions, the only admissible rule identifies the choice set with the set of efficient or Pareto-optimal outcomes—those to which there is no alternative preferred by some person and dispreferred by none.[4] This rule assigns equal social welfare to all those outcomes among which any serious question of selection arises. Interpreted in terms of justice, it endorses as just any outcome so long as each alternative to it would make some person worse off. Slavery is just in any society in which the slave owners could not be fully compensated for its abolition. It seems evident that the Pareto-extension rule is inadequate.

Second, the social-preference orderings may be based on information afforded by an interpersonal measure of individual preferences. The existence of any measure enables us to represent each person's preferences by a real-valued utility function. Now, even without the assumption of interpersonal comparability, if we suppose that social preference must also be represented by a real-valued welfare function, and that social indifference between two possible outcomes follows from the indifference of all individuals between the two outcomes, then welfare must be a weighted sum of individual utilities. If we then suppose that preferences are interpersonally comparable, we may treat the weights as reducing the utilities of different individuals to the common measure that comparability affords, and social welfare is simply the sum of comparable individual utilities. These results, demonstrated by J. C. Harsanyi, constitute a proof that if social choice is to be based on social preferences derived from interpersonally comparable individual preferences, then rational social choice must be *utilitarian*.[5]

Unlike the Pareto-extension rule, the utilitarian rule enables us to distinguish, in terms of social welfare, among those possible outcomes that are serious candidates for selection. It offers, at least in principle, a workable social-decision procedure. The procedure is naturally associated with welfare rather than with justice, since it focuses entirely

---

[4]See Sen, esp. pp. 74–77, for discussion of some of the issues involved in the determination of a choice set.

[5]See Harsanyi [2], ch. 2; and Harsanyi [4], ch. 4.

on the production and not the distribution of social goods. The utilitarian rule, and indeed any rule that models social choice on individual choice, or that models social preference on individual preference, must have this productive focus. Although the utilitarian does not treat society as having a good of its own independent of the goods of the individuals who compose it, yet she does treat society as having a good comparable to individual goods with respect to its role in rational choice. She treats society as pursuing a system of ends, although a system determined by the systems of ends of its component individuals, and supposes that it is possible to substitute maximization of a single quantity for pursuit of this system of ends.

I cannot embark here on a full-scale critique of the utilitarian view, or of the deeper, underlying view that social choice and social preferences parallel individual choice and preference. But I will propose, and endeavor to make plausible, an alternative account. Once again, I appeal to Rawls for a formulation of the idea at the root of this alternative—that society is a "cooperative venture for mutual advantage."[6] Social choice must be rational from the perspective of each individual within society. If an individual is to act on, or in accordance with, the principles of social choice or of justice, then she must find that membership in society enables her to pursue her own system of ends more effectively than were she to act on her own, independently of others, in a "state of nature." We do not claim that all actual societies may correctly be characterized as cooperative ventures for mutual advantage. We do claim that societies that command the rational support of their members must be so characterized.

Society, then, does not pursue its own system of ends, even a system derived from the ends of its member individuals. Rather, social decisions, insofar as they are rational, are directed to the promotion of the several individual goods in such a way that mutual advantage is assured. Although these decisions relate to the production of benefits, yet they are also, and not merely derivatively, concerned with the appropriate distribution of the benefits that society makes possible, and the criteria for appropriateness here reflect the underlying ideas of cooperation and mutuality. Society thus aims not simply or straightforwardly at maximum welfare, but rather at fairness, and so at justice. The idea of society as a cooperative venture for mutual advantage links rational social choice with justice. And this aim of justice is to be achieved not by decision making that embodies a single, social, maximizing procedure, but rather by decision making through agreement among the individual participants in the cooperative venture.

[6]Rawls [1], p. 4.

Put differently, the principles of justice are those principles for making social decisions or choices to which rational individuals, each seeking to cooperate with her fellows in order to maximize her own utility, would agree.

III

Beginning with the idea that the theory of justice is part of the theory of rational choice, we have now come to the view that the theory of justice makes use of rational-choice procedures. For we are now supposing that the principles of justice, of rational social choice, are themselves to be treated as the solution to a problem of rational decision, or more accurately, of rational agreement among individuals. Thus, on the one hand, these principles characterize rational social activity, conceived as cooperative and mutually advantageous, in the way in which principles of expected-utility maximization characterize rational individual activity. But on the other hand, we now claim that these principles are themselves the object of a particular rational activity—that of agreeing to principles for cooperation.

Rawls poses the problem of rational agreement on principles of justice as one of individual choice. He insists that "the parties have no basis for bargaining in the usual sense."[7] The idea of agreement is idle in Rawls's theory because the individuals who are to agree on principles of justice are placed behind a veil of ignorance so thick that the differences among them are obliterated. Each person simply asks himself which principles it would be rational to accept in ignorance of all particular facts about his talents and aptitudes, traits of character, and circumstances. Each knows that since all persons are similarly ignorant, the reasoning that will convince one must convince all. Thus each may represent himself as deciding on or choosing the principles of justice from behind the veil of ignorance; the principles that anyone chooses must be those that everyone chooses.

Here we do not follow Rawls. His use of the veil of ignorance is ultimately motivated by his insistence that the parties are to seek a conception of justice appropriate to "free and equal moral persons."[8] The real differences and inequalities that characterize them are to be dismissed as morally irrelevant. Thus the principles of justice, in Rawls's view, must be related to a prior moral conception of the person. But if we insist strictly on the parallel between individual good and social justice with which we began (and with which Rawls may, to

---

[7]Ibid., p. 139.
[8]Rawls [3], p. 521.

the unwary reader, have seemed to begin), then we may not appeal to this moral conception. Rather, the human person must be viewed in the same way from the standpoint of justice as from the standpoint of good. If the individual is represented as a maximizer of expected utility, so that his good is what he chooses on the basis of overall considered preferences, then justice among several individuals must be that to which they would agree on the basis of, and only of, their overall considered preferences. Whether our concern be with individual good or with social justice, a prior moral conception of the person has not place except insofar as it may happen to enter into and to inform considered preference.

In rejecting the view that the principles of justice are to be the object of choice behind a veil of ignorance, we do not remove all constraints on the circumstances in which they are to be selected. We suppose that the principles are to provide a basis not only for making future social decisions but also for evaluating past decisions and existing institutions and practices. We shall therefore not want the selection to be influenced by actual social circumstances; we cannot allow those factors that we seek to evaluate in terms of the principles of justice to be assumed in the process of agreeing to those principles. If we were to consider an agreement in which each person assumes his existing social position, then we should in effect allow the status quo to constrain the choice of principles of justice, although we should have no reason to suppose the status quo to be itself mutually advantageous or just.

Furthermore, we shall not want the selection of principles of justice to be affected by the actual capacities of individual persons as bargainers, or by the ability each person has to advance his interests in the context of making agreements with others. The principles of rational choice are defined for an ideal decision maker; if their use must be tailored to the capacities of particular agents, yet we do not suppose that the principles themselves should be related to the imperfect rationality of real persons. Similarly, the principles of justice are defined for an ideal society, even though their application must be tailored to the capacities and circumstances of the actual members of an imperfect society. We must therefore suppose that the process of agreement leading to the choice of principles must be itself ideal, so that the parties to the agreement, whatever their actual capacities, are to be thought of as bargainers able to advance their interests equally with their fellows, and as fully and effectively as possible. We achieve this ideal conception not by placing the bargainers behind a veil of ignorance, but rather by taking each to be adequately informed not only about his own good but also about that of his fellows. Communication among the persons must be full and free; no one is able to deceive another about anyone's interests or bluff successfully about what anyone is willing to do. The process of bargaining must be thought of as effectively cost-free, so that the participants are not under pressure, and especially not under differential pressure, to reach agreement. No one is in a position to benefit by his superior ability to outwait the others. Threats are useless to ideally rational bargainers, for insofar as a threat involves the claim that one will act in a non-utility-maximizing way unless some other person accedes to one's wishes, everyone knows that no one would carry out such a threat, so that the attempt to threaten would be idle. In these several ways, then, we require that the process of bargaining exhibit procedural equality and maximum competence among the persons who are to agree on the principles of justice.

It does not follow, either from the insistence that social contingencies shall not affect the process of bargaining or from the requirement that as bargainers individuals be ideally competent, informed, and rational, that the natural capacities of the actual members of society are also irrelevant to the agreement. Just as each person in determining his own good takes his particular capacities and interests into account, so each person in agreeing on social justice must be expected to take his capacities and interests into account. But no one is thereby able to tailor principles to his own differential advantage, since each is equally able to demand that his capacities and interests be recognized in the content of agreement. Each bargainer thus serves as an ideal representative of the particular person he will be in the social world to be shaped by the agreed principles of justice; thus fairness is assured at the procedural level.

Before I offer an account of bargaining that will enable us to characterize the particular agreement leading to principles of justice, let us note that in that agreement there must be a fundamental parallel between the bargaining process and the bargaining outcome. If society is a cooperative venture, then the principles of social choice must be principles for making cooperative or agreed decisions. If these principles are selected by agreement, then they must implicitly characterize the process by which they are selected. We may illustrate this by reference to Rawls's argument. The principles that rational persons would choose behind a veil of ignorance must parallel the principles that guide the reasoning of such persons in making their choice. Rawls supposes that the two principles of justice central to his theory are themselves a special case of a more general principle, the lexical difference principle, which expresses a *maximin* requirement; the minimum level of welfare received by any party to the agreement is to be maximized.[9] Now the reasoning that, according to Rawls, leads to the choice of the principles of justice is *maximin* reasoning: choose the outcome that maximizes one's minimum benefit. It is hardly surprising that persons who reason in this way would choose maximin principles. The principles of rational social choice thus reflect the principles of rational individual choice by which they are selected. In our account, the principles of rational social choice will instead reflect the principles of rational bargaining—the principles that each individual rationally follows in entering into agreements with his fellows.

IV (*in part*)*

In bargaining, it is natural and seemingly necessary to think of each person as beginning from a base point—a prebargaining payoff that is not called into question by the bargaining situation and that must be realized for the particular individual to be willing to accept any bargain. In our problem the prebargaining payoff may be associated with what each person could expect to gain from her own efforts in the absence of any agreed or cooperative interaction. Or more precisely, the prebargaining payoff may tentatively be so identified; we shall have to ask whether there are other constraints that must be imposed on it. For the present we simply assume that the base point is fixed in some way for each person.

It is then natural to think of each bargainer as advancing a claim, reflecting her desire to gain as much as possible from agreement, but constrained by the recognition that others must not be driven away from the bargaining table. Since those others must expect to benefit from any bargain into which they willingly enter, they could not be expected to entertain a claim acceptance of which would leave them with a payoff less than they would expect from no agreement, and so less than that afforded by their base point. The desire to benefit maximally, and the need to reach agreement, thus fix each person's claim as the most that she could receive from any possible outcome that affords every other person at least as much as her base-point payoff. Individual expected-utility maximization and mutual advantage prove to be not only necessary but also sufficient to determine all claims.

[9]Rawls [1], pp. 83, 152–153.

Note: Sections IV and V are a brief version of the account of the theory of rational bargaining in Gauthier [5], pp. 129–146. I have included only those paragraphs of IV that sketch my view informally and that also are necessary for reading the final sections of the essay; the reader may turn to "Bargaining and Justice" for a full formal account.

However, we must beware lest we understand the fixing of claims in an overly simple way. In a situation involving more than two persons, each person's claim must be restricted to those parts of the overall cooperative venture to which she contributes. Otherwise, even if all others were better off than in the absence of any venture, yet some would be worse off than with a modified cooperative venture that would exclude the particular person whose claim is in question. One's claim must not be so great that it would be advantageous for others to exclude one from the bargaining table; one must avoid driving them away and one must also avoid being driven away or excluded oneself. Although this is implicit in the idea of mutual advantage, exclusive attention to two-person agreements might lead us to overlook the full extent of the constraint that mutuality entails.

Claims, even though they are compatible with mutual benefit, will in general be incompatible one with another; each will demand the most that would be compatible with her participation in a mutually advantageous venture. Thus to reach agreement bargainers must offer concessions. Given that no one wishes to concede—given that any concession represents acceptance of a diminished payoff—then rational bargainers will endeavor to minimize their concessions. Now the magnitude of a concession is established not with reference to some absolute scale of utility but rather with reference to the particular bargaining situation; concession is a measure of the *proportion* between the part of one's claim that one abandons, and the entire claim, or gain over one's base-point payoff, that one originally advances. Since the bargainers are equally and fully rational, the maximum concession—the greatest proportion of her original claim that any bargainer gives up—must be minimized. Since all benefit from reaching agreement, some set of concessions is rational for all to accept, but a particular set is rational for all only if any alternative would require a concession at least as great as the maximum in the given set.

In bargaining, therefore, rational persons will act on a principle of *minimax concession*—the greatest or maximum concession must be a minimum. This principle may be formulated equivalently as a principle of *maximin relative benefit:* We may measure the relative benefit of an agreement to an individual as the proportion her actual gain over the base-point payoff bears to the potential gain represented by her claim. Relative benefit is thus the proportion of potential benefit that one actually receives. And we may now relate rationality, as expressed by minimax concession, to fairness or justice, which we claim is captured by maximin relative benefit. If an agreement is to be considered fair by those party to it, then no one may receive a relative benefit smaller than necessary—smaller than the minimum relative benefit of that outcome which, in relation to the other possible outcomes, has the greatest or maximum minimum relative benefit. Given that all persons benefit from reaching agreement, some set of relative benefits must be fair, but a set is fair only if any alternative would afford some person a relative benefit no greater than the minimum in the given set. Maximin relative benefit ensures that no one's advantage is sacrificed to benefit someone who, relative to the context of agreement, is better placed.

The principle of minimax concession, or maximin relative benefit, is uniquely acceptable to every party in the bargaining situation. Developing a contrast suggested by T. M. Scanlon, we may ask whether a principle is acceptable because any individual "judges that it is one he could not reasonably reject whatever position he turns out to occupy," or whether it is acceptable because "it would be the rational choice for [any individual] behind the veil of ignorance," or in ignorance of the position he is to occupy.[10] In our view the latter, which is of course what Rawls supposes, is insufficient to establish the impartiality requisite for justice. Impartiality requires acceptability in every position rather than acceptability in ignorance of one's position. The former does and the latter "does not take seriously the distinction between persons," to turn against Rawls the criticism that he levels at the utilitarians.[11] There is no reason to suppose that a principle that would be acceptable to any person in a hypothetical state of ignorance of all particulars would be acceptable to every person in every possible position that the principle would license. And so there is no reason to suppose that such a principle is truly impartial. Only acceptability from every standpoint that satisfies the principle can meet the demand—both rational and moral—that we make on justice. The idea of rational agreement by all persons on a principle demanding that the greatest concession anyone makes be minimized, or ensuring that the smallest relative benefit anyone receives be maximized, addresses the demand for acceptability from every standpoint.

VI

Several problems remain. First, I have left to one side the question of what constraints, if any, are to be imposed in determining the base point for rational agreement on the principles of justice. Is the base point to be identified simply with the outcome if each seeks to max-

[10]Scanlon, pp. 124–125.
[11]Rawls [1], p. 27.

imize his own utility in the absence of agreement? Second, I have not considered the problem of compliance with the decisions reached in accordance with the principle of minimax concession. From the standpoint of a particular individual, those actions required of him as part of a cooperative scheme to realize maximin relative benefit need not be those supported by expected-utility maximization. Why then should he comply with the requirements of the scheme? Individuals may have to forgo what we have accepted as individually rational if they are to do what we have claimed is collectively rational. And third, I have not determined the scope of the principles of justice. I have not considered what types of issues are to be decided by an appeal to minimax concession. Here I can only sketch an approach to these difficult questions.

The first two issues are connected. The rationale for compliance with principles of justice is related to the selection of the base point from which concession, or relative benefit, is calculated. As an initial approximation, the base point may be associated with the payoff each person could expect in the absence of cooperation. Society would then be viewed as a venture beneficial to each person, not in comparison with no interaction, but in comparison with noncooperative interaction, with others. But will such a venture be welcomed by each participant? Suppose that there are some persons who prefer cooperation to noncooperation, but who also prefer no interaction to noncooperation, and perhaps even to cooperation. From their standpoint society is a venture entered into primarily to reduce the costs imposed on them by state-of-nature interaction of a noncooperative kind. But their willingness to participate in such a venture, and in a particular distribution of benefits from it, may then be dependent on the presence of whatever factors forced them to acquiesce in the disadvantageous interactions of the state of nature. They may insist that they have no reason to participate *voluntarily* in social cooperation unless the benefits they receive are related to an agreement they would make either from a base point of *no* interaction or from a base point determined by noncooperative interaction that they would consider advantageous in relation to no interaction. Although we cannot argue this point here, we should maintain that voluntary compliance with the terms of cooperation—and so compliance with the principles of justice or social choice—is rational in general only if the base point is not itself considered disadvantageous in relation to no interaction. And this is in effect to say that the state of nature, as determining the base point for social agreement, is to be conceived in Lockean rather than in Hobbesian terms.

An example may suggest the rationale for this position. Consider the present situation in South Africa. We may suppose that interaction between blacks and whites is largely noncooperative and imposed by the power of the whites. Suppose that a sophisticated defender of the South African system were to point out that everyone, black and white alike, could benefit were the repressive apparatus required to maintain the present system of apartheid to be dismantled and replaced by genuine interracial cooperation. Of course, our defender would insist, the present distribution of goods and services must be taken as the base point; each person is to get what he now has, plus the cooperative payoff resulting from dismantling the repressive apparatus.

Black South Africans would be unlikely to give such a proposal serious consideration. Were the present coercive framework of interaction to be dismantled, they would not find it rational voluntarily to maintain a system resting on the distribution of benefits and costs that apartheid upholds. They would not agree to a cooperative venture taking the present noncooperative state of affairs as the base point.

A second example is suggested by the initial rise and suppression of the Solidarity trade union in Poland. As the repressive apparatus maintaining the power of the Communist minority was relaxed, it became evident that the members of Solidarity were not prepared to accept the existing distribution of power as the base point from which future social cooperation would proceed. Hence, martial law temporarily brought the radical innovation of free workers in a workers' state to an end.

Introduction of the Lockean state of nature moralizes the base point for social cooperation. Thus moral factors enter into the derivation of the principles of justice. But the manner of their entry must be carefully noted. Only those moral considerations are introduced that are necessary to attain rational compliance with the principles. In effect, the principles of justice have moral force; they require each person to refrain from seeking his greatest expected utility if and insofar as this would conflict with carrying out decisions based on the principles. For this to be rational, a further moral factor must be introduced—the requirement that no one benefit at the expense of others in any interaction taken for granted in determining the base point. But this moral factor is introduced only to ensure the rationality of compliance with the principles of justice. Thus it, like the principles themselves, are ultimately derived from purely rational considerations. It is not introduced as an independent moral element in the argument in the way in which Rawls introduces the conception of moral persons or in which Nozick introduces natural right. It is not

an a priori constraint on what each person may do, unmotivated by
the idea of a cooperative venture for mutual advantage.[12]

I have offered no demonstration that, to be rational, compliance
requires the Lockean constraint on the base point for agreement. I
have not demonstrated that compliance, insofar as it overrides individual expected-utility maximization, is *ever* rational. The arguments
needed to establish the position sketched here must be reserved for
another occasion.

VII

What is the *scope* of social choice? In conceiving of society as a
cooperative venture for mutual advantage, we immediately limit *social*
choice, and so the principles of justice, to those contexts in which each
person rationally forgoes *individual* choice based on principles of expected-utility maximization. Each must expect to benefit from cooperation. Thus pure redistribution—redistribution from the base
point established in a Lockean state of nature—cannot be a matter of
rational social concern, and it cannot be justified by an appeal to
rational principles of justice or social choice. Pure redistribution must
be the effect of private charity, not public justice.

There are two primary aims that afford persons reason to agree to
and comply with principles of social choice: to ensure protection and
to increase production.[13] *Protection* is to be understood not primarily
in reference to external threats, but internally; society protects each
of its members against the force and fraud that characterize the interaction of persons in a Hobbesian state of nature. In effect, the
protective role of society is to guarantee a Lockean framework for
interaction. But in providing this guarantee there are, strictly speaking, no alternatives among which society may choose, no goods whose
distribution raises a problem of social choice. Justice requires that
each individual's fair base point be maintained. Insofar as there are
ways of accomplishing this that differ significantly for the individuals
protected, we must suppose that in affording protection society also
provides further goods the distribution of which does give rise to a
genuine problem of social choice. But then this further distribution is
not itself part of the strict assurance of protection, and it must be
assessed rather by the standards appropriate to production. The protective role of society may best be conceived as the guarantee of *rights*.

The goods of *production* fall along a continuum whose end points

[12]See Rawls [3], esp. p. 520; and Nozick, esp. ch. 3.
[13]The protective/productive distinction is from Buchanan, pp. 68–70.

are those familiar categories distinguished by the economist—private and public. Given that protection is assured, so that force and fraud are eliminated from the interactions of the members of society, then purely private goods are efficiently produced through invisible hand processes in which each seeks her private gain—or, in other words, through interaction in which each seeks to maximize her expected utility. But there is then no place for social choice in determining the production and/or distribution of these goods. Given the efficiency of the market in which only individual decisions are required or permitted, it is not possible that each should expect to benefit from superseding individual decision by social decision. The market ensures mutual advantage—that is, a Pareto-optimal outcome—without any need for cooperation, and it does so in a manner that, being dependent only on the voluntary choices of individuals, transmits the moral characteristics of its starting point to its outcome. If each individual's base point satisfies the Lockean constraints, then no question of justice arises with respect to efficient market interaction.

Public goods, however, raise different problems. If each person acts privately to maximize her expected utility, then the possibilities of free-riders and parasites lead characteristically to the underproduction of public goods and overproduction of public bads. There will be too few lighthouses and too much air pollution. Here, then, is a further role for social choice, and here the principles of justice come into their own. In deciding how public goods are to be produced and distributed in excess of the quantities that individuals would voluntarily supply if each were to maximize her expected utility in the absence of cooperative arrangements, we must appeal to the principle of minimax concession.

In a recent book Andrew Levine attacks the coherence of liberal democracy, basing part of his argument on the claim that liberalism constrains the scope of democratic choice.[14] But of course the core idea of liberal democracy is to combine the requirement that social choice equally reflect each person's concerns and interests with a clear limitation on the sphere appropriate to such choice. This limitation is effected by an appeal to the idea of individual liberty. We make it more precise by replacing the idea of liberty with that of voluntary *ex ante* acceptance of social-choice, rather than individual choice, procedures. An individual's liberty is guaranteed insofar as the scope of social choice is determined by an appeal to what she would rationally

---

[14]See Levine; for example, p. 152: "The liberal democratic project is feasible only at the tremendous cost, indeed the impossible cost for any democrat, of abandoning the substance of the democratic component."

accept as an improvement on the Lockean state of nature. We have argued that an individual—any individual—would rationally accept the social provision of public goods, on the basis of minimax concession or maximin relative benefit, but reject the social provision of purely private goods. In the nineteenth century the workings of liberal democracy were clearly flawed by a failure to accept fully the role of society in the provision and distribution of public goods. This failure continues to infect libertarian theory. In the twentieth century the flaw has increasingly been a failure to accept fully the role of the market in the provision of private goods, which infects socialist and welfare-state theory. But the liberal democratic project is in essence the political embodiment of the conception of society as a cooperative venture for mutual advantage, which is itself the key to understanding the theory of justice as part of the theory of rational choice. What remains is to find a battle cry more inspiring than "To each so that the minimum proportion of potential benefit is maximized."

[9]

Bargaining and Justice

My concern in this paper is with the illumination that the theory of rational bargaining sheds on the formulation of principles of justice. I first set out the bargaining problem, as treated in the theory of games, and the Nash solution, or solution F.[1] I then argue against the axiom, labeled "independence of irrelevant alternatives," which distinguishes solution F, and also against the Zeuthen model of the bargaining process which F formalizes.[2]

I then characterize an alternative solution, G, and relate it to the Kalai-Smorodinsky axiomatization.[3] Unfortunately, as Alvin Roth has shown, solution G and the Kalai-Smorodinsky axioms part company when they move beyond two-person bargaining games; I mention Roth's result and its implications for both solution G and the axiomatization.[4] This leads me to propose a modification of G, solution G', which has been at the center of my own inquiries into bargaining, although for some time I failed to realize that G' was not, or at least not always, G.[5] I develop a Zeuthen model of the bargaining process which corresponds to G', and show its appealing features.

G' in hand, I note a startling resemblance between it and Rawls's

First published in *Social Philosophy and Policy* 2 (1985), reprinted with permission of Basil Blackwell Ltd, Oxford, and the Social Policy Center, Bowling Green State University.

[1]See Nash [2]; also Roth, pp. 4–19.
[2]See Zeuthen, pp. 104–121. For the relation between Nash and Zeuthen, see Harsanyi [1].
[3]See Kalai and Smorodinsky.
[4]See Roth, pp. 98–109.
[5]Solution G' appears (although not under that label) initially in Gauthier [6]. See also Gauthier [12]; and [5], ch. 5.

difference principle; this enables me to make the transition between bargaining and justice.[6] A bargaining model of morality captures, as a decision-theoretic model does not, Rawls's essential, but too often ignored, requirement that moral theory "take seriously the distinction between persons." And it permits a decisive rebuttal, both of the claim that "average-utilitarianism" correctly captures moral or social rationality, and of the claim that maximin principles provide an irrational basis for *moral* choice.[7] The result will not be to vindicate Rawls's aberrant Kantianism but rather to defend the contractarian theory that might have been developed from the insights in his early papers, most especially "Justice as Fairness."[8] Indeed, the result will be to defend precisely the moral theory that I have been developing.[9]

I turn now to the bargaining problem. Consider a finite set of actors, *n* in number, each of whom defines a Von Neumann-Morgenstern utility-function as a measure of his or her preferences over a continuous but bounded range of possible outcomes (continuity may be assured by treating any lottery over outcomes as an outcome).[10] Each outcome may then be represented as a point in *n*-dimensional utility-space, and the set of outcomes constitutes a compact, convex region in that space. Suppose that any point in this region may be realized by agreement among the actors; we may then call it the *bargaining region*, S. Suppose also that, should the actors fail to agree, the outcome will be a designated point in S, d. Then the bargaining problem, classically conceived, is the problem of determining a point of agreement, x, as a function of the bargaining region S and of the disagreement point d: $f(S,d) = x$. We suppose that the disagreement point is not Pareto-optimal in S, so that there is a point y in S such that $y > d$.

Here, a few notational points are in order. For any point x in utility-space, we write $x = (x_1, x_2, \ldots, x_n)$, where x_i is the utility of x to the i-th individual. We write $x > y$ if and only if for each i, $x_i > y_i$. And we write S^+ for the set of points x in S such that $x > d$.

The Nash solution, or solution F, to the bargaining problem may be simply characterized as follows:

$$F(S,d) = x, \text{ such that } \prod_{i=1}^{n} (x_i - d_i) > \prod_{i=1}^{n} (y_i - d_i) \text{ for all } y \, (\neq x) \text{ in } S^+,$$

---

[6]For the difference principle, see Rawls [1], esp. pp. 75–83.

[7]The quotation is from Rawls [1], p. 27. The views to be rebutted are advocated in particular by John C. Harsanyi; see esp. Harsanyi [2], pp. 37–63.

[8]See Rawls [2]. Rawls's Kantianism is emphasized in Rawls [1], pp. 251–257; and [3].

[9]The full account of this theory is in Gauthier [5].

[10]A Von Neumann–Morgenstern utility-function is one having the expected utility property; see Harsanyi [4], p. 32.

where $(x_i - d_i)$ is a measure of the gain to the i-th player of the outcome x over the disagreement outcome d. Thus, the Nash solution maximizes the geometric average of the gains realized by the actors in relation to what they would have achieved without agreement.

John F. Nash proved that solution F is uniquely determined by four axioms. Three of these I propose to accept as uncontroversial:

Pareto-optimality: if $f(S,d) = x$, then $-\exists$ y: y $\in$ S and y $>$ x.
Symmetry: if (S,d) is symmetric and if $f(S,d) = x$, then for all i, j, x_i $= x_j$.
Independence of Equivalent Utility Representations: let (S',d') be obtained from (S,d) by positive linear transformations of the actors' utility-functions: if $f(S,d) = x$, then $f(S',d') = x'$, where x' is obtained from x by the same transformations.

The appeal of Pareto-optimality is evident. Without it, some person will fail to obtain a utility that he might have obtained at no cost to the others. Symmetry seems an evident requirement; if nothing in the information enables us to distinguish the actors, then the solution equally should not distinguish them. And independence of equivalent utility representations reflects the fact that Von Neumann-Morgenstern utility-functions are defined only up to a positive linear transformation. The bargaining outcome should not be affected by the purely arbitrary choices of zero-point and unit in the individual utility-functions that may be used indifferently to measure the same preferences.

The fourth axiom is rather different:

Independence of Irrelevant Alternatives: let d$\in$T $\subset$ S: if $f(S,d) = x$ and if x$\in$T, then $f(T,d) = x$.

This condition, to be distinguished from the Arrovian condition of the same name, is an application of Sen's rationality property *alpha* to the bargaining problem.[11] Property *alpha* states that a best item in any set must be a best item in any subset of which it is a member. The rationale for its application to the bargaining problem would seem to be this. Consider the solution to a bargain over a given range of outcomes and with a fixed disagreement point. Suppose that the range is restricted, without affecting the disagreement point, and that the original solution falls within the restricted range. Then, surely, it should be the solution to the restricted bargain. In the original bar-

[11]See Sen, p. 17. For the Arrovian "independence of irrelevant alternatives" condition, see Arrow, pp. 26–28.

gain, it was selected over all of the alternative outcomes now available; what reason could there now be for selecting one of those alternatives? The axiom states that removing alternatives should not affect the bargaining solution, unless either the original solution is removed, or the disagreement point is affected.

We stated the axiom in terms of contracting the bargaining region; we may reformulate it in terms of expanding the region. Let $T \subset S$: if $f(T,d) = x$, then $f(S,d) = y$ where either $y = x$, or $y \notin T$. Suppose that the range of available outcomes is expanded, without affecting the disagreement point. Then, surely, the solution to the original bargain should still be selected over any alternatives previously available; what reason could there be for selecting one of those alternatives? The axiom states that adding alternatives should not affect the bargaining solution, unless either one of the added alternatives is selected, or the disagreement point is affected.

Sen's *alpha* property is a condition on the presence of a maximal element in a set. An element that is maximal in relation to given alternatives must remain so in relation to any subset of those alternatives. If we suppose that the solution to the bargaining problem should involve the selection of a maximal element from the available alternatives, then we shall expect Sen's *alpha* property to be satisfied by the solution. Any maximizing problem involves the selection of a maximal element, and so it must have a solution satisfying *alpha*.

But maximization is not a direct concern in bargaining. Each bargainer has a maximizing concern—a concern with maximizing his own payoff—but there is no ground for the supposition that these unite into a single maximizing concern to be resolved in bargaining. The bargaining problem is primarily distributive, a problem of determining the size of the slices into which a pie is to be divided. It is not purely a distributive problem, because the size of the pie may be affected by the way in which it is sliced. But the distributive aspect is clearly focal; each bargainer cares about the size of the pie only insofar as it affects the size of his slice.

The supposition that what the bargainers aim at is the maximization of some quantity, such as the geometric average of the gains, rests on a fundamental misconception about distributive problems. Underlying standard bargaining theory, and also the economic version of utilitarian moral theory, is the attempt to convert a question of distribution into one of production—to represent a concern with the division of some quantity as a concern with maximization. Maximization, as a feature of individual behavior, is, understandably, deeply rooted in economic thought. And the search for maximizing solutions to problems is mathematically appealing; maximization is generally well behaved. But the attempt to provide a maximizing solution to the bargaining problem resembles the attempt of the drunk to find his watch under the lamp post rather than in the shadows where he dropped it: "There's more light here." I return to this inappropriate insistence on maximization again before our inquiry is concluded.

The weakness of the Nash solution may be appreciated from another perspective if we consider the Zeuthen model of the bargaining process to which it corresponds. The model is most easily constructed for two-person bargaining, and I shall restrict my attention to that case. Faced with a possibly variable pie to be divided, two bargainers— let them be management and labor—advance proposals, which we may suppose take the form of a set of payoffs, one to each party. If their proposals are incompatible, agreement will be reached only through concessions. Zeuthen provides a measure of concession, and a rule for determining, given that measure, who should concede.

Let management's proposed outcome be $m = (m_1, m_2)$, where m_1 is management's payoff, and m_2 is labor's. Let labor's proposed outcome be $l = (l_1, l_2)$. The disagreement point—the expected outcome if no bargain is reached—is $d = (d_1, d_2)$. Then the Zeuthen formula for measuring the concession that would be involved were management to accept labor's proposal is $(m_1 - l_1)/(m_1 - d_1)$, where $(m_1 - l_1)$ represents what management would forgo in accepting labor's proposal, and $(m_1 - d_1)$ represents management's proposed gain in relation to disagreement. The Zeuthen formula measures the concession as the proportion of this total gain that would be forgone. Similarly, labor's concession is $(l_2 - m_2)/(l_2 - d_2)$. Now, the larger the concession, the less willing one is to make it. Therefore, Zeuthen argues that the party whose concession, as measured by the ratios of the Zeuthen formula, is smaller, must make a concession—that is, must put forward a revised proposal. And the revised proposal must be such that the other party will be required to make the next concession; otherwise the initial party would simply have to make a further concession or accept the other's proposal. Thus let $(m_1 - l_1)/(m_1 - d_1)$ be smaller than $(l_2 - m_2)/(l_2 - d_2)$. Management must make a concession; it puts forward a new proposal, say $m' = (m'_1, m'_2)$ such that $(l_2 - m'_2)/(l_2 - d_2)$ is smaller than $(m'_1 - l_1)/(m'_1 - d_1)$. Labor must now offer a concession; the process continues until one party is unable to make a concession forcing the other to a further concession, and can only accept the other's proposal. At that point agreement is reached.

By simple algebraic manipulation, it is easily shown that if management's current proposal is m^* and labor's is l^0, management must make a concession if $(m^*_1 - d_1)(m^*_2 - d_2)$ is smaller than $(l^0_1 - d_1)(l^0_2 - d_2)$, and labor must make a concession otherwise. Agreement clearly results on that proposal $x = (x_1, x_2)$ such that for any y ($\neq x$) in S^+, $(x_1 - d_1)(x_2 - d_2) > (y_1 - d_1)(y_2 - d_2)$. And this is solution F.

Let us reflect on the bargaining process just sketched. I have no objection to the use of the Zeuthen formula as a measure of concession, or to the Zeuthen rule for determining who must concede, given meaningful proposals and a meaningful disagreement point. But in the process as sketched, the proposals play no role. The bargainers converge on the same outcome, whatever their proposals at any stage may be, as long as each always proposes an outcome at least as favorable to himself as the outcome provided by solution F. The series of proposals and concessions seems to model a process of bargaining, but, given that the proposals play no role in determining the outcome, the concessions from meaningless proposals are equally meaningless, and so the modeling is entirely spurious.

Although in the model we talk of concessions, when the outcome is reached we are unable to determine whether one party has conceded more than the other. It is not possible to add together the several concessions that each party makes, since each concession is measured only relative to the proposal at the stage in the bargaining process when it occurs. Even if there were but one stage, and so one concession by each party, the measure of their concessions would depend on the particular proposals they had happened to advance. These proposals play a dummy role, however, and do not affect the outcome. By a suitable choice of proposal, one can make one's concession appear as large or as small as one pleases. And so concession is given no real significance in the Zeuthen model corresponding to solution F.

I turn now from solution F to solution G. To characterize solution G, we introduce the ideal point. For a bargaining situation (S,d) we write the ideal point as $\bar{x}(S) = (\bar{x}_1, \bar{x}_2, \ldots, \bar{x}_n)$, where $\bar{x}_i = \max \{x_i / x \epsilon S^+\}$. The ideal point would represent that outcome, normally inaccessible and so not part of the bargaining region, at which each actor i would receive the greatest payoff that he could receive from any outcome in the bargaining region, given that every other actor j must receive at least his disagreement payoff d_j. Obviously, if uninterestingly, we should require that if $\bar{x}(S)\epsilon S$, then $f(S,d) = \bar{x}(S)$.

The introduction of the ideal point enables us to capture directly the relevant maximizing considerations. Each individual bargainer seeks to do as well for himself as possible; each, therefore, seeks his greatest utility, given that a bargain is possible at all. And so each seeks the utility he would receive at the ideal point. In rejecting the relevance of the ideal point, solution F excludes the individual maximizing concerns of the bargainers in favor of an ungrounded, joint maximizing concern. Solution G makes no such error.

We now characterize solution G: $G(S,d) = x$, such that x is the maximal point (in S) for which, for all i, j, $(x_i - d_i)/(\bar{x}_i - d_i) = (x_j - d_j)/(\bar{x}_j - d_j)$, where $(x_i - d_i)$ represents an actor's gain from the outcome x in relation to disagreement; $(\bar{x}_i - d_i)$ represents an actor's gain from the ideal point in relation to disagreement, and so his gain from the most he could receive from any outcome in S^+, in relation to disagreement; and $(x_i - d_i)/(\bar{x}_i - d_i)$ thus represents the proportion of possible gain that is afforded to actor i by outcome x. The solution G equalizes proportions of possible gain, and equalizes them at the maximum level.

G may seem a very plausible solution to the bargaining problem. Each person wants as big a slice of the pie for himself as possible. Solution G divides the pie into slices, each of which represents the same proportion of its recipient's maximal share—the share one could get leaving others with as much pie as in the absence of agreement. And no pie is left over—the slices are as large as possible, given that each is to be the same proportion of its recipient's maximum as every other slice.

Ehud Kalai and Meir Smorodinsky have provided a very neat axiomatization of solution G for two-person bargains. The first three axioms are the same as those for solution F: Pareto-optimality, symmetry, and independence of equivalent utility representations. But instead of the independence of irrelevant alternatives, which gives solution F its maximizing character, solution G satisfies a monotonicity condition. I shall follow Alvin Roth in stating the weakest such condition satisfied by G, because it relates the solution directly to the ideal point, and because it is intuitively clearer than the actual Kalai-Smorodinsky condition:

Restricted Monotonicity: let $T \subset S$: if (T,d) and (S,d) are such that $\bar{x}(T) = \bar{x}(S)$, then $f(S,D) \geq f(T,d)$.

The very plausible idea expressed by this condition is that, if a bargaining situation is enlarged without changing either the disagreement point or the ideal point, the solution to the enlarged bargain should afford each actor a payoff at least equal to what she would receive from the solution to the original bargain.

Appealing as solution G and the Kalai-Smorodinsky axiomatization may be, they coincide only for two-person bargains. Solution G is well defined for all bargains but, as we shortly note, it loses its appeal for certain bargains involving three or more persons. And the Kalai-Smorodinsky axiomatization, alas, gives rise to an impossibility theorem for *n*-person bargains. Not all four of the axioms can be simultaneously satisfied for all bargains in which three or more persons are involved.

The argument here is from Roth, whose example I adapt for illustration. Consider a three-person bargain, T, with a bargaining region the convex hull formed by the points (0,0,0), (1,0,1), and (0,1,1), and d = (0,0,0). It is evident that the Pareto-optimal points fall on the line joining (1,0,1) to (0,1,1), so that any solution satisfying Pareto-optimality must afford the third person a utility = 1. The ideal point, $\bar{x}(T) = (1,1,1)$.

Now, consider a game S with a bargaining region formed by the points (0,0,0), (1,0,1), (0,1,1), and (1,1,0), and d = (0,0,0). The ideal point, $\bar{x}(S) = (1,1,1)$. Note that S contains T. S is a symmetric game; thus, the only solution satisfying the symmetry axiom must be f(S,d) = (2/3,2/3,2/3). But since S contains T and has the same disagreement and ideal points, by the restricted monotonicity axiom f(S,d) $\geq$ f(T,d), and so $f_3(S,d) = 1$. Thus Pareto-optimality, symmetry, and restricted monotonicity cannot all be satisfied.

Consider the solution G for these bargaining games. For S, unsurprisingly, G(S,d) = (2/3,2/3,2/3). This is the maximal point x such that $(x_1 - d_1)/(\bar{x}_1 - d_1) = (x_2 - d_2)/(\bar{x}_2 - d_2) = (x_3 - d_3)/(\bar{x}_3 - d_3)$. But for game T, perhaps surprisingly, G(T,d) = (0,0,0) = d. The disagreement point is the only point in T such that the actors receive equal proportions of their possible gains. For game T, the solution G is not Pareto-optimal.

We should not be prepared to sacrifice Pareto-optimality, at least not in a normative theory of bargaining. Solution G must therefore be rejected—although we may want an acceptable solution to be identical with G for two-person bargains. And the monotonicity axiom must also be rejected because, in conjunction with the three axioms we accept as uncontroversial, it yields an impossibility theorem. What is to be done?

I propose the following modification of solution G; let us call it solution G':

G'(S,d) = x, such that $\min_i (x_i - d_i)/(\bar{x}_i - d_i) > \min_j (y_j - d_j)/(\bar{x}_j - d_j)$ for all y ($\neq$ x) in S^+.

Recall that $(x_i - d_i)/(\bar{x}_i - d_i)$ represents the proportion of i's maximum gain that he receives from outcome x. Thus $\min_i (x_i - d_i)/(\bar{x}_i - d_i)$ represents the smallest, or minimum, proportion of possible gain yielded by outcome x to any person. G' therefore requires that the minimum proportion of possible gain yielded by the bargaining outcome be greater than the minimum proportion of possible gain yielded by any alternative outcome in the bargaining region. The worst-off person, in terms of the proportion of gain from bargaining that she receives, must be as well-off as possible.

The solution G' satisfies our three uncontroversial conditions—Pareto-optimality, symmetry, and independence of equivalent utility representations. It does not satisfy Sen's *alpha* property as applied to the bargaining problem; it is not a maximizing solution. And it is not monotonic, even in the restricted sense satisfied by G. We may easily verify, however, that if solution G is Pareto-optimal, then $G(S,d) = G'(S,d)$. For let $G(S,d) = x$. If x is Pareto-optimal, then for all y $(\neq x)$ in S, there is some person j for whom y_j is less than x_j. But then $(y_j - d_j)/(\bar{x}_j - d_j)$ must be less than $(x_j - d_j)/(\bar{x}_j - d_j)$. Since solution G yields equal proportions of possible gain to all, for all persons $i,(x_j - d_j)/(\bar{x}_j - d_j) = (x_i - d_i)/(\bar{x}_i - d_i)$. And so $\min_i (x_i - d_i)/(\bar{x}_i - d_i)$ is greater than $\min_j (y_j - d_j)/(\bar{x}_j - d_j)$. But then $G(S',d) = x$.

At this point I should produce the axiom that, added to Pareto-optimality, symmetry, and independence of equivalent utility representations, yields solution G'. But instead, I offer a Zeuthen model of the bargaining process corresponding to solution G'.

Each bargainer makes a proposal, and each proposes that she receive the greatest utility compatible with every other person receiving at least the disagreement payoff. In other words, each person proposes her ideal payoff. Now, let x be any outcome in S^+; then the concession required by person i if she accepts x, as measured by the Zeuthen formula, is clearly $(\bar{x}_i - x_i)/(\bar{x}_i - d_i)$—the proportion of her proposed gain over the disagreement payoff that she forgoes. As before, the larger one's concession, the less willing one must be to make it. Consider, therefore, the largest, or maximum, concession required for agreement on an outcome; if the outcome is x, then this will be $\max_i (\bar{x}_i - x_i)/(\bar{x}_i - d_i)$. The person who must make this largest concession will be least willing to agree on outcome x. Now, compare the largest concessions required for each of the possible outcomes. We may suppose that these represent the maximum degree of resistance to agreement on each outcome. The Zeuthen argument is, clearly, that the outcome exciting the least maximum degree of resistance must be accepted; the person required to make the maximum concession needed to yield this outcome is more willing to concede than any person required to make the maximum concession needed to yield any other outcome. Thus, the outcome with the least, or minimum, maximum concession is the bargaining solution, or, in other words, the outcome x such that $\max_i (\bar{x}_i - x_i)/(\bar{x}_i - d_i) < \max_j (\bar{x}_j - y_j)/(\bar{x}_j - d_j)$ for any outcome y $(\neq x)$ in S^+.

But $(\bar{x}_i - x_i)/(\bar{x}_i - d_i) = 1 - (x_i - d_i)/(\bar{x}_i - d_i)$. Thus, maximizing the former is equivalent to minimizing the latter. And minimizing the maximum value of the former for outcomes in S^+ is equivalent to maximizing the minimum value of the latter for these outcomes. Therefore, the requirement that the maximum concession be minimized is equivalent to the requirement that the minimum proportion of possible gain be maximized. And so the solution yielded by our Zeuthen model is solution G'.

Indeed, we may derive solution G' from the following postulates about rational behavior in bargaining:

(1) Each person must propose the greatest utility for herself compatible with no person expecting less utility than from disagreement.

(2) Given proposals satisfying 1, each person must suppose that there is a set of concessions leading to an outcome in the bargaining region such that every rational person is willing to make the concession required of her in the set, provided every other person is so willing.

(3) Each person must be willing to make a concession (provided others are similarly willing) if its size (as measured by the Zeuthen formula) is not greater than the size of the largest concession that she supposes that some rational person is willing to make (again, provided that others are similarly willing).

(4) No person is willing to make a concession if she is not required to do so by conditions 2 and 3.

Every set of concessions leading to an outcome in the bargaining region requires a concession at least as large as the minimum maximum concession. From condition 2, each person must suppose that every rational person is willing to make the concession required of him by a set containing a concession at least as large as the minimum maximum concession. This means that some rational person is willing to make a concession at least as large as the minimum maximum concession. By condition 3, each person must be willing to make a concession at least as large as the minimum maximum concession. Since this suffices to yield agreement on an outcome in the bargaining region, conditions 2 and 3 cannot require any person to be willing to make a concession larger than the minimum maximum concession, and so, by condition 4, no person is so willing. Thus, rational bargainers reach agreement on, and only on, an outcome requiring a concession no larger than the minimum maximum concession, or, in other words, rational bargainers reach solution G'.

If we reflect on the Zeuthen model corresponding to solution G', we note that the magnitude of each person's proposal enters into the measurement of concession and so proves directly relevant to the solution. Each individual has good reason to propose as much utility for himself as is compatible with no one losing utility by agreement. The relevance of the ideal point to the bargaining solution thus corresponds to the demand in the model that each person propose his greatest feasible utility. Since the proposal each person makes is meaningful, the concession each then makes is also meaningful. And since each person makes but one, we may readily determine the total magnitude of his concession. Indeed, the bargaining solution depends directly on these magnitudes; we compare them and select that outcome requiring the minimum maximum total concession.

It might be thought that the Zeuthen model corresponding to solution F is more realistic than that corresponding to solution G' because it represents bargaining as a multistage process, rather than as a single-stage process. But the stages of that model are, as we have seen, without significance. The outcome to be reached is fixed without regard either to the proposals made or to the particular sequence, single-stage or multistage, of concessions made from those proposals. If we suppose that the Zeuthen rule for determining concessions is to be applied to determine the overall or total concessions to be made by the several parties to a bargain, then we find that it yields a meaningful one-stage representation of the bargaining process supporting solution G'.

In solution G' and in the associated Zeuthen model, we compare the proportionate gains, or equivalently the concessions, made by all of the parties to a bargain. We should note, first, that these comparisons are strictly independent of equivalent utility representations; the arbitrary choices of zero-point and unit in the individual utility-functions have no effect on the magnitudes compared. We should also note that these comparisons are not interpersonal utility comparisons. We do not suppose that persons making equal concessions, as measured by the Zeuthen formula, give up equal amounts of utility, whatever that would mean. We do not suppose that persons obtaining different proportions of possible gain obtain similarly different amounts of utility. If our disagreement payoffs are $0, and your ideal payoff is $500 and mine $50, then we receive equal proportions of possible gain if you get $300 and I get $30; we do not suppose that the utility value of money is ten times for me what it is for you.

In our argument, we give no meaning to interpersonal comparisons of utility. Each person's utility is a measure of outcomes based on that person's preferences. There is no common measure involved. The notion that utilities are interpersonally comparable rests on sheer confusion; it involves the illegitimate supposition that utility is a measure of something like the extent of overall preference-satisfaction obtained by a person. Perhaps we could introduce such a measure by treating objects of preference as possible worlds, requiring each person to order all possible worlds, and then normalizing each person's resulting utility-function to a 0–1 scale. But carrying out this Herculean task would shed not the slightest light on the bargaining problem. Bargainers have no reason to be concerned with comparative overall preference-satisfaction.

Solution G′ introduces maximin or minimax considerations into bargaining. We suppose that rational bargainers will agree on an outcome that maximizes the minimum proportion of possible gain or minimizes the maximum concession. We should at once notice the connection between solution G′ and John Rawls's difference principle. Suppose that we apply G′ to the distribution of social values. The difference principle, it will be remembered, states that the minimum representative share of some subset of social values is to be maximized. As Rawls notes, his general conception of justice, that "All social values . . . are to be distributed equally unless an unequal distribution of any, or all, of these values is to everyone's advantage," is "simply the difference principle applied to all primary goods."[12] Now, as formulated by Rawls, the difference principle does not distinguish between the share of social values, or primary goods, or whatever, that would be obtained without social cooperation and the share obtained through cooperation. By introducing the disagreement point, solution G′ enables us to take account of this difference; we suppose that each person seeks to maximize her gain over the outcome of no cooperation and so is concerned with her share of socially or cooperatively produced values. Identifying the disagreement point with the outcome of no cooperation, solution G′ yields a distribution of the cooperative *product.*

Furthermore, Rawls requires an interpersonal comparison of values, or primary goods, to determine the minimum share under different social arrangements, selecting that arrangement in which the least share is maximized. By invoking the notion of proportionate shares, solution G′ enables us to avoid this problem of interpersonal comparison and, furthermore, to avoid the exploitation of the more-advantaged that Nozick and others have criticized in Rawls's argument. But here my concern is not to berate Rawls for supposing that social cooperation should involve compensation. Rather, let us note that the solution G′, as applied to agreement on the distribution of social values, works in a way similar to Rawls's difference principle, of which it may be considered a generalization. The difference principle would result from G′ in the special case in which: first, what was to be distributed could be made the object of interpersonal comparison; second, in terms of that comparison, persons would suffer equally at the disagreement outcome; and third, also in terms of that comparison, persons would benefit equally from the ideal point.

Rawls supposes, or supposed, that the difference principle, requiring the maximization of the minimum share of some subset of social values, is itself chosen by a decision process conducted in accordance with a maximin principle of choice. John Harsanyi has correctly and decisively shown the irrationality of such a principle for the individual decision making to which Rawls appeals.[13] As a critique of Rawls, Harsanyi's argument turns out to be futile because, as Rawls's later writings make evident, the decision process is not part of the core of his moral theory but rather only part of its dispensable heuristic.[14] How we get the difference principle is, for Rawls, less important than that we get it—since this principle relates to his Kantian conception of moral persons. But we are concerned with bargaining and justice, not with Kantian moral persons. And we are now in a position to see that Harsanyi's criticism (decisive as it is against the supposition that moral principles, or principles of justice, may be arrived at through a process of individual decision making based on maximin reasoning) would be entirely beside the point had Rawls developed the original contractarian insight of his theory and taken seriously the idea of bargaining, as the procedure by which principles of justice are selected. For in bargaining we do not have an individual decision maker, or even a group of individual decision makers, concerned with maximizing some single quantity. As I have argued, the attempt to invoke Sen's *alpha* property in the guise of Nash's axiom of the independence of irrelevant alternatives is simply an attempt to fit bargaining into a maximizing straitjacket. Although rational, individual decision making is correctly represented by a maximizing model, bargaining is not, and in bargaining the use of maximin considerations comes into its own. For in bargaining the distinction between persons is, and is to be, taken seriously, and the maximization of a single quantity, however conceived, fails to do this. In requiring that slices of the pie be determined by a maximin principle, in which each person is assured that the smallest proportionate gain is as large as possible, each is assured that his concerns are not being sacrificed to those of any other person. No maximizing procedure can do this.

Let me emphasize that my argument is not a criticism of maximization where it belongs. Economics, and rational choice, are properly

---

[13]See n. 7 for reference.
[14]Note the absence of the decision process in Rawls [3].

concerned with maximization; as a first approximation, one might endorse Jon Elster's view that "man may indeed be seen as a *globally maximizing machine.*"[15] But individual maximizers, interacting, do not a single maximizer make. My argument is a criticism of the imperialism of maximization that is represented, in our concern with bargaining and justice, by Nash's solution F, and by John Harsanyi's utilitarian moral theory.[16] Both of these confound distribution with production and mutual agreement with individual decision. They are paradigmatic cases of barking brilliantly up the wrong tree.

As preliminary to what follows, I want to distinguish clearly between the procedure in accordance with which principles of justice or, more generally, moral principles, are selected, and the content of the principles. We may bring the distinction into focus by a contrast between Harsanyi and Rawls. Harsanyi supposes that the "function . . . that [an] individual . . . will use in evaluating various social situations from a moral point of view will be called his *social welfare function*" as contrasted with the utility-function that he uses in evaluating situations from his personal point of view.[17] The social welfare function is, Harsanyi argues, the function an individual would use were he evaluating situations from a personal point of view, but from behind a veil of ignorance in which he assigned equal probability to occupying each of the positions in society with the preferences and capacities of the person in that position. In effect, we may say that, for Harsanyi, a moral principle corresponds to the principle for rational individual choice under complete ignorance of one's position among those affected by the choice. The principle, he claims, is the principle of maximizing average expected utility (where obviously interpersonal comparability of utility must be assumed), and it is determined by considering choice in complete ignorance of one's position.

Rawls does not identify the principles of justice with the principles one would use in choosing from behind a veil of ignorance. Rather, the principles of justice are the objects of such choice. Thus, for Rawls, the principles an individual would use for his most basic evaluations of social situations—the principles of justice—are not identical with the principles he would use for making individual decisions behind a veil of ignorance. They are, instead, the principles he would choose for social evaluation from behind that veil. For Harsanyi, moral principles are those that would characterize individual choice behind a veil of ignorance; for Rawls, moral principles are those that would be chosen from behind such a veil.

---

[15]Elster, p. 10.
[16]Perhaps the best statement of Harsanyi's theory is in Harsanyi [3].
[17]Harsanyi [4], p. 50.

We should expect that the principles one would choose from behind a veil of ignorance would be related in a significant and deep way to the principles one would employ in choosing. Thus, we could recast Harsayni's argument into a Rawlsian form and claim that, reasoning in accordance with the principle of expected utility-maximization, one would choose principles for maximizing average utility if one were choosing in ignorance of one's identity. We could also recast Rawls's argument into Harsanyian form and claim that, reasoning on a maximin principle from behind a veil of ignorance, one would evaluate social situations from the perspective of the position receiving the maximin share—thus arriving at the difference principle. The more specific features of Rawls's two principles of justice depend, as Rawls makes clear, on further limiting assumptions.

Although we can move back and forth between the two approaches exemplified by Harsanyi and Rawls, we should keep procedure separate from content, and in our present inquiry we must focus on procedure. It is, of course, not to be taken for granted that a procedural derivation of moral principles, or of principles of justice, is appropriate. But it is, I think, natural to suppose this if one begins with the idea that individuals are concerned with realizing a conception of their own, individual good—a conception that need not be a selfish one, but one that does not necessarily harmonize fully with the conceptions of others—and with the idea that society is, as in Rawls's useful phrase, a "cooperative venture for mutual advantage," where mutual advantage is to be related to the concern of each individual to realize her own good.[18] The claim is that, through social cooperation, each of us is better able to realize, or able to realize to a greater extent, a conception of our own good than would be possible in the absence of such cooperation. However, it is clearly necessary, if there is to be social cooperation, that certain principles be accepted as determining the institutions and practices of the society within which cooperation is to be effected. Given that each individual is concerned to advance her own good, and that society is conceived as promoting mutual advancement, it is natural to suppose that the acceptability of social principles must be related to agreement among individuals. Acceptable principles are those individuals would agree to under suitably constrained circumstances.

We shall return to the implications of this reference to constraint. First, let us trace the implications of the idea that the principles should be the object of agreement. This must immediately suggest the relevance of rational bargaining. The outcome of a bargain may reflect the circumstances in which the parties find themselves, but the

[18]Rawls [1], p. 4.

idea of a bargain is independent of circumstances. We suppose that the principles of justice constitute the solution to an appropriately specified bargaining problem, and so, given our acceptance of solution G', we suppose that the principles of justice may be represented as maximizing the minimum proportionate gain expected by the parties to the bargain. Principles of justice are principles for maximizing minimum proportionate gain.

If, indeed, G' is the rational solution to the bargaining problem, then an outcome maximizing minimum proportionate gain must be rationally acceptable from the standpoint of every individual. Each person, recognizing the equal rationality of all, considers it rational to tailor her own proposal and concession so that minimum proportionate gain is maximized. Thus, an agreement based on solution G' is fully impartial, not in abstracting from the interests of the individuals concerned but in giving recognition to each of their interests in a way rationally acceptable from the standpoint of each. In bargaining, we attain impartiality among real persons by taking their distinctness seriously.

To be sure, we need not suppose that all real-life bargaining exhibits the impartiality of solution G'. For in real-life bargaining, the differential bargaining skills of the bargainers will lead to solutions that often differ markedly from G'. Furthermore, G' is impartial given the circumstances of bargaining. If you are holding a gun to my head, the agreement we may reach may be rational and impartial in relation to that initial situation, but questions about its impartiality are apt to arise. Remember that we have yet to talk about suitably constrained circumstances.

Rawls makes a fatal misstep in his argument to the principles of justice when he supposes that, persons being placed behind a veil of ignorance in order to secure an appropriate agreement, they are left with "no basis for bargaining," so that their agreement may be represented as one individual's choice. Thus, Rawls says that, "If anyone after due reflection prefers a conception of justice to another, then they all do, and a unanimous agreement can be reached."[19]

Even behind a veil of ignorance, however thick, each person must be aware that he is concerned with realizing a conception of his own good. Without this, the parties have no basis for agreement; they would have no interest in reaching agreement or in anything else. But given this, each must be concerned with reaching an agreement that maximally advances his own interests, and each must recognize the equal and parallel concern of every other person. The only way in

19Rawls [1], p. 139.

which an individual can rationally protect his unknown conception of the good that he would advance is by bargaining to an agreement that—because it is rationally acceptable from the standpoint of every bargainer—is rationally acceptable from the standpoint of his own conception of the good, whatever it may be. (The only condition required here is that each person's conception of the good be such that it can be advanced by a cooperative venture for mutual advantage. This, it will be remembered, is given in the way our problem is posed.) In this bargaining, the distinction between persons is preserved. Thus, the procedure by which the principles of justice are determined respects, as Rawls's own procedure does not, our individuality. Rawls sacrifices the distinction between persons behind the veil of ignorance when he replaces bargaining by individual choice. Then, to protect his theory from the apparently utilitarian consequences of this sacrifice, he supposes that the choice of principles is made in accordance with what, as Harsanyi has correctly argued, is a highly irrational rule. Had Rawls carried through the idea of a bargain, he could have preserved the distinctness of persons and derived a maximin principle with solution G'.

In might be thought that there are two quite different procedures for arriving at principles of justice from behind a veil of ignorance— one, which I have developed, based on bargaining, and another, found in different versions in Rawls and Harsanyi, based on individual decision. But, in my view, the only possible procedure is based on bargaining. Individual choice of principles of justice behind the veil is impossible, because one would lack a sufficient basis for making such a choice—a system of aims, or a coherent set of preferences, or a conception of one's own good. One chooses rationally by maximizing utility, which is a measure of outcomes based on preference; one can then normally set about to maximize utility only if one has a known set of preferences over which one may define a utility-function. And the veil of ignorance denies one knowledge of one's preferences.

Harsanyi seeks to escape this impasse by supposing that, behind the veil, one assumes an equal chance of being each person, with that person's preferences, and then one chooses by maximizing average utility—the average level of preference-satisfaction. But the equiprobable mix of each person's set of preferences is not itself a coherent set of preferences; it does not afford a conception of any person's own good. Even if one can define a measure of outcomes, called average utility, based on the equiprobable mix of each person's set of preferences, this measure is not itself utility, and maximizing it is irrelevant to rational choice.

Were there a principle, the choice of which would maximize not average utility but one's expected utility, whatever one's preferences were, then even behind the veil of ignorance one would have sufficient basis for rationally choosing it. One would need to know only that one had a set of preferences, and not what those preferences were. But no principle or set of principles of justice is best from every standpoint, or best advances one's own good whatever that good might be.

Turning Rawls around, then, I claim that, behind the veil of ignorance, persons seeking social principles or principles of justice have no basis for anything but bargaining. Seemingly paradoxically (but only seemingly so), they cannot choose but they can agree. They cannot choose because choice is rational only from a determinate standpoint, a known set of preferences, however indeterminate the prospects over which one chooses. But they can agree because agreement is rational from every standpoint, and so from whatever standpoint each unknowingly occupies. Only the idea of agreement makes possible the unanimity required for rationally arriving at principles of justice behind a veil of ignorance.

We have identified the procedure by which principles of justice are to be selected. As the outcomes of a rational bargain, we know that they must satisfy the maximin requirements of solution G'. We must now consider the light shed on principles of justice by the rider that they be the outcome of a bargain in suitably constrained circumstances. Here, the basic point is that the circumstances must be such as to assure the *ex ante* character of the agreement. The circumstances must, then, abstract from all actual advantages enjoyed and disadvantages suffered under existing social arrangements; these are not bargaining counters appropriate to an agreement deciding on or evaluating social arrangements. Thus, the disagreement point for a bargain yielding principles of justice must be a state of nature—a condition characterized by the absence of social cooperation—and not a particular, historically given state of society.

I shall not attempt here to show that a Lockean, and not a Hobbesian, state of nature affords the appropriate disagreement point.[20] What I shall note is that the abstraction required to yield suitably constrained circumstances leads to an identification between the procedures leading to agreement and the content of the principles that are the objects of agreement. Since no basis for establishing a more determinate content is available, we can say only that the principles of justice that satisfy the requirements of solution G' must be principles that evaluate and determine social institutions and practices in terms

[20]I endeavor to show this in Gauthier [5], ch. 7.

of solution G'—in terms, that is, of the extent to which the institutions and practices assure maximin proportionate gain, taking the absence of social cooperation as the disagreement point from which gain is measured.

If we equate these principles with the idea of a social welfare function, then we may conclude that a social welfare function should not be a maximizing function. Our argument shows that it is quite mistaken to relate each person's moral choices to a function defined over a set of preferences, moral or impartial rather than personal, but satisfying the usual axioms for rational behavior under risk. Harsanyi, who has been foremost in maintaining this view, insists that morality should exhibit the same form of rationality as individual decision making.[21] But I note once more that this is to introduce maximizing requirements in the wrong place. The individual seeks to maximize her own utility—seeks to realize to the fullest possible extent a conception of her own good. Morality is not concerned with maximizing some quantity analogous to individual good; rather, morality is concerned with the way in which the benefits society makes possible are distributed among individuals, each pursuing his own good. Morality relates this distribution to agreement among those individuals. And so the rationality of moral choice is assured, not by modeling it on the rationality of individual, personal choice under risk, but rather by modeling it on the rationality of a bargain. Each should chose morally in such a way that the socially agreed upon standard of maximizing minimum proportionate gain is realized. The maximin character of solution G' carries over to determine the nature of moral choice by the individual who seeks to act in accordance with the principles of justice. This represents the application of solution G' to social practices and institutions.

Morality—or at least that part of it constituted by justice—is a matter of agreement. And, although agreement is arrived at by individual maximizers, it is not an agreement to maximize anything. Each is concerned with his share of social goods, which contributes to the realization of his own concept of the good life. There is no greater whole of which these good lives are a part. As Robert Nozick says, "There are only individual people, different individual people, with their own individual lives."[22] When these people agree, they agree on a mode of cooperation that better enables each of them to assure that his life is a good one by his own standards. The rational way to do this

[21]"I propose to consider *ethics*, also, as a branch of the general theory of rational behavior, since ethical theory can be based on axioms which represent specializations of some of the axioms used in decision theory" (Harsanyi [2], p. 97).

[22]Nozick, p. 33.

leaves the person who receives the least extensive share of social benefit, measured in relation to what he might have received, with the
knowledge that any alternative social arrangements would have afforded someone a yet smaller share.

If my argument has been successful, I have shown how a theory of
bargaining is linked to a theory of justice. In developing both, I have
taken "seriously the distinction between persons."[23] Agreeing that
productive concerns and individual decisions are to be linked to a
conception of maximining rationality, I have nonetheless shown that
distributive concerns and moral decisions are to be linked to a conception of maximining rationality—a conception, however, that is itself
linked to maximization by the argument that individually rational
bargainers would reach agreement on maximizing minimum propor-
tional gain. Thus, I have shown the congruence of three fundamental
ideas: the individual, as a rational being, concerned with realizing a
conception of her own good; society, as a cooperative venture that
contributes to the realization of these several goods; and morality, as a
set of principles agreed to by rational individuals and requiring that
society contribute to individual realization in a way that maximizes the
minimum proportionate gain. Such are the fruits of solution G'.

[23]Rawls [1], p. 27.

RATIONALITY

[10]

Reason and Maximization

I

Economic man seeks to maximize utility. The rationality of economic man is assumed and is identified with the aim of utility-maximization.[1] But may rational activity correctly be identified with maximizing activity? The object of this essay is to explore, and in part to answer, this question.

This is not an issue solely, or perhaps even primarily, about the presuppositions of economics. The two great modern schools of moral and political thought in the English-speaking world, the contractarian and the utilitarian, identify rationality with maximization and bring morality into their equations as well. To the contractarian, rational man enters civil society to maximize his expectation of well-being, and morality is that system of principles of action which rational men collectively adopt to maximize their well-being.[2] To the utilitarian, the rational and moral individual seeks the maximum happiness of mankind, with which he identifies his own maximum happiness.[3]

Neither school identifies rationality with the straightforward aim of individual utility-maximization; this is the position of egoism, which each criticizes. But the criticism is that egoism is self-defeating; if the result of unrestrained individual utility-maximizing activities were the

Reprinted with permission of the *Canadian Journal of Philosophy*
[1]Cf. Winch, "We assume that individuals behave rationally and endeavour to maximize utility" (p. 25). Also cf. Arrow, pp. 3, 21.

[2]Cf. Hobbes [4], chs. 14, 15, and 17, for the classic statement of contractarian theory. Also cf. Baier, pp. 308–315.

[3]Cf. Mill, ch. 3.

greatest utility for each, then neither the contractarian nor the utilitarian would find any need for morality or civil society. It is rational to maximize one's utilities, but it is not rational to do this by a straightforward policy of individual utility-maximization. In examining the connection of rational activity with maximizing activity, this paradox must be elucidated.[4]

But this is not all. For although I show that we can define a quite precise conception of maximizing activity, which resolves this paradox, and which should satisfy the conception of rationality which the economist, the contractarian, the utilitarian, and even the egoist, actually share (although perhaps only the contractarian correctly understands it), this conception of reason, and its associated conception of man, remain problematic. My concern is to show precisely what is involved in identifying rational activity with maximizing activity, indeed to develop the best possible case for this identification, so that it will be easier to see, on the one hand, its real practical consequences, and, on the other hand, its ideological underpinning. But I can only point to these further matters in this present essay.

I take for granted that the primary subject of action, or activity, is the individual human person. And I presuppose that it is primarily to the individual that we ascribe rationality. To speak of a rational action, or rational activity, or a rational morality, or a rational society, is to speak of rationality in a way which must be derived from our conception of a rational individual or person. This is a very important presupposition, but one which I leave unexamined here, save to remark that it does not, in itself, imply that our conception of a rational person is of an atomic individual, capable of existing independently of other persons or of society.

Since our concern is with rational activity, our first task is to connect this activity to the rational person. What must a person do, *in virtue of being rational?* The first point to note is that rationality is not an individuating characteristic of persons. It is the individual who is rational, but *qua* rational, one individual is the same as another. Hence any answer to this question must be the same for all persons: what one person must do, in virtue of being rational, is to be characterized in the same way as what any other person must do, in virtue of being rational.

The second point is another presupposition, perhaps *the* presupposition of what I call the modern Western view of man. To characterize a person as rational is not to relate him to any order, or system,

4Cf. Gauthier [4].

or framework, which would constrain his activities. It is not, as Plato thought, to relate man to the Good. It is not, as Saint Thomas thought, to relate man to God. It is not, as Kant thought, to relate man to the Kingdom of Ends. To characterize a person as rational is not then to determine his ends either positively, in terms of a goal or goals to be sought, or negatively, in terms of beings (such as other persons) to be respected.

In calling this the modern Western view of man, I do not intend to claim that it has been embraced by all Western thinkers; Kant and Hegel are obvious counterexamples. What I am claiming is that this presupposition underlies our scientific theories and our social practices. It is part of the way in which each of us understands, unreflectively, in practice, what it is to be human. To demonstrate this would require a historical and social inquiry falling quite outside the scope of this essay. What I wish to do is to develop some of the implications of this presupposition—implications which are relevant to an assessment of our understanding of what it is to be human. For it is this understanding which ultimately is called into question by an inquiry into rationality and maximization.

Given this supposition, the strict answer to the question, What must a person do, solely in virtue of being rational? is: Nothing. Reason of itself determines no actions. The modern Western view of man implies at least part of the Humean view of reason, that it is the slave of the passions.[5] Reason takes the ends of our activities as given, and determines the means to those ends.

On this instrumental view of reason, to characterize a man as rational is to characterize the way in which he goes about his activities. And so our first question about rational activity is replaced by the question, How must a man act, in virtue of being rational? What, in other words, is the *rational manner* of acting?

II

The immediate consequence of the instrumental view of reason is that rationality is, or at least involves, efficiency. The rational person endeavors to select those actions which achieve her ends, and which achieve them with the minimum expenditure of time and effort. She does what is necessary to secure what she wants, and no more than is necessary.

But efficiency is not the whole of the rational manner of acting. The

[5]Hume [1], bk. II, pt. III, sec. III.

interesting problems of practical reason arise because we cannot secure all of what we want. We have incompatible ends, so that the means which bring about one exclude another. We have ends to which there are no available sufficient means, and which therefore are at least partially unattainable. We have open ends, such as happiness, to which no set of means can be complete.

The identification of rationality with maximizing activity requires the reduction of problems about incompatible or unattainable ends to problems about a single open end, characterized in a purely formal way. That is, we suppose that there is a single measure of an individual's ends, which can be applied to evaluate the contribution each of the actions possible for her in a situation makes to the overall realization of her ends. A rational person then endeavors to select the action, or one of the actions, which maximizes this contribution.[6]

When a person acts, she brings about one of a number of outcomes, each of which is possible in her situation. To deny this is to deny the real possibility of action; it is to take a fatalist view with regard to human behavior. The outcome actually brought about need not be known to, or intended by, the person acting, but she conceives herself to be acting only insofar as she forms some expectation of the outcome, or of a probability distribution over possible outcomes, and can distinguish this object of her expectation from other outcomes or probability distributions over outcomes, which she believes to be also possible in the situation. The object of the person's expectation, whether an outcome or a probability distribution over outcomes, may be termed the *expected outcome;* thus for example if a coin is tossed to determine how it lands, the expected outcome is a 50 percent probability of heads and a 50 percent probability of tails. The act selected, then, is selected to bring about the expected outcome, rather than other possible outcomes, and this expected outcome is the preferred outcome.

Preference in this sense is intentional, manifested in what a person actually takes herself to be doing. Her preferences cannot necessarily be inferred from the outcomes really possible in her situation, and the outcome actually brought about; it is her conception of the possibilities, and of the expected outcome, and indeed of the action itself, which is decisive. What an individual expects as the outcome of what she takes herself to be doing is what she prefers among the conceived possibilities.

[6]This is too direct a statement of the connection between reason and maximization; it applies to what I call independent action but not to what I distinguish as interdependent action. See V–VII infra. Similarly, the discussion of preference must be modified to fit interdependent action; see n. 16 infra.

Intentional preference need not correspond to attitudinal preference. A person may favor one outcome over others yet act consciously and intentionally to realize one of the outcomes not favored. The problems that arise in accounting for the gap between attitudinal and intentional preference, which are of course similar to those that arise in accounting for weakness of will, are not of concern here. But the failure of this correspondence indicates a failure of rationality; the rational person acts, or at least intends to act, in accordance with her attitudes. This is not to say that attitudinal preference is more rational than intentional; no standard for the rationality of either intentional preference or attitudinal preference, taken in itself, has yet been introduced. It is only to say that the correspondence of the two is rational, the divergence, irrational.

A person's preferences, whether intentional or attitudinal, may depend on her knowledge and reflection. This dependence provides us with a standard for preferability. One outcome is preferable to another, for a person, if she would prefer it, given full knowledge and reflection. The very real problem of what constitutes fullness of knowledge and reflection is another matter which must be excluded from this essay. And a person is rational, only insofar as her preferences correspond to her subjective judgment of what is preferable— only, then, insofar as what she takes herself to do corresponds to what she judges she would do, and what she favors corresponds to what she judges she would favor, given full knowledge and reflection.

Preferability provides a standard for the rationality of both intentional and attitudinal preference. But this standard is fully compatible with the supposition that the rationality of a person is not determined by the ends she seeks. The rationality of a person, on this view, depends on whether the ends she seeks are those which she judges she would seek under conditions ideal in certain respects. Reason does not assess a person's ends in relation to some standard beyond her passions (in the Humean sense). Rather, reason assesses a person's ends in relation to the standards implicit in the passions themselves, the standards of consistency between intention and attitude, and conformity of both to ideal intention and attitude. Bringing these standards together, a person is a rational agent only if her actions conform to what she supposes she would do and favor were she sufficiently informed and reflective.

III

Rationality in action is thus more than mere efficiency. But there are further conditions arising from our understanding of preferences.

Although reason as instrumental imposes, and can impose, no restraints on the content of particular preferences, it does impose restraints on the relations among the contents of different preferences.[7]

I have said that the rational man acts to bring about that outcome which he prefers, among those which he believes are open to him. Thus he must be able to compare the possible outcomes in any situation to determine that which he prefers to the others. Let o_i and o_j be any two outcomes which logically are alternative possible outcomes for some situation. Then since there is no reason in principle why a person might not be restricted to a choice between these two outcomes, he must be able to determine a preference between them. We require a *connectivity* condition: If o_i and o_j are any alternative possible outcomes for any situation, then any rational person A must either prefer o_i to o_j, or o_j to o_i, or be indifferent between them.

This may seem an innocuous requirement, although it assumes a single dimension of comparison among our ends. A second, obviously less innocuous condition, but one equally necessary if one is to select a most preferred outcome in any situation, is that one's preferences not be cyclic. If I prefer apples to pears, pears to peaches, and peaches to apples and am in a situation in which I must select one of these three fruits, then no selection is most preferred—for any outcome, there is some other outcome which I prefer to it. To avoid this we require a *transitivity* condition: If o_i, o_j, o_k are any alternative possible outcomes for any situation, then if any rational person A does not prefer o_j to o_i, and o_k to o_j, A does not prefer o_k to o_i. (This slightly awkward formulation is required to ensure that transitivity extends to indifference.)

These conditions are sufficient to induce a weak ordering of the possible outcomes in any situation, in terms of an individual's preferences. They do not, however, establish a quantitative measure of preference, which is necessary if rational action is to be identified with maximizing action. Three further conditions are needed to do this.

These further conditions depend on the concept of a *lottery* among outcomes. A lottery is simply a probability distribution over the members of a set of possible outcomes. For example, suppose that I am to receive a fruit, selected at random, from a plate on which there are four apples, two pears, and six peaches. Then there are three possible outcomes—receiving an apple, a pear, a peach—and random selection of a fruit from the plate represents a lottery over these outcomes, with probabilities one-third for apple, one-sixth for pear, and one-half for peach. The conditions then are these:

[7]For a fuller discussion of preference and utility, cf. Luce and Raiffa, ch. 2, and works referred to therein.

Substitution: If o_i and o_j are any alternative possible outcomes or lotteries for any situation, and if any rational person A is indifferent between them, then o_i may be substituted for o_j in any lottery or situation without affecting A's preferences.

Unique indifference: If o_i, o_j, and o_k are any alternative possible outcomes or lotteries for any situation, and if any rational person A prefers o_i to o_k and does not prefer o_j to o_i or o_k to o_j, then there is a unique lottery over o_i and o_k which A considers indifferent to o_j.

Positive correlation: If o_i and o_j are any alternative possible outcomes for any situation, and if any rational person A prefers o_i to o_j, then if l_m and l_n are any two lotteries over o_i and o_j, A prefers l_m to l_n if and only if the probability of o_i in l_m is greater than in l_n.

The interpretation of the last two conditions may be assisted by an example. Suppose I prefer apples to pears and pears to peaches. Then the unique indifference conditions requires that there be a single, unique lottery among apples and peaches which I consider indifferent to pears. And the positive correlation condition requires that I prefer a lottery affording me a 50 percent chance of an apple and a 50 percent chance of a pear to one affording me a 40 percent chance of an apple and a 60 percent chance of a pear.

All of these conditions lack intuitive plausibility in one respect—a respect in which the earlier transitivity condition is also defective. For all require that we have unlimited powers of discrimination in matters of preference. If I prefer apples to pears, then according to the positive correlation condition I must prefer a lottery among apples and pears affording me a 50.00002 percent chance of an apple to one affording me a 50.00001 percent chance. But my powers of discrimination do not enable me to detect any practical difference between the two lotteries.

It is not possible to remedy this difficulty within the compass of this essay. We may take our conditions, then, as representing an ideal of reason with respect to preference. A person is rational, insofar as his preferences are concerned, to the extent to which they satisfy these conditions.

We are now able to introduce the measure of a man's ends, which is termed *utility*.[8] To determine such a measure for the members of any set of alternative possible outcomes is to determine a *utility-function* for the members of the set. Let $o_1, \ldots, o_n$ be any set of alternative pos-

---

[8] A more formal treatment would require a proof that the conditions given are necessary and sufficient for the introduction of a utility-function.

sible outcomes, ordered so that no member of the sequence is preferred to any preceding member by the person in question, A. If A is indifferent between o_1 and o_n, then he is indifferent among all the possible outcomes, and a utility-function is defined for the members of the set simply by assigning the same number—any number will do—to each. But suppose that A is not indifferent among all the possible outcomes. Let each outcome be replaced by the unique lottery over o_1 and o_n to which it is indifferent for A; for any outcome o_i let this lottery be $(p_i o_1 + (1 - p_i) o_n)$. Then U is a utility-function for A over $o_1, \ldots, o_n$ if and only if:

(1) $U(o_1) = u_1$, where u_1 is any real number;
(2) $U(o_n) = u_n$, where u_n is any real number smaller than u_1;
(3) $U(o_i) = U(p_i o_1 + (1 - p_i) o_n) = p_i U(o_1) + (1 - p_i) U(o_n) = p_i u_1 + (1 - p_i) u_n = u_i$.

If U is a utility-function for A over the members of any set of outcomes, then any positive linear transform of U, that is, any function

$$U^* = aU + b \ (a > 0)$$

is also a utility-function for A over these outcomes.

A person is a rational agent, then, only if a utility-function can be defined over the alternative possible outcomes in any situation, as a measure of his preference among those outcomes. And so the identification of rationality in action with the aim of individual utility-maximization now seems to be complete. A rational individual, I concluded in section II, identifies his intentional preference, his attitudinal preference, and his supposition of what he would prefer given full knowledge and reflection. For him we may speak simply of preference, referring to all of these. A rational individual, I have now concluded, is one whose preferences can be measured by a utility-function, or, in other words, one whose preferences can be replaced functionally by numerical utilities. Bringing these conclusions together, a rational individual is one whose intended actions conform to his numerical utilities, that is, one who acts to bring about an expected outcome with utility at least as great as that of any outcome he considers possible in the situation. Thus the rationality condition established by identifying rational activity with maximizing activity is: *A person acts rationally only if the expected outcome of his action affords him a utility at least as great as that of the expected outcome of any action possible for him in the situation.*

This development of rationality from efficiency to utility-maximization is by no means unproblematic. As I have indicated, the argument of II rests on the assumption that there is a single dimension of comparison among our ends, a dimension which I have labeled preference. And the argument of III requires two further assumptions. The first is that preference can be represented as a continuum, rather than, say, a mere ordering. The second is that this continuum has no necessary upper bound, that the formal end, utility, is open. In any particular situation there is a maximum possible utility, but the pursuit of utility is unending. These assumptions are, of course, part of the orthodox conception of economic man, and of the contractarian and utilitarian views which are its alternative elaborations in the realm of morals and politics. But they are not entailed by the conception of reason as instrumental.

IV

Is utility-maximization always possible? If rationality is identified with the aim of individual utility-maximization, and if there are situations in which it is not possible to maximize one's utilities, then there are situations in which it is not possible to act rationally. This is not a conclusion one would willingly accept. Hence a proof of the possibility of utility-maximization, in all situations, is required.

But this task is beyond the compass of this essay. Here, I can consider only three types of situations. The first, and simplest, is that in which the person knows the full circumstances in which she is to act, and the effects of her (intended) action on those circumstances; hence she is able to correlate a determinate outcome with each of her possible actions. This case is unproblematic. The utility of each outcome may be related to the corresponding action, and utility-maximization is achieved by selecting that action, or one of those actions, with greatest utility.

The second case is that in which the person is uncertain about either the circumstances, or the effects of her action in those circumstances. To each of her possible actions she is able to correlate not a determinate outcome but only a determinate set, each member of which is the outcome resulting from a particular combination of circumstances and effects possible given the action. If we suppose, however, that she can make some estimate of the probabilities of these various possible circumstances and effects, then she can correlate a unique expected outcome with each possible action, the expected outcome being the appropriate probability distribution over the set of outcomes.[9] And the utility of this expected outcome (its expected utility)[10] may be determined from the utilities of the outcomes belonging to the set; it is simply the sum of the products of the probabilities and utilities of all the members of the set. This expected utility may then be related to the corresponding action, and utility-maximization is achieved by selecting that action, or one from those actions, with greatest expected utility.

The third, most difficult case is that in which there is more than one person, each rational, and the outcome is the product of their actions in the circumstances.[11] I shall not demonstrate that utility-maximization can be achieved, but only that one problem which arises from the interaction of the persons can be resolved. To illustrate the problem, consider the simplest possibility—two persons, A and B, each able to correlate a determinate outcome with each pair consisting of a possible action for A and a possible action for B. Suppose now that A expects B to perform some one of her actions—or, failing this, assigns a probability to each of B's possible actions, so that he expects, as it were, a probability distribution over B's possible actions. In either case, he can correlate an expected outcome with each of his possible actions and proceed as before to maximize.

But A must take B's rationality into account. Since B is rational, A must suppose that the action he expects B to perform will maximize B's expected utility, given the action B expects A to perform. A's intended action, then, is utility maximizing for A against that possible action of B which A expects B to perform, which in turn is conceived by A as utility maximizing for B against that possible action of A which A expects that B expects A to perform. Now let us make one further, crucial, simplifying assumption. Let us suppose that A assumes that B's expectation is correct. That is, the possible action of A, which A expects that B expects A to perform, is A's intended action. Hence A's action is utility maximizing for A given that action of B which A expects B to perform, which in turn is utility maximizing for B given A's action. Hence from A's point of view (and also, of course, from B's, which is assumed to be exactly parallel), each action must be utility maximizing for the agent given the other's action.

It is not obvious that this requirement can always be satisfied. In-

---

[9]I shall not consider the possibility of utility-maximization if the agent is unable to make any estimate of the probabilities of the various circumstances and effects.

[10]A person prefers greater utility to less and is indifferent between equal utilities, whether these utilities are actual or expected. This is assured by the way in which her utility-function is generated from her preferences. Hence the introduction of expected utility makes no difference to the argument; it is in no sense inferior to actual utility.

[11]This is the situation analyzed by the mathematical theory of games, to which I owe many of my arguments and concepts.

deed, it cannot be, unless each person is able to select not only from her possible actions but also from all probability distributions over her possible actions, in deciding what to do. To show this, let us consider a simple example. Suppose that A and B find themselves in a situation in which each has but two alternative possible actions. Let these be a_1 and a_2 for A, b_1 and b_2 for B. There are four outcomes, one for each pair of possible actions, which we represent as $o_{11} = a_1 \times b_1$, and similarly o_{12}, o_{21} and o_{22}. Now let there be a utility-function for each person such that the utilities of the outcomes are as shown in this matrix, A's utilities appearing first:

	b_1	b_2
a_1	$o_{11}(0,3)$	$o_{12}(3,2)$
a_2	$o_{21}(1,0)$	$o_{22}(2,1)$

It is evident by inspection that if A expects B to perform b_1, A should perform a_2, but if B expects A to perform a_2, B should perform b_2. On the other hand, if A expects B to perform b_2, he should perform a_1, but if B expects A to perform a_1, she should perform b_1. There is no pair of actions such that each is utility maximizing against the other.

However, if we allow probability distributions over actions, there is such a pair. For if A expects B to randomize on an equal basis between b_1 and b_2, then any of his possible actions is utility maximizing, and if B expects A to randomize on an equal basis between a_1 and a_2, then any of her possible actions is utility maximizing. Hence the probability distributions $(1/2a_1 + 1/2a_2)$ and $(1/2b_1 + 1/2b_2)$ are utility maximizing against each other.

I shall say that the members of an n-tuple of actions, one for each of the n agents in a situation, are in *mutual equilibrium* if and only if each member of the n-tuple maximizes the respective agent's utility, given the other members of the n-tuple. It has been shown by Nash that, if we include probability distributions over possible actions as themselves possible actions, then in every situation with finitely many persons, each with a finite range of actions, there is at least one n-tuple of possible actions, such that its members are in mutual equilibrium.[12] Hence one condition which is necessary if each action is to be utility maximizing can be satisfied.

This completes my argument here for the possibility of utility maximization. The important conclusion for present purposes is that, in a situation involving several persons in which each assumes the cor-

[12]Nash [1].

rectness of the others' expectations, each must expect all of the actions to be in mutual equilibrium, if each is to maximize her utilities. If then we suppose that each person can determine correctly the actions of all persons, the identification of rationality with the aim of utility-maximimization entails that for rational persons in situations of interaction, all actions must be in mutual equilibrium.[13]

V

Moral philosophers have not been slow to challenge the identification of rationality with individual utility-maximization.[14] To maximize one's utilities is to act prudently, in that extended sense of the term which has become philosophically commonplace, or to act from self-interest, where self-interest is taken to embrace all one's aims, and not only one's self-directed aims. To identify rationality with the aim of utility-maximization is then to identify it with prudence, and insofar as morality is distinct from prudence, to distinguish it from morality. The moral man is not always rational, and the rational man not always moral. To many persons these consequences are unacceptable. Moral philosophers have responded in various ways; the most radical response has been to deny the rationality of utility-maximization.

Not all forms of this denial concern our present argument. But one of the principal objections to the rationality of utility-maximization rests on the insistence that reason and utility are indeed related, but in a way which is deeper than and incompatible with the relationship we have developed. And this type of objection we must consider.

Note first that it is in general not possible for every agent in a situation to achieve his maximum utility. Let us say that an outcome is best if and only if it affords each person in the situation at least as great a utility as that afforded him by any other outcome; then in general no outcome in a situation is best. Hence it would be futile to suppose that we should seek always to bring about best outcomes. However, in every situation there must be at least one outcome, and there may be many outcomes, which afford each person a *maximum compossible utility,* that is, the greatest utility each can receive, given the utilities received by the others. Such outcomes are termed *optimal* or *efficient;* an outcome is optimal if and only if there is no alternative possible outcome affording some person a greater utility and no person a lesser utility. It may seem evidently reasonable to require that in

[13] I shall not consider the possibility of utility-maximization in the case in which not all agents correctly assume that all expectations are correct.
[14] Cf. Moore, secs. 58–61; also Brandt, pp. 369–375.

any situation, every person should act to bring about an optimal outcome. For if the outcome is not optimal, then some persons might do better, yet no person does worse.

With the conception of optimality established, the first step of the objection is to point out that individual utility-maximization may lead to a non-optimal outcome. The well-known Prisoner's Dilemma is sufficient to show this.[15] The Dilemma is found in any situation which can be represented by such a matrix as this:

	b_1	b_2
a_1	$o_{11}(1,1)$	$o_{12}(10,0)$
a_2	$o_{21}(0,10)$	$o_{22}(9,9)$

It is evident on inspection that whatever B does, A maximizes his utility by his action a_1. Similarly, whatever A does, B maximizes her utility by her action b_1. Hence if we identify rationality with utility-maximization, and assume A and B are rational, they will achieve the outcome o_{11}, with a utility of 1 to each. But o_{22} would have afforded each a utility of 9. The actions a_1 and b_1 are in mutual equilibrium and indeed are the only actions in mutual equilibrium in this situation, but their outcome is not optimal. Hence we have a situation in which the requirement that individual utility-maximizers act in mutual equilibrium is incompatible with the proposal that the outcome of interaction be optimal.

Only in some situations will individual utility-maximization lead to a non-optimal outcome. But since the possibility of these situations cannot be ruled out, individual utility-maximizers cannot reasonably suppose that in the long run they will do as well for themselves as possible. Whenever they find themselves in an interaction situation in which no equilibrium n-tuple of actions leads to an optimal outcome, they will act to bring about an outcome which denies at least some of them utilities which they might have attained without any utility cost to the others.

But do persons behave irrationally in bringing about a non-optimal state of affairs? This has not yet been argued, so that the objection is incomplete. Consider, then, the following argument, which purports to show that because the policy of individual utility-maximization leads, in some situations, to non-optimal outcomes, it is therefore not rational.

What is rational for one person is rational for every person. Hence what is correctly judged rational for one person must be judged ra-

---

[15]The Prisoner's Dilemma is attributed to A. W. Tucker.

tional for every person, on pain of error. And what one person correctly judges rational, every person must judge rational, on pain of
error. Suppose then that some person, A, correctly judges himself
rational to maximize his own utility. Then he must judge each person
rational to maximize his (that person's) utility. And every person must
judge each person rational to maximize his own utility.

What constraint does the identification of rationality with the aim
of utility-maximization impose on this judgment? Since there is in
general no best outcome, the constraint may not require that every
person suppose his own utility maximized by that policy of action he
judges rational for each to follow. But the constraint must surely
require that every person expect for himself the maximum utility
compossible with that received by each other person, from that policy
of action he judges rational for each person. Thus, if every person
correctly judges each person rational to maximize his own utility, then
the policy of individual utility-maximization must afford every person
maximum compossible utility, or in other words, individual utility-
maximization must yield optimal outcomes, and only optimal outcomes. But we have shown that individual utility-maximization does
not always yield optimal outcomes. Therefore every person does not
correctly judge each person rational to maximize his own utility. Person A does not correctly judge each person rational to maximize his
own utility. And so A does not correctly judge himself rational to
maximize his own utility.

This argument captures a way of thinking about the universality of
rational judgments which is supposed to rule out the rationality of
prudence. But it is a bad argument. It will be recalled that I have
presupposed that we ascribe rationality primarily to the individual
person. Our concern is with practical reason, and so with the rational
agent. On the instrumental conception of reason, the rationality of an
agent is shown by the relation between the actions he takes himself to
perform, and his ends, his basis of action. If we consider this basis of
action to enter into his point of view, then we may say that the rationality of an agent is determined by assessing his intended actions in
relation to his point of view.

This is not to say that what is rational from one point of view is not
or may not be rational from another point of view. What is rational is
rational *sans phrase*. But it is the point of view of the agent which
determines, from every point of view, whether his actions, and he
himself, are rational. If a person A is to assess the rationality of another person B, then it is the relation of B's actions to B's utility, and
not the relation of B's actions to A's utility, which is relevant.

The fallacy in the argument just outlined is now easily detected.
The fallacious step is the claim that every person must expect for

himself the maximum utility compossible with that received by each other person, from that policy of action he judges rational for each person. A's maximum compossible utility is not the relevant criterion for assessing the rationality of the actions of persons other than himself, and hence not the relevant criterion for assessing the rationality of a policy of action insofar as it determines the actions of other persons.

In explicating practical rationality, the argument fails to take seriously the position of the *agent*. The question whether the aim of utility-maximization is rational is the question whether it is rational to *act* in a maximizing manner. It is not the question whether it is rational to act and to *be acted on* in this manner, for this question makes no sense. There is no way of being acted on which is as such either rational or irrational; there is no *rational patient* corresponding to the *rational agent*. There is, of course, the question whether utility-maximization is the most *desirable* way to act and be acted on, and this indeed is the question which is answered negatively by consideration of the Prisoner's Dilemma, for it is in part whether one's utility is maximized, given the utilities received by the other persons, if one acts and is acted on in accordance with the tenets of individual utility-maximization. But the answer to this question does not answer the question how it is rational to act, unless the way in which one acts determines the way in which others act. If in choosing how to act, one chooses how one is to be acted upon, then one's role as patient becomes relevant to one's role as agent. But this is to go beyond the argument we have considered.

VI

Let us then turn to the supposition that the way in which one acts determines the way in which others act, and *vice versa*. So far we have considered only *independent* action, action in a manner which each person selects for herself. But we may contrast this with *interdependent* action, action in a manner on which all agree.[16] Interdependent action is action in *civil society*, by which I understand a common frame-

---

[16]For interdependent action we modify our account of preference in the following way. What the agent takes herself to be doing can be coupled with her beliefs and the agreed manner of action to determine her intentional preference. Her attitudinal preference can be coupled with her beliefs and the agreed manner of action to determine a strategy. She is rational only if this strategy corresponds to what she takes herself to be doing. What she supposes she would do, were she sufficiently informed and reflective, can then be used to determine intentional preferability; what she supposes she would favor under these ideal conditions can be used to determine a strategy. She is rational only if what she favors and what she would favor determine the same strategy, which corresponds to what she takes herself to be doing and also to what she would do.

work of action. Independent action, then, may be termed action in a *state of nature*.

Since reason is the same for all, rational persons must adopt the same manner of action if they share the same condition. But this does not obliterate the distinction between independent and interdependent action. Independent rational persons will each *separately* adopt the same manner of action. Interdependent rational persons will *collectively* adopt a common manner of action. Interdependent persons will act in the same manner *because* all have agreed so to act; if they are rational, they will act because all have rationally agreed so to act.

What is the rational manner of interdependent, or agreed, action? This question would seem to be equivalent to, on what manner of action is it rational to agree? The identification of rationality with the aim of utility-maximization provides at least a necessary condition for rational agreement.[17] It would not be rational to agree to a way of acting if, should that way of acting be adopted, one would expect a utility less than the maximum compossible in the situation with the utility afforded by the agreement to every other part. And so it is rational for all concerned to agree to a way of acting only if, should it be adopted, each person may expect the maximum utility compossible, in the situation, with that utility which each other person expects. Or in other words, an agreed way of acting is rational only if it leads to an outcome which is optimal so far as the parties to the agreement are concerned.

Individual utility-maximization does not guarantee an optimal outcome. Thus, although in a particular situation, an agreement that each person seek to maximize her own utilities may lead to an optimal outcome, such an agreement will not in general lead to an optimal outcome, and so it is not, in itself, rational. But if it is not rational to agree to individual utility-maximization as such, then individual utility-maximization cannot be the rational manner of interdependent action. The argument against the identification of rationality with the aim of utility-maximization, misapplied to independent action, succeeds for interdependent action.

Indeed, it seems that the identification of rationality with the aim of individual utility-maximization leads to a contradiction. Consider any situation, such as that exemplified by the Prisoner's Dilemma, in which there is at least one outcome which affords greater utility to each person than the outcome of rational independent action. Then it is evidently possible to specify at least one agreement such that the outcome of acting on it affords each party to the agreement an ex-

---

[17]I shall not introduce a sufficient condition in this paper.

pected utility greater than that which he can expect by independent action. Hence if each person in the situation is rational, each must be willing to enter into some agreement. But if one enters an agreement rationally, then one must act rationally insofar as one acts in accordance with the agreement, at least if the circumstances remain as one envisages them in entering the agreement. Hence it must be rational for each person in the situation to act in accordance with some agreement.

Since the outcome of any agreement which each enters rationally must be optimal, the agreed actions of the persons cannot be in mutual equilibrium. Thus the agreement must require at least one party to it to act in such a way that the expected outcome does not afford her a utility at least as great as that of the outcome of some other action open to her. But then it cannot be rational for her to act in accordance with the agreement. Therefore there is at least one party to the agreement for whom it is both rational and not rational to act in accordance with the agreement. This is a contradiction; therefore either it is rational for such a person not to enter the agreement, or it is rational for her to keep the agreement. But the condition established in III, that a person acts rationally only if the expected outcome affords her a utility at least as great as that of the expected outcome of any possible action, is violated in either case. Therefore rationality cannot be identified with the aim of individual utility-maximization.

This last argument is again fallacious. A rational person must be willing to enter into an agreement only if entry would afford her a greater expected utility than any alternative action. But since in a situation of the type under consideration, any agreement leading to an optimal outcome would require some person to act irrationally, then, if every person is rational, the agreement must be violated. And so such an agreement must fail to secure its intended outcome. But then the actual expected outcome of entering the agreement need not afford each party a greater utility than the expected outcome of independent action. Since this can be known at the time of making the agreement, it is not the case that each person could rationally expect a greater utility from entry than from nonentry. And so it is not the case that it must be rational for each to enter an agreement. It would be rational for each to enter into an agreement were it rational for each to keep it, but since it is not rational for each to keep it, it is not rational for each to enter it.

Our reply defends the consistency of identifying rationality with the aim of utility-maximization only at the cost of denying the possibility of rational interdependent action in any form which genuinely differs from rational independent action. A rational agreement cannot require any person to perform an action which does not lead to an expected outcome with utility for her at least as great as the utility of the expected outcome of any action possible for her. Agreement, then, cannot enable people to escape from Prisoner's Dilemma situations. In such situations any mutually beneficial agreement would require each person to act irrationally, and so no one has reason to make such an agreement.

We seem obliged to conclude, with Hobbes,[18] that people cannot escape the state of nature by agreement alone. Of course, if by agreement actions can be made literally interdependent, so that what each party to the agreement does actually depends on what every other party does, then independent violation is impossible, and the agreement may prove effective. Or if by agreement the actions possible for each party may be altered, so that it is no longer possible for each to violate in a utility-maximizing manner, then the agreement may prove effective. Or again, if by agreement the utilities of some of the possible outcomes may be altered, so that the action which one would rationally perform in the absence of agreement no longer leads to an outcome with maximum possible utility, then also the agreement may prove effective. But in each of these cases the effectiveness of the agreement is secured by eliminating any conflict between the action required by the agreement, and the action which leads to an outcome with maximum expected utility for the agent. The agreement will then permit each person to seek to maximize her own utilities, but will impose constraints which ensure that this pursuit of individual utility-maximization will in fact lead to an optimal outcome.

But it would be a counsel of despair to conclude that rational interdependent action is impossible. The straightforward identification of rationality with the aim of individual utility-maximization, although not inconsistent, is nevertheless inadequate because it denies the possibility of agreements which require one or more of the parties to refrain from the maximization of individual utility, yet secure to each of the parties greater utility than is possible without such agreement. This inadequacy does not, however, show that rationality is not connected with maximizing activity. For it is just because those persons who identify rationality with straightforward individual utility-maximization will not always achieve optimal outcomes, that their conception of rationality is inadequate. I shall, therefore, attempt to formulate more adequately the connection between rationality and maximizing activity and then demonstrate that this more adequate conception can in fact be derived from an initial acceptance of the view that a

---

[18]Cf. Hobbes [4], chs. 14, 15, and 17.

person acts rationally only if the utility to her of the expected outcome of her action is as great as possible.

VII

Suppose that we restrict the rationality condition established in III to independent action. Thus it reads: a person acting independently acts rationally only if the expected outcome of his action affords him a utility at least as great as that of the expected outcome of any action possible for him in the situation. And suppose that we formulate a parallel condition for interdependent action, based on the claim that it is rational to agree to a way of acting only if, should that way of acting be adopted, one's expected utility would be the maximum compossible with the expected utility of each other party to the agreement. The condition would be: *A person acting interdependently acts rationally only if the expected outcome of his action affords each person with whom his action is interdependent a utility such that there is no combination of possible actions, one for each person acting interdependently, with an expected outcome which affords each person other than himself at least as great a utility, and himself a greater utility.*

Note that this latter condition in effect implies the former. For to act independently is to act interdependently with oneself alone. Hence by the condition for interdependent action, one acts rationally only if the expected outcome of one's action affords one (as the sole person with whom one is acting interdependently) a utility such that one has no possible action with an expected outcome affording one greater utility. And this is equivalent to the condition of independent action.

It is therefore possible to eliminate the phrase "acting interdependently" from the formulation of the new condition. It is then a general alternative to the unrestricted condition established in III. This new condition requires each person to seek to maximize his utility, not given the *actions* of all other persons in the situation but rather given the *utilities* of those with whom he acts interdependently, and the actions of any other persons—persons not party to the agreement. This condition does not represent a policy of utility-maximization, as ordinarily understood. Nevertheless, the policy following from this condition is clearly intended to maximize the agent's overall expected utility, by enabling him to participate in agreements intended to secure optimal outcomes, when maximizing actions performed in the absence of agreement would lead to non-optimal outcomes. Hence I propose to term this the condition of agreement-constrained utility-maximization, or, for short, the *condition of constrained maximization*. And by constrained maximization, I mean that policy, or any policy, which requires individual utility-maximization in the state of nature and agreed optimization in society.

Agreed optimization, I should note, is not a determinate policy of social action. In most situations there are infinitely many expected outcomes which are optimal; an agreement must single out one such outcome for each situation to which it applies and require the actions which lead to that outcome. The condition of constrained maximization must be combined with a condition of agreement, to test the rationality of policies of action. We may assume that a rational condition of agreement will require that the expected outcome afford each party to the agreement greater utility than the expected outcome of independent action, for otherwise a rational person will not enter an agreement. But this generally allows considerable opportunity for negotiation, and no test has been provided for the rationality of such negotiation. To provide such a test is to determine the rational distribution of those utilities which are the product of agreement, or, in other words, to determine the rational manner of cooperative activity. This task, which may also be expressed as the task of developing a theory of distributive justice, I have attempted elsewhere.[19]

Leaving aside this question, then, how can we defend constrained maximization? If we identify rationality with the aim of individual utility-maximization, we are led, as I have shown, to the condition of III, which may be termed the *condition of straightforward maximization*. A policy of straightforward maximization requires individual utility-maximization under all circumstances and thus destroys the real possibility of society as a condition in which men act differently than in the state of nature.

We resolve this problem by introducing a new consideration. Suppose a person is to choose his conception of rationality. In such a situation of choice, the several possible actions have, as their outcomes, different possible conceptions of rationality. Hence his action, in choosing, is open to rational assessment. What conception of rationality is it rational for him to choose?

This may seem an impossible question to answer. For, it may be urged, one can only assess the rationality of a choice given some conception of rationality. But if the choice is among such conceptions, by what conception can one make the assessment? It might be suggested that one should assess one's choice by the conception chosen; it is rational to choose a conception of rationality if, given that conception of rationality, it is rational to choose it. This condition, however,

[19]Cf. Gauthier [6] and "Justice and Natural Endowment," above; more recently Gauthier [5], esp. ch. 5.

seems to be necessary rather than sufficient. If the choice of a certain conception of rationality is not rational, given that conception, then it is surely not a rational choice. But there may be several incompatible conceptions of rationality, each of which is self-supporting in the manner just considered.

Let us return to our point of departure—economic man. The traditional view of his rationality is expressed by the condition of straightforward maximization. We shall assume this condition and ask what conception of rationality one should choose to afford one the expectation of maximum utility. Is it rational for economic man to choose to be a straightforward maximizer? Or is the form of rationality traditionally ascribed to him not self-supporting?

Our previous arguments make the answers to these questions evident. If we compare the effects of holding the condition of straightforward maximization, with the effects of holding the condition of constrained maximization, we find that in all those situations in which individual utility-maximization leads to an optimal outcome, the expected utility of each is the same, but in those situations in which individual utility-maximization does not lead to an optimal outcome, the expected utility of straightforward maximization is less. In these latter situations, a constrained maximizer, but not a straightforward maximizer, can enter rationally into an agreement to act to bring about an optimal outcome which affords each party to the agreement a utility greater than he would attain acting independently. Now it does not follow from this that such an agreement will come about, for at the very least the status of the other persons in the situation— whether they are straightforward or constrained maximizers, or neither—will be relevant to what happens. And even if an agreement is reached, a constrained maximizer is committed to carrying it out only in the context of mutual expectations on the part of all parties to the agreement that it will be carried out. It would not be rational to carry out an agreement if one supposed that, because of the defections of others, the expected outcome would afford one less utility than the outcome one would have expected had no agreement been made. Nevertheless, since the constrained maximizer has in some circumstances some probability of being able to enter into, and carry out, an agreement, whereas the straightforward maximizer has no such probability, the expected utility of the constrained maximizer is greater. Therefore straightforward maximization is not self-supporting; it is not rational for economic man to choose to be a straightforward maximizer.

Is it, then, rational for economic man to choose to be a constrained maximizer? Is there any other conception of rationality, adoption of which would afford him the expectation of greater utility? It is evident that in the context of independent action, either maximizing conception affords one the expectation of the greatest utility possible. In the context of interdependent action, one's expectation of utility will depend on the type of agreement one makes. We have noted that the condition of constrained maximization does not determine this. But the constrained maximizer is committed only to make and carry out agreements which afford him the expectation of greater utility than independent action.

Here then I can argue only that to choose to identify rationality with constrained maximization, insofar as it commits one to seek optimal outcomes, may well afford one an expectation of utility as great as is afforded by the choice of any other conception of rationality, and at least affords one the expectation of greater utility than to choose to identify rationality with straightforward maximization. Hence a rational person who begins by adopting the policy of individual utility-maximization, in accordance with the condition of straightforward maximization, will, following that policy, choose a different conception of rationality and will prefer a policy which requires agreed optimization whenever possible, to his original policy and possibly to any alternative policy.

VIII

The supposition that a person chooses, or can choose, her conception of rationality raises many problems which fall outside the scope of this essay. Some may argue that the supposition is unintelligible, insisting that, whatever the status of other norms, the norms of rationality are given and not chosen. Now there is a sense in which this is so from the standpoint of each individual, even on our position. For a person does not and cannot begin by selecting a conception of rationality *in vacuo*. Rather, she begins and must begin with a conception which she does not choose but which affords her the rational basis for a further choice, which may confirm the original conception or may set it aside in favor of a different conception. But the initial conception itself need be given only from the individual's standpoint. Conceptions of rationality are, I should suppose, not fixed in human nature, but rather the products of human socialization. There seems to me little doubt that the conception of rationality has undergone social change, that neither in classical nor in medieval society was rationality identified with maximizing activity. But I have claimed that in our society the received conception, which most persons do accept initially given their socialization, does identify rationality with maximizing activity. And this identification is usually expressed by the condition of straightforward maximization.

Far from supposing that the choice of a conception of rationality is unintelligible, I want to argue that the capacity to make such a choice is itself a necessary part of full rationality. A person who is unable to submit her conception of rationality to critical assessment, indeed to the critical assessment which must arise from the conception itself, is rational in only a restricted and mechanical sense. She is a conscious agent, but not fully a self-conscious agent, for she lacks the freedom to make not only her situation but herself in her situation, her practical object. Although we began by agreeing, with Hume, that reason is the slave of the passions, we must agree, with Kant, that in a deeper sense reason is freedom.

In philosophical literature, the classic example of the person who is bound by his conception of reason is Hobbesian man, the self-maintaining engine. The restricted rationality of Hobbesian man becomes evident in Hobbes's insistence that, although men recognize the rational necessity of interdependent action, the necessity, in other words, that each man should covenant with his fellows "to lay down [his] right to all things; and be contented with so much liberty against other men, as he would allow other men against himselfe,"[20] yet "the Validity of Covenants begins not," and so interdependent action is impossible, "but with the Constitution of a Civill Power, sufficient to compell men to keep them."[21] Men recognize the rationality of entering society, but force, not reason, is required to keep them there.

Hobbesian man is unable to internalize the social requirement that he subordinate his direct pursuit of survival and well-being to the agreed pursuit of optimal outcomes which best ensure the survival and well-being of each person. Thus in our terms Hobbesian man actually remains in the state of nature; the civil power, the Sovereign, can effect only the appearance of civil society, of interdependent action. The real difference between the state of nature and civil society must be a difference in man, and not merely in the external relations of men.

While acknowledging Hobbes's masterful portrayal of the straightforward maximizer, we must offer a different conception of rational man. To the received conception of economic man, we must add Rousseau's recognition that the "passage from the state of nature to civil society produces in man a very remarkable change, in substituting justice for instinct in his conduct, and giving his actions the moral-

---

[20]Hobbes [4], ch. 14.
[21]Ibid., ch. 15.

ity which previously they lacked."[22] This passage introduces the last of the concepts we must relate to the identification of rational activity with maximizing activity, the concept of morality. We must conclude by giving economic man a moral dimension.

In our argument, two contexts of action have been distinguished: independent action, in which each person determines his own principle of action, which has been identified with the state of nature, and interdependent action, in which all act on a common principle, which has been identified with civil society. The rational policy of independent action is individual utility-maximization; the rational policy of interdependent action is, or rather involves, agreed optimization. Both of these policies satisfy the condition of constrained maximization, which I have argued best expresses the identification of rational activity with maximizing activity. Only the first of these policies satisfies the more usual condition of straightforward maximization, which I have argued is inadequate because it rules out rational interdependent action. Economic man is usually assumed to accept the condition of straightforward maximization; if we are to continue to identify him with rational man, we must suppose instead that he accepts the condition of constrained maximization.

The policy of individual utility-maximization may be identified with prudence, provided we think of the prudent man as characterized by an exclusive and direct concern with what *he* wants, whatever that may be, and not necessarily by a concern for himself as the object of his wants. The policy of agreed optimization may be identified with morality. For if it be agreed that morality must be rational, or at least not anti-rational, and that morality involves some restraint in the pursuit of one's wants and desires, then agreed optimization is the only candidate. For on the condition of constrained maximization, it is rational to restrain one's pursuit of one's own aims only to fulfil an agreement to seek an optimal outcome unattainable by independent utility-maximization.

Morality may thus be placed within the bounds of the maximizing activity of economic man, given our enlarged conception of economic man, and yet distinguished from prudence, from the direct pursuit of one's wants and desires. The moral man is no less concerned with his own well-being than is the prudent man, but he recognizes that an exclusive attention to that well-being would prevent him from participation in mutually beneficial agreements.

We might then express the relation between prudence and morality accurately, if apparently paradoxically, by saying that the prudent

[22]Rousseau [2], I, viii, translation mine. Cf. Baier, pp. 311–315.

man considers it rational to *become* moral, but not rational to *be* moral. On prudential grounds he can justify the adoption of moral, rather than prudential, grounds of action, but only if he does adopt moral grounds, and so becomes a moral man, can he justify a moral, rather than a prudential, policy of action.

In this essay I have not attempted to develop an adequate theory of either prudential or moral action. In situations in which people interact independently, rational persons with full knowledge will perform actions in mutual equilibrium, but I have not considered the problem of coordination, which arises in those situations in which there is more than one set of possible actions in mutual equilibrium. In situations in which men interact interdependently, rational persons with full knowledge will perform actions leading to an optimal outcome, but as I have indicated previously, I have not considered the problem of cooperation, or distributive justice, which arises in selecting a particular optimum.

We must not expect that an account of morality, based on agreed optimization, will necessarily resemble our existing conception of morality. There is little reason to suppose that our present conception has developed to correspond to rationality, conceived as identified in any way with utility-maximization. In particular, it is evident that morality, as agreed optimization, can concern only the production and distribution of those benefits which people can secure for themselves only by agreement; it cannot concern those benefits which people can or could secure for themselves independently. Our present conception of morality is by no means limited in this respect.

The implications of a rational morality, given the identification of practical rationality with any form of maximization, have not, I think, been adequately understood by our utilitarian and contractarian moral theorists.[23] But these implications are in fact quite straightforward consequences of the conception of man with which this essay began. The morality, and the rationality, with which we have been concerned, are the morality and rationality of economic man, and it is to the adequacy of economic man, as our conception of what it is to be human, that we must turn if rationality as constrained maximization, and morality as agreed optimization, should seem questionable doctrines.

[23]John Rawls and R. M. Hare are two leading examples. For Rawls the identification is quite explicit; cf. Rawls [1], pp. 142–143. For Hare it is more difficult to document, but it is surely implicit; cf. Hare [1], chs. 6 and 7, esp. pp. 92–93, 122–123. "Justice and Natural Endowment," above, attempts to show Rawls's failure to grasp the implications of rational morality. To show Hare's failure is certainly not the work of a footnote, but, in a phrase, he goes astray because his universal prescriptivism conflates agent and patient; cf. V supra.

[11]

The Incompleat Egoist

I. What Can an Egoist Do?

1. "Egoism . . . is the doctrine which holds that we ought each of us to pursue our own greatest happiness as our ultimate end."[1] Thus G. E. Moore, who proceeded to charge this doctrine with "flagrant contradiction."[2] "The egoistic principle," Brian Medlin asserted, "is inconsistent."[3] In leveling these accusations, Moore and Medlin have been representative of a host of philosophers who have found egoism wanting in rationality. But why accuse the egoist? Left to himself, surely he seeks only to do as well for himself as possible, and this intent, if not wholly attractive, seems to fall squarely within the confines of the economist's utility-maximizing conception of practical rationality—hardly, then, what we should expect to find contradictory or inconsistent.[4] Philosophers are blessed with both talent for and desire of finding paradox where other mortals suspect none, yet

Reprinted with permission of the University of Utah Press from the *Tanner Lectures on Human Values*, vol. 5 (University of Utah Press and Cambridge University Press, copyright 1984).

[1]Moore, p. 96.

[2]Ibid., p. 102.

[3]Medlin, p. 118.

[4]Note that the egoist's aim is not dictated by the utility-maximizing conception of practical rationality. What is rational, according to this conception, is to do as well as possible—to maximize some measure defined over the possible outcomes of one's actions. The characteristics of the measure to be maximized are left largely unspecified by this maximizing requirement. The egoist adds to the idea of doing as well as possible the specification that the measure be self-directed, so that he may do as well *for himself* as possible.

what, *rationally,* could be at fault with the attempt to do as well for oneself as possible?

As a philosopher, I have up my sleeve what, if not truly paradoxical, should seem unexpectedly puzzling. But the questions I shall raise about egoism come, not from the traditional philosophical repertoire, but rather from the theory of rational choice. More particularly, although the lone egoist will pass rational scrutiny, yet when put with others of his persuasion, in interaction in which each seeks to maximize his own happiness, grounds for challenging the rationality of egoism appear. And these grounds concern, not so much the egoist's concern with his own happiness, but rather his maximizing principle of choice. Something is amiss in our account of practical rationality.

2. Let us then focus briefly on the theory of rational choice. We may first recall a dictum laid down by John Rawls: "The theory of justice is a part, perhaps the most significant part, of the theory of rational choice."[5] I shall interpret this dictum in a quite un-Rawlsian way, and in order to sketch my interpretation I must temporarily set egoism to one side; but before doing this, let us note an immediate connection between Rawls's claim and our concern with the rationality of egoism. If the theory of justice is literally a part of the theory of rational choice, and so much a part that justice proves to be required in rational choice, then it would seem that either justice is compatible with egoism, or that egoism is not compatible with rationality. If the former is implausible, then we may expect the case for the rationality of justice to be linked to the case against egoism. And both will depend on a proper understanding of rational choice.

Before concluding our reflections we shall indeed have proceeded from an argument against the rationality of egoism to an argument linking, not only justice, but morality, with rational choice. But that link comes at the end of a long chain. Here let us reflect on what Rawls said and generalize it to what I believe—that moral theory as a whole is part of choice or decision theory. What I believe, however, is *not* what Rawls believes.

I treat moral principles as principles *for* rational choice. In a very general and important type of interaction, which I shall call *cooperative,* a rational actor would—I claim—base her choice among possible actions on a moral principle, provided she expected others to do likewise. In section five of this part I shall consider what a principle for choice, or for action, is, and in the second part I shall explain why a rational actor would base choices on principles appropriately characterized as moral.

[5]Rawls [1], p. 16.

Rawls treats the principles of justice, not as principles *for* rational choice, but as objects *of* rational choice.[6] This is a very different matter. For Rawls the principles of justice determine the basic structure of society. He asks, what principles, constitutive of society, would a rational individual choose in the "original position," behind a veil of ignorance making her unaware of her identity except as a free and equal person. Rawls identifies the principles so chosen with the principles of justice. This is how he connects the theory of justice with the theory of rational choice.

Note the differences between us. Rawls asks: *what* would rational actors choose behind a veil of ignorance? He answers: they would choose the principles of justice. I ask: *how* would rational actors choose in cooperative interaction? I answer: they would choose on the basis of moral principles. For Rawls the principles of justice constitute the *solution* to a particular problem of rational choice.[7] For me moral principles are used by persons in *solving* certain problems of rational choice. Rawls uses principles of rational choice as tools in developing his theory of justice. I develop moral theory as part of the theory of rational choice—as part of the theory that determines what principles a rational actor would use in choice.

There is a second equally important difference between Rawls's attempt to use rational choice in characterizing justice and my attempt to develop morality as part of rational choice. And this difference bears directly on my concern with egoism. The theory of rational choice examines two significantly different forms of agency, parametric and strategic.[8] The parametric actor chooses in an environment that, whether its characteristics be known to her or not, she treats as fixed in relation to her choice. Her choice is a response to circumstances that are not, or are not considered to be, responsive to her as choosing. The strategic actor chooses in an environment that is responsive to her as a chooser. She relates her choices to an environment that includes other actors seeking to relate to her choices. Egoism, we shall find, succeeds for parametric choice but fails for strategic choice.

To illuminate the difference between parametric and strategic choice, consider a simple illustration. Jane must choose whether to go to Ann's party. She wants to go, but only if Brian will not be there. In case one, Jane expects Brian to go to Ann's party unless his father needs him to deliver pizza, a matter having nothing to do with Jane. Whether Brian is needed to deliver pizza is, for Jane, an unknown but

[6]My account here reflects Rawls [1], secs. 2–4.
[7]See Rawls [1], sec. 20.
[8]For this distinction between parametric and strategic, see Elster, pp. 18–19, 117–123.

fixed circumstance. If she considers it likely that he is needed, she will choose to go to Ann's party; if she considers it unlikely, she will choose not to go. Jane faces a problem of parametric choice.

In case two, Brian must also choose whether to go to Ann's party. He does not want to go unless Jane will be there. Here Jane chooses on the basis of her expectation of Brian's choice, and Brian chooses on the basis of his expectation of Jane's choice. Thus Jane chooses on the basis of her expectation of a choice based on an expectation of her choice. And Brian chooses similarly. Each faces a problem of strategic choice.

Rawls relates the principles of justice, not to strategic, but to parametric choice. This may seem surprising, since he supposes that the principles would be agreed to by all rational persons in the original position. And so it may seem that each seeks to relate her choice of principles to the choices of others who are themselves seeking to relate their choices to her choice. But Rawls emphasizes that this appearance of strategic interaction is misleading.[9] Behind the veil of ignorance, persons are identically situated, not only in their objective circumstances but also subjectively, in that each is completely ignorant of her capacities and interests and so is unable to distinguish herself from her fellows. They have, then, no basis for bargaining with one another, and agreement on the principles of justice may be represented by the choice of a single representative individual. The problem of rational choice to be solved is therefore one of individual decision under extraordinary uncertainty. And this is a problem of parametric choice.

I relate moral principles to strategic choice. As I shall argue, moral principles direct choice in cooperative interaction in which each person, fully aware of her particular circumstances, capacities, and concerns, seeks to relate her actions to those of others in ways beneficial to each. The rationale for moral principles—and the irrationale, we may say, for egoistic principles—emerges from an examination of the structure of such interaction.

At the end of our enquiry I shall return to this difference between Rawls and myself—a difference that also distinguishes my contractarian approach to moral theory from the utilitarian argument of John Harsanyi.[10] I suggest that there is a deep incoherence in the attempt to relate moral principles to parametric choice, since parametric choice does not fully accommodate the interaction of rational beings. Strategic rationality, which focuses on this interaction, is not

[9]See Rawls [1], p. 139.
[10]See Harsanyi [2], esp. chs. 2 and 6, secs. 1–5.

fully egoistic, and moral theory is properly based on the failure of strategic egoism.

3. Once again I have indicated a destination. At the end of our brief journey we should understand more clearly both why egoism fails and how morality relates to strategic choice. At the beginning we must relate egoism to parametric rationality.

I shall assume that rational parametric choice may be represented by a simple maximizing model. That is, I shall suppose that a parametrically rational actor behaves as if he is maximizing the expected value of some function defined over the possible outcomes of his choices. For the model adequately to represent risky and uncertain choices, in which the actor does not know the outcome of each possible choice but rather is able to assign to each only a probability distribution over possible outcomes,[11] the function must be uniquely defined up to a positive linear transformation, so that it affords an interval measure of the outcomes. A familiar example of an interval measure is temperature; the zero-point and the unit may be selected arbitrarily, but once selected the unit is constant.

I shall not ask whether rationality in parametric choice is fully captured by maximization. For our purposes we need not decide whether an actor is rational insofar as he maximizes, without consideration of what he maximizes. Thus I shall take maximization only as necessary for parametric rationality. But I shall make one further, crucial assumption—that the value maximized by an actor is relative to him. If Mary voted for Reagan and Harry for Carter, then we may suppose that Reagan being president had greater expected value than Carter being president as an object of Mary's choice, but lesser expected value as an object of Harry's choice.

This assumption, that value is relative and that choice is based on actor-relative value, may be related to strategic as well as to parametric rationality. Although we shall find that rational strategic choice may not always be represented by a simple maximizing model, yet strategically rational actors may be considered as assigning values to the possible outcomes. In interaction the interval measures defined by the several actors over possible outcomes are logically independent one from another. Brian's most valued outcome may be, and indeed is, Jane's least valued outcome. An outcome has no single value but a set of values, one for each actor, or indeed for each person affected by it, and there is no relationship a priori among the members of the set.

The egoist, whom we kept in a secondary role in our discussion of

---

[11]We speak of risk if the probabilities are objective, of uncertainty if they are subjective.

rational choice, has now reappeared, slightly disguised, as a species of parametrically rational actor. We first introduced the egoist as the person who pursues his own greatest happiness. He is a maximizer, albeit of a rather specific quantity—his own happiness. But for our purposes we may generalize from this characterization and think of the egoist as maximizing whatever actor-relative value he pleases— perhaps his own happiness, perhaps not. He is then simply the person whose interests, whatever they may be, have no necessary link with the interests of his fellows, so that his values provide a measure of states of affairs quite independent of their values. This generic account affords a very weak characterization of an egoist, and indeed even an excessively weak one, since it admits to the egoistic ranks persons whose interests are other-directed, provided only that their other-directed interests are not simply dependent on others' interests. But it is all that our argument will require. Our egoist then is simply a maximizer, or would-be maximizer, of actor-relative value. He satisfies the necessary condition of parametric rationality.

Before proceeding to face the egoist with the problems of interaction, I should note, out of fairness to G. E. Moore, that in introducing the maximization of actor-relative value I have already embraced what to him was the contradictory feature of egoism. For Moore, "The *good* of [something] can in no possible sense be 'private' or belong to me; any more than a thing can *exist* privately or *for* one person only."[12] Moore could allow that a state of affairs might further the well-being of one person but not that of another. He could allow that a state of affairs might be good in that it furthered one person's well-being and bad in that it hindered another's. But he denied that a state of affairs could be good in relation to the person whose well-being it furthered and bad in relation to the person whose well-being it hindered. Rather he insisted that it must be good absolutely insofar as it hindered one person's well-being and bad absolutely insofar as it hindered another's.

Moore's position might be formulated as a claim about the universality of reasons for choosing or acting. On this view, for any states of affairs p and q, if there is a person X who is able to choose between p and q and has a reason for choosing p over q, then any person Y able to choose between p and q has a reason for choosing p over q. This position is embraced by many philosophers other than Moore, such as R. M. Hare and Thomas Nagel, but in embracing actor-relative value I propose to ignore it.[13]

[12]Moore, p. 99.
[13]See Hare [2], esp. chs. 5–7; and Nagel, esp. ch. 10.

On my view reasons for choosing have only a weaker universality. For any states of affairs p and q, if there is a person X who is able to choose between p and q and has a reason for choosing p over q, then there is some relation R holding among X, p, and q, such that, for any person Y who is able to choose between p and q, (1) R need not hold among Y, p, and q, but (2) if R does hold among Y, p, and q, then Y has a reason for choosing p over q. The actor-relativity of reasons is assured by founding them on a relation between the actor and the objects of choice that does not hold for every person by virtue of holding for some person.

Suppose that Moore and I agree that enhancing my prospects of survival is a reason for me to choose to have a site for the disposal of nuclear wastes located in the Antarctic rather than in Allegheny County. We might expect that for Moore this would instantiate the claim: for all persons X and Y and all states of affairs p and q, if p affords X greater survival prospects than q, Y has a reason for choosing p over q. For me it instantiates the claim: for all persons X and states of affairs p and q, if p affords X greater survival prospects than q, then X has a reason for choosing p over q.

If Moore were right, and reasons were not actor-relative, then the maximization of some actor-relative measure of possible outcomes would be an irrational basis for choice. Not only egoism, but the entire edifice of the standard theory of rational choice, the theory that characterizes parametric rationality, would collapse. This affords an easy, but in my view unpersuasive, refutation of egoism. In granting actor-relative value, I concede egoism the initial stage of the argument concerning its rationality.

4. We are now ready to ask: what happens when the egoist, or more generally the parametrically rational actor, finds herself interacting with others of her kind? Does the endeavor to maximize actor-relative value involve her in contradiction? Or inconsistency? Or some other form of irrationality? Is it always possible for her to put her egoism into practice? And if, or when, it is possible, is it always rational, or at least not irrational, for her to maximize?

In answering, or trying to answer, these questions, we must focus not on interaction in general but on strategic interaction. Were the egoist not faced with strategic problems, problems in which she seeks to adapt her choice to the choices of others adapting their choices to hers, the issues we shall raise would not appear. To the extent to which interaction is not conceived in strategic terms, egoism seems fully, and perhaps even paradigmatically, rational.

This is an historically important consideration. For the most thoroughly studied form of interaction, that which occurs in the perfectly competitive market, is parametric and not strategic in character. Although each actor in the market is interacting with others of his kind, yet each chooses in a fixed environment. The firm seeks to maximize profits given known costs of factor supply and known prices reflecting aggregate consumer demand. The consumer seeks to maximize the value of her commodity bundle given known commodity prices. Since choices have fixed and indeed known outcomes, market interaction may be represented by a model that dispenses with interval measures of those outcomes in favor of weak orderings. A world conforming in every detail to the ideal of the perfectly competitive market would not raise the problems that we shall examine. Egoism is rational within the framework of the market, as Adam Smith implicitly recognized in his doctrine of the Invisible Hand, and the modern appeal of egoism is not unrelated to the dominance of the market framework in our practical thought.

But not all economic behavior is perfectly competitive, and not all behavior is economic. The market adequately models only a limited range of interaction. In adopting the title *Theory of Games and Economic Behavior*, Von Neumann and Morgenstern were calling attention to the insufficiently understood strategic dimension found in most interaction.[14] And it is this dimension that interests us, as we examine the problems that arise in attempting to extend the simple maximizing model of parametric rationality to accommodate strategic choice.

We shall discover two principal and distinct issues. The first is expressed in the claim that egoism is *inconsistent*—or unable always to give consistent guidance to choice. The second is expressed in the claim that egoism is *self-defeating*—that egoists fall farther short of their objectives than do some non-egoists. The first charge, we shall find, has no simple resolution. The second charge will be sustained, and in sustaining it we shall come to the constructive problem to which our argument is propaedeutic—to the development of moral theory as part of rational choice. We shall then understand why the strategically rational actor must be, or at least must become, a moral actor.

Let us now illustrate the two charges that we shall assess. I shall then spend the remainder of this part in examining inconsistency, leaving self-defeatingness to its successor.

The claim that egoism is inconsistent may be illustrated by our original example of strategic choice. Jane and Brian must each choose whether to go to Ann's party. Each, we suppose, has two and only two

---

[14]Von Neumann and Morgenstern's study is the seminal work from which studies of strategic rationality have developed.

choices—to go, or not to go. If both choose to go, then Jane has chosen wrongly; she wants to go to the party, but only if Brian is not there. If neither chooses to go to the party, then Jane has also chosen wrongly; she wants to go to the party if Brian is not there. If one chooses to go and the other chooses not to go, then Brian has chosen wrongly; he wants to go to the party if and only if Jane is there. Whatever Jane and Brian choose, one of them fails to maximize his or her value. Hence one has failed to satisfy the requirements of egoism. But this failure is unavoidable. The requirements, then, can not always be satisfied. Egoism, and indeed the maximization of actor-relative value, is inconsistent.

The claim that egoism is self-defeating may be illustrated by an example long familiar among game theorists and now widely known to philosophers—the Prisoner's Dilemma. Jack and Zack are prisoners charged with a serious crime; each must choose between a confession that implicates the other and non-confession. If only one confesses, he is rewarded for turning state's evidence with a light sentence, while the other receives the maximum. If both confess, each receives a heavy sentence, but short of the maximum. If neither confesses, each will be convicted on a lesser charge and receive a sentence slightly heavier than that which would reward turning state's evidence. Jack reasons that, if Zack confesses, then he avoids the maximum sentence by confessing himself, whereas if Zack does not confess, then he gains the lightest sentence by confessing. Whatever Zack does, Jack does better to confess. Zack of course reasons in a parallel way. Given that neither is able to affect the other's choice by his own, each does better to confess, whatever the other may choose to do. Jack and Zack each maximizes his value by confessing. Each receives a heavy sentence. If neither had confessed, each would have received a lighter sentence. Jack and Zack have both satisfied the requirements of egoism and have reached a mutually costly outcome. The requirements, then, should not always be satisfied. Egoism is self-defeating.

5. To charge egoism with both inconsistency and self-defeatingness may seem excessive. If egoism fails in that it makes demands that cannot be met, then why consider whether those demands are also self-defeating? The answer, of course, is that the charge of inconsistency does not affect every situation in which persons may endeavor to act egoistically. Only in some interactions, such as that of Jane and Brian, does egoism fail to direct choice.

We must be clear about the nature of this failure. Either Jane or Brian does not realize her or his most preferred outcome, but this is not sufficient to show failure of choice. If Brian chooses to go to Ann's party, then Jane, whatever she chooses, cannot realize her most preferred outcome, which is to be at the party without Brian. If Jane chooses to stay home, then Brian, whatever he chooses, cannot realize his most preferred outcome. In these cases, one person's most preferred outcome is excluded by the other's choice. Failure to realize one's most preferred outcome thus need not show that one has chosen wrongly and does not in itself raise a problem for egoism. Some persons may take egoism to be inconsistent because egoists have incompatible objectives, so that not all can succeed. But the mere existence of incompatible objectives does not prevent any individual from doing as well for himself as possible, where what is possible must be determined in part by the choices of others. However, in the situation we are examining, either Jane or Brian fails to do as well as possible given the other's choice, and it is this failure, to choose what will maximize one's value given the possibilities left open by the choices of others, that is at the root of the charge that egoism is unable always to give consistent directives.

The inconsistency of egoism thus seems to arise in the following way. The egoist would be a maximizer of actor-relative value in strategic interaction. What is required for one to be such a maximizer? It would seem that one must always choose what maximizes one's value given the choices of the others. Our example shows that it may be impossible for everyone to make such a choice. *Any* person can make such a choice; given the choices of others any person has a maximizing alternative. But not *every* person can make such a choice. Not everyone can always be a maximizer of actor-relative value in strategic interaction. Egoism, in requiring this, is inconsistent.

This argument moves too quickly. In a world of risk and uncertainty, even the parametrically rational actor can not ensure that he maximizes actor-relative value. Given his estimate of the probability of alternative circumstances, he can maximize *expected* actor-relative value, but in choice he can set his sights no higher. Similarly, the strategically rational actor must be satisfied if he maximizes expected value. And to do this, he need not always choose what maximizes his value given the choices of the others, but only what maximizes his value given the choices he expects the others to make. If Jane supposes it unlikely that Brian will choose to go to the party, then she may maximize her expected value by choosing to go. If Brian supposes it likely that Jane will choose to go to the party, then he may maximize his expected value by choosing to go. Jane will then be disappointed by the outcome, but her choice, it may seem, satisfies the requirements of egoism. We have found no reason to claim that not everyone can be a maximizer of expected actor-relative value in strategic choice, even if some must be disappointed by the outcome.

But this rejoinder also moves too quickly. Let us suppose that Jane and Brian know each other to be would-be maximizers of actor-relative value. Then for each to maximize expected value, each must choose on an expectation about the choice the other will make based on an expectation about what his or her own choice will be. If Jane chooses to go to the party, she does so expecting Brian to choose not to go because he expects her to choose not to go. If Jane chooses to stay home, she does so expecting Brian to choose to go because he expects her to choose to go. Whatever she chooses, Jane must base her choice, if it maximizes her expected value, on an expectation that requires Brian to have a mistaken expectation about her choice. And similarly, Brian must base his choice on an expectation that requires Jane to have a mistaken expectation about his choice.

We may now give a more satisfactory explanation of the failure that seems to make egoism inconsistent. The egoist would maximize expected actor-relative value in strategic choice. Thus he must seek to maximize his value given the choices he expects to be made by others who seek to maximize their values given the choices they expect to be made by others, himself included. But the following three propositions can not all be true:

(1) An egoist always chooses to maximize value given the choices he expects others to make.
(2) An egoist always expects other egoists to choose to maximize value given the choices they expect others, himself included, to make.
(3) In satisfying 1 and 2, an egoist is never required to suppose that the expectations of other egoists are mistaken.

The failure of egoism thus lies in the necessity of attributing mistaken expectations to others in situations such as that of Jane and Brian, in order to suppose that each person chooses to maximize actor-relative value given the choices he expects the others to make.

Let us introduce some useful terminology for expressing what we have argued. An action maximizing the actor's value in interaction with others is a *best response* to the others' actions. An egoist chooses an expected best response. In some situations no set of actions, one for each person, is a set each member of which is a best response to the other members. In the terminology of the theory of games, a set of mutual best responses is a *Nash-equilibrium* set;[15] in some situations

---

[15]The term "Nash-equilibrium" refers to John F. Nash, who is responsible for the core result concerning equilibrium in strategic interaction to be discussed in the next section.

there is no Nash-equilibrium set of actions. In such situations egoists can all choose expected best responses only if some have mistaken expectations. The existence of a Nash-equilibrium set of actions is a necessary condition for successful and informed egoistic choice.

Let us treat a *principle for choice* as a function that takes sets of alternative actions into subsets of themselves. (For any set S, the corresponding subset is then termed the *choice set*, C(S).) A principle is *complete* for any domain if and only if it takes each member of the domain into a nonempty subset. A principle is *egoistic* only if it takes each set S into a subset C(S), the members of which maximize some measure defined over S. In a community of sufficiently informed egoists, a principle that determines a choice for each person involved in an interaction must determine choices that maximize each person's value given the other choices it determines. In other words, a principle that includes in its domain all of the sets of alternative actions making up an interaction must take each set into a subset which has as members only actions belonging also to Nash-equilibrium sets for the interaction. Since for some interactions there is no Nash-equilibrium set, there can be no egoistic principle for choice defined over the domain consisting of all sets of alternative actions in all possible interactions. There can be no egoistic principle of choice complete for all strategic interaction. This gives precise sense to the accusation that egoism is inconsistent.

6. Having called the resources of the theory of rational choice to our aid, we now find that they open unexpected complexities in our attempt to assess the consistency of egoism. Only the first round of our discussion is completed; we begin the second round by turning from *actions* to *strategies*. A strategy is a lottery or probability distribution over possible actions. To this point we have thought of each actor choosing among possible actions; let us now enlarge the choice space and think of each actor choosing among possible strategies. To choose an action is in effect to choose a strategy assigning that action a probability 1 and each alternative a probability 0. Such a strategy is termed *pure*. But there are countless *mixed* strategies which assign a positive probability to each of two or more alternative actions.

We have supposed that each actor may be represented as seeking to maximize the value or expected value of a function that provides an interval measure of possible outcomes. The value assigned to each *action* is the weighted sum of the values of its possible outcomes, where each weight represents the probability of the outcome given performance of the action. The value assigned to each *strategy* is then the weighted sum of the values of its possible actions, where each

weight represents the probability assigned to the action by the particular strategy. We now suppose that the egoist seeks to maximize some
actor-relative value in choosing among her possible strategies.

With this supposition we may, surprising as it might seem, rescue
the egoist from the charge of embracing an inconsistent basis of
choice. For more than thirty years ago John F. Nash proved that, in
any interaction among finitely many persons, each with only finitely
many actions or pure strategies, there is at least one Nash-equilibrium
set of strategies.[16] Or in other words, there is at least one set of
strategies, one for each actor, each of which is a best response to the
other members of the set. And the existence of such a Nash-equilibrium set satisfies our requirement for egoistic choice that is both
maximizing and correctly informed.

If we would apply the existence of a Nash-equilibrium set of strategies to resolve the problem of choice facing Jane and Brian, we must
provide each with an interval measure of possible outcomes. Rather
than doing this and solving the resulting mathematical problem, we
shall develop intuitively the idea of determining a pair of strategies,
each of which is a best response to the other. Suppose that Jane
despairs of concealing her strategy choice from Brian. She expects
that, should she select a strategy giving a high probability to going to
Ann's party, Brian will respond by choosing to go to the party so that
the likely outcome will be undesirable for her. And she expects that,
should she select a strategy giving a low probability to going to Ann's
party, Brian will respond by choosing not to go to the party, so that
once again the likely outcome will be undesirable. What then is she to
do? She needs a strategy that leaves Brian indifferent between choosing to go to the party and choosing not to go, that affords him the
same expected value whatever he chooses. Similarly, Brian needs a
strategy that leaves Jane indifferent between choosing to go to the
party and choosing not to go. If Brian is indifferent as to his choice of
strategy, then any strategy is a best response for him; similarly, if Jane
is indifferent as to her choice of strategy, then any strategy is a best
response for her. Therefore if each chooses a strategy that leaves the
other indifferent, each strategy must be a best response to the other,
so that the pair constitutes a Nash-equilibrium set.

Jane does not first form an expectation about Brian's choice of
strategy and then choose her best response to it. Instead she chooses a
strategy that leaves Brian nothing to choose among his responses.
And Brian chooses a strategy that leaves Jane nothing to choose
among her responses. In situations such as the one we are consider-

[16]See Nash [1].

ing, it is always possible to find a strategy that leaves the other indifferent, and such strategies are mutual best responses, so that successful egoistic choice seems possible.

If we make not implausible assumptions about the relative values, to Jane and to Brian, of the possible outcomes of their choices, we might find that Jane should choose a mixed strategy with probability 2/7 of going to the party and 5/7 of not going, and that Brian should choose a mixed strategy with probability 3/5 of going to the party and 2/5 of not going.[17] And these strategies would constitute the unique Nash-equilibrium pair. If either were able to calculate one of these strategies, she or he would have sufficient knowledge of the situation to calculate the other. Neither Jane nor Brian need be concerned to conceal the choice of strategy from the other. Of course, at some point each must determine what actually to *do*—no doubt using a handy pocket randomizing device appropriately programmable for any lottery. We must suppose that the outcome of this determination remains unknown to the other until the action is actually carried out. In supposing that each chooses a strategy, we suppose that each considers the other's choice of a strategy, forming expectations about it but not any more determinate expectations. If Brian could know that Jane's handy randomizer said "Go!", then, rather than consulting his own, he would simply head for Ann's party.

We have no reason to assume that Jane and Brian actually have the information about each other's values needed to calculate strategies in Nash-equilibrium. And this is a very simple interaction. In more complex situations the procedure required to determine strategies in Nash-equilibrium may be more difficult, even if the information needed is available. We know from Nash's proof that there must be at least one Nash-equilibrium strategy set, but this knowledge may have no practical application. Thus I make no claim about the ability of actual egoists to choose best response strategies. But there is a fundamental difference between recognizing that failure does occur and demonstrating that it *must* occur. There is a principle for choice

[17]These mixed strategies yield equilibrium for the following case. Arbitrarily assigning the value 1 to an actor's most favored outcome, and 0 to the least favored outcome, we find that an interval measure of Jane's preferences assigns 1 to going to Ann's party if Brian does not, 1/2 to not going if Brian goes, 1/4 to not going if Brian does not, and 0 to going if Brian goes. And we find that an interval measure of Brian's preferences assigns 1 to going to Ann's party if Jane goes, 1/2 to not going if Jane does not, 1/10 to going if Jane does not, and 0 to not going if Jane does. Jane's mixed strategy affords Brian an expected utility of 5/14 whatever he does, and Brian's mixed strategy affords Jane an expected utility of 2/5 whatever she does. Note that the utility values for Jane and Brian are *not* interpersonally comparable; we may not infer that Jane may expect to do better from the situation than Brian from the fact that 2/5 is greater than 5/14.

among strategies that includes in its domain all of the sets of alternative strategies making up an interaction, and that takes, as values, subsets each of which has as members only strategies belonging also to Nash-equilibrium sets for the interaction. Egoists are no longer set a task that is insoluble in principle.

To avoid possible misunderstanding, note that the strategic consistency of egoism can in no way affect the impossibility, in some situations, of actually selecting only actions that meet the egoistic requirement. When Jane and Brian actually act, and discover what each other does, then one will not maximize value given the other's behavior. Moving to the strategic level does not enlarge the actual possibilities for action, and so does not affect the impossibility of successful informed maximization by both Jane and Brian in terms of their actions. But if each selects a strategy that is a best response to the other's selection, then each will know that whatever the outcome, she or he maximized expected value. Neither will judge his or her choice to have failed *as a choice*.

Before we conclude this round of our argument, we should admit that we have not shown the existence of a principle for egoistic choice among strategies that includes all sets of alternative strategies in all interactions in its domain. All that we have shown is that the requirement that the strategies selected by the principle for any interaction form a Nash-equilibrium set can be satisfied. But we must not suppose that a sufficient principle of egoistic choice would simply require each actor to select a strategy—any strategy—belonging to such a set. For although this would suffice in the simple situation we have considered, in which there is but one Nash-equilibrium pair of strategies, yet in other more complex situations there may be a multitude of sets, each of which contains only strategies that are best responses to each other, but such that a strategy belonging to one Nash-equilibrium set is not a best response to strategies belonging to other Nash-equilibrium sets. Consider, for example, a situation in which several persons want to meet but are indifferent among several possible meeting-places. If each chooses to go to the same possible meeting-place, then each action is a best response to the others; if each chooses to go to a different meeting-place, then the actions are not best responses. We have not considered how egoists, embarrassed by such riches, would select among different sets of actions or strategies in Nash-equilibrium. Thus the present round of our argument concludes only with the judgment that the accusation of inconsistency against egoism is not proven. We have a Scots verdict.

7. An exhaustive examination of the problems created for egoists

by the existence in some situations of several sets of actions or strategies, each in Nash-equilibrium, is beyond the scope of our present
enquiry. I shall focus on but one such problem, arising from the
plausible requirement that egoists coordinate their choices to bring
about a mutually superior Nash-equilibrium, should one exist and
should each stand to lose from the failure to coordinate.[18]

Let us begin by considering a simple game. Two players are each
given a coin and must choose whether to show heads or to show tails.
No communication between them is permitted; each must choose in
ignorance of the other's choice. If both show the same, then each wins
a sum of money, but the sum is larger if both show heads. If one shows
heads and the other shows tails, then each loses a sum of money. In
this game there are two pairs of actions in Nash-equilibrium—each
showing heads, and each showing tails. But the former pair is a superior equilibrium, dominating the latter, since the outcome if each
shows heads has greater value for each player than the outcome if
each shows tails. A principle of choice for egoists must surely accommodate this. We might initially suggest that such a principle must
require the selection of strategies that will ensure coordination on a
superior equilibrium, should there be one and should it satisfy certain
accessibility considerations that we may ignore here.[19] Thus we suppose that in this game rational egoists choose heads.

A variant on our game may suggest that the proposed coordination
requirement is too strong for egoists. Suppose that each player gains a
sum of money if the other shows heads and loses an equivalent sum if
the other shows tails. In this game every pair of strategies is in Nash-
equilibrium, since each player is entirely indifferent about his own
choice; what he gets is determined by what the other does. There is a
unique equilibrium superior to all others, arising if each player shows
heads. But the requirement that players coordinate on this equilibrium is egoistically unmotivated. Neither player has any incentive
to show heads, since showing tails would neither reduce his expected

---

[18]The problem discussed in this section is essentially the same as that discussed in
Gauthier [9]. This earlier paper examines certain details not treated here but focuses
less clearly on the issue identified here as the consistent application of a principle for
choice to an interaction and its sub-interactions.

[19]Consider a situation with three outcomes resulting from sets of strategies in Nash-
equilibrium. Let the outcomes be p, q, and r, and let p and q be indifferent (from the
standpoint of each individual) but superior to r. If communication is impossible, and if
neither p nor q possesses any naturally salient feature, then coordination may be
possible only on the inferior equilibrium r, because its very inferiority distinguishes it,
whereas nothing distinguishes p from q. Here p and q are effectively inaccessible;
without communication neither can be singled out as a target for coordination.

value nor affect the occurrence of equilibrium. In this game we have no reason to suppose that rational egoists would choose heads rather than tails.

Intuitively, we want to treat coordination on strategies belonging to a set in superior Nash-equilibrium as an egoistic requirement only if defection from such coordination would reduce the defector's expected value. I shall not however attempt to formulate this requirement precisely, since it will be clear, in the situation we are about to consider, and that poses a problem for the consistency of egoism, that coordination is egoistically motivated.

Consider now a more complex game, in which three players, A, B, and C, are each given a coin, and must choose, without communication, whether to show heads or to show tails. The values, or payoffs, of the possible outcomes of the different combinations of actions are shown in this table:

Action (=Pure strategy)			Payoff		
A	B	C	A	B	C
H	H	H	$1.00	$1.00	$1.00
H	H	T	$1.50	$1.50	0
H	T	H	−$1.50	−$1.50	0
T	H	H	−$1.50	−$1.50	0
H	T	T	$1.50	−$3.00	$1.00
T	H	T	−$3.00	$1.50	$1.00
T	T	H	$1.50	$1.50	0
T	T	T	$1.00	$1.00	$1.00

In this game there is a single set of strategies in Nash-equilibrium; each player shows heads. This is easily verified; showing heads is each player's best response if the others show heads, so the set is in equilibrium. It is unique since, given any other set, at least one player would do better to change her response, so the other set of strategies is not in Nash-equilibrium.

Let us suppose then that A expects C to show heads. For A reasons that if expectations are correct, and if each choice is a best response to the others, then the strategies must be in Nash-equilibrium, and showing heads yields the unique Nash-equilibrium. But then she notes that *if* C shows heads, then she and B would each do better were they to show tails. For then they would take C's winnings and add them to their own, gaining $1.50 instead of $1.00. Taking C's choice as fixed by the requirement of equilibrium, and focusing then solely on the interaction between A and B, the payoffs for the possible outcomes are shown in this table:

Action		Payoff	
A	B	A	B
H	H	$1.00	$1.00
H	T	−$1.50	−$1.50
T	H	−$1.50	−$1.50
T	T	$1.50	$1.50

In this sub-game there are two pairs of strategies in Nash-equilibrium—each player shows heads, and each shows tails. But the latter pair dominates the first; it is a superior equilibrium. And coordination on it is egoistically motivated; each stands to gain from achieving coordination and to lose if she defects from it. If A expects B's reasoning to parallel her own, then she concludes that, given that C may be expected to show heads, then she should show tails with the expectation that B also will show tails.

But C's deliberation need not have ceased with the realization that the requirement of equilibrium determines that she show heads. For if she correctly anticipates the reasoning of A and B, leading them to coordinate on tails, then she must conclude that she too should show tails. If she expects them to show tails, then showing tails is her best response, enabling her to keep a gain of $1.00 rather than losing it to A and B. But then if A and B anticipate this further deliberation by C, they should coordinate on heads; expecting C to show tails, they realize that their strategy pair showing heads now dominates the pair showing tails, since it enables them to recapture C's gain. And if C anticipates this further deliberation on the part of A and B, then, expecting them to show heads, she too should show heads. Thus she returns to the set of strategies in Nash-equilibrium, the point of departure for the circle that we have traced.

Crucial to the argument implicit in our discussion of this game is a claim about the consistency required for a principle of choice to be successfully employed. Suppose that a principle includes in its domain all of the sets of strategies constituting an interaction. Thus for each actor it yields a subset of his strategies as his choice set. Let each subset contain a single strategy; this will arise if the principle satisfies the Nash-equilibrium requirement and the situation has a unique Nash-equilibrium. Suppose that one actor chooses the unique strategy in his choice set, as the principle requires. Taking that choice as a fixed circumstance, apply the principle to the reduced interaction among the remaining actors. Then our claim is that, if the principle is consistent, it must yield, for each remaining actor, a choice set that contains the strategy in his original choice set. The principle must yield consistent guidance, whether an actor apply it directly to his choice of strategy in an overall interaction, or whether, taking for granted that some others will conform to it, he apply it to his choice of strategy in the resulting sub-interaction. A principle that says, "Everyone should show heads, but if actor C shows heads then everyone else should show tails," is inconsistent.

If we accept this view of consistency, then no egoistic principle of action can be both complete and consistent. An egoistic principle must satisfy the equilibrium requirement, that strategies chosen in an interaction be mutual best responses, and the coordination requirement, that strategies chosen yield a superior equilibrium, if one exists and defection from it would be costly to the defector. A complete principle of choice for interaction must yield a nonempty choice set for each set of strategies in each possible interaction. A consistent principle of choice must yield compatible choice sets when applied to an interaction as a whole and to any reduced sub-interaction resulting from taking its application to some of those interacting as given. Our game of matching coins shows that egoism, completeness, and consistency are jointly incompatible.

Egoists seek individually advantageous responses to the actions of their fellows and mutually beneficial coordination among their actions. These goals prove to be in conflict in situations such as the game we have discussed. Of course, the failure to attain a goal can be accepted. But we have shown that in some situations, some actors cannot do as well for themselves as possible, given what the others do. If A, B, and C do not all show heads, then at least one could do better given the possibilities left open by the others' choices. If A, B, and C do all show heads, then A and B could coordinate on a mutually better outcome. In such a situation, egoism makes inconsistent demands and so fails.

8. So what can an egoist do? Why, she can do her best. But we now know that this answer misleads. We have discovered situations in which not everyone *can* do her best. *Any* person can do her best, but *not every* person can. If we ask, what can *egoists* do, we must not reply that *they* can do their best.

Let us change the question. What can egoists choose? If we take strategies as the objects of choice, then we can answer: they can choose their best. But again we know that the answer misleads. We have discovered situations in which everyone can choose her best, given all other choices, but only if some fail to coordinate their choices on what is, for them, mutually best. And were they to succeed in coordinating, then some individual would fail to choose her best.

Taken individually egoists can choose their best; taken, let us say, coordinatively, not all egoists can.

Faced with the complexities of strategic interaction, the egoist must soon lose the naïve hope of formulating a complete and consistent principle for choice satisfying the conditions implicit in her egoistic stance. The problem proves less tractable than either philosophical critics or proponents of egoism have recognized. Perhaps, then, the first lesson for the would-be egoist is to place less trust in the words of philosophers and pay closer attention to the structures of interaction exhibited by game theorists. But the message our game-theoretic inquiry conveys must surely dishearten her: anyone may do her best, but not everyone.

Yet may not her dismay and puzzlement remain only that? The demonstrably impossible is, simply, impossible. The egoist can do her best. That the structures of interaction constrain doing one's best in initially unexpected ways neither contracts nor expands the real horizons that egoists, in their actions and choices, have always faced.

This would dismiss too easily the import of our argument. Egoists, and not egoists alone but all would-be maximizers of actor-relative value, have been on the whole unaware of the structure of their predicament. They have recognized problems arising from the incompatibility of their professed values; some have interpreted this incompatibility as a sign of irrationality, some have seen it only as the basis of inevitable frustration. They have not, however, recognized the constraints that exist on doing, and choosing, one's best. They have not recognized that the very correctness of the expectations persons may form about the choices of those with whom they interact may ensure that someone must fail to *do* what would maximize her value, given the possibilities left open to her by those expected choices. They have not recognized that a full awareness of the possibilities for advantageous coordination may ensure that either someone fails to choose what would maximize her value given the choices of others, or that some fail to choose what would be mutually maximizing given the choices of others.

A principle that prescribes a choice for each and then, on the assumption that some follow it, prescribes a different choice for the others, forces more than dismay and puzzlement on those who would adhere to it. The inconsistency of egoistic principles requires us to think again about certain failures of interaction, to reappraise what goes wrong in the light of the inescapable nature of certain conflicts. Even if anyone can do her best, the fact that not everyone can do her best forces us to reconsider the attribution of responsibility for failure in situations comparable to those we have examined. We excuse, or partially excuse, a person's failure to achieve her objective, if we find that she did her best; must we now excuse a person's failure to do her best, if we find that not everyone could?

Here I leave these and other implications of our discussion of the inconsistency of egoism to the reader's reflection. Perhaps, just as we found a partial remedy for the failure of egoistic choice among actions by considering choice among strategies, so we might be able to find a partial remedy for the conflict between individual maximization and mutual coordination. We must not draw too firm a conclusion to our treatment of the consistency of egoism, and so we must hesitate in assessing its implications for such issues as the attribution of responsibility. But we put these issues aside in part because an even more pressing question awaits us. If there are limits to what egoists can do and can choose, yet in many situations all can indeed do their best. But should they? The would-be egoist who as yet sees no reason to change her ways may yet have to reconsider if those ways can be shown to be self-defeating.

II. What Should an Egoist Do?

1. "The very *raison d'être* of a morality is to yield reasons which overrule the reasons of self-interest in those cases when everyone's following self-interest would be harmful to everyone."[20] As a claim about actual moralities, this statement by Kurt Baier may well be false, or at most a very partial truth. But as a claim about rational morality—about a morality that would be acceptable to rational actors—this statement is, I believe, the exact truth. A rational morality is a constraint, or set of constraints, on the maximization of actor-relative value with which it is rational for would-be maximizers of such value to agree and comply.

But how can it be rational for maximizers to constrain their maximizing activity—or, more specifically in terms of our inquiry, for egoists to constrain their egoism? I propose to answer this question. But for some years I thought no answer was possible. Indeed, I said as much.

When I first considered Kurt Baier's conception of morality, I found myself trying to understand the conflict between reasons of self-interest and overriding reasons, and I wrote, and read, a paper in which the issues became obscured in a labyrinth of words. After listening to those words, Howard Sobel took me aside and, quickly

---

[20]Baier, p. 309.

sketching a matrix on a sheet of paper, said, "Look! You're talking about the Prisoner's Dilemma." And I looked, and it was as if scales fell from my eyes and I received sight.[21]

But at first I saw poorly. I saw in the Prisoner's Dilemma a clear representation of the conflict between interested reasons and moral or cooperative reasons, but neither seemed overriding. I saw a conflict between two conceptions of rationality—the one individual and prudential, the other collective and moral. And I said that "the individual who needs a reason for being moral which is not itself a moral reason cannot have it. . . . For it is more than apparently paradoxical to suppose that considerations of advantage could ever of themselves justify accepting a real disadvantage."[22] I was wrong. It is that supposedly genuine paradox that I want now to confute—to show that one can and does have a non-moral reason for being moral, a reason that must be recognized even by the egoist.

Egoism is self-defeating. The objective of the egoist is to do as well for himself as possible, to maximize actor-relative value. More typically we think of the egoist as identifying his interest or his advantage with what he values, so that his objective is simply to maximize that interest or advantage. But the egoist falls short of this objective—and falls farther short than some who are not egoists. Reflecting on his maximizing objective, the egoist finds reason to change his ways, casting off the egoistic scales from his eyes and seeing as a moral being— even as a being who accepts real disadvantages. The egoist, embarked on the journey of rational choice, finds, contrary to all expectation, that his destination is moral theory.

To show that egoism is self-defeating is no simple matter. As we shall see, it is not enough to show that egoists, in maximizing actor-relative value, fail to do as well for themselves *collectively* as they might. It is not enough to show, in Baier's words, that "everyone's following self-interest would be harmful to everyone." We must rather show that each person's following self-interest is harmful to himself, that each fails to do as well for himself *individually* as he might. Only an argument addressed to the individual egoist can hope to show that *his* ways are self-defeating. But we may begin from the perspective of everyone, from the failure of egoists to do as well for themselves as possible, and then show how this perspective may be linked to that of the individual. And so we may begin with the Prisoner's Dilemma.

2. If philosophers have paid little attention to considerations of

[21]The incident described here occurred at the University of California, Los Angeles, in November 1965.
[22]Gauthier [4], p. 470.

Nash-equilibrium in examining the consistency of egoism, they have become quite familiar with the Prisoner's Dilemma as exhibiting the seemingly self-defeating character of egoistic behavior. Let us review exactly what the Dilemma shows. Each prisoner—Jack and Zack as I called them in the preceding part—has a strategy that is a best response to whatever strategy the other chooses. This strategy is confession. But the outcome if each chooses his best response is disadvantageous to both. Both would do better if both chose the alternative strategy—non-confession or silence. Each does best to confess whatever the other does, but each does better if neither confesses than if both confess.

We need another piece of terminology to talk about the Dilemma—Pareto-optimality.[23] An outcome is Pareto-optimal if and only if no feasible alternative affords some person greater value and no person lesser value. Or, assuming a link between value and preference, if and only if no alternative would be preferred by some and dispreferred by none. An equivalent formulation is that an outcome is Pareto-optimal if and only if every feasible alternative that affords some person greater value also affords some other person lesser value.

Consider the outcomes possible for Jack and Zack. If both confess, each receives a heavy sentence, but short of the maximum. If neither confesses, each receives a light sentence, but exceeding the minimum. If one confesses and the other does not, the one confessing receives the minimum sentence and the other receives the maximum. Let us assume that their values are related inversely to the length of their sentences. Then if we consider in turn each pair of outcomes, we find that in every case Jack prefers one member of the pair and Zack the other, except that both prefer the outcome if neither confesses to the outcome if both confess. The outcome of mutual confession is therefore *not* Pareto-optimal; there is an alternative affording both greater value. Every other outcome *is* Pareto-optimal; for each such outcome, every alternative affording one prisoner greater value affords the other lesser value.

But the strategies leading to confession are in Nash-equilibrium; each is the best response to the other. And since each is the unique best response whatever the other prisoner chooses, no other set of strategies is in Nash-equilibrium. The outcomes thus divide into two exclusive and exhaustive sets—the set of Pareto-optimal outcomes and the set of outcomes resulting from strategies in Nash-equilibrium. That the sets are exhaustive is not a common characteristic of structures of interaction. But that the sets are exclusive is common, or

[23]The term "Pareto-optimality" refers to Vilfredo Pareto, who did not talk about optimality at all, but rather ophelimity.

at least not uncommon, and represents that feature of the Prisoner's Dilemma that makes it a supposed dilemma. For if, as I have argued, informed egoists are restricted to outcomes resulting from strategies in Nash-equilibrium, then in such situations as the Dilemma, egoists are barred from Pareto-optimality. Each may succeed in doing as well for herself as she can, but everyone could do better.

An outcome may be conceived in two quite different ways, each important to rationality. On the one hand, an outcome may be conceived as the product of the members of a set of strategies; on the other hand, it may be conceived as a set of payoffs. Conceived as the product of a set of strategies, we say that it is in Nash-equilibrium if and only if each strategy maximizes the actor's value given the other strategies. Considered as a set of payoffs, we say that it is Pareto-optimal if and only if each payoff maximizes the recipient's value given the other payoffs.[24] No complete principle for choice in interaction takes every set of alternative strategies into a (nonempty) choice set, some member of which belongs also to a Nash-equilibrium set that yields a Pareto-optimal outcome. No complete principle can ensure both Nash-equilibrium and Pareto-optimality in every interaction. This is the impossibility theorem, illustrated by the Prisoner's Dilemma, that egoists and all maximizers of actor-relative value must face.

Note that this impossibility does not reveal a further inconsistency in egoism. The problem here is not similar to those discussed in the preceding part. There is no difficulty in formulating an egoistic principle for choice in the Prisoner's Dilemma and similar situations of incompatibility between equilibrium and optimality. The equilibrium requirement for an egoistic principle is straightforwardly satisfied, with no need to resort to strategies rather than to actions as the objects of choice. And the equilibrium requirement suffices to determine an egoistic principle; coordination is irrelevant in the Dilemma. The coordination requirement for egoistic principles of choice that I introduced in the preceding part applies to certain situations with more than one Nash-equilibrium strategy set. But in the Dilemma there is only one equilibrium set. Egoists, as maximizers of actor-relative value, are able to coordinate their strategies only within the limits allowed by the requirement that each actor consider her strategy to be a best response to the strategies she expects the others to choose. If, as in the Dilemma, each actor has a unique best response whatever she expects the others to choose, then coordination has no place.

Let us illustrate the difference between a simple coordination prob-

---

[24]This is true only if payoff functions are continuous. More generally, an outcome is Pareto-optimal if and only if each payoff maximizes the recipient's value on condition that no other payoff is decreased.

lem and the Dilemma by contrasting two games. First, consider again
the two-person game of matching coins that served in part I, section
7, to motivate the coordination requirement, here with determinate
monetary values.

Action		Payoff	
A	B	A	B
H	H	$2	$2
H	T	−$2	−$2
T	H	−$2	−$2
T	T	$1	$1

Here each does best to show what the other shows; this assures equilibrium. Both do better if both show heads than if both show tails;
mutually beneficial coordination thus enables the players to select
among the equilibrium strategy sets. But now consider this Dilemma-
type game:

Action		Payoff	
A	B	A	B
H	H	$2	$2
H	T	−$3	$3
T	H	$3	−$3
T	T	$1	$1

Here again both do better if both show heads than if both show tails.
But this consideration never enters into an egoistic principle for
choice. For each does best to show tails whatever the other does; this
alone assures equilibrium. And so the equilibrium requirement leaves
no room for other considerations. Egoists should *not* show heads,
because showing heads does not lead either player to do as well for
herself as she can. The outcome of egoistic behavior may well be
regarded by the players as unfortunate, but in choosing tails, each
does her best for herself. But should she? Should she *be* an egoist?

Before attempting to answer this question, we must generalize from
the particular structure of the Dilemma to the underlying conflict
between Nash-equilibrium and Pareto-optimality that it illustrates.
And we must not misunderstand the nature of this conflict. An egoist
concerned to maximize actor-relative value is utterly indifferent to
both equilibrium and optimality. She cares only for her own payoff. If
the strategies of others are given, then she chooses that strategy most
profitable to herself; if all behave in this way, then Nash-equilibrium is

the unintended result. If the payoffs of others were given and she were to choose among payoffs, then she would choose that most profitable to herself; if all behaved in this way, then Pareto-optimality would be the unintended result. The egoist is concerned with payoffs, but since choice determines actions or strategies, she can express her concern with payoffs only in her choice among strategies. What the Dilemma reveals is that in some situations, her choice does not give effective expression to her concern. Selecting among strategies, the egoist may be unable to maximize her payoff given the payoffs of others, and so may be unable to obtain some benefit that she could enjoy at no cost to others. Let us then say that the egoist faces *strategy–payoff conflict*. This is the general problem that the Dilemma reveals.

3. How important is strategy–payoff conflict? Grant that its occurrence must complicate life for egoists and indeed for all maximizers of actor-relative value. But does it occur, except in the structures of interaction studied by game theorists? If it is a phenomenon of no practical significance, then it can hardly serve as the basis for an argument that egoism is self-defeating.

It does occur. Indeed, strategy–payoff conflict is a fundamental phenomenon of social life. It constitutes the core of the problem of ensuring the optimal supply of public or collective goods. It explains the sub-optimality that characteristically results from failures to internalize effects—the coincidence of net social costs from pollution with net individual benefits to polluters. It is at the heart of Garrett Hardin's tragedy of the commons,[25] and helps explain John Kenneth Galbraith's observation that an affluent society enjoys "private opulence and public squalor."[26] It enables us to understand why even a government that spent its funds wisely would need an I.R.S. to collect them. Free-riders and parasites flourish in the context of strategy–payoff conflict.

Its importance, widely recognized today, was long obscured in much of our social and economic thought. There are two principal reasons for this. First, economists since Adam Smith have tended to focus unduly on the perfectly competitive market—from which strategy–payoff conflict is blissfully absent. As Russell Hardin has dramatically expressed it, the Prisoner's Dilemma is the back of the Invisible Hand.[27] In the perfect market the Invisible Hand ensures that if each pursues his own interest, the social interest is furthered, albeit unintentionally. We may make this more precise by saying that market

[25]See G. Hardin.
[26]See Galbraith, p. 257. He does not, however, focus on this explanation.
[27]See R. Hardin, p. 7.

activity—in which each individual seeks to maximize the value of a function defined over the goods he consumes and the factor services he provides—leads to an outcome on society's utility-possibility frontier, so that no person's position could be improved without worsening that of some other person. The equilibrium resulting after all voluntary exchanges is Pareto-optimal.

Were the world to be, as some economists of the Chicago school are alleged to suppose that it is, a perfectly competitive market, then egoists would have no reason to change their straightforwardly maximizing ways. The Prisoner's Dilemma would be a logical curiosity, revealing the possibility of interactions, happily never realized, in which egoists would fail to end up on the utility-possibility frontier and so would fail, collectively, to do as well for themselves as possible. But illuminating as the market is in showing us the possibility of interactions that give rise to no problems for maximizers of actor-relative value—indeed, illuminating as the market is in revealing to us a type of interaction that would not need to be guided by those principles, constraining maximizing behavior, that constitute a rational morality—yet to most of us the real world does not seem to be a very close approximation to the realm of perfect competition. And so we expect to face strategy–payoff conflicts, both in our everyday interactions and in the design of the social institutions that frame those interactions.

But even when we turn away from the perfect market, we encounter a second factor that has obscured our awareness of this conflict. For awareness of the failure of the market as a model for much of our social interaction does not entail awareness of the core problem facing non-market public or collective behavior. There is a strong temptation to suppose that, just as a rational individual will, within the limits of available information, so choose that he does as well for himself as possible, so a group of rational individuals will also choose that they do as well for themselves as possible. We extrapolate from individual action to group or collective action.

Mancur Olson, Jr., in his book *The Logic of Collective Action*, seems to have been the first to recognize the general fallacy involved in this extrapolation.[28] Here I shall illustrate it with an example adapted, not from his work, but from that of Russell Hardin.[29] Suppose that ten units of a pure public good in full joint supply are available to a community of ten persons. Each unit costs $5 and affords each member of the community a benefit of $1. Each must decide whether to

[28]Olson; the fallacy is spelled out in the introduction, pp. 1–2.
[29]R. Hardin, pp. 25–28.

contribute $5 to the social provision of the good. If all contribute, total benefit is $100 and cost $50, for a net social benefit of $50 and a net benefit to each individual of $5. If no one contributes, then net social and individual benefit are both $0. Nevertheless, no one who seeks to maximize his payoff will contribute. Each reasons that n other persons will contribute, where n takes a value from 0 to 9. If he also contributes, net social benefit is $10(n + 1), divided so that net benefit to each contributing individual is $(n − 4) and to each non-contributor $(n + 1). If he does not contribute, net social benefit is $10n divided so that net benefit to each contributing individual is $(n − 5) and to each non-contributor, $n. Thus, if he contributes, his net benefit is $(n − 4); if he does not contribute, his net benefit is $n. For all possible values of n, $n is greater than $(n − 4), so he chooses not to contribute.

The parallel with reasoning in the Prisoner's Dilemma should be evident. Given a pure public good, each individual chooses to ride free; of course the result is that there is nothing on which to ride. I have considered only an artificially simple case; in more realistic cases in which the value of each unit of the good diminishes as more units are obtained, it may be that some units will be bought by individuals who find it worth their while to pay the entire cost of supplying the unit to everyone, but before optimal supply is reached, each will prefer to ride free at the current level of supply rather than to contribute an additional unit.

Recognition of the problem of collective action should dispel any temptation to suppose that my argument is addressed not to us but only to very different persons—to egoists. We are, all of us, maximizers of actor-relative value—or a near approximation thereto—in many of our interactions. And we all face the problem of collective action posed by the back of the Invisible Hand. When we do, our behavior tends to be, as the egoist's must be, self-defeating. Or so I claim. I must now make the claim good.

4. That egoism is self-defeating in situations involving strategy–payoff conflict may seem evident. For the outcome of egoistic interaction affords each actor a payoff less than she might obtain without the payoff of any other actor being in any way diminished. Everyone could gain; net benefits are possible but not provided. Each, then, does not do as well for herself as possible, and so egoistic behavior defeats its own end. The egoist aims at maximizing her value and achieves less than the non-egoist who aims instead at Pareto-optimality.

We should not be convinced by this argument. *Each* does not *get* as much as possible, and *all* do not *do* as well for themselves as possible; it does not follow that *each* fails to *do* as well for herself as possible. To show that egoism is self-defeating we must consider, not its overall result, but the situation of the individual who must choose her response to the choices she expects her fellows to make. To consider the plight of egoists solely from the overall or collective standpoint is to commit a version of the fallacy exposed by Olson in his analysis of collective action. Naïvely, we supposed that a group of individuals maximize their overall net benefit in the same way that a single individual does. Realizing this to be fallacious, we may then suppose that an individual will fail to maximize net benefit in the same way that a group does. But just as what is maximizing from the standpoint of an individual need not be so from the standpoint of a group, so what is self-defeating from the standpoint of a group need not be so from the standpoint of an individual member. And only from this latter standpoint can we show an egoist that her way of acting is self-defeating.

The egoist tells us that we have shown nothing of the kind. She chooses her best response given her expectations of what the others will do. What more can she do for herself? The problem, if indeed it is a problem and not a simple misfortune, is that the choices of others lead to her getting less than she might, given their payoffs. She is the victim of their choices, not her own. They do not seek to victimize her; each in turn simply chooses as best he can for himself. Each is the victim of choices that do not take his benefits and costs into account. But to be victimized is not to engage in self-defeating behavior. Indeed, were the egoist to complain to her fellows that they did not consider her costs and benefits, they would rightly reply that, were they to take more than their own interests into account, then they would truly be engaged in self-defeating behavior.

Egoists are defeated by the existence of strategy–payoff conflict. But no individual egoist is defeated. No individual can improve her own lot. The remedy is not for individuals to choose differently, in a non-egoistic way, but rather for them to prevent strategy–payoff conflicts from arising. Those who would otherwise expect to find themselves paying the costs of such conflicts may have good reason to provide for sanctions, through binding agreements or external enforcement, that alter the payoffs so that strategies in Nash-equilibrium lead to a Pareto-optimal outcome. These are the classic devices, proposed by Thomas Hobbes long before the theory of games revealed the precise structure giving rise to conflict. Covenants—but not covenants without the sword, for they are but words of no strength to secure a man—and the sovereign who enforces covenants and structures social institutions to prevent free-riding bring order to the egoists' world.[30] These precau-

---

[30]See Hobbes [4], chs. 15 and 17.

tionary devices themselves involve costs that egoists would prefer to avoid, and Hobbes may be accused of failing to give sufficient consideration to these costs,[31] but the world is under no obligation to accommodate itself to all of our preferences. There is nothing self-defeating in the need to cope with structures of interaction that in themselves impede persons seeking the greatest possible realization of their actor-relative values.

The charge that egoism is self-defeating seems to rest on confusion. We must distinguish between the choices of individuals and the structures within which they choose. The claim that egoism is self-defeating is a claim about the effects of egoistic choices. It can not be supported merely by pointing to the effects of strategy–payoff conflict. These effects determine the possibilities for choice; within these the egoist does the best she can. She would do better were the possibilities otherwise, were the world a perfect market.

The sensible egoist may of course seek to convince her fellows that egoism is a self-defeating policy. Aware of the costs they inflict on her, she may in her own interest seek to persuade them not to impose such costs. She may appeal to the idea of strategy–payoff conflict in the hope of convincing them that, since everyone ends up worse off than need be, their egoism is self-defeating. But her appeal is purely specious, intended to secure for herself the benefits of non-egoistic behavior by others, while continuing clear-headedly to displace what costs she can upon them—save that she must appear to practice what she preaches to enhance the effectiveness of her preaching. The claim that egoism is self-defeating is, it may now seem, not merely a misunderstanding of the nature of strategy–payoff conflict but also the egoist's deliberate distortion of its real character.

5. The egoist's defense is mistaken. He does not do as well for himself as he could. The reader will no doubt be on his guard when I claim this; perhaps I am the egoist seeking to sucker him with my honeyed words. Against this suspicion I can but offer argument. And the key to my argument is this. An egoist will of course maximize actor-relative value whenever he can. Putting to one side those situations in which egoism may fail to offer consistent guidance to choice, let us agree that in each situation the egoist chooses a best response to the choices he expects others to make, and that *in those situations* he can do no better. But his very way of choosing affects the situations in which he may expect to find himself. And the effects are to his disadvantage. The egoist makes the most of his opportunities, but as an

---

[31]But Hobbes does give some consideration to this matter. At the end of *Leviathan*, ch. 18, he notes that "the estate of Man can never be without some incommodity or other," and goes on to compare the costs of government with those of civil war and the absence of all authority.

egoist he finds those opportunities inferior to those of a non-egoist—
not, to be sure, just any non-egoist, but one whom I shall call the
cooperator. In making this clear we show the self-defeating character
of egoism.

In the Prisoner's Dilemma we may distinguish a cooperative and a
noncooperative strategy for each actor. In the tale of Jack and Zack,
the noncooperative strategy is of course to confess; the cooperative
strategy is to remain silent. We may be thankful if prisoners prove to
be noncooperators, if there is no honor among thieves, but in general,
and always from the standpoints of those concerned, noncooperation
is costly. Two cooperators will each do better than two noncooperators. The problem, as we have seen, is that a noncooperator paired
with a cooperator will do better still, and at the cooperator's expense.

Suppose then that an actor is *conditionally* disposed to cooperate in
Prisoner's Dilemma situations, and more generally in all situations
involving strategy–payoff conflict. She does not unthinkingly opt for
a cooperative strategy. Instead, she forms an expectation about the
strategy choices of her partners (or opponents) and conforms her
own choice to that expectation. She chooses cooperation as a response
to expected cooperation, and noncooperation as a response to expected noncooperation.

How does her conditionally cooperative disposition affect her
payoffs? At first glance it may seem that it must reduce them. If she
expects the other to choose a noncooperative strategy, then she maximizes her expected payoff by her own choice. But if she expects the
other actor to cooperate, then she does not maximize her expected
payoff and so gains less than were she consistently to choose
noncooperation.

But this argument fails to take into account the disposition of the
other actor or actors. Suppose that the other actor is also conditionally
disposed to cooperation. Then were she disposed not to cooperate,
and could expect him correctly to read her intention, she would expect him also not to cooperate and so would expect to end up at the
mutually disadvantageous outcome of strategies in Nash-equilibrium.
But if she is disposed to cooperate, and again expects the other correctly to read her intention, then she expects him to cooperate and so
she expects to end up at a mutually advantageous Pareto-optimal
outcome. Among conditional cooperators, expectations about others'
choices and dispositions to choose oneself are so related that each may
benefit from interaction in ways that noncooperators cannot parallel.

The egoist seeks to maximize actor-relative value given his expectations about the strategies others will choose. But their choices, and so
his expectations, may be affected by his egoistic, maximizing policy;

others, anticipating his choice, respond in a maximizing manner. The cooperator refrains from seeking to maximize value given her expectations about the strategies others will choose. And their choices, and so her expectations, may be affected by her cooperative policy; other cooperators, anticipating her choice, respond in a cooperative manner. And so egoism is self-defeating. Our argument rests on a comparison between the effects of choosing on a maximizing, noncooperative basis, and the effects of choosing on a conditionally cooperative basis. Although the conditional cooperator refrains from making the most of her opportunities, yet she finds herself with opportunities that the egoist lacks and so may expect payoffs superior to those that he can attain.

Of course the conditional cooperator may err. She may fail to recognize the willingness of others to cooperate with her and so treat them as egoists. She may fail to recognize the egoism of others and, treating them as cooperators, be taken advantage of by them. Unless cooperators are reasonably capable of both identifying one another and singling out noncooperators, their conditional disposition may prove disadvantageous. This is an empirical matter. However, given the real benefits of cooperation, we should expect would-be conditional cooperators to seek to improve their abilities both to identify the dispositions of those with whom they interact and to make their own disposition known. Although the actual advantageousness of conditional cooperation depends both on these abilities and on the proportion of cooperators in the interacting population, yet the potential advantageousness of the disposition is not empirically based, but reflects the logical structure of interaction. Ideally, an individual whose objective is egoistic, to do as well for himself as possible, must expect to do better, not as an egoist, but as a cooperator.

I claim, then, that given the capacity to choose between egoism and conditional cooperation, and given also sufficient ability to identify the dispositions of others and to make oneself identifiable in turn, a rational person will choose to dispose herself to conditional cooperation. This choice is itself an egoistic one; she maximizes her expected actor-relative value in so choosing among possible dispositions to choose. But its effect is to convert her from an egoist to a cooperator, to a person who, in appropriate circumstances, does not choose egoistically.

Before considering objections to this argument, I should note that it does *not* depend on the supposition that one may expect to find oneself in an indefinite sequence of strategy–payoff conflicts, so that by choosing to cooperate in a particular situation one affects the expectations, and so the choices, of others in subsequent situations.

There has been considerable discussion of the importance of reputation in iterated or repeated Prisoner's Dilemmas and in situations in which one benefits from a credible deterrent threat—for example the market-entry situation discussed in Reinhard Selten's "Chain-store Paradox."[32] But our concern is not with reputation or threat. The rationale for choosing conditional cooperation over egoism does not depend on the supposition that one can gain long-term benefit by acquiring a reputation for making cooperative choices. My argument may be applied to a one-shot conflict.[33]

Suppose that each person were to know—we need not mind how—that once and only once in her life would she face a strategy–payoff conflict. If she could reliably identify the disposition of the other actors in that situation and could expect them to identify hers, then she would have reason to dispose herself to conditional cooperation. For were she able to do so, then, if her partners in the situation were also conditional cooperators, she would do better than were she a noncooperator. And were her partners noncooperators, then, since she would so identify them, she would do no worse than had she remained an egoist. Note that in this situation, if she finds herself among cooperators, she clearly does *not* maximize actor-relative value, whether in terms of her short-run expectations in the particular situation, or in terms of her long-run expectations for the remainder of her life. If she is genuinely disposed to cooperate, then in appropriate circumstances she does not behave in any way as an egoist.

Let us now turn to objections. It will no doubt be said that, although it may be rational to pretend to be a cooperator, yet it is not rational actually to be one. The rational egoist will not give up his egoism however much he may appear to do so. Now I do not deny that there can be circumstances in which pretense would be the rational policy for a maximizer of actor-relative value. But no argument has been, or can be, given to show that this must always be the case. Perhaps pretense will not work—the detecting capacities of others are too good. Or perhaps the psychological strain of pretense is simply too great. The best way to reap the advantages of cooperation may be to be a genuine cooperator. The honesty that is the best policy may prove to be the honesty that, once adopted, cannot be cast aside.

It may then be said that our argument shows that the egoist must recognize the benefits, in appropriate circumstances, of disposing himself to conditional cooperation. But then egoism is not self-defeat-

---

[32]See Selten.
[33]For the application to deterrence, see my "Deterrence, Maximization, and Rationality," below.

ing. Rather it contains the resources for its own reform. The truest egoism is conditional cooperation. This objection interprets egoism very differently than I have done. In considering whether egoism is self-defeating, as in considering whether it is inconsistent, I have focused on an egoistic principle for choice among strategies or actions. I have shown that it is self-defeating to be unconditionally disposed to act on such a principle—that is, on a principle satisfying the condition that it take each set of alternative possible strategies for an actor into a subset, the members of which maximize some actor-relative measure defined over the original set. I take egoism to be the unconditional disposition to act on such a principle. The person who, for whatever reason, chooses not to act on such a principle, chooses not to be an egoist. Her reason for so choosing may itself be egoistic, as may her choice not to be an egoist. But it is what she chooses, and not why or how she chooses it, that is decisive here; she is not an egoist if she does not choose an egoistic principle for choice.

Egoism does indeed contain the resources for its own reform. The egoist is able to recognize the self-defeating character of his disposition to choose, and so has reason to select an alternative disposition. But the reform that the egoist carries out is not one internal to his original egoistic position. Choosing conditional cooperation is the egoist's last act as an egoist, and in that act the self-defeating character of egoism is affirmed.

6. By limiting the pretension of egoism we enhance the prospect for morality. Were egoistic principles of choice not self-defeating, the moralist would find herself compelled to reject either an actor-relative conception of value or a maximizing conception of rationality. Morality, as I understand it here, provides an *internal* constraint on the straightforward attempt to do as well for oneself as possible. An internal constraint is one that falls between the actor's evaluation and her choice—a constraint, then, on her principle for choice, the function taking her sets of alternative strategies into choice sets. Such a constraint has no claim to the egoist's consideration. He does not consider the imposition of an *external* constraint unjustified, since for him all justification is actor-relative and those imposing the constraint may well find that it promotes their ends. But an external constraint affects either one's range of options, and so the strategies among which one can choose, or the value one may expect from the outcome of some of one's options. An external constraint thus leaves the egoist free to choose on the basis of his maximizing principle, and so leaves his egoism intact. But voluntary adherence to a constraint on maximization—a constraint leaving one's range of options and their values unaffected—is incompatible with egoism. If morality provides

such an internal constraint, then a moral principle for choice must be incompatible with, and so an alternative to, an egoistic principle.

To avoid possible misunderstanding, let me note that in treating morality as an internal constraint on straightforward maximization, I am offering a necessary, but not a sufficient, characterization. Not every conceivable internal constraint would be moral. I can not here offer a full account of what must be added to the idea of an internal constraint to capture the concept of morality; what I shall add will relate morality to cooperation.

In rejecting egoism the moralist has traditionally employed one or both of two lines of attack. The first turns on the egoist's conception of actor-relative value. As I noted in the first part, some, such as G. E. Moore, profess to find this conception self-contradictory, insisting that value must be absolute. Thus they accuse the egoist of maximizing the fulfillment of his interest rather than maximizing what is truly good. His interest may be part of this good, but no more part than the interest of anyone else. Others argue that the egoist mistakes his apparent interest for his true interest and claim that each person's true interest is linked to a transcendent, non-relative value in such a way that the conflict between the apparent interests of individuals is replaced by the harmonization of their true interests. This I believe to be the position Plato advances in the *Republic;* thinkers of this persuasion accuse the egoist of maximizing the fulfillment of apparent good rather than true good.

The second line of attack turns on the egoist's conception of maximizing rationality. Some, such as Kant, would argue that the egoist mistakenly supposes reason to be merely instrumental, determining the means appropriate to given ends, so that he fails to recognize that reason has a practical role quite independent of that set it by interest.[34] Morality, on this view, arises from the ascription to practical rationality of the same universality found in theoretical rationality. As theoretical reason discovers descriptive or explanatory laws, so practical reason discovers prescriptive or justificatory laws. The egoist's commitment to maximization is thus rejected as insufficient for the universality inherent in true rationality.

Neither of these lines of attack on egoism seems promising to me. Fortunately, I need not argue that claim here; it would be absurd and

---

[34]This paragraph is intended as an interpretation of Kant's position as he develops it in the *Groundwork of the Metaphysic of Morals* and the *Critique of Practical Reason*, but it is not my concern here to offer any defense of whatever controversial features the interpretation contains. Whether or not the account is faithful to Kant, it seems to me to raise important questions about the instrumentality of practical reason, and the connection of practical and theoretical reason, that deserve non-Kantian answers.

presumptuous to think that I could dispose of two of the main traditions of moral thought in a few words. Instead I can bypass them. Allowing the egoist his conception of actor-relative value and of maximizing rationality, I have shown that if he does not give up his egoism in favor of conditional cooperation, then he bars himself from opportunities for advantageous interaction with his fellows. Adherence to a principle for choice that places appropriate constraints on maximizing behavior may be expected to benefit the adherent. And so I find a place for internal constraint, for a non-maximizing moral principle for choice, by arguing from the egoist's premises to the rejection of his conclusions.

I can then suggest that my attack on the egoist requires assumptions far weaker than those necessary to the attacks mounted by traditional moralists. Where they assault his position from without, seeking to batter down his premises, I undermine it from within, showing that the premises give it no support. I need neither absolute value nor universalized rationality. I can then suggest that moral theorists have resorted to these lines of attack because they have not seen the possibility of defending morality by fighting the egoist on his own ground. And so I can suggest that the appeal of both the Platonic and the Kantian traditions has depended on the failure to recognize a third way by which the moralist may snatch value and reason from the egoist's grasp.

To add substance to these suggestions, let us see how the failure of egoism offers some positive insight into the place morality can occupy. The egoist fails satisfactorily to resolve strategy–payoff conflicts. I have characterized the disposition needed for such resolution as conditionally cooperative. Cooperation is more than mere coordination; the cooperator selects a course of action promoting mutual benefit and adheres to it against the temptation of individually advantageous defection. Thus cooperation requires a real measure of constraint. If we relate morality to the disposition to cooperate, then moral theory will be, or at least will include, that part of the theory of rational choice that is concerned with the formulation of principles for cooperative interaction. These principles perform the traditional constraining role of morality in such a way that their rationality must be recognized by all those who, sharing the egoist's view of value and reason, realize the self-defeating character of his choices.

In the Prisoner's Dilemma the selection of cooperative strategies is unproblematic. But this is not generally true in strategy–payoff conflict. In the Dilemma there is but one plausible way of cooperating, for there is but one outcome that is both Pareto-optimal and mutually advantageous in comparison with the equilibrium outcome of egoistic behavior. But in most strategy–payoff conflicts there are many ways of cooperating—many outcomes that are both optimal and superior for each person to what she could expect were each to seek directly to maximize value. Moral principles must enable us to select among these possibilities. If they are to be used effectively as an alternative to general egoism, then they must be reasonably simple and clearly established in accepted social practices and institutions. Cooperation depends on the ability of each cooperator to anticipate the choices of her fellows, and this is possible in general only if those choices reflect widely shared principles.

We should expect moral principles for mutually beneficial cooperation to require such traditional virtues as truth-telling and promise-keeping, as honesty, gratitude, and reciprocal benevolence. But we should not expect all of traditional morality to pass the scrutiny imposed by the cooperative standpoint. In relating morality to rational choice we seek to derive principles independent of any appeal to established practice. We are not concerned with reflective equilibrium.[35] Although it would be surprising, did no commonly recognized moral constraints relate to mutually beneficial cooperation, yet traditional morality as such may be no more than a ragbag of views lacking any single, coherent rationale. My account of morality does not attempt to refine our ordinary views, but rather to provide constraint with a firm foundation in rational choice.

7. The role of moral theory is to provide a reflective and critical standard by which existing moral practices may be assessed and revised. The standard for this reflection and criticism is provided by the individual who asks herself what she may rationally put in the place of an egoistic principle—what principle of choice, if adhered to by everyone, would be acceptable to her. And she must consider not only herself but everyone else; since her adherence to the principle is to be conditional on her expectation of others' adherence, she must expect those others also to be convinced of its acceptability.

Each person prefers to cooperate with others on terms as advantageous to herself as possible. But each must recognize that everyone has this preference. And so no one can expect others, insofar as they are rational, to accept terms of cooperation less advantageous than the least advantageous terms she herself will accept. The recognition of mutual rationality leads to the requirement that moral principles be mutually acceptable.

Schematically we may represent the question of determining a mu-

---

[35]For the claim that moral theory is concerned with reflective equilibrium, see Rawls [1], pp. 20–21, 48–51.

tually acceptable principle for cooperative choice in the following way. Let C be the set of feasible principles, and assume that the egoistic principle e is a member of C. Let each person i define an interval measure v_i representing the value to her of each member of C; thus for any principle p belonging to C, $v_1(p)$ is i's evaluation of p. Let $v(p)$ be the set of all individual evaluations $v_i(p)$; we shall call it the *value-representation* of p. And let V(C) be the set of all value-representations $v(p)$; in other words,

$$V(C) = \{v(p) : p \text{ is a member of C}\}$$
$$v(p) = \{v_i(p) : i \text{ is a person}\}.$$

Now the acceptability of a principle of cooperative choice depends first on its affording each person greater expected value than does egoism. Beyond this, we may suppose that its acceptability must depend on comparing individual evaluations of the principle with evaluations of its alternatives. In other words, our problem is to select a principle r on the basis of its value-representation $v(r)$, in relation to the members of the set of value-representations V(C), and the particular requirement that for each individual i, $v_i(r)$ is greater than $v_i(e)$, which we may write as: $v(r)$ is greater than $v(e)$. But this problem is isomorphic with the usual formulation of the bargaining problem in game theory: to determine an outcome, defined in terms of its values, as a point of mutual agreement, given a set of possible outcomes and a fixed outcome representing no agreement.[36]

In section 2 of the first part I distinguished my view of the relation between rational choice and moral theory from that held by John Rawls. I claimed that moral principles are principles *for* choice, used to select among possible actions or strategies, whereas Rawls treats the principles of justice as objects *of* choice. And I claimed also that moral principles relate to strategic rationality, and so to situations in which each person chooses on the basis of his expectations of others' choices, whereas Rawls relates the principles of justice to the solution of a problem of parametric rationality in which the circumstances of choice are treated as uncertain but fixed. We may now see that the distinction between my view and that of Rawls is somewhat more complex than I previously suggested. Moral principles are indeed principles *for* choice, and for strategic choice. They are principles for choice in cooperation. But they are also objects of choice, in that moral principles would be *agreed to* by rational persons, considering possible alternatives to the egoistic principle for situations in which

---

[36]For an account of the bargaining problem, see Luce and Raiffa, pp. 124–126.

strategy–payoff conflict makes cooperation desirable. They are the principles for choice that would be chosen by all rational persons in situations in which everyone's choosing on the basis of an egoistic principle would be harmful to everyone.

But if moral principles are objects of choice as well as principles for choice, note that they are not the objects of a parametric choice. I have argued that the problem of selecting moral principles is iso-morphic to the bargaining problem, and this is one of the central questions in the theory of strategic choice. It seems to me extraordi-nary that given the role of moral principles in interaction, those theo-rists who have wanted to relate moral theory to the theory of rational choice, such as John Rawls and John Harsanyi, have not recognized that the theory of bargaining, of strategic agreement, offers the ap-propriate point of linkage.[37]

In proposing that we consider moral principles as the outcome of a rational bargain, I am not suggesting that morality is a matter of bargaining skills, as these are ordinarily understood. No doubt the principles that would result were actual persons to negotiate among themselves would reflect the differing abilities of the persons and the initial advantages or disadvantages that each would bring to the bar-gaining table. But although moral principles are of course to be ap-plied by actual persons in their real interactions with their fellows, the bargain by which I suppose them selected is not itself actual. We must abstract from the real situation of actual individuals in two important ways. First, since the principles chosen are to be used as a standard for assessing social practices and institutions, they must be chosen from a position *prior* to the existing social structure. Individuals are to be thought of as choosing principles for their interaction *ex ante,* so that they cannot bargain from the particular advantages or disadvantages that the actual workings of society have conferred upon them. Each may bring only her natural assets to the bargaining table. And second, the choice of principles is to be determined by the requirement of bargaining theory rather than by actual negotiation among imper-fectly rational actors, so that each person is in effect represented at the bargaining table by an ideally rational self, and no question of differential bargaining skills arises. Moral principles are those to which our rational selves would agree, *ex ante,* for the regulation of our cooperative interactions.

Ideally rational selves do not, however, exist behind a Rawlsian veil of ignorance. Rationality here, as throughout my argument, is instru-

---

[37]Rawls does argue for his focus on individual decision rather than bargaining in sec. 24 of Rawls [1]. Harsanyi never considers that ethics and bargaining might be related.

mental. Each person's rational self is fully informed about her abilities and interests. Thus the idea of a bargain satisfies the condition, stated but not in my view observed by John Rawls, that moral theory "take seriously the distinction between persons."[38] A rational bargain is rational from the standpoint of each person party to it; the bargain determining moral principles is thus *ex ante* rational for every person. The demand that moral theory be part of the theory of rational choice keeps the individual not simply as a free and equal moral person,[39] but in all the richness of her talents and interests, her capacities and concerns, her distinctness from her fellows, as the focal point of morality.

8. And so I claim that our argument vindicates morality by appealing directly to each one of us. Not only does each of us do better by disposing oneself to conditional cooperation with others, but the terms of that cooperation are determined by an agreement to which each of us is fully party. Each of us may then begin as an egoist, seeking to do as well for oneself as possible, and supposing that this maximizing objective must guide each choice, each action. But the argument I have sketched in these lectures should lead us out of egoism; without abandoning the objective of doing as well for oneself as possible, each of us must recognize that the direct translation of that objective into a principle of choice is self-defeating. The morality of conditional cooperation offers the correct translation of the egoist's objective into action.

So what should an egoist do? Why, he should become a cooperator and consent to morality. Here I have only begun the task of illuminating that morality by an appeal to the theory of rational choice. My principle task has been a preliminary one—to sketch the incompleat egoist so that, in seeing what he lacks, we might better be able to seek out the compleat moralist.

---

[38]Rawls [1], p. 27.
[39]The phrase "free and equal moral person" comes from Rawls; it constitutes one of the central themes of Rawls [3].

[12]

Coordination

I

In the days when the Great Central and the Midland ran competitive services from Leicester to London, I agreed to meet your train when you came up from Leicester. "It arrives at 12.5," you said in your letter. But you neglected to mention which station, and only on the morning of your journey did each of us realize that this matter had been left open. You intended to travel from Leicester Central, it being more convenient for you than London Road, and you supposed that I would be able to infer your intention by consulting Bradshaw,[1] and noting a 12.5 arrival from Leicester at Marylebone. But on consulting it yourself you discovered, to your dismay, that there was also a 12.5 arrival from Leicester at St. Pancras, and that the Midland train was slightly faster. Of course, I also consulted Bradshaw, and so on that fateful morning we faced this situation:

	You travel from Leicester	
	Central	London Road
I go to Marylebone	we meet	we don't meet
I go to St. Pancras	we don't meet	we meet

If you could have known that I would go to Marylebone, you would have followed your original intention and traveled from Leicester Central. If you could have known that I would go to St. Pancras, you would have changed your plans and traveled from London Road. If I

Reprinted by permission of *Dialogue*.
[1]*Bradshaw's,* pp. 549, 643.

could have known you would travel Great Central, I would have gone to Marylebone; if I could have known you would travel Midland, I would have gone to St. Pancras. But neither could know what the other would do.

Our problem was one of coordination. We wanted to coordinate our actions so that we should meet at the same London station. But we failed to solve our problem. For you decided, not knowing what I would do, to travel from the more convenient station, and I decided, not knowing what you would do, to meet the faster train. We failed also to solve the ensuing problem of coordination—when I did not meet you at Marylebone, you, flustered, took a cab to St. Pancras, and when you did not arrive at St. Pancras, I, gallantly, took a cab to Marylebone.

The rest of this melancholy tale does not concern us here. What does concern us is the nature of the problem which it illustrates. The problem of coordination has been discussed by several thinkers, notably T. C. Schelling and David Lewis.[2] But their purposes in discussing it, and their understanding of it, are both somewhat different from mine. My main purpose is to show how problems of coordination are to be resolved within the framework of an account of rational action, as rational action is commonly understood. But in doing this, I shall shed light on some problems classified traditionally within moral philosophy, the questions of the rationale of truth-telling and promise-keeping. And this light will make clear that such current views of these problems as that of D. H. Hodgson[3] are misconceived, that truth-telling and promise-keeping are perfectly rational activities for act-consequentialists, whether conventional act-utilitarians or maximizers of individual utility.

II

What is the problem of coordination? As a first step toward characterizing it, let us consider what occurs in successful coordination. A number of persons successfully coordinate their actions only if each acts in a way which is best, given the actions of the others. The outcome of successful coordination is the product of the members of a set of mutually best actions. In our story there are two such sets, two pairs of mutually best actions—you travel from Leicester Central and I go to Marylebone, and you travel from Leicester London Road and I go

[2]Schelling, esp. chs. 3 and 4; Lewis [1], ch. 1. The term 'salience' (secs. V-VIII infra) comes from Lewis, p. 35.
[3]See Hodgson.

to St. Pancras. We coordinate successfully only if each of us selects a member of the same pair.

This account suggests a necessary condition of successful coordination; I shall argue later that it is not sufficient. How can we specify it more fully and precisely? Consider any situation, involving two or more persons, each with two or more possible actions. Each possible outcome in the situation may be represented as the product of the members of a set of compossible actions, one for each person. To each possible outcome we may assign a value for each person. One might suppose that this value is objective, or at least intersubjective, so that each outcome need be assigned but a single value for all persons. But this is at best a dubious assumption, and I shall rather suppose that each outcome is assigned a separate value for each person. The objectivist, or intersubjectivist, position is not thereby ruled out, since it is just that special case in which the several values assigned to each outcome are identical.

The numerical values assigned to the outcomes are termed utilities. According to the conception of rationality commonly accepted in economic and social scientific inquiries, a rational person is a utility-maximizer.[4] Thus to act in a way which is best is to maximize one's utility. Successful coordination requires that each person act in a way which is best, given the actions of the others. Hence the utility afforded each person by the outcome of his action, together with the actions of the others, must be at least as great as the utility afforded him by any of his possible actions, together with the same actions of the others. Or in other words, the utility for any person of the outcome of successful coordination must be at least as great as the utility for that person of any other outcome differing only with respect to his own action. We say that such an outcome is in equilibrium, or is an *equilibrium outcome*. For such an outcome is stable, in that no person can increase his utility by unilaterally acting differently, the actions of the other persons remaining fixed. Successful coordination, then, results only if the outcome of the actions in a situation is in equilibrium.

Hence the problem of coordination is, at least in part, the problem of selecting actions so that their outcome is in equilibrium. At this point it might seem reasonable to divide this problem into two—the problem of *tacit* coordination and the problem of *explicit* coordination. Procedures which enable persons not in communication, one with

---

[4]See my "Reason and Maximization," above, on the relation between rationality and utility-maximization. I do not regard the maximizing conception of practical rationality as fully satisfactory, but its entrenchment in our thought makes it the appropriate starting point for this inquiry, and its inadequacies do not manifest themselves at the fairly simple level of a theory of rational coordination.

another, to select their actions so that the outcome is in equilibrium, may seem to be very different from those which make use of communication. But we shall not emphasize this difference. For we shall restrict our attention to situations in which all persons are sufficiently informed about the circumstances to share, and to know that they share, a conception of the situation which is common at least to the extent of awareness of the equilibria and their relative utilities to the several persons. In many situations, such as that in our story, it is plausible to suppose such a common conception. And when it is, then although the difference between tacit and explicit coordination is very important in practice, it is of little theoretical significance. Devices which promote explicit coordination work in much the same way as devices which promote tacit coordination among sufficiently informed persons.

Of course there are problems of coordination which arise for persons who lack a common conception of their situation. But we must attempt to analyze the problem in the simpler, more "ideal" case in which such a conception is assumed, before we can hope to consider other cases. In this sense I am endeavoring to develop a theory of ideal coordination, recognizing its very imperfect applicability to the real world.

Let us turn to two problems which concern the equilibrium condition of successful coordination. First, is it always possible to ensure that the outcome of the actions in a situation is in equilibrium? Is there an equilibrium outcome for every situation? The answer to this question depends on what we are willing to accept as an outcome. If we define an outcome strictly as the product of the members of a set of possible actions, and understand by a possible action what a person actually can do, then the answer is negative—there need be no equilibrium outcome in a situation. (Consider, for example, a game in which we match pennies; you win if we both show heads or both show tails; I win if one of us shows heads and the other tails. You maximize your utility by showing what I show, and I maximize my utility by showing what you do not show.) However, if we extend the class of possible actions to include all randomizations, that is, probability distributions, over possible actions (so that in the example, every randomized selection between heads and tails will constitute a possible action), and the class of possible outcomes to include all products of the members of compossible sets of these possible actions, then it has been shown by J. F. Nash that there is at least one equilibrium outcome in every situation.[5] But we need not give a definite answer to the

[5]Nash [1].

question. For we may say that a coordination problem can arise only if, among whatever the persons concerned take to be possible outcomes, there is at least one equilibrium.

Second, we must note that rational maximizers will not always wish to secure an equilibrium outcome. In some situations there are non-equilibrium outcomes which afford everyone a utility greater than that afforded by any equilibrium outcome. More precisely, an outcome is said to be *optimal* (in the Pareto sense) if and only if there is no possible outcome affording some person a greater utility and no person a lesser utility. Then in some situations the class of equilibrium outcomes and the class of optimal outcomes are mutually exclusive.[6] In such situations rational persons will realize that independent maximizing actions—actions intended to maximize the agent's utility given the expected actions of the others—are mutually unprofitable in terms of their maximizing objective. They will wish to agree, whether explicitly or tacitly, on a common principle of action which will afford them an optimal outcome. They may not always be able to achieve such an agreed basis of action. But insofar as they seek to do so, their problem is one not of coordination but of cooperation—acting together to secure a mutual benefit unavailable to those who act independently to secure individual benefit. This problem is not our concern. We shall restrict discussion to situations in which either it is not advantageous or not possible to cooperate in attaining an optimal non-equilibrium outcome.

Thus the problem of coordination is the problem of deciding how to act in situations with at least the following characteristics:

1. There is at least one equilibrium outcome.
2. Either there is at least one optimal equilibrium outcome, or the persons are unable to seek agreement on acting to secure an optimal outcome.

III

In a situation in which but one outcome is in equilibrium, the problem of coordination is easily solved. Provided this equilibrium is optimal, and provided every person takes every person to be rational and to be aware of the unique equilibrium, then it is rational for each person to perform that action which has the equilibrium as one of its possible outcomes. Every person being rational, every person will act on this principle, and successful coordination will result.

[6]A. W. Tucker's Prisoner's Dilemma is the classic example of such a situation. See p. 221 above.

However, in many situations more than one outcome is in equilibrium. Consider first a game in which we are financed by a bank to match pennies, with the following payoffs, mine appearing first:

	You show heads		You show tails	
I show heads	5¢	5¢	−25¢	−10¢
I show tails	−10¢	−25¢	0	0

In this game there are two outcomes in equilibrium—the outcome if each shows heads, and the outcome if each shows tails. Now it is evident that *if* I knew or believed that you would show tails, then I should show tails, and similarly, if you knew or believed that I would show tails, you should show tails. However, each of us is better off if each shows heads, and each knows this. Furthermore, we assume that each knows this—before playing we observed each other being shown the payoff matrix. Each also is certain that the game is honest, and that each is concerned with her own monetary gains and losses in a straightforward way, so that the table of payoffs reflects utilities. I do not, for example, suspect you of trying to maximize my losses, by planning to show tails on the assumption that I shall show heads.

Given this mutuality of knowledge and—as far as the equilibria are concerned—of interest, and the mutuality of knowledge of interest, each of us may treat the situation *as if* his decision were a common decision. If I choose to show heads, I choose the outcome which pays each of us 5¢; if I choose to show tails, I choose the outcome which pays each of us nothing. Hence as a rational maximizer I choose to show heads, and so do you. Insofar as we are rational, we will solve this coordination problem in the mutually best way, without any need for communication between us.

If each of us were to show tails, we should not solve our coordination problem. Since we would have satisfied the condition established in the preceding section, that condition is insufficient. It is not enough that each of us act in a way which is best, given the actions of the other. What further condition is required for successful coordination in situations such as this?

Let us say that an equilibrium is *best* if and only if it affords each person in the situation at least as great a utility as any other equilibrium. Then it seems evident that we want to require that persons act to secure a best equilibrium, should there be one, in order to coordinate their actions successfully. For reasons to be considered in section V, this requirement would be too strong. But for the present, we may at least require that persons act to secure a best equilibrium, if there is one and only one.

Hence we introduce a *principle of coordination:* in a situation with one and only one outcome which is both optimal and a best equilibrium, if each person takes every person to be rational and to share a common conception of the situation, it is rational for each person to perform that action which has the best equilibrium as one of its possible outcomes. This is the principle on which we must act to resolve the coordination problem in our game. Note that it contains, as a special case, the principle for successful coordination if there is but one equilibrium, for a unique equilibrium is by definition best.

Note also that this principle can not be extended in a direct way to cover situations with more than one best equilibrium. If each person performs an action which has a best equilibrium as a possible outcome, and if there are several best equilibria, then the outcome need not be a best equilibrium. However, in section V, I shall show that the problem of coordination in situations with several best equilibria can in fact be reduced to the problem in situations with one best equilibrium, so that no further principle is required.[7]

IV

Before continuing to develop the theory of rational coordination, I propose to apply that portion of it so far outlined. The overall aim of the applications of the theory which I consider in this paper is to show that certain practices which conventionally are regarded as moral, prove to be at least in part exercises in rational coordination. These practices, truthful communication and promising, are of particular interest in that they have recently been the subject of extended discussion by D. H. Hodgson.[8]

Hodgson tries to show that "in regard to both promise-keeping and truth-telling, the *expectations* upon which the comparatively good consequences of such acts depend could not be promoted in" an act-

---

[7]Note that the principle of coordination may not be applied to a situation in the following iterated manner. Suppose a situation with three or more people, and a unique best equilibrium, so that the principle determines a particular action for each. Now take the action so determined for one of the persons as a fixed circumstance, eliminating that person from consideration as an agent. Consider the reduced situation involving the remaining two or more people. In this reduced situation there may be a unique best equilibrium differing from the best equilibrium in the situation prior to reduction. If the coordination principle were applied to this reduced situation, it would determine a different action for each of the persons involved than that determined for them in the situation prior to reduction. This is clearly inadmissible, so we must not apply the principle to situations reduced by taking the actions which it requires for certain persons as fixed circumstances. The general problem which is created by reduction is discussed in Gauthier [9], and "The Incompleat Egoist," above.

[8]Hodgson. Numbers in parentheses following quotations refer to pages from this book.

utilitarian society. Therefore "the making of promises and the communication of information would be pointless in our act-utilitarian society, so that these practices would not be engaged in", and "there could be no human relationships as we know them" (44–45)

How do the problems of an act-utilitarian society relate to the theory of rational coordination? The persons considered in our theory are rational maximizers of individual utility. Each decides what to do, in each situation, by considering the utilities of the expected outcomes of her possible actions—that is, by considering certain of the consequences of her possible actions. Hence these persons are act-consequentialists. If each were to make an initial assessment of her individual utilities, which we might term private utilities, and then compute her actual utilities by summing the private utilities of all those involved in the situation (invoking some interpersonal measure of utility), then our persons would be act-utilitarians, concerned to maximize total utility. Hence we may say that act-utilitarians are a particular variety of the type of persons our theory considers.

I shall then use the theory of rational coordination to show that both the making of promises and the communication of information are possible and rational practices for utility-maximizers, and so, contrary to Hodgson, for act-utilitarians. In this section I shall begin the examination of truthful communication.[9]

Hodgson's argument may, I believe, be set out in six steps. The first five of these are acceptable, whether applied, as by Hodgson, to act-utilitarians, or generalized to all utility-maximizers. The argument is as follows:

(1) "In our act-utilitarian society, it would be pointless to attempt to communicate information to another . . . unless a person sometimes took information communicated to him as more likely to be true than false" (42).

(2) "One would never so take information if it were known that there could be no good reason for doing so" (ibid.).

(3) "There would be good reason for taking information communicated to one as being true rather than false if and only if (in the informant's belief) it would have 'very best' consequences to tell the truth" (43).

(4) This is "dependent upon a person's believing what he is told, upon his taking the information communicated as true rather than false: unless he would do this, it could not have very best consequences to tell him the truth" (44).

---

[9]A very brief sketch of the type of argument I employ is found in Mackie, pp. 290–291. I was, of course, unfamiliar with Mackie's argument when the principal draft of this paper was completed in July 1973.

(5) Thus "the informant . . . could reason that if the other would take his information as true rather than false, it might have very best consequences to tell the truth, and that if he supposed that the other would so take his information and concluded that it would have very best consequences to tell the truth, then there would be good reason for the other so to take the information. But (as both would know), the informant could equally reason that if he supposed that the other would take his information as false and concluded that it would have very best consequences not to tell the truth, then there would be good reason for the other to take the information as false" (ibid.).

(6) "We conclude, therefore, that in our act-utilitarian society, no one could take information communicated to him as more likely to be true than false (or vice versa); and that therefore it would be pointless to attempt to communicate information to another" (ibid.).

Hodgson's argument, in brief, is that the act-utilitarian principle is insufficient to generate a practice of truthful communication. It is equally rational, for an act-utilitarian, to tell the truth and to believe what is told, and not to tell the truth and not to believe what is told.

Hodgson's argument is, I believe, open to two quite distinct interpretations.[10] The first may be represented in our terminology by this matrix:

	B believes A		B disbelieves A	
A tells the truth	u_1	v_1	u_2	v_2
A does not tell the truth	u_3	v_3	u_4	v_4

For Hodgson the utilities must be interpersonally comparable, and each of the sums $(u_1 + v_1)$ and $(u_4 + v_4)$ must be greater than each of the sums $(u_2 + v_2)$ and $(u_3 + v_3)$. If we suppose the argument applicable to all utility-maximizers, then (u_1, v_1) and (u_4, v_4) must be equilibria, so that A's utility u_1 is greater than u_3, and u_4 is greater than u_2, and B's utility v_1 is greater than v_2, and v_4 is greater than v_3. Not all of these relationships will hold in every case; for example, sometimes I may want to deceive you, so that u_3 is greater than u_1. But these cases are exceptional, and neither enter into nor affect Hodgson's argument.

Evidently it has very best consequences, for act-utilitarians in particular and for maximizers of individual utility in general, to tell the

10The second interpretation was first suggested to me by André Gombay, in discussing an earlier version of this paper. It was advanced more directly as *the* interpretation of Hodgson's argument in a communication from David Braybrooke, whose comments were very helpful in leading me to the present section VII of this chapter.

truth if and only if one is believed, and not to tell the truth if and only if one is not believed. But does it follow, as Hodgson claims, that one cannot select rationally between these two possibilities?

We must ask, as Hodgson does not, about the relationship between $(u_1 + v_1)$ and $(u_4 + v_4)$, and, in generalizing the argument, about the relationships between u_1 and u_4, and v_1 and v_4. Is it better for A to tell B the truth and to be believed, or not to tell B the truth and not to be believed? Clearly the former, given that A's concern is to communicate information. And is it better for B to believe A and to be told the truth, or not to believe A and not to be told the truth? Again clearly the former, given that B's concern is to acquire information. So it is generally better, for A, for B, and overall, that A tell B the truth and B believe A than that A not tell B the truth and B disbelieve A.

Hence we have a situation with a unique *best* equilibrium outcome, an outcome which results if A tells B the truth and B believes A. And this outcome is of course optimal. This situation then poses a coordination problem of the type considered in section III; A and B coordinate their actions successfully if and only if A tells B the truth and B believes A. As rational persons this is what they must do. A has reason to tell B the truth because she expects B to believe her, and B has reason to believe A because he expects A to tell him the truth, and both expectations arise because both know (and both know that both know) that each benefits more if A tells the truth and is believed, than if A does not tell the truth and is disbelieved.

But is this argument a reply to Hodgson? Hodgson insists that we "consider a society in which everyone accepts the act-utilitarian principle as his only personal rule, and attempts always to act in accordance with it" (38). And he then argues that this principle is indeterminate with respect to truthful communication. In our argument, we suppose that everyone accepts also the principle of coordination. But this principle is not a consequence of the act-utilitarian principle, which, as Hodgson states it, is the following: "An act is right if and only if it would have best consequences, that is, consequences at least as good as those of any alternative act open to the agent" (1).

Our argument shows not that Hodgson is wrong but that his position does not rule out act-utilitarianism, or more generally act-consequentialism, in any genuinely important sense. For he does not show that the act-utilitarian principle is inconsistent, that it requires incompatible actions or rules out all actions in certain circumstances. Nor does he show that the principle cannot be supplemented by a further principle or principles, entirely compatible with it, and serving only to determine a particular action in those situations left indeterminate by the act-utilitarian principle itself. And this is precisely what the coordination principle does. It is strictly compatible with the act-utilitarian principle; the members of a society of rational coordinators will find that all of the actions required by their principle have consequences at least as good as those of any alternative actions open to them. But it determines particular actions in those situations, or at least in some of those situations, left unresolved by the act-utilitarian principle.

Furthermore, the coordination principle completes the act-utilitarian principle in a manner consonant with the spirit of act-utilitarianism. What distinguishes the act-utilitarian, or more generally the act-consequentialist, is, first, that he attends to, and only to, the consequences of particular actions, and, second, that he is concerned with the maximization of utility. The coordination principle satisfies these two requirements. A person who is a member of a society in which the act-utilitarian principle is accepted will always act to secure an outcome which is best, in relation to the alternative outcomes he might secure given the actions of the others. A person who is a member of a society in which both the act-utilitarian and the coordination principle are accepted will always act to secure an outcome which is best among those outcomes which are best in relation to the alternative outcomes which might be secured given the actions of the others. The coordination principle actually carries further the aim of utility-maximization than does the act-utilitarian principle, or its more general act-consequentialist analogue.

But before concluding that truthful communication is a possible and rational practice for act-consequentialists, we must consider a second interpretation of Hodgson's argument. This may be represented by the matrix:

	B believes what he is told		B believes the negation of what he is told	
A tells B the truth	u_1	v_1	u_2	v_2
A tells B the denial of the truth	u_3	v_3	u_4	v_4

The relationships among the utilities which hold in the first interpretation hold also in this interpretation, and as well $u_1 = u_4$ and $v_1 = v_4$, for information is communicated equally well if the truth is told and believed, or if the truth is denied and the negation believed. Hence the two equilibria, (u_1, v_1) and (u_4, v_4) are thus equally best, and the principle of coordination is of no direct use in enabling persons to decide between them. We must, then, defer further consideration of communication and truth-telling until we have shown how to solve the problem of coordination in situations with several best equilibria.

V

The key concept to be introduced in extending our theory of rational coordination is that of *salience*. I shall show how the selection of one of the equilibria as salient enables the persons in the situation, without any communication, to reduce the problem of what to do to the simple problem of selecting that course of action which has a unique optimal best equilibrium as one of its outcomes.

Suppose that we formalize the situation envisaged in our original story in terms of numerical utilities. Meeting, of course, must be assigned a greater utility than not meeting. Let us assume first that we are indifferent about where we meet (if we do meet), and about where we are if we do not meet. Then there are only two values to be assigned for each of us, one to meeting and one to not meeting. Since all positive linear transformations of utility assignments are equivalent, these values may be any numbers whatsoever, as long as the greater number in each case is assigned to meeting. Let us then represent the situation by this matrix:

	You travel from Leicester			
	Central		London Road	
I go to Marylebone	5	5	0	0
I go to St. Pancras	0	0	5	5

It might be objected that, since Leicester Central is more convenient for you than London Road, your utility should be slightly greater if you travel from Leicester Central, so that the situation should be structured rather like this:

	Central		London Road	
Marylebone	5	6	0	0
St. Pancras	0	1	5	5

This situation has a unique best equilibrium. However, we assume that the greater convenience for you of Leicester Central is unknown to me, and known by you to be unknown to me. Hence you know that as far as I know there is nothing to choose between your traveling Great Central and your traveling Midland. Thus the greater convenience of the one cannot enter into that representation of the situation which we share, and it is that common representation which must be the basis for coordination in the absence of communication.

Let us now change one factor in the situation. So far as we both can know, we are indifferent about where we meet, but suppose now that each of us knows that each of us would prefer to be at St. Pancras rather than Marylebone should we fail to meet—it is closer to your favorite bookshop and to my favorite pub. Then we may represent the situation like this:

	Central		London Road	
Marylebone	5	5	0	1
St. Pancras	1	0	5	5

There are still two best equilibria. But this situation lacks the bedeviling symmetry of our original story. Going to St. Pancras provides me a better payoff, if we fail to coordinate, than going to Marylebone; traveling from London Road offers you a better payoff, if we fail to coordinate, than traveling from Leicester Central. We could then expect to coordinate on meeting at St. Pancras; this would be the salient outcome. Why is this so?

Before attempting an explanation, let us consider two other ways in which one of the best equilibria may be salient. Suppose first that each of us had inspected Bradshaw more closely and noticed that the Midland ran considerably more frequent and generally faster trains between Leicester and London than the Great Central. Each of us might reasonably (and correctly) have inferred that most people traveling between the two cities journeyed on the Midland. Knowing that this information was available to each of us, each of us might have considered the Midland the salient choice for coordination, although our utilities would have been in no way affected.

Suppose next that on the day of your journey you wired me, "Meet me at Marylebone." Here communication would make the Great Central the salient choice. But your telegram would not affect our utilities; we should each do just as well if you traveled on the Midland and I went to St. Pancras. Your wire would make meeting at Marylebone the salient outcome, but why and how does this provide a rationale for coordination?

One explanation of the role of salience in facilitating coordination among rational persons is based on the claim that it enables them to generate expectations which converge on the salient equilibrium. Each expects every other person to select an action with this equilibrium as a possible outcome, and so selects such an action himself. This explanation may seem to fit the first of the three examples just outlined. For the greater desirability to each of us of being at St. Pancras, should we fail to meet, makes the expected utility of going to St. Pancras, and your traveling from Leicester London Road, respectively greater than the expected utility of my going to Marylebone, and your traveling from Leicester Central, should each of us suppose the other to be indifferent between his actions. And this difference in expected utility, given an initial expectation of indifference, provides expectations which converge on meeting at St. Pancras rather than at Marylebone.

But even if we accept the possibility of converging expectations in this case, we can not in general explain the role of salience by convergence. For an argument parallel to Hodgson's, which we rejected when applied to a situation with one best equilibrium, seems valid when applied to a situation with several best equilibria. To show this, consider how the greater volume of traffic on the Midland between Leicester and London is supposed to enable us to form expectations converging on meeting at St. Pancras. If I suppose that it is more likely than not that you will travel on the Midland, then I maximize my expected utility by going to St. Pancras. If you have reason to suppose that I consider it more likely than not that you will travel on the Midland, you may expect me to go to St. Pancras and so maximize your expected utility by traveling on the Midland. But I, being rational, will suppose it more likely than not that you will travel Midland, only if I can reasonably believe you to have reason so to travel. This reason, it is claimed, is generated by the salience of the Midland, which in the example arises from our awareness that it carries the greater volume of traffic. But this salience does not affect your utilities. Hence it can give you a reason for traveling on the Midland only if you have reason to expect me to be influenced by it, or if you have reason to expect me to expect you to be influenced by it.[11]

In other words, the salience of the Midland gives you a reason for traveling from London Road only if I believe it gives you such a reason, or if it gives me a reason for going to St. Pancras rather than Marylebone. Since I am rational I believe that it gives you a reason only if it does. Therefore it gives you a reason only if it gives me a reason for going to St. Pancras. But equally it gives me such a reason only if it gives you a reason for traveling from London Road (or again, if you believe it gives me a reason, which, since you are rational, reduces to the first alternative). Rational maximizers of utility cannot use additional information, not incorporated into the utilities of the situation, to generate expectations which converge on one of several best equilibria. So the salience of the Midland, based on mutual knowledge of the greater volume of traffic which it carries, does not in itself give either of us a reason for selecting one course of action rather than another.

[11]Note that it would not be admissible to add a further principle requiring, say, that each person perform that action with the salient outcome as one of its outcomes, if there is a unique salient outcome. For such a principle might well be incompatible with the act-utilitarian principle, and even if it were restricted to avoid such incompatibility, it would not be based on the utilities of the consequences of particular actions.

A similar argument shows that your wire does not provide us with expectations converging on meeting at Marylebone rather than at St. Pancras, at least unless it affects our utilities. Thus salience does not in general enable rational persons to generate mutually supporting expectations which converge on the salient equilibrium. But this conclusion, although valid, is irrelevant. For it is based on a misconception of the way in which salience does enable persons to coordinate their actions. Salience could work, in the way in which we have shown it does not work, only if it were to affect the utilities of those involved. But actually it works by enabling them to substitute, for their original conception of their situation, a more restricted conception in which the problem of several best equilibria does not arise.

Several best equilibria are too many of a good thing. You and I want to meet in London. We want, then, one meeting place. Our problem is that we have two equally good meeting places. What we need is a way to restructure our conception of the situation so that we are left with but one. We must restrict the possible actions which we consider, in such a way that we convert our representation of the situation into one with but one best equilibrium. This restriction in our conception of what we may do, far from being disadvantageous, is what makes successful coordination possible.

We effect the necessary restriction by singling out some characteristic of some one equilibrium outcome. This characteristic then determines a new conception of the situation in which each person has but two courses of action—to seek an outcome with that characteristic, or to ignore that characteristic in what he does. So conceived, the situation has but one best equilibrium—that outcome which results if each person performs his "seeking" action, or, in other words, that outcome with the characteristic sought. Successful coordination in this restricted situation is then achieved by acting in accordance with the principle established in section III.

But how is the characteristic which determines the restricted situation to be singled out? It cannot be by agreement. For if the persons could agree on the restricting characteristic, they could equally agree on a principle of action which would remove the need for coordination. Each person must be able to single out the restricting characteristic independently of the others, and yet each must expect that all will single out the same characteristic. Coordination on the characteristic is required for coordination in action. Necessarily, therefore, the restricting characteristic is salience. For the salient outcome is, by definition, that which is apprehended as standing out from the others. Salience provides the natural basis for coordination. If we were not able to apprehend salience, we should be unable to coordinate our actions in situations with several best equilibria.

The apprehension of salience is itself not, or at least not only, a rational apprehension. And our capacities for apprehending salience are not identical. The presence of salience is often a matter of degree; in some situations salience may provide a partial ordering of the best equilibria. On occasion no best equilibrium may be salient, or several may stand out as equally salient. Thus the use of salience to restrict situations with more than one best equilibrium does not guarantee successful coordination. If in some situations it enables each person confidently to conceive the possible actions in such a way that they yield one best equilibrium outcome, yet in many situations it permits only an uncertain or partial restriction of the possible actions. But there is, and can be, no alternative characteristic on which we might base procedures for coordination.

Let us, however, focus on the successful use of salience to achieve coordination and show precisely how it restricts the agents' conceptions of a situation, so that there is but one best equilibrium rather than several. Turning again to our story, represented in the initial matrix in this section, we suppose that each of us notes the greater frequency of Midland trains between Leicester and London, so that meeting at St. Pancras is the salient outcome. I now restrict my actions to seeking the salient outcome, and ignoring it, instead of going to St. Pancras and going to Marylebone. I seek the salient outcome, of course, by going to St. Pancras, but I ignore it not by going to Marylebone but by randomizing on an equal basis between going to St. Pancras and going to Marylebone. You restrict your actions similarly, so that the situation now becomes:

	You seek	You ignore
I seek salience	we meet	50% chance we meet
I ignore salience	50% chance	50% chance

or, in terms of utilities:[12]

	You seek		You ignore	
I seek	5	5	$2^{1/2}$	$2^{1/2}$
I ignore	$2^{1/2}$	$2^{1/2}$	$2^{1/2}$	$2^{1/2}$

[12]The matrix values are calculated as follows. The outcome if each of us seeks the salient outcome is the same as the outcome if I go to St. Pancras and you travel from London Road. The outcome if I seek the salient outcome and you ignore it is an equiprobable mix of the outcomes of my going to St. Pancras and you traveling from London Road, and my going to St. Pancras and you traveling from Leicester Central. Its utility to each is thus the sum of half of the utilities of these outcomes. The utilities of the outcome if I ignore salience and you seek it are determined similarly. The outcome if each of us ignores the salient outcome is an equiprobable mix of the four possible outcomes; its utility to each is thus the sum of one-quarter of the utilities of each of these outcomes.

If you wire, "Meet me at Marylebone," the structure of the situation will be similar, and the matrix identical, but the salient outcome will of course be meeting at Marylebone rather than at St. Pancras. If, on the other hand, what is involved in salience is the preference each of us has for being at St. Pancras rather than at Marylebone should we fail to meet, so that the situation is represented in the third matrix in this section, the new matrix becomes:

	You seek		You ignore	
I seek salience	5	5	3	$2\frac{1}{2}$
I ignore salience	$2\frac{1}{2}$	3	$2\frac{1}{2}$	$2\frac{1}{2}$

In each case there is but one best equilibrium, and in this last case there is only one equilibrium, in the restricted conception of the situation. Hence successful coordination is easily achieved.

Our examples so far have illustrated the resolution of coordination problems involving several best equilibria by singling out one of the best equilibria as salient. However, in some cases another equilibrium, rather than one of the best, proves to be salient. Consider a situation in which we each have three possible actions, with these utility payoffs:

	Your #1		Your #2		Your #3	
My #1	3	3	0	0	0	0
My #2	0	0	2	2	0	0
My #3	0	0	0	0	3	3

With no further information and no communication, the outcome of our second actions presents itself as salient just because its payoffs differ from those of the other two equilibria. We ignore salience by randomizing equally over all of our actions; hence the restricted situation is:

	You seek		You ignore	
I seek salience	2	2	$\frac{2}{3}$	$\frac{2}{3}$
I ignore salience	$\frac{2}{3}$	$\frac{2}{3}$	$\frac{8}{9}$	$\frac{8}{9}$

There is one best equilibrium in the restricted situation; we coordinate successfully in attaining it, even though it is not a best equilibrium in the situation as conceived prior to restriction.

Successful coordination thus depends on conceiving a situation in such a way that it has but one best equilibrium. If there are several best equilibria, the salience of one of these equilibria, or, failing this, the salience of some other equilibrium, may be used to reconceive the situation as having but one best equilibrium. Successful coordination requires that all the persons involved in the situation apprehend the same outcome as salient; if they do not, or cannot, then coordination is a matter of chance, not of reason.

VI

The last extension of our account of coordination which I shall attempt here is to situations in which there are several equilibria, but no best equilibrium or equilibria. Such situations, if they can not be resolved by an agreement to seek an optimal outcome not in equilibrium, pose more than a problem in coordination. For in choosing among non-best equilibria, the preferences of those involved in the situation must be opposed.

However, such situations will pose a coordination problem, in addition to what we may term a bargaining problem. And insofar as coordination is involved, the procedures developed in section III and V are required; the persons involved must use salience to establish a common conception of the situation involving but one best equilibrium outcome and then act to bring about this outcome. As an example of such a situation, consider this variant of our story. We seek to meet, but I prefer to meet at St. Pancras, whereas you prefer to meet at Marylebone. If we fail to meet, each prefers to be at St. Pancras. This matrix will plausibly represent the situation:

	You travel from Leicester			
	Central		London Road	
I go to Marylebone	5	6	0	1
I go to St. Pancras	1	0	6	5

Since each of us prefers to be at St. Pancras if we do not meet, meeting at St. Pancras is the salient equilibrium. The restricted conception of the situation is thus:

	You seek		You ignore	
I seek salience	6	5	$3^{1/2}$	$2^{1/2}$
I ignore salience	3	3	3	3

Since there is but one equilibrium outcome, coordination presents no problem. Although our preferences for a meeting place are opposed, our interest in meeting is sufficiently strong that it overrides this opposition, and the advantage accrues to me given our mutual preference for being at St. Pancras if we do not meet.

But consider another situation, Suppose that we have some reason to meet. I want very much to go to your house, where you will be obliged to entertain me, and you want very much to go to my house, where I will be obliged to entertain you. Neither of us wants to entertain the other, so that each would prefer to stay home and not to meet than to meet the other in his own house. And each of us wants least of all to go to the other's house and find him not there. Although our preferences thus display a similar order, their relative strengths are somewhat different, giving rise to the situation represented in this matrix:

	You stay home		You go to my house	
I stay home	3	2	2	5
I go to your house	4	1	0	0

Meeting at my house and meeting at your house are both in equilibrium. Suppose now that I wire you, saying, "Let's meet at your house." You have no time to reply. Hence meeting at your house is the salient outcome. But the situation restructured by salience is:

	You seek		You ignore	
I seek salience	4	1	2	$^{1}/_{2}$
I ignore salience	$3^{1}/_{2}$	$1^{1}/_{2}$	$2^{1}/_{4}$	2

The outcome if each seeks salience, that is, meeting at your house, is of course in equilibrium. But so is the outcome if each ignores salience and randomizes between staying home and going to the other's house. And neither equilibrium is best; I prefer the salient outcome whereas you prefer to ignore it. In this situation my attempt to achieve coordination by making one of the equilibria salient need not be successful, for the restructured situation does not have one best equilibrium.

Our examples show that in some situations the coordination problem dominates the bargaining problem, whereas in other situations the bargaining problem dominates the coordination problem. I shall not pursue the relation of coordination and bargaining beyond these examples. Although they raise an important issue, they introduce nothing new into our positive theory of rational coordination.

VII

We are now in a position to complete our argument in support of the rationality and desirability of the practice of truthful communication for rational utility-maximizers in general, and act-utilitarians in particular. The problem which we faced at the end of section IV might be expressed in this way. Hodgson's argument purports to show that it is not possible to choose rationally between two ways of communicating that-*p*: stating that-*p* and believing what is stated, and stating that-not-*p* and believing the negation of what is stated. Each is equally effective; hence act-utilitarians, and more generally act-consequentialists, are, like Buridan's ass, suspended between the two ways, unable to employ either.

We now employ salience to resolve this situation. Stating that-*p* and believing what is stated is more direct way of communicating that-*p* than stating that-not-*p* and believing the negation of what is stated. Hence salience attaches to the outcome of telling the truth and believing what is told.

A second argument will reinforce this conclusion.[13] There are circumstances in which it is possible to verify whether stating that-*p* is to be taken as a way of communicating that-*p*, or a way of communicating that-not-*p*. I say, "The cat food is in the cupboard and the cat is not in the kitchen," and you look and see whether the cat food is in the cupboard and the cat not in the kitchen, or whether the cat food is not in the cupboard and the cat is in the kitchen. If act-consequentialists tell the truth in these situations, they thereby make telling the truth and believing what is told salient, not just for such situations but in general. In this way they develop the practice of communicating information by telling the truth. Indeed, this is presumably how we develop this practice with children. That stating that-*p* is to be understood as asserting that-*p* and not as asserting that-not-*p*, or for that matter asking-whether-*p* or a host of other possibilities, is established, at least in part, by making statements in contexts in which the communicative function is evident to creatures with our capacities.

The use of salience to restructure a situation in such a way that the principle of coordination may be applied to it is again to go beyond the simple application of the act-utilitarian, or act-consequentialist, principle. We can conceive of creatures whose imaginative capacities would not enable them to employ salience in this way. Nevertheless, we do apprehend salience, and our use of it, like our use of the principle of coordination itself, is fully in the spirit of attention exclusively to consequences of particular actions and concern for utility-maximization which characterizes Hodgson's, and our, persons.

Hence I conclude that it is generally advantageous and rational for maximizers of utility to coordinate their communicative actions on telling the truth and believing what is told. There are of course situations in which telling the truth and believing what is told do not yield the best outcome for both informant and informee, and in such situations informant may not tell the truth, or informee may not believe

[13]Cf. Lewis [1], pp. 36–51.

what he is told. But these situations are exceptional. The communication of information by telling the truth and believing what it told is a possible and rational practice for maximizers of utility. Truth-telling is a rational virtue.

VIII

The second application of the theory of rational coordination which I develop here is to show that at least a rudimentary form of promising is not only possible but also rational and desirable for all act-consequentialists.[14] Indeed, the practice of promising is one of the fundamental ways in which we effect the successful coordination of our actions.[15] Although, as I indicated in section IV, Hodgson rejects promise-keeping along with truth-telling, I shall not examine his particular arguments, since they parallel those which we have considered in discussing the possibility of communication. I instead show directly the possibility and desirability of the practice of making and keeping promises.

If I promise you that I will do something, then the promise, if genuine, must have at least two effects. First, it must provide me with a reason for performing the promised act, a reason which I did not have prior to promising. And second, it must provide you with a reason for expecting that I will perform the promised act, a reason which you did not have prior to my promising. These effects may not be sufficient—they may no exhaust the effects which a genuine promise must have; but they are at least necessary.

The second effect would seem to depend upon the first. That the promise gives me a reason for performing is your further reason for expecting my performance. Hence we need explain only how a promise affords the promiser a reason for performing. And this may seem to be impossible on act-consequentialist grounds. How can the making of a promise change the situation in such a way that I, the promiser, am given a reason for performing? No appeal to the expectations of you, the promisee, will suffice, for your expectation must be grounded on my reason, and cannot, therefore, ground it.

If making a promise affects my utilities—if, for example, I value promise-keeping—then of course my promise gives me a new reason to perform the act promised. But why should I assign an additional value to the act which keeps a promise, over and above the value I

---

[14]This rudimentary form is related to the "low view" of promises discussed by McNeilly.

[15]Narveson argues this point informally.

assign to it apart from its relation to the promise? And are we to suppose that a promise gives the promiser a reason for performing, only if she happens to place a special value on promise-keeping? This would be clearly unsatisfactory. The special value we normally expect to be attached to promise-keeping itself derives from the reason which the promise provides for performing, and so cannot ground that reason.

Why, then, does the making of a promise give the promiser a reason for keeping it? The answer may be found in our discussion of salience. If I promise you that I will perform some action, then I make the outcome of my doing that action salient. In promising I change, not the utilities in the situation in which we find ourselves, but our conception of that situation. My reason for performing the act promised is that in the situation conceived in terms of the promise, the promised act leads to the unique best equilibrium outcome. And this reason is provided by the making of the promise, for in the situation conceived apart from the promise, no act leads to a unique best equilibrium outcome.

We would meet tomorrow; we seek to coordinate our actions so that we are in the same place at the same time. I promise you that I will be in my office at 2 P.M. This makes meeting in my office at 2 P.M. salient. Previously, any pair of actions which resulted in our meeting led to an outcome which was, as far as our desire to meet was concerned, a best equilibrium outcome. But now one pair of actions—each of us going to my office to be there at 2 P.M.—is singled out. The utility, to each of us, of the outcome of this pair of actions is quite unchanged. But we are able to restrict a vast range of possible actions, with many pairs leading to a best equilibrium but with no way of selecting among them, to a range in which each of us has but two actions—seeking and ignoring the salient outcome—with one pair leading to the unique best equilibrium.

My suggestion, then, is that the primary function of the practice of promising is to serve as a device for coordination. We promise to do certain things in order to make an outcome salient in a situation in which otherwise we should be unable to coordinate our actions to secure a mutually advantageous outcome. Thus if we ask why, in general, we should keep our promises, the answer is evident. Suppose I make you a promise. Then in most situations, I do best to keep the promise if and only if you expect me to keep it, and I do best not to keep it if and only if you expect me not to keep it. Similarly, you do best to expect me to keep it if and only if I keep it, and you do best to expect me not to keep it if and only if I do not keep it. But each of us does better if I keep it and you expect me to keep it than if I do not keep it and you expect me not to keep it. The situation may therefore be represented in this way:

	You expect me to keep my promise	You do not expect me to keep it
I keep my promise	Best for each	Worst for me
I do not keep it	Worst for you	

This information is enough to show that both the outcome if I keep my promise and you expect it, and the outcome if I do not keep my promise and you do not expect it, are in equilibrium, but that the former is the unique best equilibrium. Hence as rational persons, I must keep my promise and you must expect me to keep it.

It is evident that not all of our practice of promising is captured in this account. Although making a promise gives the promiser reason to perform and the promisee reason to expect performance, the account provides no ground for the claim that making a promise puts the promiser under an obligation to perform, or gives the promisee a right to the performance. The terms 'obligation' and 'right' suggest the overriding of considerations of individual utility, which is no part of the present account. An individual maximizer of utility will have no reason to keep her promise if she finds her utilities change so that the outcome of keeping the promise and being expected to keep it is no longer more advantageous to her than the outcome of breaking the promise yet being expected to keep it. Promising as discussed here simply enables persons to coordinate on mutually advantageous outcomes; it does not enable them to override considerations of individual advantage.

Act-utilitarians could use promising as a device for coordinating on outcomes with maximum total utility, without particular regard to individual utilities. A utilitarian has reason to keep a promise, even should she find that her own utility is not maximized by keeping it should the other expect it, as long as total utility is maximized by keeping it. But even so, it is difficult to envisage how promising, for the act-utilitarian, would create obligations and rights in the way in which we ordinarily suppose that promising functions.

This raises questions which go far beyond the scope of a study of coordination. It may be that our ordinary conception of promising is rationally indefensible just because it treats promising as more than a coordinating device.[16] But the only conclusion to be drawn here is

---

[16] Or it may be that our conception of rationality is inadequate. A utility-maximizing conception of rationality may be incompatible with our ordinary conception of obligations and duties; if so, one must be abandoned. But which one?

that what is at least a rudimentary practice of promising is available to, and rational for, maximizers of utility, as a means of coordinating their actions to bring about states of affairs which are as mutually advantageous as possible.

IX

An inquiry about coordination is not an inquiry into an aspect of morality. The persons with whom we have been concerned are maximizers of individual utility; each acts to secure as much as possible of what he values, whatever that may be. The virtues which are appropriate to these persons are prudential, in that extended sense of the term which philosophers use to contrast with what is moral. The condition in which these persons live is the state of nature, that condition in which each person acts independently in a manner which he decides for himself, rather than the state of society, the condition in which persons act interdependently in a manner on which all agree.[17]

I have argued that the practice of communicating information, with its virtue of truth-telling, and the practice of promising, with its virtue of promise-keeping, are rational for these persons. Therefore communicating and promising are not essentially, or even primarily, moral practices. Truth-telling and promise-keeping are not primarily moral demands. The practices, and hence the virtues, are prudentially based.

Our inquiry thus reveals the richness, perhaps the unexpected richness, of the state of nature. Coordination is possible for rational persons in the state of nature, and coordination brings them to the best possible equilibria. This is necessary to mutually advantageous human interaction. It is not sufficient; the richness of the state of nature must not be overstated. Coordination is not cooperation; in the state of nature persons are barred from optimal outcomes not in equilibrium, and hence from all optimal outcomes in those situations in which no equilibria are optimal.[18]

If the principal aim of this paper is to exhibit the rationale of coordination, and thus to establish a fundamental principle of rational action, the secondary aim is to exhibit part of the boundary between the state of nature and society, between prudence and morality, and thus to distinguish more clearly what receives prudential justification from what requires moral justification. Coordination, and with it truth-telling and promise-keeping, are the culmination of prudence.

[17]Cf. "Reason and Maximization," above, secs. VI, VIII.
[18]I discuss the problem of securing an optimal outcome in the absence of optimal equilibria in Gauthier [6] and elsewhere; see esp. Gauthier [5].

[13]

Deterrence, Maximization,
and Rationality

I

Is deterrence a fully rational policy? In our world deterrence works—sometimes. But in a more perfect world, in which actors rationally related their choices to their beliefs and preferences, and in which those beliefs and preferences were matters of common knowledge, could deterrence work? Some say no.[1] Others hold a conception of rationality that would commit them to saying no, were they to consider the issue.[2] I say yes. Deterrence can be part of a fully rational policy. I propose to demonstrate this.

At the heart of a deterrent policy is the expression of a conditional intention. An actor A expresses the intention to perform an action x should another actor B perform an action y. If B would do y did A not express her intention, then we may say that A's expression of intention deters B from doing y. In expressing her intention as part of a deterrent policy, A seeks to decrease the probability of B's doing y by increasing his estimate of her conditional probability of doing x should he do y.

We need better labels than x and y if our talk about deterrence is to be perspicuous. In at least some situations, A's deterrent intention is *retaliatory;* A expresses the intention to retaliate should B do y. So let us call x *retal.* And what A seeks to deter is an action that would

Reprinted by permission of the University of Chicago Press (copyright © 1984), Rowman & Littlefield, and the Center for Philosophy and Public Policy, University of Maryland.

[1]One who says no is Schell, pp. 201–204.

[2]Among these others are game theorists who insist that strategic rationality demands perfect equilibria.

advantage B in relation to A; let us then call y *advant*. We shall then say that an actor A expresses the intention to *retal* should another actor B *advant*.

A seeks to affect B's estimate of her conditional probability of *retal* should he *advant*. Why does she expect her expression of conditional intention to have this effect? Let us suppose that A and B are rational; on the received view of rationality, an actor seeks to maximize expected utility, the fulfillment of her preferences given her beliefs. If A expects to affect B's estimate of what she will do, then she must expect to affect his beliefs about her preferences and/or beliefs. Or so it seems.

A wants to deter B from *advant*. She believes that B is less likely to *advant* if he expects her response to be *retal* than if he expects a different response, *nonretal*. She therefore expresses the intention to *retal* should he *advant*. For this to affect B, it would seem that he must take her expression of intention to indicate her preference for *retal* over *nonretal*, given *advant*. Perhaps A does have this preference and so seeks to inform B that she prefers *retal*. Perhaps A does not have this preference but seeks to deceive B into supposing that she prefers *retal*. But in either case the deterrent effect of her expression of intention would seem to require that B be initially uninformed, or at least uncertain, about her preference. Were he informed of her preference, then his estimate of her conditional probability of choosing *retal* should he *advant* would be unaffected by any claim she might make about her intention.

But is this so? Must the actor to be deterred be initially uncertain about the preferences of the would-be deterrer? Let us consider the matter more closely. We suppose that B knows A's preferences between *retal* and *nonretal*, given *advant*. If she prefers *retal*, then his knowledge should suffice to deter him from *advant*, supposing that his preferences are such that he can be deterred at all. A needs no deterrent policy. If she prefers *nonretal*, then how can her expression of the conditional intention to *retal* should he *advant* be credible? How can it affect his estimate of what she will do?

First we might suppose that, although A prefers *nonretal* to *retal* ceteris paribus, yet she also prefers being a woman of her word. She may value sincerity directly, or she may find it instrumentally useful to her. In expressing her intention to *retal* should B *advant*, she stakes her reputation for being a woman of her word, and B, knowing or believing this, realizes that by expressing her intention she has transformed the situation. She prefers *nonretal* to *retal*, but she also prefers honoring a commitment leading to *retal* to dishonoring a commitment even if it brings about *nonretal*. Her expression of conditional intention does not affect her preferences but brings a different set into play and so affects B's estimate of the utilities of the courses of action open to her should he *advant*.

Second, A may be imperfectly rational, unable fully to control her behavior in terms of her considered preferences. If B *advants*, then her cool preference for *nonretal* may be overcome by anger, or rage, or panic, so that she may *retal*. In this case we should no doubt say, not that A expresses a conditional intention to *retal*, but rather that she expresses a warning that she will, or may, find herself choosing *retal* should he *advant*. Fortunately for A, her inability to control her behavior stands her in good stead, enabling her to deter, or at least to seek to deter, B from *advant* by warning him of her probable folly should he do it. Such an inability may seem suspect, as altogether too convenient, making us hesitant to accept this apparent mode of deterrence at face value.

Third, A's expression of intention may not stand alone but may activate forces themselves beyond her control, which may make *nonretal* less desirable, or *retal* more desirable, than would otherwise have been the case. Perhaps A has made a side bet which she loses should she fail to abide by her stated intention, or perhaps she has insured herself against the costs of having to carry out what otherwise would be an unprofitable course of action. And fourth, in expressing her intention, A may also delegate her power to choose; some other person, or some preprogrammed device, capable of ignoring her preferences, will ensure that if B *advants*, *retal* will ensue. These complicating cases will play no part in our discussion. My interest in this paper is in deterrent policies that do not call into play external factors no longer within the actor's control.

My interest is also in genuine expressions of intention, and not in warnings. No doubt we are not always in such control of our actions that our cool, long-term, considered preferences prevail. But as I have noted, there is something suspect about arranging to gain from this lack of control, about extracting rational advantage from seeming irrationality. I shall consider would-be deterrers who are able to carry out what they intend and who form their intentions on a rational, utility-maximizing basis. A then does not warn B but coolly informs him that she will deliberately *retal* should he *advant*.

And lastly, my interest is not in the provision of deterrent information about preferences. Rather we shall examine situations in which there is no doubt, in the minds of those concerned, that, at least if other things are equal, the would-be deterrer A disprefers *retal* to *nonretal*, should B *advant*.

It would therefore seem that we are left with but one possibility for a deterrent policy among rational persons informed of each other's preferences and beliefs. We must suppose that the would-be deterrer prefers to be a person of her word. A, in expressing her conditional intention, must transform the situation, preferring to abide by her commitment even though, ceteris paribus, she would prefer the outcome of ignoring the commitment. She prefers *nonretal* to *retal*, but having expressed the intention to *retal* given *advant*, she prefers to carry out her intention to ignoring it, should her attempt to deter fail.

Although some deterrent policies may seem to invite this characterization, there are, in my view, insuperable difficulties with it, if we insist firmly on the full rationality of the actors. Of course, since we impose no a priori constraints on the content of preferences, an actor may simply take satisfaction in making commitments which she then carries out. But why would a rational actor choose to make commitments to dispreferred courses of action? Perhaps she finds masochistic satisfaction in making and carrying out such commitments. But if deterrent policies are rational only for a peculiar variety of masochist, then most real-world examples of such policies survive only because of irrationality. Let us not be so hasty to judge them. I shall suppose that in general, the actor's concern is with the instrumental and not the intrinsic benefits of adhering to an expressed intention. What are these benefits? What does A gain if she actually responds to *advant* by *retal*, having expressed the intention so to respond?

If B *advants*, then A's attempt to deter him has failed. Any gain that would compensate for the cost of *retal* must then derive from further, future consequences of choosing *retal* that extend beyond the particular deterrent situation. Presumably these consequences are the effects of carrying out her expressed intention, on the deterrent value of expressing similar intentions in other situations. If A *retals*, showing that her expression of intention was seriously meant, then future, similar expressions of intention should have a greater effect on others' expectations of what she will do than if she fails to *retal*.

But among fully rational persons is this effect possible? If A is rational, then B rationally expects her to do what she believes will maximize her expected utility. What she has done in the past may provide information about her preferences and beliefs, but we are supposing these to be common knowledge. How then can what A has done affect B's expectation of what she will do in the future? He expects her to maximize her expected utility; how can what she has done affect her expected utility? We are not concerned with behavior that alters the payoffs or outcomes possible for A. If in choosing *retal* A neither informs B about her preferences nor alters the possible outcomes of her future choices, then B has no reason to take what she has done into account in forming his expectations about what she will do in the future. A rational observer, informed of A's preferences, could only interpret her choice of *retal* as a lapse from rationality, in no way affecting expectations about her future choices on the supposition that they will be made rationally.

The only expectation one can rationally form about rational utility-maximizers is that they will seek to maximize expected utility. The only reputation they can rationally gain is the reputation for maximizing expected utility. If carrying out an expressed intention is not itself utility maximizing, then it can have no effect on the expectations of rational and informed persons that would suffice to make it utility maximizing.

To suppose otherwise is to fail to think through the forward-looking implications of maximizing rationality. A utilitarian, dedicated to collective maximization, cannot have reason to keep his promises in order to gain a reputation as a promise-keeper among a community of utilitarians, although he may have reason so to act among us non-utilitarians. Similarly, an individual utility-maximizer can have no reason to carry out her intentions, in order to gain a reputation as a woman of her word, among a community of informed individual utility-maximizers, although she may have reason so to act among less rational persons. We seem then to have exposed a deep irrationality at the core of deterrent policies. Leaving aside the provision of information about one's preferences, or the issuance of a warning about one's irrationality, or the invocation of factors beyond one's control that would determine one's response, we seem forced to conclude that A cannot expect B to alter his estimate of her conditional probability to *retal* should he *advant*, on the basis of her expressed intention to *retal*, if ceteris paribus she would prefer *nonretal*. And so A cannot expect to decrease the probability of B choosing *advant* by her expression of conditional intention; she is not able to deter, or rationally to attempt to deter, B from *advant*.

II

Or so it would seem. I shall show that things are not what they seem and that it may be rational to adopt a deterrent policy committing one to the performance of a disadvantageous, non-utility-maximizing action should deterrence fail. But before turning to this demonstration, let us pause to entertain the possibility that my argument has been mistaken and that A might have reason to carry out an otherwise disadvantageous expressed intention because of its effect on expectations about her future behavior. It is clear that this can be relevant to the rationality of a deterrent policy only if A is concerned about future deterrence.

Although our analysis of deterrence is intended to apply generally, yet I am particularly concerned with the rationality of deterrent policies in the context of relations among those nations possessing nuclear weapons. More precisely, I am concerned with a policy which has as its core the expressed intention to respond to a nuclear strike with a counterstrike. I shall call this the policy of "nuclear retaliation."

To exemplify this policy and set it in the context of deterrence, let us suppose that one nation—call it the SU—is perceived by another nation—call it the US—to constitute a nuclear threat. The US fears that the SU will launch a nuclear strike, or, perhaps more plausibly, will credibly threaten to launch such a strike should the US refuse some demand or resist some initiative, or, perhaps more plausibly still, will act in some way inimical to the interests of the US that could be effectively countered only in a way to which the SU might respond with a nuclear strike. The US seeks to deter the SU from a policy that would or might lead to a nuclear strike, whether unconditionally or as a result of US refusal to acquiesce in or endeavor to counter some SU initiative. To do this, the US announces the intention to resist any SU initiative even if resistance invites a nuclear strike and, should a strike occur, to retaliate even if this provokes full-scale nuclear combat. In talking about the "strike policy" of the SU, and the "retaliatory policy" of the US, I shall intend the policies just sketched. In particular, a strike policy may center on the threat to strike should some demand not be met, and a retaliatory policy may center on the refusal to submit to such a demand even though a nuclear exchange may result.

Now it is possible that the US prefers suffering a nuclear strike to submitting to a demand by the SU. And it is possible that the US prefers retaliating against a nuclear strike, with the prospect then of fighting a nuclear war, to accepting passively a single strike and so, effectively, cutting its nuclear losses by capitulating. But suppose, plausibly, that the consequences of nuclear warfare are such that the US would always prefer less nuclear devastation to more; nevertheless it seeks to deter the SU from a strike policy by expressing the intention to choose its less preferred retaliatory response. It is then engaged in just the type of deterrent policy that we have put rationally in question. And it seems clear that an appeal to future expectations would not here provide ground for altering US preferences in order to defend deterrence in terms of future effects. For the US to claim that, despite its preference for minimizing nuclear devastation, retaliation would be advantageous in the long run because it would make the future use of a retaliatory policy credible and so effective would be to overlook the probable lack of a relevant long run. After a nuclear exchange, future expectations, if any, would likely have very little basis in the policies of the nations prior to the exchange. Thus, even if in some cases a deterrent policy could be rationalized by an appeal to future expectations, nuclear retaliation lacks such a rationale.

Retaliation would therefore seem to be an irrational policy. If submission is preferred to retaliation, as minimizing the expected nuclear devastation one suffers, then the expression of the conditional intention to retaliate would lack credibility. The US could not expect to affect the SU's expectations about US behavior by expressing such an intention, and so the US could not decrease the probability of the SU's pursuing a strike policy by announcing its own policy of nuclear retaliation. Among sufficiently rational and informed nations, nuclear deterrence must fail. If it succeeds in the real world, then the expressed intention not to submit and to retaliate must serve, it seems, to inform the potential attacker of the would-be deterrer's real preferences, or to deceive the attacker about those preferences, or to warn the attacker to expect an irrational response to a strike policy.

But this conclusion is mistaken. We have reached it by focusing entirely on the benefits and costs of actually carrying out the conditional intention that is the core of a deterrent policy. We have failed to consider the benefits and costs of forming or adopting such a conditional intention. The argument against the rationality of nuclear retaliation, or more generally against a deterrent policy, has this structure: it is not utility maximizing to carry out the nonsubmissive, retaliatory intention; therefore it is not rational so to act; therefore it is not rational to form the intention; therefore a rational person cannot sincerely express the intention; therefore another rational and informed person cannot be deterred by the expression of the intention. The structure of the argument that I shall present and defend is: it may be utility maximizing to form the nonsubmissive, retaliatory intention; therefore it may be rational to form such an intention; if it is rational to form the intention, it is rational to act on the intention; therefore a rational person can sincerely express the intention; therefore another rational and informed person can be deterred by the expression of the intention. We shall of course have to consider why this argument succeeds and the former argument fails.

I shall therefore defend the rationality of deterrent policies and, more particularly, of nuclear retaliation. But my defense is a limited one. Indeed, among rational and informed actors, a policy of pure and simple deterrence is not rational, although it may be rational as part of a larger policy directed, among other things, at the obsolescence of deterrence. Putting my position into a historical context, I shall defend Hobbes's formulation of the first law of nature: "That every man, ought to endeavour Peace, as farre as he has hope of obtaining it; and when he cannot obtain it, that he may seek, and use, all helps, and advantages of Warre."[3] Deterrence is both an advantage of war and, among rational actors, a means to peace. Or rather, some deterrent policies may have these features. But as a means to peace, a deterrent policy looks to its own supercession. For recognition of the rationality of deterrence is inseparable from recognition of the rationality of moving, not unilaterally but mutually, beyond deterrence.

III

To give precision to our analysis of deterrence, I shall focus on situations with a very simple structure. An actor who, consistently with our previous usage, we call B, has a choice between two alternatives, y and y', where y corresponds to *advant*. If he chooses y, then another actor, A, knowing B's choice, has a choice between two alternatives, x and x', where x corresponds to *retal* and x' to *nonretal*. If B chooses y', then A may or may not have a choice between x and x' or other alternatives; initially we need suppose only that some outcome is expected. There are, then, three possible outcomes relevant to our analysis: yx, or *advant* followed by *retal*; yx', or *advant* followed by *nonretal;* and y'—, or B's choice of his alternative to *advant* followed by a possible but unspecified choice by A. Each actor orders these possible outcomes; for simplicity we assume that neither is indifferent between any two. There are then six possible orderings for each actor, and so thirty-six different possible pairs of orderings.

Only one of these thirty-six pairs determines a deterrent situation. Consider first A's orderings. Since she seeks to deter B from *advant,* she must prefer y'—, the expected outcome if B chooses his alternative action, to both yx and yx'. And since she seeks to deter B from *advant* by expressing a conditional intention to *retal* contrary to her known preferences, she must prefer yx' to yx. Now consider B's orderings. Since A seeks to deter him from *advant* by expressing her conditional intention to *retal,* he must prefer yx' to yx. If A has any need to seek to deter B from *advant,* then he must prefer yx' to y'—, and if she is to have any hope of deterring him, then he must prefer y'— to yx. A's ordering is: y'— > yx' > yx; B's ordering is yx' > y'— > yx.

Let us take a brief, closer look at the outcome if B chooses y'. I shall

[3]Hobbes [4], ch. 14.

not pursue the implications of this discussion in the present paper, although it raises issues of some interest and importance. If deterrence is to be possible, then, should B choose y', A must have a choice w (where this includes the limiting case in which she has no alternative to w) such that she prefers y'w to yx' and he prefers y'w to yx. If for every alternative w' such that A prefers y'w' to yx', B prefers yx to y'w', then, much as A might wish to deter B from choosing y she has no conditional intention sufficient. If for every alternative w" such that B prefers y'w" to yx, A prefers yx' to y'w", then even though A may have a conditional intention sufficient to deter B she has no interest in using it.

Suppose then that A prefers y'w to yx', and B prefers y'w to yx. If B also prefers yx' to y'w, then A will seek to deter B from choosing y. But the expression of a conditional intention to choose x in response to y, even if fully credible, may be insufficient to deter B. For A may have an alternative w' to w such that A prefers y'w' to y'w, but also such that B prefers yx to y'w'. Where B to choose y' in response to A's conditional intention to respond to y with x, then he would expect A to choose w' rather than w, so that he would be worse off than if he had ignored A's attempt to deter. However, were A to combine her expression of conditional intention to choose x in response to y with the credible expression of a conditional intention to choose w in response to y', then B, preferring y'w to yx, would choose y'. In this case A is able to deter B only if she is able to combine her threat with an offer—an offer to refrain from her utility-maximizing choice in order to leave B open to her threat. Note that, although A's offer requires her not to choose her utility-maximizing response to B's choice of y', by making it she may expect an outcome y'w which affords her greater utility than the outcome yx' which she would otherwise expect. Note also that B would prefer A not to be in a position to make such an offer.

It will be evident that A's conditional intention to choose a non-maximizing w in response to y' raises precisely the same problem of rationality as her conditional intention to choose a non-maximizing x in response to y—*retal* in response to *advant*. In both cases she must form an intention to choose a course of action in itself non-maximizing, as part of a policy intended to maximize her expected utility. I shall not address the problem of non-maximizing offers in this paper, but an argument for the rationality of deterrent threats can easily be applied to the offers as well.

Before proceeding to that argument let us relate our abstract treatment of deterrence to the particular issue of nuclear retaliation. In the terms in which we have posed that problem, the US corresponds to actor A, the SU to actor B. The policy of nuclear retaliation by the US corresponds to x or *retal;* the strike policy for actor B corresponds to y or *advant.* Recall that "strike" and "retaliation" are shorthand for more complex policies; the core of a strike policy may be the threat to launch a nuclear strike should some initiative be resisted; the core of a retaliatory policy may be the refusal to acquiesce in such a threat— with, of course, the intention to retaliate should such refusal lead to a strike.

I suppose then that the US orders the possibilities: no strike > strike and no retaliation > strike and retaliation. The first preference is evident; the second preference follows from the assumption that the US wishes to minimize nuclear devastation, given that retaliation, as we have characterized it, increases its expectation of suffering such devastation. And I suppose that the SU is perceived by the US to order the possibilities: strike and no retaliation > no strike > strike and retaliation. As I noted in the preceding paragraph, a strike policy may center on a threat; the SU's supposed first preference need not indicate a passion for blood but only a desire to get its way by resorting to whatever threat may be needed. The SU's second preference follows from the assumption that it too wishes to minimize being the victim of nuclear devastation.

These preference orderings satisfy the requirements for a deterrent situation. I suppose that they are a plausible schematic representation of the preferences that have been ascribed to possible real-world counterparts of the US and the SU. Thus our argument for the rationality of deterrent threats is not intended to be an inquiry into merely possible worlds. However, some of the points raised abstractly in this section should be borne in mind in any attempt to apply our argument. In particular, it is worth noting that the SU may suppose that the US has several possible responses to its no-strike policy, some of which, such as a unilateral US strike, might indeed be worse from its perspective than a strike policy coupled with US retaliation. Effective deterrence by the US may then require an offer sufficient to allay SU fears of possible unilateral US action in response to a no-strike policy. I shall not pursue this matter here, but it is essential to be aware that the components of an effective policy of nuclear deterrence are matters that require the most careful evaluation.

IV

The key to understanding deterrence, or, for that matter, the key to understanding all forms of interaction, such as agreement, that require constraints on directly maximizing behavior, is that in interaction the probability that an individual will be in a given situation or type of situation may be affected by the beliefs of others about what that individual would do in the situation. B's willingness to put A in a situation, to face A with a choice, will be affected by his belief about how she will act in that situation, how she will choose. His belief about how she will act will be affected by his assessment of her intentions. In particular, if he knows that she is fully in control of what she does, he will, ceteris paribus, expect her to do what she conditionally intends to do should she be in that situation. Hence the probability of A being in a given situation, insofar as her being in that situation is determined by the actions of B, is affected by A's prior intentions about what she will do in that situation.

It is of course true that, if A is rational, then her intentions must be those that it is rational for her to hold. But neither A nor B can ascertain the rationality of her intentions merely by considering the actions to which various possible intentions might commit her, and their payoffs. If B's beliefs about A's intentions partially determine what situations she will be in, then A, in forming her intentions, must consider the situations she may expect to face given the possible intentions she might form, and the payoffs from those situations. It may be tempting to suppose that it is rational to form an intention if and only if it would be utility maximizing to execute the intention. Instead we argue that it is rational to execute an intention if and only if it is utility maximizing to form it.

Let us then examine the calculations of a rational actor choosing among possible intentions. I shall restrict our analysis to the simplest case, corresponding to our analysis of deterrent situations in the preceding section. Suppose then that A must decide whether to adopt the intention to do x in a situation characterized by the performance of some action y by another actor B. Let $u(yx)$ be the utility she would expect were she to do x given y. Let x' be the alternative intention to x so that $u(yx')$ is the utility she would expect were she to act on x' given y. Let $u(y')$ be the utility she would expect were B not to do y. And let p_x be the probability that B will do y should A adopt the intention to do x given y, and $p_{x'}$ the probability that B will do y should A adopt the intention to do x' given y.

Then A's expected utility should she intend x is

$$p_x u(yx) + (1 - p_x)u(y').$$

And her expected utility should she intend x' is

$$p_{x'} u(yx') + (1 - p_{x'})u(y').$$

Our concern is with the rationality of a deterrent policy. Hence we suppose that A does not want to be faced with y, which corresponds to *advant,* so that her utility $u(y')$ is greater than both $u(yx)$ and $u(yx')$. Furthermore, we suppose that doing x, which corresponds to *retal,* is not utility maximizing for A, so that $u(yx')$ is greater than $u(yx)$. And finally, A must suppose that intending x should B do y reduces the probability of his doing y, so that $p_{x'}$ is greater than p_x.

Since A prefers facing y' to doing x' given y, and doing x' given y to doing x given y, there must be some lottery over facing y', and facing y with the intention of doing x, that A considers indifferent to the certainty of facing y with the intention of doing x'. Let p be the probability of facing y' in that lottery. Then we may express the utility of facing y with the intention of doing x', $u(yx')$, in terms of the utilities of facing y', $u(y')$, and of facing y with the intention of doing x, $u(yx)$:

$$u(yx') = pu(y') + (1 - p)u(yx).$$

Without loss of generality for our argument we may set $u(y') = 1$, and $u(yx) = 0$. Then:

$$u(yx') = p.$$

And so A's expected utility if she intends x given y is

$$1 - p_x.$$

And her expected utility if she intends x' given y is

$$p_{x'}p + (1 - p_{x'}).$$

Suppose that A maximizes her expected utility by forming the intention to do x should B do y, that is, by forming the intention to *retal* should B *advant.* Then it must be the case that

$$(1 - p_x) > [p_{x'}p + (1 - p_{x'})].$$

Or equivalently:

$$[(p_{x'} - p_x)/p_{x'}] > p.$$

To interpret this condition, we note that avoiding y constitutes "deterrent success," whereas facing y and doing x constitutes "deterrent failure." Facing y and doing x' we may identify with nondeterrence. Then p is that probability of deterrent success, where the alternative is deterrent failure, that makes a deterrent policy indifferent to nondeterrence from the standpoint of the prospective deterrer. We may therefore call p the "minimum required probability" for deterrent success; it reflects the value of nondeterrence relative to deterrent success and failure. The expression $[(p_{x'} - p_x)/p_{x'}]$ is the "proportionate decrease" in the probability of being in the situation that the prospective deterrer would avoid, that is achieved by her policy of deterrence. Thus the condition states that, for a deterrent policy to be rational, the proportionate decrease that it effects in the probability of facing the undesired action, *advant,* must be greater than the minimum required probability for deterrent success.

Consider a simple example. B, a university professor in Boston, is offered a position in Dallas. His wife, A, wishes to deter him from accepting the appointment and so tells him that, if he accepts it, she will leave him and remain in Boston, even though she would prefer to accompany him to Dallas. Then if A is indifferent between a lottery that would offer a 70 percent chance that B would stay in Boston and a 30 percent chance that he would go alone to Dallas, and the certainty that both would go to Dallas, .7 is a minimum required probability for deterrent success. If A supposes that there is a 50 percent chance that B will accept the appointment in Dallas if she will accompany him, but only a 10 percent chance that he will accept it if she won't, then the proportionate decrease effected by deterrence in the probability that he will accept the appointment is $(.5 - .1)/.5$, or .8. Since .8 is greater than .7, A indeed maximizes her expected utility by her adoption of a deterrent policy, requiring her to form the conditional intention not to accompany B should he accept an appointment in Dallas.

Consider now the application of our analysis to the policy of nuclear retaliation. Deterrent success for the US lies in not facing a strike policy by the SU—a policy that intends directly, or threatens and so intends conditionally, a nuclear strike. Deterrent failure lies in being faced with such a policy and being committed to a retaliatory response—to ignoring any threat by the SU and to responding to a nuclear strike by a counterstrike. Nondeterrence lies in facing a strike policy by the SU without being committed to a retaliatory response, and so it involves acceptance of the lesser evil between acquiescing in whatever initiative the SU takes and engaging in retaliation. Given these alternatives, we may suppose that, although deterrent success is of course preferred to nondeterrence, both are strongly preferred to deterrent failure. It may indeed be better to let the Reds have their way than to be among the nuclear dead. Thus a substantial decrease in the probability of facing a strike policy by the SU is required if the deterrent policy of nuclear retaliation is to maximize the expected utility of the US and so be rational to adopt.

I shall not try to estimate the extent of this decrease or, equivalently, the minimum required probability for deterrent success. This is a difficult empirical question. What is clear is that a merely ordinal ranking of preferences over possible outcomes does not afford sufficient information to assess the rationality of a deterrent policy, either in general or in the specific case of nuclear retaliation. An actor might prefer, and strongly prefer, to avoid facing a situation brought about by some other actor doing y, but the proportionate reduction in the probability of facing y that could be effected by a deterrent policy might not be worth the expected cost of facing it with the deterrent intention. The benefits of deterrent success must always be balanced against the costs of deterrent failure, and only the relevant probabilities of being in the undesirable situation, both with and without a policy of deterrence, together with an interval measure of utility in terms of which we may calculate the minimum required probability for deterrent success, enable us to calculate the balance of benefits and costs. If our argument shows that deterrent policies in general, and nuclear retaliation in particular, may be utility maximizing, it also shows that such policies may *not* be utility maximizing, and it may be extraordinarily difficult to determine, in a particular case, whether deterrence or nondeterrence is less disadvantageous.

But while I want to emphasize this cautionary note, I do want to insist that my argument refutes the claim that deterrence is necessarily an irrational policy because carrying out the deterrent intention is not utility maximizing. The argument for the irrationality of deterrence looks only to the costs of deterrent failure. Because there are such costs, it rejects the policy. My argument, on the other hand, relates the probability-weighted costs of deterrent failure to the probability-weighted benefits of deterrent success, in order to assess the rationality of forming the conditional, non-maximizing intention which is the core of a deterrent policy. I claim that if it is rational to form this conditional, deterrent intention, then, should deterrence fail and the condition be realized, it is rational to act on it. The utility cost of acting on the deterrent intention enters, with appropriate probability weighting, into determining whether it is rational to form the intention. But once this is decided, the cost of acting on the intention does not enter again into determining whether, if deterrence fails, it is rational to act on it. Acting on it is part of a deterrent policy, and if expected utility is maximized by forming the conditional deterrent intention, then deterrence is a rational policy.

V

Let us turn to some possible objections to this argument. We may forestall one counterargument by noting that, of course, if one is able to achieve the same deterrent effect by pretending to form a conditional non-maximizing intention as by actually forming it, then such pretense would be rational. Even if pretense offers a lesser deterrent effect, its lesser possible costs may make it rational. But there is no reason to suppose that pretense must always have as great a net benefit as the actual formation of an intention. It must be judged on the same, utility-maximizing basis as the real thing.

An objector may insist that pretense can be rational because it does not commit one to non-maximizing behavior, but that a genuine commitment to non-maximization cannot be rational. If it is rational to form an intention that commits one to what, ceteris paribus, would not maximize one's utility, then the utility of forming the intention must affect the utility of carrying it out, increasing it so that execution is utility maximizing. The US would, in the abstract, prefer not to engage in a nuclear exchange with the SU. Our objector admits this but urges that if a nuclear exchange arises from a rational policy of deterrence, then the US would prefer to maintain that policy and so prefer to engage in the exchange. On his view, preference for forming a conditional intention entails preference for executing it should the condition be met.

But what reason has he for claiming this, other than his insistence on a simple, and in my view simpleminded, account of the connection between utility maximization and rationality?[4] I have shown that the adoption of an intention can be utility maximizing even though acting on it would not be, at least considered in itself. Why then should we suppose that, because adoption is utility maximizing, implementation magically becomes utility maximizing? Why should we suppose that a preference for adopting or forming an intention must carry with it a preference for implementing or executing the intention? The two preferences are logically and actually quite distinct. We may grant that

[4]If preference is necessarily revealed in behavior, then choosing a nuclear exchange shows that one prefers it to one's alternatives. Conceptually, we can (and many economists and game theorists do) fit preference and choice so tightly together that nothing could count as non-utility-maximizing behavior. But this mode of conceptualization is a Procrustean bed for the treatment of such issues as the rationality of deterrence.

in most situations one prefers to adopt an intention because one would prefer to execute it. But my argument is intended to show that this connection does not hold between conditional intentions and their implementation in deterrent situations. I have shown why the connection does not hold—because adoption of the intention affects one's expected utilities by affecting the probability that the condition for implementation will be realized.

Our objector must surely take another and stronger tack. If he allows our argument about the rationality of adopting a non-maximizing intention, then he must claim that it may be rational to adopt an intention even though it would be, and one knows that it would be, irrational to act on it should the condition for implementing it be realized. If our objector takes this tack, then he acknowledges the rationality of some deterrent policies, but nevertheless insists that these policies, although fully rational, involve the performance of irrational actions if certain conditions are satisfied. How then does his position differ from mine, in which I claim that deterrent policies may be rational, and if rational, involve the performance of actions which, in themselves and apart from the context of deterrence, would be irrational, but which, in that context, result from rational intentions and so are rational?[5] Surely he grants the substance of my argument but expresses his agreement in a misleading and even paradoxical way, insisting that actions necessary to a rational policy may themselves be irrational. To assess an action as irrational is, in my view, to claim that it should not be, or have been, performed. If our objector accepts deterrent policies, then he cannot consistently reject the actions they require and so cannot claim that such actions should not be performed.

Suppose, then, that our objector confronts my position head on and rejects the rationality of deterrent policies. He insists that the execution of an intention must take precedence, rationally, over its adoption. He must insist that it is rational to form an intention if and only if one maximizes one's expected utility both in forming it and in executing it. If either condition fails, then formation of the intention is not rational.

This objector insists that the rationality of an action is always to be assessed *from here*, in the words of Bernard Williams.[6] The rationality of an action is to be assessed from the point at which the question, not of intending it but of performing it, arises. And this is, I think, the

[5]How his position may differ is made clear by Lewis [2]. I begin a rejoinder to Lewis in Gauthier [8].
[6]Williams, p. 35.

heart of the matter. In taking this position the objector applies the utility-maximizing standard of rationality in the way generally approved by economists, decision theorists, and game theorists. But he, and they, are mistaken. The fully rational actor is not the one who assesses her actions from here but rather the one who subjects the largest, rather than the smallest, segments of her activity to primary rational scrutiny, proceeding from policies to performances, letting assessment of the latter be ruled by assessment of the former.

A utility-maximizing policy may include non-utility-maximizing performance. Deterrence exemplifies this. The expected utility of a policy is the sum of the probability-weighted expected utilities of the performances it allows or requires. The apparent paradox, that a utility-maximizing policy may contain non-utility-maximizing performances, is resolved in the realization that altering the performances need not be independent of altering their probabilities. An assessment that begins and remains at the level of the performances neglects this crucial fact. And so the actor who assesses the rationality of his actions only from here, from the point at which the question of performance arises, may expect a lesser overall utility than the actor who assesses the rationality of her actions in the context of policies, who adjusts performances so that the probability-weighted sum of their utilities is greatest.

Our objector will say that the policy maximizer allows her choices to be ruled by the dead hand of the past, whereas he, the performance maximizer, lives and chooses in the present. But our objector is mistaken. Unable to escape the burden of choice, the performance maximizer must, choosing in the present, keep in mind that his attempt to maximize utility in the present performance is constrained by his future attempts to maximize utility on the occasion of each successive performance. He is ruled by the unborn, and perhaps never-to-be-born, hands of his possible futures. And his yoke is the worse. Maximization is the policy maximizer's goal, but the performance maximizer's fate.[7]

Before leaving our objector to that fate, let us note carefully that the reply to him does not insist that one should maximize in the long run rather than the short run. The would-be deterrer who fails to deter and who must then make good on her threat in order to carry out her conditional intention, is not maximizing at all. Her reason for sticking to her guns is not to teach others by example, not to improve her prospects for successful deterrence in the future, or anything of

[7]I expand on this point in Gauthier [8].

the sort. Her reason is simply that the expected utility or payoff of her failed policy depended on her willingness to stick to her guns.

Let us suppose that each person or nation—each actor—knew (never mind how!) that but once in his life he would be in a situation in which, by convincing another actor that he would respond in a non-maximizing way to a possible choice of the other, he could increase his expected utility by reducing the probability that the other would make that choice. Here, if the other is not deterred, carrying out the non-maximizing response can, *ex hypothesi*, have no effect on the actor's credibility or on future deterrence. Yet he can hope to deter only if the other believes that he will, or at least may, make that non-maximizing response. And adopting a genuine policy of deterrence may be the only way of bringing about that belief, or increasing its strength, in the other person. Even in this one-shot situation, a deterrent policy, committing one to a non-maximizing choice should deterrence fail, may be utility maximizing. If I have convinced you of this, then I have accomplished my most important task in this essay, because only those convinced can have a proper understanding, not only of deterrence, but also of the whole range of situations, including most prominently generalized Prisoner's Dilemmas, in which policies that require non-maximizing behavior are utility maximizing, and so rational.[8] And what these policies effect is throughout the same—to alter the probabilities of an actor's being in certain situations, facing certain choices. Only in understanding this do we begin to appreciate the true characteristics and complexity of utility-maximizing rationality.

VI

I have referred in passing to the expression of a conditional intention to *retal* as a threat. And the argument that I have advanced for the rationality of a deterrent policy is indeed an argument for the rationality of threat enforcement. If the expected gain from deterrence exceeds the expected cost of carrying out the deterrent threat, where each expectation is probability weighted, and if no less costly means of deterrence is available, then the rational actor sincerely threatens and enforces her threat should it fail to deter.

Not all threats, we may pause to note, are properly deterrent. The kidnapper threatens the parents of his victim with the death of their

---

[8]I discuss this, although obscurely, in "Reason and Maximization," above, pp. 227–230. Matters should be clearer in Gauthier [5], ch. 6.

child should they fail to pay; it would be perverse to say that he seeks to deter them from nonpayment. But I shall not attempt an analysis of threats here. My purpose in introducing the conception of threat is to broaden the perspective of our analysis so that it embraces both threatener and threatened, and in this perspective we shall find a new and problematic dimension in our argument.

If we think of nuclear retaliation as a policy of threat enforcement, yet we must note immediately that it is also a policy of threat resistance. The US threatens nuclear retaliation to deter a strike by the SU, but a strike policy, as we have described it, may center on the issuance of a credible threat of nuclear attack should some initiative be opposed, and retaliation thus embraces resistance to such a threat. In the context of nuclear deterrence each party may be viewed both as threatener and as threatened, both as a potential threat enforcer and as a potential threat resister. Not all threat situations involve this symmetry, but the standpoints of threatener and threatened are themselves significantly parallel. For each must decide whether to adopt an intention—to enforce a threat or to resist a threat. The enforcer seeks to avoid that situation in which enforcement would be required; the resister seeks to prevent that situation in which resistance would be required. The argument of section IV may be adapted to show the rationale for both threat enforcement and threat resistance. Since, taken together, enforcement and resistance make threat behavior unprofitable, the existence of parallel rationales may cast doubt on the rationality of any policy involving threats, and so on a policy of deterrence.

Let us consider briefly how the argument of section IV applies to enforcement and resistance. Both the would-be threat enforcer and the would-be threat resister seek to reduce the probability of being in an undesirable situation (having one's threat ignored/facing a credible threat) by expressing a conditional intention to respond in a mutually costly way in that situation. Enforcement/resistance success lies in avoiding the undesirable situation; enforcement/resistance failure lies in having to carry out one's conditional intention. The minimum required probability for enforcement/resistance success is defined as the probability of that success in the lottery between success and failure that the enforcer/resister considers indifferent to no enforcement/no resistance. A policy of threat enforcement/threat resistance is rational only if the proportionate decrease that it effects in the probability of having one's threat ignored/facing a credible threat is greater than the minimum required probability for enforcement/resistance success.

The parallel rationales that can be constructed for threat enforcement and threat resistance may seem to show the overall irrationality of threat behavior. For if both enforcement and resistance are rational, then either the worst case prevails, in which a threat is issued, ignored, and executed, or the prethreat situation prevails, no threat being issued since, if it were, it would be ignored and then executed. But although there is a deep irrationality in threat behavior, the parallel rationales do not themselves suffice to demonstrate it. For they show only that the structure of the argument for enforcement is the same as that for resistance. They do not show that, in a given situation, threat enforcement and threat resistance are equally rational or irrational.

We may illustrate this by our core example—nuclear deterrence. Suppose that the SU were to announce a policy of deterrence-resistance. It will carry out, or threaten, a nuclear strike if it considers that a retaliatory response would be costly to the US—if it believes that the maximizing US response would be acquiescence or submission.

As we noted in section III, the SU is perceived to prefer strike and no retaliation to no strike, and no strike to strike and retaliation. Given these preferences, a policy of deterrence-resistance is rational for the SU only if the proportionate decrease that it effects in the probability of a US policy of retaliation is greater than the minimum required probability for the success of deterrence-resistance. But this is the probability of strike and no retaliation in that lottery between strike and no retaliation, and strike and retaliation, that the SU finds indifferent to the certainty of no strike. No strike represents, in effect, acceptance of the status quo; we may plausibly suppose that the SU would require a very high probability of gain—of the US acquiescence entailed in strike and no retaliation—and a correspondingly low probability of loss—of the nuclear exchange entailed in strike and retaliation—before it would be indifferent between such a lottery and the status quo. We may plausibly suppose that deterrence-resistance will not seem to the SU to be a utility-maximizing policy.

The US, as we also noted in section III, is supposed to prefer no strike to strike and no retaliation, and strike and no retaliation to strike and retaliation. Thus as we established in section IV, deterrence is a rational policy for the US only if the proportionate decrease that it effects in the probability of a strike policy by the SU is greater than the probability of no strike in the lottery between no strike and strike and retaliation that the US finds indifferent to the certainty of strike and no retaliation. Although we have refrained from attempting to estimate this probability, except to suggest that it is likely to be high, yet we may note that strike and no retaliation represents, not the status quo, but a real worsening of the situation of the US. Even though a nuclear exchange is a greater worsening, yet we may plausibly suppose that the US would not require a very high probability of maintaining the status quo implicit in no strike, and a very low corresponding probability of loss through nuclear exchange, to be indifferent between such a lottery and the loss implicit in no retaliation. Although any firm judgment must be beyond armchair competence, it may well be the case that nuclear retaliation is a rational policy for the US, although resistance to deterrence is not a rational policy for the SU.

Thus the parallel between the rationales for threat enforcement and threat resistance does not in itself show the irrationality of a policy of deterrence. However, even if threat behavior is rationally justifiable from the standpoint of a particular actor, there is a need for mutually agreed measures to remove the threat-inviting context. Fundamental to Hobbes's analysis of the state of nature is the need to exit through the acceptance of mutual constraints.[9] The state of nations and, more especially, of nuclear powers is our nearest analogue to the state of nature, and Hobbes's advice applies to it. The need to rely on deterrence is a sign of the presence of peril sufficient to justify an agreement removing or minimizing the need. This will be my final theme in this paper; even if deterrence not only may be, but is, a rational policy for the US, the nuclear status quo that demands deterrence is not a rational state of affairs.

VII

Threat behavior is nonproductive, and indeed counterproductive, if we take its effects on all persons into account. This does not result directly from the intentions of the actors involved. The person who issues a threat seeks to increase her expectation of benefit, but only by reducing the expectation of the party threatened. The threat enforcer's willingness to risk an unfavorable outcome lowers the prospects of the person threatened and thus brings about a redistribution of benefits and costs. But a redistribution need not be a reduction of net benefit. The threat resister simply seeks a restoration of the status quo; given a threat, his strategy is redistributive, but taken in a larger context, it is intended as a counter that renders threats ineffective. The threat resister, through his willingness to risk an unfavorable outcome, seeks to restore his initial expectation of benefit, but not by reducing the prethreat expectation of the prospective threatener. Again, there need be no reduction in net benefit.

---

[9]This is the import of Hobbes's second law of nature; Hobbes [4], ch. 14.

However, if in an ideal world threat behavior might avoid mutual costs, yet in the real world we must expect that from time to time either a threat enforcer or a threat resister will be called on to make good on a conditional non-maximizing intention. And when this occurs, the result is sub-optimal. The payoff from a failed threat, or from failed threat resistance, is less desirable to each party than either the payoff expected in the absence of any threat or the redistributed payoff resulting from a successful threat. Insofar as threat behavior involves a real risk of such a sub-optimal result, it must be regarded as *ex ante* disadvantageous from the standpoint of any actor who is sufficiently uncertain about future prospects. Only someone who could expect to be especially favorably placed with respect to successful threatening would lack *ex ante* reason to agree to eschew threat behavior. Rational persons will therefore find the mutual avoidance of threat behavior to be an appropriate matter for agreement.

We should note here a contrast between threat situations and collective goods situations. Where the possibility of providing collective goods is present, rational persons can expect to benefit from mutual agreement to assure the optimal provision of these goods, even though such provision may require non-maximizing behavior. For the outcome of individually maximizing behavior in such situations is typically sub-optimal; each party stands to gain from making and adhering to an optimizing agreement in comparison to the expected outcome of no agreement. Here non-maximizing behavior is set in a productive context. But in threat situations, the non-maximizing behavior required to make the issuance of or resistance to threats rational is not productive. The parties to such behavior are not enabled to reach outcomes mutually preferable to those they would otherwise expect; instead, they are likely to reach outcomes mutually less preferable. Hence actors faced with the problem of providing collective goods have reason to enter into agreements calling for non-maximizing behavior, whereas actors faced with the problem of threats have reason to enter into agreements calling for the renunciation of policies with non-maximizing threat components. Faced with collective goods problems, rational actors will agree mutually to constrain their directly maximizing dispositions. Faced with threat problems, rational actors will agree mutually not to constrain their directly maximizing dispositions in ways that would make credible threats possible.

Deterrence, as a typical policy of threat enforcement and threat resistance, is itself clearly unproductive. But in considering the terms on which it should rationally be renounced, it is essential to recognize its role in stabilizing human interaction. For the threat implicit in nuclear deterrence is not a threat against social order but rather a threat intended to maintain the conditions under which viable and fair social order is possible.

We may appeal here to a normative idea clearly formulated by John Rawls, that society is "a cooperative venture for mutual advantage."[10] This idea immediately suggests a baseline condition for social interaction: no person or other social actor is entitled to benefit at the expense or cost of another, where both benefit and cost are measured against a no-interaction baseline. That is, no actor is entitled to make himself or herself better off than could be expected in the absence of interaction, by policies or performances that render other actors worse off than they would expect to be in the absence of interaction. A refusal to accept or abide by this condition is an indication of an unwillingness to interact cooperatively with others—an unwillingness, in Hobbesian language, to seek peace and follow it.

Now a policy that includes a willingness to resort to an initial nuclear strike, even if only in the event of a failed threat, is clearly ruled out by this condition. For the effect of such a policy is clearly to worsen the situation of the victim in a way that exceeds what he could expect in the absence of interaction. And the policy cannot itself be treated as defensive, as merely preventing the actor from having his own position worsened through interaction with the victim. An aggressive strike policy is one that seeks to better the condition of its holder through measures that worsen the condition of those against whom it is directed. To resort to such a policy is to reject the prospect of cooperative interaction with others.

Nuclear retaliation, as a deterrent policy, is directed at protecting the retaliator from being victimized by any actor willing to engage in a first strike. It is, then, not to seek to redistribute benefits in a way more favorable to the would-be deterrer than could be expected in the absence of interaction but, rather, to ensure that her situation is not worsened in terms of that baseline. It is directed at upholding, rather than subverting, the requirement that human society be a cooperative venture for mutual advantage.

In itself, of course, nothing could be less cooperative, less directed at mutual advantage, than the use of nuclear weapons. But a retaliatory, deterrent policy is directed at preventing such use—directed at maintaining those conditions in which societies may be brought to recognize the benefits of cooperation. A policy of nuclear deterrence clearly has failed if a nuclear exchange occurs. But the serious alternative to such a policy, in the absence of agreement to eschew all threat behavior, can only be the willingness to accept victimization, to

[10]Rawls [1], p. 4.

suffer passively a nuclear strike or to acquiesce in whatever the potential striker demands as the price of its avoidance.

Morality, in my view, follows rationality. Practical rationality is concerned with the maximization of benefit; the primary requirements of morality are that in maximizing benefit, advantage must not be taken and need not be given.[11] Nuclear deterrence, despite its horrific character, is then a moral policy—a policy aimed at encouraging the conditions under which morally acceptable and rational interaction among nations may occur. If we agree that the idea of society as a cooperative venture for mutual advantage, and the related proviso against benefiting through interaction that worsens the condition of others, express a fundamental moral ideal, then the willingness to maintain those conditions under which this ideal may be realized, and the refusal to acquiesce in measures that would subvert it, must themselves be the objects of moral approval rather than censure.

Rational nations, recognizing the need to seek peace and follow it given the costs of war, can unilaterally renounce the first use of nuclear weapons and thereby end all strike policies. Rational nations can mutually agree to destroy their holdings of nuclear weapons, at least insofar as these weapons are directed against each other, and so can end all deterrent policies. Since the knowledge that brought nuclear weapons into being will not disappear, we cannot expect a world fully free of nuclear threats. We can only minimize a peril that cannot be exorcised. But to understand the conditions under which we may rationally agree to the mutual abandonment of deterrent and other threat policies, we must first understand the rationale of deterrent policies and the role of these policies in maintaining the conditions of acceptable international interaction. Hobbes conjoins two fundamental requirements in relating the law and the right of nature: "To seek Peace, and follow it" and "By all means we can, to defend our selves."[12] Hobbes understands that these requirements are mutually supportive; a correct understanding of nuclear deterrence supports his view.

[11]Neither utilitarians nor Kantians will find this conception of morality to their taste. I cannot defend it here, but see Gauthier [5].
[12]Hobbes [1], ch. 14.

IDEOLOGY

[14]

The Social Contract
as Ideology

The conception of social relationships as contractual lies at the core of our ideology. Indeed, that core is constituted by the intersection of this conception with the correlative conceptions of human activity as appropriative and of rationality as utility maximizing. My concern is to clarify this thesis and to enhance its descriptive plausibility as a characterization of our ideology, but to undermine its normative plausibility as ideologically effective.

I

The thesis refers to our ideology. There are two terms here which require immediate clarification; the first is "our." Philosophers habitually use the first-person-plural pronoun; its use demands specification. Who are "we"? In this essay, first-person-plural references are intended to denote those persons who have inhabited Western Europe, who are descended from such inhabitants, or who live or have lived in social structures developed from those of Western Europe during the past three to four hundred years. I am supposing, without further defense, that these persons share certain ideas and certain ways of thinking and behaving that permit the attribution to them of an ideology.

"Ideology" is the second term which requires clarification. It has not been employed with great consistency or clarity by social thinkers.[1] It picks out some aspect of our consciousness, frequently pe-

[1]For some brief characterizations of ideology, see Waxman, pp. 3–4. Superstructure and false consciousness are, of course, part of the Marxian account of ideology. The

joratively, whether because of its allegedly derivative character (super-structure) or its allegedly misleading character (false consciousness). Although the demise of ideology as a determinant of social values and practices has been widely celebrated, more recent reports suggest that the celebrations may themselves be ideological in character. My use of the term is intended to retain the place of ideology in consciousness, and indeed perhaps to ensure the permanence of that place, without pejorative commitment.

Ideology is part of the deep structure of self-consciousness.[2] By self-consciousness I understand that capacity of human beings to con-ceive themselves in relation to other humans, to human structures and institutions, and to the nonhuman or natural environment, and to act in the light of these conceived relationships. Exhibited in these thoughts and activities is a conception of the self-as-human. This conception need not be, and typically is not, actually expressed in self-consciousness. Rather, it must be inferred from a person's actual thoughts and activities, insofar as they concern himself, his fellows, his society, and his world, as that underlying structure of ideas which affords their most economical foundation. This conception of self-as-human is thus a theoretical construct that we attribute to the ground of self-consciousness to explain its content, the surface of overt thought and action. This theoretical construct is what I refer to as ideology.

A conception of oneself as a person may be part of the content of consciousness. But this conception is not what I refer to as ideology, for it need not be identical with that conception which is exhibited in one's other thoughts and activities. Of course, ideology must afford the foundation for one's conscious self-awareness, but this does not preclude a difference, and even a contradiction, between the content of the ideological substructure and the content of overt self-aware-ness. As with language, deep structure and surface structure must be distinguished, and their characteristics may be found to be opposed.

This similarity of language and consciousness is not accidental; in my view, self-consciousness depends on the actualization of linguistic capacity. Both language and consciousness have the deceptive ap-

---

demise of ideology was celebrated in Bell, and discussed in Waxman. Note such titles as "The End of Ideology as Ideology" by Robert A. Haber, "The Anti-Ideology Ide-ologues" by Michael Harrington, "The End of 'The End of Ideology'" by Donald Clark Hodges.

[2]My sketchy characterization of ideology needs to be amplified and embedded in a theory of consciousness. There is, of course, no space for that here. What I have to say owes much to my reading of Dennett, esp. ch. 6. But I should not want to suggest that Dennett would accept parenthood for my ideas.

pearance of transparency; both conceal a deep structure which unconsciously affects conscious activity. Ideology is not, or at least need not be, false consciousness, but it is necessarily prereflective consciousness. It can be the subject of reflection; it can be brought to the surface of our thought, as indeed this essay is intended to exhibit. But its role does not require this reflection or an assessment of its validity or truth. Whether its role can be affected by reflection—whether the deep structure of self-consciousness can be affected by bringing it to the surface—is a matter to which I shall allude in the course of this essay, although it may be exhibited more fully by the response to an inquiry into ideology rather than by the inquiry itself.

The structure of the ideas that comprise an ideology is not idiosyncratic. Persons who differ fundamentally in the ideological grounds of their activities would find interaction and communication difficult, if not frequently impossible. Whatever their supposed purpose, one of the main functions of social institutions is, and must be, to maintain and transmit a common ideology among those who compose a society. Without the effective functioning of such institutions, a society would rapidly disintegrate as its members ceased to be able to interact.

However, I do not suppose that a single, invariant structure of ideas holds for all persons in all times and places. My basic thesis presupposes only the existence of a common structure for us, that is, for modern Western Europeans and their descendants and offshoots.

The articulation of an ideology, like the articulation of any deep structure, cannot be expected to be an easy task. Many recent studies, especially in moral philosophy but also in political philosophy, have tended to ignore it. They have focused on the language or the logic of morals and politics and on practical, moral, and political reasoning, but frequently they have examined only the surface structure, the ideas we consciously express about ourselves. John Rawls's *A Theory of Justice* is a pioneering work in many respects, but in none more important than in its awareness of the significance of deep structure, although Rawls seems to suggest that this structure is invariant for human beings and not relative only to our own society.[3] And it is most

---

[3] "Now one may think of moral philosophy . . . as the attempt to describe our moral capacity. . . . This enterprise is very difficult. For by such a description is not meant simply a list of the judgments on institutions and actions that we are prepared to render, accompanied with supporting reasons when these are offered. Rather, what is required is a formulation of a set of principles which, when conjoined to our beliefs and knowledge of the circumstances, would lead us to make these judgments with their supporting reasons were we to apply these principles conscientiously and intelligently. . . . The principles which describe them [our moral capacities] must be presumed to have a complex structure, and the concepts involved will require serious study.

"A useful comparison here is with the problem of describing the sense of gram-

noteworthy that in articulating this deep structure, he is led to develop, once again in the history of our political thought, the theory of the social contract.

II

The theory of the social contract has been advanced in more and less embracing forms. Thomas Hobbes and John Locke are classic exponents of these contrasting approaches. Since my concern is primarily with the Hobbist variant, I shall begin with a brief sketch of its alternative.

Locke supposes that a certain group of men, namely landed proprietors, those who have successfully appropriated or inherited real property or estate, contract together for mutual protection and well-being.[4] Their contract brings civil government into existence, but civil government is not, in Locke's view, the only or the primary ground for social relationships among human beings. Locke's landed proprietors are heads of households, and their household relationships—of man with wife, father with child, and master with servant—are prior to and indeed fall outside of the contractual relationship which gives rise to political society. Furthermore, although here Locke is less explicit, it seems evident that landed proprietors enter into relationships of sociability, one with another, which are neither conditions nor consequences of the contract among them. And their relations one with another, and with other human beings, explicitly fall under the divine law of nature, which regulates conduct outside political society, in the state of nature, as well as conduct within it.

Hobbes's theory affords an altogether larger scope to contractual relations.[5] Indeed, for Hobbes, relations among human beings are of two kinds only: relations of hostility, which obtain in and constitute the state of nature, and relations of contract, which obtain in and constitute the state of society. In the state of nature, every man has the right to do whatever he will in order to preserve and benefit himself;

---

maticalness that we have for the sentences of our native language. . . . This is a difficult undertaking which . . . is known to require theoretical constructions that far outrun the ad hoc precepts of our explicit grammatical knowledge. A similar situation presumably holds in moral philosophy. . . . A correct account of moral capacities will certainly involve principles and theoretical constructions which go much beyond the norms and standards cited in everyday life" (Rawls [1], pp. 46–47). Other relevant passages are on pp. 126–128, 137–138, and 143–145.

[4]Locke [4], especially Second Treatise, chs. 7–9. See also ch. 2 for discussion of the law of nature.

[5]Hobbes [4], esp. chs. 13–17 and 20.

the result is the state of war "where every man is Enemy to every man." To bring this self-defeating condition to an end, every man is supposed to contract with his fellows to establish a commonwealth under a single and all-powerful sovereign. Only within a commonwealth is any sociability possible. The family is itself a miniature commonwealth; the father, or sometimes the mother, is sovereign, and the children are supposed to contract with their parent to obey in return for being allowed to live, in the way in which the vanquished in war contracts with the victor. And this latter contract, of vanquished with victor, which establishes sovereignty by acquisition, is explicitly stated by Hobbes to constitute the relation between servant and master. The contractual relationship among men, in establishing political society, is thus the model on which all other human relationships are interpreted.

It is Hobbes's radical contractarianism which I am attributing to our ideology. To make this attribution is to hold that our thoughts and activities, insofar as they concern ourselves and our relationships, are best understood by supposing that we treat all of these relationships as if they were contractual. Only the relation of hostility is excluded from the scope of contract, and only it is natural to man. All other human relationships are treated as essentially similar in character, and all are conventional, the product of human agreement.

The theory of the social contract, as part of our ideology, is not concerned with the objective character of social institutions and relationships. It is not a piece of speculative, but purportedly actual, history or sociology. Contractarians do not suppose, either explicitly or implicitly, that human society originated in a contract, or is now maintained by contract. They do not suppose that children contract with their parents. To suppose that the theory of the social contract must be intended to explain the origin of actual societies is to confuse deep structure with surface structure; our contractual conception of human relationships may ground an explanation which makes no appeal to contract.

The theory itself concerns the rationale of relationships among persons, and between society and its members, rather than the cause of those relationships. The justification of rights and duties, institutions and practices, is to be found by regarding them as if they were contractual, and showing the rationality of this hypothetical contractual base. Of course, a theory of rationale does have an explanatory function. Were the theory true, then fully self-conscious beings whose social environment was entirely the product of their deliberate choice would only relate contractually one to another. For such beings the theory of the social contract, and indeed our entire ideology, would not be a theoretical construct, but rather the conscious basis of their social thought and practice. As part of our ideology, then, the contract theory rationalizes social relationships by providing an ideal, nonactual explanation of their existence.

In attributing this ideology to us, I am not defending it. I am not claiming that society is to be understood, or ought to be understood, as if it were contractual. It may well be absurd to so understand society. What I am doing is claiming that our thoughts and actions are to be understood as if we supposed that all social relationships were to be rationalized in contractual terms. Note that "as if" plays a dual role in my account: our conscious thoughts, and overt actions, are to be explained *as if* we held the theory of the social contract, that is, the theory that all social relationships are to be understood *as if* they were contractual.

I should not want to argue that radical contractarianism of a Hobbist kind has unequivocally dominated our thoughts and practices. Rather, I believe this to be the final form of the contractarian conception of society, the form toward which it develops as an ideology, gradually increasing its influence on our thoughts and leading us to abandon earlier ideas of human relationships as natural or supernatural rather than as conventional. I believe, although I cannot fully defend this belief here, that our society is moving toward a more Hobbist position. Evidence for this may be found in political life, for example in the "social contract" proposals of the British government under former prime minister Harold Wilson. But the most significant recent evidence is found in the extension of contractarian thought to family and domestic life. We may cite the arguments and practices of those who seek to divest the marriage contract of its religious and moral overtones, to treat it as the ordinary contract which, they argue, it really is. We may cite those who suppose that housework should be paid for, or that childraising is but one occupation among many possible vocations and that those who do it, too, should be remunerated. And we may cite the words of a Montreal woman on the "jock circuit" (the circuit of those who offer nonprofessional diversion to professional athletes): "In a way, it's a sort of business arrangement—but then, aren't all man-woman relationships?"[6]

On reflection, we may disavow contractarianism. We may insist that there is more to human relationships than the conventions which result from agreement. The contractarian can admit this, as long as he holds that these other features of human relationships are nones-

---

[6]The source for this is one of the magazines distributed in Canada with the Saturday newspaper. The magazine has found its way from my desk into a bundle of old newspapers, leaving behind only the quote.

sential, a sentimental residue from the past, or an emotional patina which affords a more pleasing aura to an otherwise bare artifice. But the contractarian can also maintain that we delude ourselves, and that indeed our ideology induces us to preach what we do not practice. The practice of contractarianism may indeed be most effective if it is explicitly denied. The surface structure induced by the ideology may have a content incompatible with it.

This suggests a different linkage between ideology and false consciousness than the Marxian identification. Ideology, deep structure, may give rise to false consciousness, as surface structure. If so, then presumably bringing the ideology to consciousness, surfacing it, will undermine its effectiveness, for the contradiction between the ideology and our conscious conceptions will become patent.

In appraising contractarianism in this essay, I shall not go beyond questions of logical coherence and practical effectiveness. The further question of truth or validity is a difficult one for any ideology. The problem, at least in part, is that social institutions, practices, and relationships do not exist independently of human activity and human thought. Hence the view of these relationships presented by an ideology may be confirmed, for its adherents, because they act to constitute their relationships in accordance with it, while it may be disconfirmed, for its opponents, because they act to constitute their relationships on a quite different basis. No doubt many social theorists would insist that institutions and practices have an objective character quite independent of the thought and intent of those persons involved in them and that ideology may falsify this objective character. But it will not do simply to insist that human relationships are not, in fact, to be explained as they are ideologically conceived, since ideology concerns rationale rather than literal explanation. To say that an ideology is false or invalid must, then, be to say that the rationale it provides for society is *incompatible* with the literal truth about that society. But how are we to determine incompatibility between the "as-if" and the "is"? This question I raise only to put aside.

III

To conceive all social relationships as contractual is to suppose that men, with their particular human characteristics, are prior to society. The contract theory expresses this priority in temporal terms, giving us the picture of men in a state of nature entering society on the basis of a contract. But, as I have pointed out, the language of the theory is the language of ideal explanation; the men in the state of nature are not ourselves. The theory does not require that actual human individuals are temporally prior to their society; here, as elsewhere, temporal priority is a metaphor for conceptual priority.

What contractarianism does require is, first of all, that individual human beings not only can, but must, be understood apart from society. The fundamental characteristics of men are not products of their social existence. Rather, in affording the motivations that underlie human activity in the state of nature and that are expressed in natural hostility, they constitute the conditions of man's social existence. Thus man is social because he is human, and not human because he is social. In particular, self-consciousness and language must be taken as conditions, not products, of society.

But more than this is implicit in contractarianism. It would be compatible with the claim that the individual is prior to society, to suppose nonetheless that human sociability is itself a natural and fundamental characteristic of individuals, which expresses itself directly in social relations among human beings. And this is denied by contract theory in its insistence upon the essentially conventional character of society. Men who were naturally sociable would not need to contract together in order to form society and would not rationalize society in contractarian terms. Although contract might be the foundation of government, as in Locke, society would not be a purely artificial creation. Contract as the foundation of all society is required only by men who are not inherently sociable.

Furthermore, radical contractarianism is incompatible with the view that men undergo fundamental change in becoming members of society. Men's reasons for contracting one with another are supposed to arise out of their presocial needs in the state of nature. If contractarian ideology is to be effective in rationalizing social relationships, then these needs must be represented not as only presocial but as permanent, so that the reasons for entering the contract will also be reasons for maintaining the society created thereby. Society is thus conceived as a mere instrument for men whose fundamental motivation is presocial, nonsocial, and fixed. If men are, in fact, socialized beings, so that human nature is in part a social product, then contractarian ideology must conceal this, representing social needs as if they were the product of presocial nature. Rousseau may use the device, and even the title, of the social contract, but the theory which he formulates tends to subvert contractarian ideology in its overt distinction of social man from natural man.[7]

_____

[7]"This passage from the state of nature to civil society produces in man a very remarkable change, in substituting justice for instinct in his conduct, and giving his actions the morality which previously they lacked. . . . If the abuses of this new condition did not often degrade him below that from which he has come, he should bless

Although the contractarian cannot represent man as a social being he need not deny, as Hobbes may seem to, that human beings as we know them, within society, do display sociable characteristics.[8] The contractarian need but insist that man is sociable only because he creates society; human sociability is the product, and not the condition, of social existence. And as the product of what is itself conventional, this sociability is but an accidental attribute of human nature, an overlay on a fundamentally and permanently nonsocial character, possessing a merely conventional existence.

The correlate of the claim that man is nonsocial by nature is, of course, the claim that society is not, and cannot be, an end in itself. Man's social existence is not self-justifying. In offering an effective rationale for society, the contractarian must face the charge that because society is conventional, it is therefore arbitrary. Thrasymachus argued this against Socrates;[9] today there is a strong tendency to extrapolate from the contractarian, conventionalist view of such fundamental human relationships as male and female, or parent and child, to the contention that such relationships are arbitrary. The debate about the relation between *physis* and *nomos* has not advanced greatly in the past twenty-four hundred years. But to suppose that what is conventional must therefore be arbitrary is entirely contrary

---

unceasingly the happy moment . . . which, from a stupid and limited animal, made an intelligent being and a man" (Rousseau [2], bk. I, ch. 8, my translation). Also, "He who dares undertake to create a people ought to feel himself capable of changing, so to speak, human nature, of transforming each individual, who by himself is complete and solitary, into part of a larger whole from which he receives almost his very life and being, of changing his constitution to strengthen it, of substituting an interdependent and moral existence for the physical and independent existence which we all have received from nature. It is necessary, in a word, that he remove man's own powers, in order to give him ones which are foreign to him and which he can not use without the help of others" (bk. II, ch. 7, my translation).

It should be noted here that Rawls subverts contractarianism in a way very similar to Rousseau. Having determined one's fundamental legitimating principle for society (for Rousseau, that social relationships respect liberty in avoiding the dependence of one man on another; for Rawls, that social relationships embody mutual respect), one then introduces a "most favored" initial situation, in which persons would rationally choose a society based on the legitimating principle. One then supposes that in society, human beings are so socialized that their self-conception comes to center on that legitimating principle; hence they will consider their social relationships to be those they would have chosen. Thus the principle acquires a contractarian rationale.

But the rationale is spurious; since the initial situation is selected to ensure the "correct" choice, the act of choice is evidently neither necessary nor sufficient to justify the legitimating principle. The real character of the theory then emerges when one asks for the grounds of the legitimating principle.

[8]"Men have no pleasure, (but on the contrary a great deal of griefe) in keeping company, where there is no power able to over-awe them all" (Hobbes [4], ch. 13).
[9]Plato, 338d–339a.

to the spirit of contractarianism, which finds only in convention a sufficient rationale for society.

To consider society arbitrary is to suppose that it affords no sufficient fulfillment or meets no fundamental need of most or all of its members. To avoid the charge of arbitrariness, then, the contractarian must relate the conventional character of society to a natural base in human nature. He must show society to be the indirect, rationalized expression of natural and essential human characteristics. In this way, by showing that society has, and must have, instrumental value to the naturally nonsocial human being, the contractarian justifies society to the individual and thus resolves what has been the central problem in our political philosophy.

But how does the contractarian show that society must have instrumental value to human beings? I shall argue that he relies on the view that human activity is basically appropriative, thus establishing one of the links set out in my original thesis. Before I can make this argument convincing, however, I must first sketch part of the outline of a general formal theory of human interaction. By attending to the requirements of this theory, I shall seek to develop a conception of human good which will assure to society a sufficient instrumental value.

IV

Consider any situation in which there are several persons, each with several possible actions, and in which the outcome, as it affects each person, depends on the particular combination of actions performed. I shall define the *state of nature* as that relation holding between any two persons in the situation if and only if each acts on an independently selected principle of action, and *society* as that relation holding between any two persons in the situation if and only if both act on a mutually selected principle of action.[10] Note that, so defined, the state of nature and society are exclusive, but not exhaustive, alternatives. Both exclude fundamentally unequal relationships in which there is a one-way dependence in the selection of principles of action. (It is perhaps worth mentioning that thinkers like Thrasymachus assume such a one-way dependence in arguing for the arbitrariness of society.)

Suppose that in a given situation, every person is in the state of

---

[10]To act on a mutually selected principle of action is to act on the basis of a choice, made by each person, of a single set of actions, one for each person in the situation; until all choose the same set, no one acts.

nature with respect to every other person. I shall call the outcome of the actions performed in this full state of nature the *natural outcome*. That is, the natural outcome results if each person acts on a principle of action which he selects for himself independently of the others. It is evident that a society will be considered arbitrary by those persons for whom the outcome of social action is worse than the natural outcome. Hence, a nonarbitrary society must improve on the natural outcome for everyone.

The outcome of a situation is *optimal* (in the Pareto sense) if and only if any alternative outcome which would be better for some person would be worse for some other person. If the natural outcome is optimal, then every alternative must make someone worse off, and so it is not possible for society to improve on the full state of nature for everyone. A society embracing all of the persons in the situation would either bring about the natural outcome, which would make the existence of the society pointless, or some outcome worse for some persons than the natural outcome, which would make the society arbitrary from their standpoint.

A nonarbitrary society embracing all of the persons in a situation is therefore possible only if the natural outcome of the situation is not optimal. Of course, not every society conceivable in such a situation will be nonarbitrary. The mutually selected principle of action must be such that the outcome is better for some persons, and at least as good for all persons, as the outcome in the full state of nature. It is reasonable to require further that the outcome of society be itself optimal, for otherwise some persons will consider it arbitrary, not because it is worse for them than the natural outcome but because it is worse for them than some alternative which would leave everyone else at least as well off.

In addition to optimality, the stability of an outcome is of importance in analyzing nonarbitrary societies. An outcome is *stable*, or in equilibrium, if and only if no one person can bring about an alternative outcome which is better for himself by unilaterally changing his way of acting. If an outcome is not stable, then it is evident that some person or persons will be tempted to defect from an agreement to accept a principle of action which brings it about.

Situations in which the natural outcome is not optimal may be divided into three types, using the concept of stability. Note that in all such situations, there must be some outcome which is both optimal and no worse for anyone than the natural outcome.

A situation is of *type I* if and only if (1) there are some outcomes which are (a) stable, (b) optimal, and (c) no worse for anyone than the natural outcome; and (2) there is a nonempty set of outcomes, each

satisfying (1), such that no member of the set is strongly dispreferred
to any outcome satisfying (1) by any person. I shall suppose that the
persons in a type I situation will be prepared to act on any principle of
action which has as its outcome a member of the set of outcomes
specified in (2). For such an outcome will be stable and optimal, worse
for no one than the state of nature, and no one will strongly disprefer
it to any other outcome satisfying these conditions.

A situation is of *type II* if and only if (1) there are some outcomes
which are (a) stable, (b) optimal, and (c) no worse for anyone than the
natural outcome; and (2) any outcome which satisfies (1) is strongly
dispreferred by some person to some other outcome satisfying (1). I
shall suppose that the persons in a type II situation will be prepared
all to act on some member of the set of principles of mutual action
each of which has, as its outcome, a state of affairs satisfying (1). But
these persons will not be prepared, without further ado, to act on any
member of the set, since the outcome of each will be strongly dispreferred by some person or persons to the outcome of some other
member. Hence they will bargain with each other to select a principle
of mutual action from the set.

A situation is of *type III* if and only if (1) there are some outcomes
which are (a) optimal and (b) no worse for anyone than the natural
outcome, but (2) no outcome satisfying (1) is stable. In such a situation, some persons will be tempted to defect from any principle of
mutual action which has, as its outcome, a state of affairs satisfying (1),
since these persons can bring about an outcome better for themselves
by such unilateral defection. Hence I shall suppose that the persons in
a type III situation will be prepared all to act on some member of the
set of principles of mutual action each of which has as its outcome a
state of affairs satisfying (1), *provided* these persons have some guarantee that their agreement will be effective, that is, that no person will
unilaterally violate it.

The persons in a type I situation require some procedure for *coordination,* to ensure that all adhere to the same principle of action. The
persons in a type II situation require some procedure for *bargaining,*
to enable them to agree on a principle of action (and possibly a coordination procedure, if bargaining results in a set of principles, each of
which is about equally acceptable to each member of society). The
persons in a type III situation require, in addition to bargaining and
perhaps coordination procedures, some *constraining* devices, both internal ("conscience") and external ("authority"), to afford them the
guarantee that each will act to bring about the agreed outcome. The
rationale for society, and hence for the social contract on which it is

based, is thus provided by these three desiderata: coordination, bargaining, and constraint.

Following Hobbes, I shall suppose that what characterizes political society is the existence of some form of external constraint, that is, coercive authority.[11] Coercive authority induces men to conform to principles of mutual action not in themselves maximally beneficial for all persons, by imposing costs, penalties, or punishments on failure or refusal to conform. Coercive authority will appear arbitrary from the standpoint of those subjected to it if the outcome of the coerced actions is not better than the outcome these persons would achieve in the state of nature, when they are not subject to such coercion. Were it not for type III situations, coercion would be arbitrary, and anarchism might be the only defensible form of human society. Hence it is necessary to consider further the nature of human beings and the goods which they seek, if type III situations are essential to the human condition.

V

All members of society must regard coercion as both beneficial and necessary. This imposes a severe constraint on the goods which these persons seek. Were these goods strictly competitive in nature, so that no increase in joint supply was possible and any increase in one person's good entailed a corresponding decrease in the good available to some other person, then there could be no basis for mutual improvement from the outcome of the state of nature, and coercion could not be beneficial for all. Some might better their position by coercing others, but such coercion would be totally arbitrary from the standpoint of those whose position was worsened by it.

However, were the goods sought by the members of society essentially noncompetitive, so that an increase in one person's good was generally compatible with an increase in the goods available to others, then there would be little reason for anyone to prefer one optimal outcome to another, and some optimal outcomes would be stable, so that men would face only a problem of coordination. If coercion is necessary, then there must be considerable competition for the goods sought, so that despite the possibility of mutual improvement, frequently an increase in the good of one person must entail a decrease

[11]Hobbes [4], ch. 17, esp. "the agreement . . . of men, is by Covenant only, which is Artificiall: and therefore it is no wonder if there be somewhat else required (besides Covenant) to make their Agreement constant and lasting; which is a Common Power, to keep them in awe, and to direct their actions to the Common Benefit."

in the good of another. Each person's good must therefore be sharply distinct from, and in some respects opposed to, the good of others. The resources available to the members of society must be insufficient to permit the full or almost full satisfaction of everyone simultaneously, so that they face extensive conflict over the distribution of goods.

What goods satisfy these conditions? Goods such as companionship may be left aside, since only those goods which nonsocial creatures might seek can be involved. These must be goods whose supply can be increased by cooperative action, so that mutual improvement is possible. But they must be goods which are possessed or used individually, so that distributive problems can arise. And they must be goods for which the demand is unlimited, or at least always in excess of the supply, however much that supply is augmented by cooperation, so that potential distribution problems become actual.

In classifying goods, a simple Platonic schematism will serve present purposes.[12] I shall distinguish the goods of intellect, of spirit, and of desire. Men may cooperate in the pursuit of all three, but whereas the supply of such goods as knowledge and food may be increased by concerted action, only the distribution of such a good as honor is affected. Men may possess all three, but whereas the possession of food or honor is exclusive, the possession of knowledge by one person does not affect its possession by another. Hence of the three types, only goods of desire satisfy the two requirements that cooperation increase supply and that possession create distributive problems.

But are goods of desire the object of unlimited demand? Need they be in short supply? If these goods are related to physical need, to the natural appetites for food and drink, warmth, comfort, and sex, then surely they are not—as Rousseau pointed out, in criticizing Hobbes's account of the state of nature as one in which men were in constant conflict, making a coercive society the necessary instrument of peace.[13] Only a population explosion would make the goods of desire in necessarily short supply, and there is no reason to attribute that to the state of nature. Thus if man is motivated by his natural, nonsocial appetites, and material goods are considered in relation to these appetites, the demand for these goods will not usually exceed the supply,

---

[12]The classification of goods obviously corresponds to the tripartite division of the soul in Plato, 436a–441c.

[13]Hobbes "ought to say that, the state of nature being where the care of our own conservation is the least prejudicial to that of others, it was consequently the most conducive to peace and the most appropriate for mankind. He says precisely the opposite, having inopportunely introduced into the savage's care for his own conservation the need to satisfy a multitude of passions which are the work of society" (Rousseau [1], première partie, translation mine).

and no distribution problem will arise which only coercive authority could resolve.

Rousseau's own argument for the necessity of coercion is not available to the radical contractarian, since it depends on the introduction of competitive motivation in the process of socialization. There are, it would seem, two possible arguments consistent with contractarian premises: either the threat of scarcity inherent in the state of nature must be the basis for a necessarily competitive endeavor to assure oneself against its actualization or further appetites, of a kind such that scarcity of the goods satisfying them is assured, must be attributed to men in the state of nature.

Hobbes adopts the first alternative.[14] He argues that in the absence of coercive authority, the threat of scarcity among the goods of desire leads to competition for the goods of spirit. He characterizes men as seeking endless power, not because they always lack sufficient means to preserve and gratify themselves, but because they always lack the assurance that their means are sufficient.

The emergence of the desire for power turns a situation in which there is potential for cooperation into one which is actually increasingly competitive. Since the goods which preserve us are largely the same, I increase the assurance of my survival and well-being only by decreasing your assurance. Power is thus relative, so that men who seek only power must be engaged in a zero-sum conflict—one gains only at the expense of the other. This is the pure war of every man against every man. However, its outcome is to lessen every man's ability to assure his own preservation, so that the state of nature is far worse for everyone than what would result were there a coercive force sufficient to deter each from the active pursuit of unlimited power, while enabling all to cooperate in increasing the supply of those goods necessary to preservation and well-being.

Hobbes's argument for the competitive drive for power is not fully convincing. For if goods of desire are in sufficient supply in the state of nature, so that the real threat of scarcity is slight, then the cost each person incurs in embarking on the search for ever greater power— the cost of being a party to the war of every man against every man— will be greater than the risk each runs in being satisfied with his present means to preserve himself. Hence some political theorists, such as C. B. Macpherson, have argued with considerable plausibility that Hobbes's real answer to the type of criticism advanced by Rousseau is to be found, not in his explicit account of the desire for power, but in his implicit acceptance of an appetite for material goods differ-

[14]Hobbes [4], chs. 13 and 11.

ent in kind from the limited appetites for food, drink, sex, and the like, an appetite for unlimited appropriation.[15] This appetite, peculiarly characteristic of men in Hobbes's—and in our—society, is what turns the state of nature into an arena of unlimited combat. The view which explains the need for coercion is that man is by nature and necessity an appropriator.

To appropriate is to make one's own. The most complete and literal appropriation is of course appropriation into oneself—the conversion of an external object into one's body. But not all goods can be appropriated in such a way that each loses its own bodily identity; what is one's own thus extends beyond one's body to the physically distinct objects which constitute property. To appropriate is then to acquire property; the very object of appropriation is individual possession. Now there can be property in both the goods of intellect and the goods of appetite, but primarily it is the goods of desire which are appropriated and constitute property. Since the supply of these goods can be increased by cooperative action, the goods of appropriation clearly satisfy the first two conditions requisite if coercion is to be both beneficial and necessary. But do the goods of appropriation necessarily give rise to distributive problems? Are they in short supply? Why is the appetite for appropriation characteristically *unlimited*?

The natural appetites for food, drink, and sex are *satis*fiable; one eats, drinks, copulates enough, *satis*. The appetites are constantly renewed, but so are their objects, so that a balance can be achieved between supply and demand. The desire to appropriate is not similarly satisfiable; there is no natural level of satiation for appropriative activity. If one is an appropriator *by nature*, then one must continue to appropriate, or to seek to appropriate, but the objects for appropriation are not continually renewed; what one appropriates is removed from the stock of goods available for appropriation, so that, even with the increased supply of some goods made possible by cooperation, the supply is limited by the finitude of the earth, if by no previous limit of accessibility. Hence the demand for property always exceeds the supply of goods to be appropriated. The goods of desire are always scarce from the standpoint of the appropriator, and this scarcity is increased by the presence of other appropriators. Men therefore find themselves necessarily in conflict with respect to their desires for property.

The competitive search for power is easily derived from the insatiable desire for appropriation. Hence, men find themselves in an increasingly competitive situation, in which the security of their proper-

---

[15]"Hobbes . . . came nearest to postulating man as an infinite appropriator (though he did not quite do so)" (Macpherson [1], p. 29n).

ties is continually decreasing. Thus, simply in terms of the desire to appropriate and without reference to man's other natural appetites, the state of nature leads to an outcome far worse for everyone than what would result were there a coercive force sufficient to curb each man's appetite for power and to channel his desire to appropriate into an arena which is competitive yet peaceful—the marketplace rather than the battlefield.

The market is the primary social forum for the members of a society of appropriators. Their social concern for their fellows derives from their interest in appropriation and is expressed in the relationship of exchange, whereby they transfer the possession of appropriated objects. Exchange of property is the primary function of the market; its efficient organization enables the appropriators to contract one with another to maximize the production and determine the allocation of their goods. Hence within society, the primary relationships of appropriators are contractual.

One might suppose that much of the argument I have developed, in seeking to link the contractarian conception of social relationships with the appropriative conception of human activity, could have been avoided quite simply by noting that the desire to appropriate necessarily manifests itself socially as the desire to exchange. Appropriators think of their fellows as partners in exchange, and so they think of social relations as contractual. But this, although true, would not show that appropriators conceive of society itself as contractual. The radical contractarian supposes that the marketplace, the locus of contract, is itself the product of a social contract and is embedded in a coercive order which is also the product of that contract. From the claim that man is by nature an appropriator it does not follow *directly* that he finds a coercive order beneficial and necessary. My concern has been to establish this further connection, and to introduce appropriative activity as that which naturally leads to hostility among men, yet which also affords scope for mutually beneficial cooperation, thus affording sufficient rationale for coercive society.

I have not shown that conceiving human activity as essentially appropriative requires one to accept a contractarian view of society. Locke's men are primarily appropriators, but they exist within a divinely ordained framework of natural law which relates them nonconventionally to their fellows.[16] Nor have I shown that conceiving all social relationships as contractual requires one to hold that human activity is primarily appropriative, for I have not shown that no alter-

[16]Locke [4], Second Treatise, ch. 5 (on appropriation); and ch. 2 (on the law of nature).

native account of human activity would afford nonsocial individuals with a rationale for a social contract. What I have shown is that the contractarian conception of social relationships and the appropriative conception of human activity are mutually supporting. Given the undoubted historical importance of appropriative activity in our society, I conclude that within our ideology, the ideology of Western Europeans, the conceptions of appropriation and contract intersect in the person of the individual property owner, related only by convention to his fellows. I shall therefore take the first connection in my initial thesis to be sufficiently defended.

VI

To conceive all social relationships as contractual is to deny that reason either determines or presupposes an order, a rational order, within which men are related prior to any agreement among themselves. This severely constrains the contractarian conception of rationality; I shall argue that it requires that rationality be conceived as related instrumentally to the satisfaction of individual interests.

Hobbes offers a useful way of formulating the problem of relating rationality to the theory of the social contract. "That is done by *right,* which is not done against reason," Hobbes claims, so that "we ought to judge those actions only *wrong,* which are repugnant to right reason. . . . But that *wrong* which is done, we say it is done against some law. Therefore *true reason* is a certain *law.*"[17] Reason, in other words, determines a framework of rights and laws, within which all men find themselves. But surely these rights and laws must determine relationships among men, which, being grounded in reason alone, are natural rather than conventional. If this were so, then radical contractarianism would have to be abandoned in favor of the Lockean theory that contract supplements and completes man's natural social relationships. Hobbes does not accept any such relationships; how then does he accommodate reason?

Hobbes keeps his conception of rationality consistent with his contractarianism by treating reason as both individualistic and instrumental. He speaks of "that Reason, which dictateth to every man his own good," and says that "all the voluntary actions of men tend to the benefit of themselves; and those actions are most Reasonable, that conduce most to their ends."[18] Given this conception of rationality, he is able to argue that every man has an unlimited, permissive right or

[17]Hobbes [1], II. 1.
[18]Hobbes [4], ch. 15.

liberty to do all things, so that each may do as he sees fit in order to preserve and benefit himself. The laws, to which every man is naturally subject, are but "Theorems concerning what conduceth to the conservation and defence of themselves." Hence reason does not in itself determine a system of rights and laws which relate men one to another in any way other than the natural relation of hostility. The "rational" order corresponding to the unlimited right of nature is the condition of war of every man with every man.

Contrast Hobbes's conception of reason with views which suppose rational standards transcending individual interests.[19] The Stoic holds that all men, as rational, are capable of apprehending the laws of nature, in terms of which all are related as members of a cosmopolis transcending more limited, conventional societies. The medieval Christian supposes that all men, as rational, are capable of apprehending the divinely ordained laws of nature, in terms of which all are related directly to God and indirectly to their fellows. The Kantian supposes that all men, as rational, are directly related one to another as members of a Kingdom of Ends in which each must treat his fellows not merely as means but also as ends in themselves. In each case there is an order—the Stoic cosmopolis, the Christian Kingdom of God, the Kantian Kingdom of Ends—which is constituted either by or in accordance with reason, to which all men belong and within which all are related. This relationship is prior to human agreement, depending solely on man's rationality. It may of course be the basis of further, contractual relationships, but these are only of secondary importance.

Each of these positions may be brought into verbal agreement with Hobbes's claim that "those actions are most Reasonable, that conduce most to their ends," but only by equivocating on "ends." Where Hobbes speaks of the ends subjectively given by men's passions, the Stoic, Christian, or Kantian speaks of the ends objectively given by Nature, God, or Reason itself. Such objective ends constitute a natural order within which all men are related, and so each of these views is incompatible with radical contractarianism.

To specify the contractarian conception of rationality more precisely, I shall relate it to the view of human activity developed in the preceding section. A person is a rational agent if and only if he acts to fulfill his (subjective) ends as far as possible. If it be agreed, as I have argued, that the contractarian ideology involves the conception of human activity as appropriative, then a person is a rational agent if

---

[19]The comparisons in this paragraph are intended to be commonplace; I have not tied them to particular references to Stoics, medieval Christians, and Kant.

and only if he acts to appropriate as much as possible. As much what? Here, our ideology exhibits a historical development. What is to be appropriated is first thought of as real property, land or estate. The distinction between land and other forms of property is then denied, and what is to be appropriated becomes the universal measure of property, money. Finally, in a triumph of abstraction, money as a particular object is replaced by the purely formal notion of utility, an object conveniently divested of all content. The rational man is, as Samuel Gompers succinctly recognized, simply the man who seeks *more*.

Thus it follows that not only the individualistic instrumental conception of rationality, but more precisely the individualistic utility-maximizing conception, is part of the ideology of the social contract, derived by means of the appropriative conception of human activity which is historically central to our ideology. But more than this may be said about reason, for it is not a merely derivative conception in contractarian thought.

I have argued that the appropriative conception of human activity, although consonant with contractarian thought, does not in itself require a contractarian interpretation of all human relationships, for it is at least possible to view man as belonging to a natural order, perhaps divinely ordained, within which he is noncontractually related to his fellows. But the instrumental conception of rationality rules out any ultimate natural or supernatural ground for human relationships. By itself, instrumental rationality does not imply any form of order or any type of relationship among human beings; it is compatible with the supposition that human existence is entirely solitary. But conjoined with the conception of human activity as appropriative, instrumental, maximizing rationality determines the hostile order of the state of nature, and this in turn makes it necessary for men to establish a conventional order among themselves by agreement or contract. Hence instrumental rationality conjoined with appropriative human nature entails contractarian society.

This concludes my exposition of the initial thesis of this essay. Radical contractarianism entails the instrumental conception of rationality; radical contractarianism together with the conception of human nature as appropriative entail more precisely the individualistic utility-maximizing conception of rationality. Conversely, instrumental rationality, together with the appropriative conception of human nature, entails the radical contractarian view that coercive society, and all social relationships, are the product of human convention. Thus society as conventional, human nature as appropriative, and rationality as maximizing cohere together at the core of our ideology.

VII

The maximizing conception of rationality is entailed by contractarianism, but it also undercuts the very possibility of rational agreement among men and thus the very possibility of contractually based society. There is an apparent incoherence in contractarian ideology to which I now turn.

Individual appropriators find themselves naturally and necessarily in conflict one with another. But individual utility-maximizers have no direct rational means for resolving their conflicts. Hobbes expresses this point clearly: "And therefore, as when there is a controversy in an account, the parties must by their own accord, set up for right Reason, the Reason of some Arbitrator, or Judge, to whose sentence they will both stand, or their controversie must either come to blowes, or be undecided, for want of a right Reason constituted by Nature; so is it also in all debates of what kind soever."[20] The Stoic, the Christian, or the Kantian may appeal to a right reason constituted by nature, as the basis of conflict resolution among human beings. But for the contractarian there is no such appeal.

Why is this important? Consider once again the functions which society must perform—coordination, bargaining, and constraint. Each of these requires procedures for decision and action which are not strictly contained in the principle of individual utility-maximization. Each then involves at least an extension in the contractarian conception of rationality. I have argued elsewhere that coordination and bargaining are fully compatible with utility-maximization.[21] These raise no problem. But constraint is not so compatible. The necessity for constraint arises when the outcome of bargaining is not stable, so that if each person acts to maximize his own utility, some persons will not act to bring about the agreed outcome. Voluntarily to act in a constrained manner is contrary to the dictates of individual utility-maximization.

Individual appropriators must enter into contractual relationships to resolve their conflicts and to bring about an optimal state of affairs, better for each than the natural outcome. But their conception of rationality leads them to violate their contracts whenever, as must often be the case, adherence would require them to abstain from directly maximizing behavior. In section IV, I insisted that agreement

---

[20]Hobbes [4], ch. 5.
[21]The argument on pp. 283–284 of "Coordination," above, may be transferred from the case of act-utilitarianism to that of individual utility-maximization, to show that coordination is a natural extension of maximization. Bargaining is discussed in Gauthier [6]; more recently in Gauthier [5].

in a type III situation—a situation in which no acceptable optimal outcome is stable—is possible only given some assurance that the agreement will be honored. This assurance requires external constraints, and thus I introduced the need for coercion. But it also needs internal constraints, the constraints of conscience, and these contradict the requirements of reason. The contractarian principle of rational action undercuts the internal constraints necessary to maintain contractual relationships.

This problem can be resolved only if it is possible to remedy the want of a right reason established by nature. The remedy can only be conventional. Natural reason, the reason of the individual maximizer, leads only to the natural relationship of hostility among men. A conventional rationality which upholds adherence to one's agreements even against the dictates of individual utility-maximization must therefore be accepted as the basis of the social contract, and so of social relationships.

Hobbes recognizes this need for a conventional standard of right reason, for he continues the passage quoted above: "And when men that think themselves wiser than all others, clamor and demand right Reason for judge; yet seek no more, but that things should be determined, by no other mens reason but their own, it is as intolerable in the society of men, as it is in play after trump is turned, to use for trump on every occasion, that suite whereof they have most in their hand." This passage contains the heart of the matter. Trump is established by the social contract, as that convention required to achieve an optimal state of affairs, better for each than the natural outcome. But each man, guided by his own reason, uses for trump his own interest. And this is intolerable, for it undercuts the contract and makes society impossible. However, Hobbes fails to establish a conventional standard of right reason, adhering to his individualist view that "those actions are most Reasonable, that conduce most to their ends." In the state of nature this is true, but as Hobbes himself recognizes, this is exactly what is intolerable in society or, indeed, intolerable if there is to be any society.

This is the point at which the theory of the social contract seems to collapse into incoherence. As I have noted, contract—the generic relationship of which the social contract is but the focal expression—is the fundamental relationship among appropriators. Their prime concern one with another is to exchange objects of appropriation, and contracts are their necessary means. But contracts are not fully self-sustaining. The society established by the social contract, market society, is from one point of view simply the network of contracts among individuals. But this network is maintained by a legal order which enforces the contracts. The contractual relationships of appropriators must be embedded within a political framework which coerces them into remaining within the market in their actions and relationships. Contractarian ideology represents this framework as itself contractual. But the condition of the market—the condition of the network of contracts—cannot itself be the product of a contract, which would be only part of that network. If the market is not self-sustaining, then it cannot be sustained by a part of itself.

The charge of incoherence operates at two levels. The argument which I have sketched suggests that radical contractarianism is incoherent as a *theory*, in providing an account of human relationships which presupposes a noncontractual base. I shall suggest that it can answer this charge. But there is a further argument which suggests that contractarianism is incoherent as an *ideology* in providing an account of human relationships which, in practice, undermines their base. I shall suggest in section IX that this charge succeeds, that the price contractarianism must pay for theoretical coherence is too great to allow it to maintain ideological effectiveness, once its adherents come to be aware of that price.

This last clause is important. Questions about the theoretical coherence of contractarianism need not affect its ideological coherence except insofar as they become questions in the minds of its adherents. Suppose it were true that contractual relationships, to be effectively maintained, must be embedded within a coercive order which itself were not contractually grounded. This would not prevent persons from conceiving of this coercive order as contractual, or from conceiving of all of their social relationships as contractual without attending to their framework. As long as the question of the coercive basis of contractual relationships did not arise in thought, the incoherence of the ideology would not be recognized, and its effectiveness would be unimpaired.

But now I want to defend contractarianism against the criticism that the instrumental conception of rationality, which it requires, must undermine the theory of the contractual rationale for society. What is essential, as Hobbes recognized, is a conventional standard of rational action, which will enjoin adherence to the social contract even when strict individual maximization calls for nonadherence, yet which itself is grounded in the individualistic utility-maximizing conception of rationality.

This may seem impossible. Surely any standard of rational action which is grounded in individual utility-maximization must have its same corrosive effect on adherence to agreements which require persons to refrain from maximizing behavior. But, I have argued elsewhere, this is not so.[22] A person who begins as an individual utility-maximizer will find it rational, on individualistic maximizing grounds, to change his very *conception* of rationality and come to adopt a conventional standard of right reason, which I have termed *constrained maximization*.

The principle of constrained maximization corresponds to straightforward individual utility-maximization in its application to state-of-nature situations, but it enjoins each person to agree with his fellows on actions leading to outcomes which are optimal and better for all than the corresponding natural outcomes, and to perform such actions within society. The rationale for the adoption of this new conception of rationality by utility-maximizers is quite simple; constrained maximizers are able to make agreements which straightforward maximizers cannot, because constrained maximizers will, and straightforward maximizers will not, adhere to these agreements, and the benefits of making such agreements are greater than the costs of adhering to them. Persons who adopt the standard of constrained maximization will find that, under widely prevailing, albeit not universal, conditions, it is rational for them to enter into and to adhere to a social contract with at least some of their fellow human beings, thereby replacing the natural relationship of hostility with the conventional relationship of sociability.

Reason itself neither determines nor presupposes any relationships among men, so that the contractarian requirement that all social relationships be conventional is not violated. But reason does lead men to enter by agreement into social relationships, and to adopt a standard of rationality which sustains these relationships rather than undermining them. Contractarian theory takes the individualistic utility-maximizing conception of rationality as the natural standard but provides for its rational replacement by a constrained maximizing conception which grounds those mutually optimizing actions to which men agree as the basis of their society.

VIII

I have distinguished two aspects of contractarian society: the market, the locus of the particular contracts which relate men as producers and distributors of goods, and the coercive order, or state, which ensures that the market does not revert to the battlefield of the state of nature. This distinction corresponds, in an interesting and important way, to the distinction which I have introduced between straightforward utility-maximization and constrained maximization.

---

[22]See "Reason and Maximization," above, esp. pp. 227–230.

Straightforward maximization corresponds to the rule of self-interest. Throughout most of human history the rule of self-interest has been considered a primary threat to society, as indeed my analysis of the problem posed to contractarianism by straightforward maximization would suggest that it is. Religion, law, morality, and tradition have combined to repress the force of self-interest. The great discovery of our society is, of course, the discovery of the social value of self-interest. The triumph of the science of economics was to demonstrate that under appropriate conditions, those of perfect competition in a free market, if each person acted purely self-interestedly, to maximize his own utilities, then the outcome would necessarily be optimal, the particular optimum depending solely on the initial positions of the persons in the market. Instead of repressing self-interest, our society has harnessed it. The benefits have been striking; critics of our society would hold that the costs have been overlooked.

Within the perfectly competitive market, straightforward individual utility-maximization is an adequate rule of reason. However, the market may fail to be perfectly competitive because of the presence of externalities—free goods or uncompensated costs, and the market is never fully self-sustaining since force and fraud always threaten it. Hence it requires to be regulated and controlled by the power of the state, and here straightforward maximization must be supplanted by constrained maximization. The distinction which I have drawn between these two conceptions of rationality parallels the distinction between the two primary sectors of contractarian society.

This may be indicated by a suitable relabeling of the two conceptions of rationality. Straightforward individual utility-maximization, the natural standard of reason, is effective in maintaining optimal productive and distributive activities for men in the market, and so may be termed the standard of *economic* rationality. Constrained individual utility-maximization, the conventional standard of reason for contractarians, is effective in maintaining the beneficial and necessary coercive order of the state against those directly maximizing actions which would restore the hostility of the state of nature, and so may be termed the standard of *political* rationality.

Since contractarian ideology is at the basis of our social thinking, it should not be surprising that the conception of society which is consonant with it proves familiar to us, in focusing on the economic, bargaining order of the market and viewing the political, coercive order of the state as sustaining the market. It should also not be surprising that contractarian society is of limited extent and is not a single society of the human race.

Not all persons need find it mutually advantageous to leave the state of nature to establish a market and a state. Only if all can improve on their original situation can all have sufficient reason to enter the social contract. If, however, the relations among some persons, or among some groups previously established by contract, are such that a gain for one must be a loss for another, then not everyone will have reason to agree to a departure from the existing state of affairs.

The implication of this for the present world situation is worth noting. On the contractarian view, it is evident that people should enter into contractual relations only with those with whom cooperation will prove profitable. Now we—Western Europeans and offshoots whose thinking is shaped by contractarian ideology—have no reason to expect it to be profitable or beneficial to us to cooperate with the overpopulated and underdeveloped peoples of much of the rest of the world. Given the finitude of the earth's resources, their gains are our losses.

To the question, Who is my neighbor? the radical contractarian has a simple answer. My neighbor, according to our ideology, is the man with whom I can make a mutually profitable agreement. Everyone else is my enemy—to be exploited if I can, to exploit me if he can. One might take as one measure of the hold of contractarian ideology upon us the extent to which this answer determines our practice, whatever we may preach.

IX

Radical contractarianism has come more and more to dominate our thoughts and actions, or so I would contend. Correlatively, contractarianism has passed increasingly from covert to overt manifestation in our self-awareness. Institutions and practices which derive their rationale from noncontractarian considerations are being discarded or rejected. The effect of this is to throw into sharp relief the contractarian conception of rationality, and its relationship to our appropriative desires.

Insofar as the two are mutually supportive, all is well. The supposition that all human relationships other than hostility are conventional, the product of mutually beneficial agreement, will sustain bargaining activity within the market, for here economic rationality and the desire to appropriate reinforce each other. But the coercive order of the state is a quite different matter, for here political rationality imposes a constraint on the unlimited appetite of the contractarian. However rational it may be to stand to one's advantageous agreements even against direct interest, yet reason is insufficient in practice to overcome the motivations which, on the contractarian view, direct our actions. Awareness of oneself as an appropriator undercuts one's willingness to accept the constraints of the political order.

Historically the political order, which is necessary to the maintenance of peace and security within society, has been supported by motivations quite different from those that enter the contractarian conception of human nature. As this conception comes to be both more overt and more pervasive, these other factors lose their hold on us, and the political order loses its motivational base.

To the extent to which it has not been self-enforcing, political society has rested on *patriotism*—the love of country which binds men to the coercive order because it is surrounded with the emotional trappings of fatherland or motherland (trappings which themselves are corroded as the contractarian conception of the family comes to the fore!). It is, I suggest, this attachment of individuals to their society which has generated sufficient voluntary support to enable coercion to be effective. To be sure, not all members of society have felt this attachment, but enough have been moved by it to permit the remainder to be constrained through the further motive of *fear*—fear of the coercive order itself.

In addition to patriotic feeling, familial feeling has been a fundamental motive supporting the political order. The effect of familial feeling has been primarily to strengthen society as an entity enduring in time. Since future generations have little to contribute to the well-being of those now alive, a contract between us and our descendants seems a tenuous basis for an enduring society. However, the transgenerational affective ties which bind together members of a family supply the motivation needed for each generation to seek the continuation of society. I shall term this motive *love* and suggest that it operates primarily at a prerational level. By this I mean that membership in the family, and the ties of love, precede, causally if not logically, the emergence of that individual self who engages in the appropriative and contractual activities of the market and aligns with others to create and maintain the state.

Patriotism and love thus maintain the enduring political basis of contractual market society. Because our ideology is part of the deep structure of our thought about ourselves, it has been possible for us to think in contractarian ways while acting on these quite uncontractarian motives. We may suppose that our ties to our fellows and our society are strictly contractual and yet act on ties which are not contractual. However, as the ideology of contract comes increasingly to manifest itself at the level of conscious thought, so that we come consciously to disavow nonappropriative motivation, patriotism and love must seem more and more irrelevant and even unintelligible. The rejection by the young of America's role in the Vietnam war and the emergence of radical feminism are manifestations of this increasingly overt contractarian consciousness.

Patriotism and love have had a further effect on the development of our society. Historically they have served, together with the fear engendered by the coercive order which they sustain, to exclude most human beings from effective membership in market society, and thus from what, to the contractarian, are the essentially human activities of appropriation and exchange. Neither workers, who have lacked control over the means of production, nor women, who have engaged in reproduction rather than production, have conceived themselves, or been in a position to conceive themselves, as full human beings in the sense implicit in radical contractarian ideology.[23] Marx, mistakenly, thought religion to be the opium of the people,[24] the real opiates, in contractarian society, have been love and patriotism. By removing wide areas of human activity, and even more important, most people, from the effective scope of the ideology, love and patriotism have enabled those remaining within its scope to conduct their appropriative activities more successfully.

Indeed, this restriction of appropriation to, largely, the male bourgeoisie has been essential to the development of our society. If every person had considered himself, or herself, to be an appropriator, in competition with every other person, then, as Hobbes insisted, only an all-powerful sovereign could have prevented endless conflict. The mode of rationality which would have led every person to make and carry out an agreement to check competition and ensure mutual advantage would have been insufficient to overcome the competitive desire to appropriate.

C. B. Macpherson, in his introduction to *Leviathan*, emphasizes this when he says: "Given the postulate that the power of every man necessarily opposed and hindered the power of other men, so that every man in society necessarily sought more power over others, *and provided* that this centrifugal force was not offset by any centripetal force, it would follow that any slackening or temporary absence of a sovereign power would tend to lead to internecine strife. What Hobbes overlooked and failed to put into his model was the centripetal force of a cohesive bourgeois class within the society."[25] The

[23]Lacking control over the means of production, workers have been required to sell their labor, and thus their claim to own their products, in order to survive. Thus they have been excluded from appropriative activity, an exclusion which continued even after they combined in trade unions, until those unions abandoned the goal of replacing the appropriative, competitive economy with a noncompetitive order, and adopted instead the aim of exercising power within the existing system. Reproduction, the activity of women, has been considered inferior and instrumental to true production. Being unable to engage in production, women have been required to sell *their* labor in order to survive; the husband has thus appropriated the children as products.

[24]Marx, introduction.

[25]Hobbes [4a], pp. 55–56; see also pp. 61–63.

male bourgeoisie have acted as a cohesive, centripetal force because they have recognized, implicitly, that they must retain appropriative activity exclusively in their hands to prevent the strife which would result from the competition of every person with every other person. But they have been able to retain appropriative activity for themselves alone, not just because of their cohesion but also because neither workers nor women have conceived of themselves as appropriators. Acceptance by workers and women of the contractarian view of human beings would lead to their refusal to remain excluded from truly human, appropriative activity.

I have suggested that the ideology of radical contractarianism is manifesting itself increasingly in our overt consciousness. And this consciousness is spreading more and more widely. In itself, the ideology embraces everyone, so that, as more and more people attain self-awareness, they do so in the terms provided by the deep structure of our thought—in the terms, then, of contractarianism.

The likely end of the current fad for liberation movements, whatever the ostensible aim of these movements, will be to extend contractarian self-awareness to new areas of human activity and new groups of human beings. Radical feminists will go the way of radical trades unionists; women will join the system rather than overthrow it. But as all persons come to consider all human relationships to be contractual, they will not achieve the happy state of ideally rational appropriators, or even the cohesive unity of the male bourgeoisie. The absorptive capacity of the system is being overstrained, so that the effect of extending contractarian ideology is and will continue to be to corrode all of those bonds which in the real world have been the underpinning of the market. Bereft of its framework, the bargaining order will collapse into competitive chaos.

Love and patriotism are myths to the contractarian. But these myths, and not reason, have been the real support for the enduring coercive order, enabling it to enlist fear and thus assure the survival of the state. And the contractarian state, rational to the constrained maximizer but effective only because of its basis in these myths, has maintained the bargaining order of the market. Remove this basis by bringing all human beings to awareness of themselves as appropriators, and the practical incoherence of contractarian ideology manifests itself in the inability of conscious contractarians to maintain the coercive basis of their social relationships. Thus the triumph of radical contractarianism leads to the destruction, rather than the rationalization, of our society, for what real men and women who believe the ideology need to keep them from the war of all against all is not reason but the Hobbist sovereign, and he is not available.

The ideology of radical contractarianism is, of course, but one among many possible ways of structuring our thought about man, society, and reason. We may see that this way of thinking is, from a practical point of view, bankrupt, and indeed that it will destroy us if we remain its adherents. But other ways of thinking, however possible they may be, are not produced to order. Faced with the falling of the dusk, the owl of Minerva spreads its wings—and takes flight.[26]

[26]"One word more about giving instruction as to what the world ought to be. Philosophy in any case always comes on the scene too late to give it. As the thought of the world, it appears only when actuality is already there cut and dried after its process of formation has been completed. . . . When philosophy paints its grey in grey, then has a shape of life grown old. By philosophy's grey in grey it cannot be rejuvenated but only understood. The owl of Minerva spreads its wings only with the falling of the dusk" (Hegel, pp. 12–13).

Hegel played a larger role in earlier drafts of this essay. The discussion of property and contract in the first part of the *Philosophy of Right* is a fundamental source for any articulation of contractarian ideology, however much Hegel rejects the view that all social relationships are contractual. But the exposition of Hegel is a problem in itself, and this essay faces enough problems, so Hegel has been unfairly relegated to a footnote.

Bibliography of Works Cited

Anscombe, G. E. M. "Modern Moral Philosophy." *Philosophy* 33 (1958). 1–19.

Aristotle. *Nicomachean Ethics.*

Arrow, Kenneth J. *Social Choice and Individual Values.* 2d ed. New York: Wiley, 1963.

Baier, Kurt. *The Moral Point of View: A Rational Basis of Ethics.* Ithaca, N.Y.: Cornell University Press, 1958.

Bell, Daniel. *The End of Ideology.* New York: Free Press, 1960.

Berman, Marshall. *The Politics of Authenticity.* New York: Atheneum, 1962.

Bradshaw's General Railway and Steam Navigation Guide. No. 921, April 1910. Reprint. Newton Abbot, England: David & Charles, 1968.

Braithwaite, R. B. *Theory of Games as a Tool for the Moral Philosopher.* Cambridge: Cambridge University Press, 1955.

Brandt, Richard B. *Ethical Theory.* Englewood Cliffs, N.J.: Prentice-Hall, 1959.

Buchanan, James M. *The Limits of Liberty.* Chicago: University of Chicago Press, 1975.

Cox, Richard H. *Locke on War and Peace.* Oxford: Clarendon Press, 1960.

Darwall, Stephen. "Kantian Practical Reason Defended." *Ethics* 96 (1985), 89–99.

Dennett, Daniel C. *Content and Consciousness.* London: Routledge & Kegan Paul, 1969.

Dunn, John. *The Political Thought of John Locke.* Cambridge: Cambridge University Press, 1969.

Elster, Jon. *Ulysses and the Sirens: Studies in Rationality and Irrationality.* Cambridge: Cambridge University Press, 1979.

Galbraith, John K. *The Affluent Society.* Boston: Houghton Mifflin, 1958.

Gauthier, David. [1] "Coordination." *Dialogue* 14 (1975), 195–221.

———. [2] "Deterrence, Maximization, and Rationality." *Ethics* 94 (1984), 474–495.

———. [3] "Justice and Natural Endowment: Towards a Critique of Rawls'

Ideological Framework." *Social Theory and Practice* 3 (1974 [pub. 1975]), 3–26.

———. [4] "Morality and Advantage." *Philosophical Review* 76 (1967), 460–475.

———. [5] *Morals by Agreement.* Oxford: Clarendon Press, 1986.

———. [6] "Rational Cooperation." *Noûs* 8 (1974), 53–65.

———. [7] "Reason and Maximization." *Canadian Journal of Philosophy* 4 (1975), 411–433.

———. [8] "Response to the Paradox of Deterrence: Afterthoughts." In *The Security Gamble: Deterrence in the Nuclear Age,* ed. Douglas MacLean (Totowa, N.J.: Rowman & Allanheld, 1984), 159–161.

———. [9] "The Impossibility of Rational Egoism." *Journal of Philosophy* 71 (1974), 439–456.

———. [10] *The Logic of Leviathan: The Moral and Political Theory of Thomas Hobbes.* Oxford: Clarendon Press, 1969.

———. [11] "The Social Contract as Ideology." *Philosophy and Public Affairs* 6 (1977), 130–164.

———. [12] "The Social Contract: Individual Decision or Collective Bargain?." In *Foundations and Applications of Decision Theory,* ed. C. A. Hooker, J. J. Leach, and E. F. McClennen (Dordrecht: Reidel. 1978), 2:47–67.

———. [13] "Thomas Hobbes: Moral Theorist." *Journal of Philosophy* 76 (1979), 547–559.

———. [14] "Why Ought One Obey God? Reflections on Hobbes and Locke." *Canadian Journal of Philosophy* 7 (1977), 425–446.

Gough, J. W. *The Social Contract.* 2d ed. Oxford: Clarendon Press, 1957.

Hardin, Garrett. "The Tragedy of the Commons." *Science* 162 (1968), 1243–1248.

Hardin, Russell. *Collective Action.* Baltimore: Johns Hopkins University Press, 1982.

Hare, R. M. [1] *Freedom and Reason.* Oxford: Clarendon Press, 1963.

———. [2] *Moral Thinking.* Oxford: Clarendon Press, 1981.

Harsanyi, John C. [1] "Approaches to the Bargaining Problem before and after the Theory of Games." *Econometrica* 24 (1956), 144–156.

———. [2] *Essays on Ethics, Social Behavior, and Scientific Explanation.* Dordrecht & Boston: Reidel, 1976.

———. [3] "Morality and the Theory of Rational Behaviour." In *Utilitarianism and Beyond,* ed. Amartya Sen and Bernard Williams (Cambridge: Cambridge University Press, 1982), 39–62. Originally published in *Social Research* 44 (1977), 623–656.

———. [4] *Rational Behavior and Bargaining Equilibrium in Games and Social Situations.* Cambridge: Cambridge University Press, 1977.

Hegel, G. W. F. *Hegel's Philosophy of Right.* Tr. T. M. Knox. Oxford: Clarendon Press, 1942.

Hobbes, Thomas. [1] *De Cive.* Translated as *Philosophical Rudiments Concerning Government and Society.* London: 1651; [1a] In *Man and Citizen,* ed. Bernard Gert (Garden City, N.Y.: Doubleday, 1972), 87–386.

―――. [2] *De Corpore Politico.* In *The English Works of Thomas Hobbes,* ed. Sir William Molesworth (London: 1840), vol. 4.

―――. [3] *Human Nature.* In *The English Works of Thomas Hobbes,* ed. Sir William Molesworth (London: 1840), vol. 4.

―――. [4] *Leviathan.* London: 1651; [4a] Ed. and intro. C. B. Macpherson. Harmondsworth, Middlesex: Penguin, 1968.

―――. [5] *The Questions concerning Liberty, Necessity, and Chance.* In *The English Works of Thomas Hobbes,* ed. Sir William Molesworth (London: 1841), vol. 5.

Hodgson, D. H. *Consequences of Utilitarianism.* Oxford: Clarendon Press, 1967.

Hume, David. [1] *A Treatise of Human Nature.* Ed. L. A. Selby-Bigge. Oxford: Clarendon Press, 1888.

―――. [2] *An Enquiry concerning the Principles of Morals.* Ed. L. A. Selby-Bigge. Oxford: Clarendon Press, 1902.

―――. [3] *Essays and Treatises on Miscellaneous Subjects.* 2 vols. London and Edinburgh: 1777.

Kalai, Ehud, and Smorodinsky, Meir. "Other Solutions to Nash's Bargaining Problem." *Econometrica* 43 (1975), 513–518.

Kant, Immanuel. [1] *Critique of Practical Reason.* Tr. Lewis White Beck. Indianapolis, Ind.: Bobbs-Merrill, 1956.

―――. [2] *Critique of Pure Reason.* Tr. Norman Kemp Smith. London: Macmillan, 1950.

―――. [3] *Groundwork of the Metaphysic of Morals.* Tr. H. J. Paton, as *The Moral Law.* London: Hutchinson, 1948.

Levine, Andrew. *Liberal Democracy: A Critique of Its Theory.* New York: Columbia University Press, 1981.

Lewis, David K. [1] *Convention: A Philosophical Study.* Cambridge, Mass.: Harvard University Press, 1969.

―――. [2] "Devil's Bargains and the Real World." In *The Security Gamble: Deterrence in the Nuclear Age,* ed. Douglas MacLean (Totowa, N.J.: Rowman & Allanheld, 1984), 141–154.

Locke, John. [1] *An Essay concerning Human Understanding* (London: 1690)

―――. [2] *John Locke: Essays on the Law of Nature.* Ed. and tr. Wolfgang von Leyden. Oxford: Oxford University Press, 1954.

―――. [3] *Letter concerning Toleration.* London: 1690.

―――. [4] *Two Treatises of Government.* Ed. Peter Laslett. Cambridge: Cambridge University Press, 1967.

Luce, R. D., and Raiffa, H. *Games and Decisions.* New York: Wiley, 1957.

Mackie, J. L. "The Disutility of Act-Utilitarianism." *Philosophical Quarterly* 23 (1973), 289–300.

McNeilly, F. S. "Promises De-Moralized." *Philosophical Review* 81 (1972), 63–81.

Macpherson, C. B. [1] *Democratic Theory: Essays in Retrieval.* Oxford: Clarendon Press, 1973.

―――. [2] *The Political Theory of Possessive Individualism: Hobbes to Locke.* Oxford: Clarendon Press, 1967.

Marx, Karl. *Contribution to the Critique of Hegel's Philosophy of Right: Introduction.*

In *Karl Marx: Early Writings*, ed. T. B. Bottomore (London: C. A. Watts & Co., 1963), 43–59.

Medlin, Brian. "Ultimate Principles and Ethical Egoism." *Australasian Journal of Philosophy* 35 (1957), 111–118.

Mill, John Stuart. *Utilitarianism*. London: Parker, Son, and Bourn, 1863.

Moore, G. E. *Principia Ethica*. Cambridge: Cambridge University Press, 1903.

Nagel, Thomas. *The Possibility of Altruism*. Oxford: Clarendon Press, 1970.

Narveson, Jan. "Promising, Expecting, and Utility." *Canadian Journal of Philosophy* 1 (1971), 220–228.

Nash, John F. [1] "Noncooperative Games." *Annals of Mathematics* 54 (1951), 286–295.

———. [2] "The Bargaining Problem." *Econometrica* 18 (1950), 155–162.

Nozick, Robert. *Anarchy, State, and Utopia*. New York: Basic Books, 1974.

Olson, Mancur, Jr. *The Logic of Collective Action*. Cambridge, Mass.: Harvard University Press, 1965.

Plato. *Republic*. Tr. Allan Bloom. New York: Basic Books, 1968.

Rawls, John. [1] *A Theory of Justice*. Cambridge, Mass.: Harvard University Press, 1971.

———. [2] "Justice as Fairness." *Philosophical Review* 67 (1958), 164–194.

———. [3] "Kantian Constructivism in Moral Theory." *Journal of Philosophy* 77 (1980), 515–572.

Roth, Alvin E. *Axiomatic Models of Bargaining*. Berlin: Springer Verlag, 1979.

Rousseau, Jean-Jacques. [1] *Discours sur l'origine et les fondements de l'inégalité parmi les hommes*. In [7], 1:118–220.

———. [2] *Du contrat social*. In [7], 2:1–136.

———. [3] *Essai sur l'origine des langues, où il est parlé de la mélodie et de l'imitation musicale*. Ed. and intro. Charles Porset. Paris: Ducros, 1970.

———. [4] *Émile*. Paris: Garnier-Flammarion, 1966.

———. [5] *Julie, ou La Nouvelle Héloïse*. Paris: Garnier-Flammarion, 1967; [5a] Tr. Judith H. McDowell. University Park, Pa.: Pennsylvania State University Press, 1968.

———. [6] *Oeuvres complètes*. 4 vols. Ed. B. Gagnebin and M. Raymond. Paris: Pléiade, 1959–1969.

———. [7] *Political Writings*. 2 vols. Ed. C. E. Vaughan. Cambridge: Cambridge University Press, 1915; New York: Wiley, 1962.

Scanlon, T. M. "Contractualism and Utilitarianism." In *Utilitarianism and Beyond*, ed. Amartya Sen and Bernard Williams (Cambridge: Cambridge University Press, 1982), 103–128.

Schell, Jonathan. *The Fate of the Earth*. New York: Alfred A. Knopf, 1982.

Schelling, Thomas C. *The Strategy of Conflict*. Cambridge, Mass.: Harvard University Press, 1960.

Selten, Reinhard. "The Chain-store Paradox." *Theory and Decision* 9 (1978), 127–159.

Sen, Amartya K. *Collective Choice and Social Welfare*. San Francisco: Holden-Day, 1970.

Shklar, Judith N. *Men and Citizens*. Cambridge: Cambridge University Press, 1969.

Shorter Oxford English Dictionary. Oxford: Clarendon Press, 1964.

Strauss, Leo. *Natural Right and History.* Chicago: University of Chicago Press, 1953.

Von Neumann, John, and Morgenstern, Oskar. *Theory of Games and Economic Behavior.* Princeton: Princeton University Press, 1944.

Warrender, Howard. *The Political Philosophy of Hobbes: His Theory of Obligation.* Oxford: Clarendon Press, 1957.

Waxman, Chaim I., ed. *The End of Ideology Debate.* New York: Simon & Schuster, 1968.

Wiggins, David. "Truth, Invention, and the Meaning of Life." In *Proceedings of the British Academy* (Oxford: Clarendon Press, 1976), 62:331–378.

Williams, Bernard. *Moral Luck.* Cambridge: Cambridge University Press, 1981.

Winch, D. M. *Analytical Welfare Economics.* Harmondsworth, Middlesex: Penguin, 1971.

Zeuthen, Frederik. *Problems of Monopoly and Economic Warfare.* London: Routledge, 1930.

Author's Bibliography, 1963–1988

(Brief reviews and nonscholarly writings omitted)

*Papers reprinted in this volume

"The Philosophy of Revolution." *University of Toronto Quarterly* 32 (1963), 126–141.

Practical Reasoning: The Structure and Foundations of Prudential and Moral Arguments and Their Exemplification in Discourse. Oxford: Clarendon Press, 1963. ix + 210.

"Rule-Utilitarianism and Randomization." *Analysis* 25 (1965), 68–69.

"The Role of Inheritance in Locke's Political Theory." *Canadian Journal of Economics and Political Science* 32 (1966), 38–45.

"How Decisions Are Caused." *Journal of Philosophy* 64 (1967), 147–151.

"Moore's Naturalistic Fallacy." *American Philosophical Quarterly* 4 (1967), 315–320.

"Morality and Advantage." *Philosophical Review* 76 (1967), 460–475. Reprinted in *Morality and Rational Self-Interest,* below, 166–180, and in *The Definition of Morality,* ed. G. Wallace and A. D. M. Walker (London: Methuen, 1970), 235–250. Excerpted in *Problems of Moral Philosophy,* 2d ed., ed. Paul W. Taylor (Encino and Belmont, Calif.: Dickenson, 1972), 530–538.

"Progress and Happiness: A Utilitarian Reconsideration." *Ethics* 78 (1967), 77–82.

"Hare's Debtors." *Mind* 77 (1968), 400–405.

"How Decisions Are Caused (but Not Predicted)." *Journal of Philosophy* 65 (1968), 170–171.

"The Unity of Wisdom and Temperance." *Journal of the History of Philosophy* 6 (1968), 157–159.

The Logic of Leviathan: The Moral and Political Theory of Thomas Hobbes. Oxford: Clarendon Press, 1969. x + 217.

"Yet Another Hobbes." *Inquiry* 12 (1969), 449–465.

Morality and Rational Self-Interest, editor. Englewood Cliffs, N.J.: Prentice-Hall, 1970. viii + 184. Contributed introductory essay, 1–23; bibliographical essay, 181–184; and "Morality and Advantage," cited above.

Comments on R. M. Hare, "Wanting: Some Pitfalls." In *Agent, Action, and Reason,* ed. R. Binkley, R. Bronaugh, and A. Marras (Toronto: University of Toronto Press, 1971), 98–108.

"Moral Action and Moral Education." In *Moral Education: Interdisciplinary Approaches,* ed. C. M. Beck, B. S. Crittenden, and E. V. Sullivan (Toronto: University of Toronto Press, 1971), 138–146.

"Brandt on Egoism" (abstract). *Journal of Philosophy* 69 (1972), 697–698.

"The Impossibility of Rational Egoism." *Journal of Philosophy* 71 (1974), 439–456.

"Rational Cooperation," *Noûs* 8 (1974), 53–65.

*"Justice and Natural Endowment: Toward a Critique of Rawls' Ideological Framework." *Social Theory and Practice* 3 (1974 [pub. 1975]), 3–26.

*"Coordination." *Dialogue* 14 (1975), 195–221.

*"Reason and Maximization." *Canadian Journal of Philosophy,* 4 (1975), 411–433. Secs. IV–VIII reprinted in *Rational Man and Irrational Society?* ed. Brian Barry and Russell Hardin (Beverly Hills, London, and New Delhi: Sage Publications, 1982), 90–106.

Critical notice of *Analytical Philosophy of History,* by Arthur C. Danto. *Canadian Journal of Philosophy* 5 (1975), 463–471.

*"The Social Contract as Ideology." *Philosophy and Public Affairs* 6 (Winter, 1977), 130–164.

*"Why Ought One Obey God? Reflections on Hobbes and Locke." *Canadian Journal of Philosophy* 7 (1977), 425–446.

Critical notice of Stephan Körner, ed., *Practical Reason. Dialogue* 16 (1977), 510–518.

"Economic Rationality and Moral Constraints." *Midwest Studies in Philosophy* 3 (1978), 75–96.

"Social Choice and Distributive Justice." *Philosophia* 7 (1978), 239–253.

"The Social Contract: Individual Decision or Collective Bargain?" In *Foundations and Applications of Decision Theory,* ed, C. A. Hooker, J. J. Leach, and E. F. McClennen (Dordrecht & Boston: Reidel, 1978), 2:47–67.

Critical notice of John C. Harsanyi, *Essays on Ethics, Social Behavior, and Scientific Explanation. Dialogue* 17 (1978), 698–706.

"Bargaining Our Way into Morality: A Do-It-Yourself Primer." *Philosophical Exchange* 2 (1979), 14–27.

"Confederation, Contract, and Constitution." In *Philosophers Look at Canadian Confederation = La confédération canadienne: Qu'en pensent les philosophes?* ed. S. G. French (Montreal: Canadian Philosophical Association, 1979), 193–199.

*"David Hume: Contractarian." *Philosophical Review* 88 (1979), 3–38.

*"Thomas Hobbes: Moral Theorist." *Journal of Philosophy* 76 (1979), 547–559.

*"The Politics of Redemption." *Revue de l'Université d'Ottawa* 49 (1979) [pub. 1980]), 329–356. Also in *Trent Rousseau Papers,* ed. J. MacAdam, M. Neu-

mann, and G. Lafrance (Ottawa: University of Ottawa Press, 1980), 329–356.

"The Irrationality of Choosing Egoism: A Reply to Eshelman." *Canadian Journal of Philosophy* 10 (1980), 179–187.

"Justified Inequality?" *Dialogue* 21 (1982), 431–443.

"No Need for Morality: The Case of the Competitive Market." *Philosophical Exchange* 3 (1982), 41–54.

"On the Refutation of Utilitarianism." In *The Limits of Utilitarianism*, ed. H. B. Miller and W. H. Williams (Minneapolis: University of Minnesota Press, 1982), 144–163.

*"Three against Justice: The Foole, the Sensible Knave, and the Lydian Shepherd." *Midwest Studies in Philosophy* 7 (1982), 11–29. Edited by P. A. French, T. E. Uehling, Jr., and H. N. Wettstein.

"Unequal Need: A Problem of Equity in Access to Health Care." In *Securing Access to Health Care: The Ethical Implications of Differences in the Availability of Health Services*, vol. 2: *President's Commission for the Study of Ethical Problems in Medicine and Biomedical and Behavioral Research* (Washington, D.C.: U.S. Government Printing Office, 1983), 179–205.

Critical notice of *Ulysses and the Sirens: Studies in Rationality and Irrationality*, by Jon Elster. *Canadian Journal of Philosophy* 13 (1983), 133–140.

*"Deterrence, Maximization, and Rationality." *Ethics* 94 (1984), 474–495. Also in *The Security Gamble: Deterrence in the Nuclear Age*, ed. Douglas MacLean (Totowa, N.J.: Rowman & Allanheld, 1985); 101–122, with "Response to the Paradox of Deterrence: Afterthoughts," 159–161. Reprinted in *Nuclear Deterrence: Ethics and Strategy*, ed. Russell Hardin, John J. Mearsheimer, Gerald Dworkin, and Robert E. Goodin (Chicago: University of Chicago Press, 1985), 99–120.

*"The Incompleat Egoist." In *The Tanner Lectures on Human Values*, vol. 5, ed. Sterling M. McMurrin (Salt Lake City: University of Utah Press; Cambridge: Cambridge University Press, 1984), 67–119.

*(in part) "Justice as Social Choice." In *Morality, Reason and Truth*, ed. D. Copp and D. Zimmerman (Totowa, N.J.: Rowman & Allanheld, 1984), 251–269.

*"Bargaining and Justice." *Social Philosophy and Policy* 2 (1985), 29–47. Also in *Ethics & Economics*, ed. E. F. Paul, F. D. Miller, Jr., and J. Paul (Oxford: Basil Blackwell, 1985), 29–47.

"Maximization Constrained: The Rationality of Cooperation." In *Paradoxes of Rationality and Cooperation: Prisoner's Dilemma and Newcomb's Problem* ed. R. Campbell and L. Sowden (Vancouver: University of British Columbia Press, 1985), 75–93. Reprinted with an added introductory section from ch. 6, secs. 2 and 3 of *Morals by Agreement*.

*"The Unity of Reason: A Subversive Reinterpretation of Kant." *Ethics* 96 (1985), 74–88.

Morals by Agreement. Oxford: Clarendon Press, 1986. ix + 367. Reprinted 1987; reprinted as paperback 1987; with corrections, 1988 (twice).

"Reason to Be Moral?" Kurt Baier Festschrift, *Synthese* 72 (1987), 5–27.

"Reply to Wolfram." *Philosophical Books* 18 (1987), 134–139.

"Taming Leviathan." Critical notice of Jean Hampton, *Hobbes and the Social*

Contract Tradition, and Gregory S. Kavka, *Hobbesian Moral and Political Theory. Philosophy & Public Affairs* 16 (1987), 280–298.

"George Grant's Justice." *Dialogue* 27 (1988), 121–134.

"Hobbes's Social Contract." In *Perspectives on Thomas Hobbes,* ed. G. A. J. Rogers and Alan Ryan (Oxford: Clarendon Press, 1988), 125–152; shorter version in *Noûs* 22 (1988), 71–82.

"Moral Artifice." *Canadian Journal of Philosophy* 18 (1988), 385–418.

"Morality, Rational Choice, and Semantic Representation: A Reply to My Critics." *Social Philosophy & Policy* 5 (1988), 173–221. Also in *The New Social Contract: Essays on Gauthier,* ed. E. F. Paul, F. D. Miller, Jr., and J. Paul (Oxford: Blackwell, 1988), 173–221.

"War and Nuclear Deterrence." In *Problems of International Justice,* ed. Steven Luper-Foy (Boulder, Colo.: Westview Press, 1988), 205–221.

Index

Library of Congress Cataloging-in-Publication Data

Gauthier, David P.
  Moral dealing / David Gauthier.
    p.   cm.
  Includes bibliographical references.
  ISBN 0-8014-2431-3 (alk. paper). — ISBN 0-8014-9700-0 (pbk. : alk. paper)
  1. Ethics.   2. Contracts.   3. Reason.   I. Title.
BJ1031.G38   1990
171—dc20
                                                    89-45975